Preparing for the Texas
PreK-4 Teacher Certification

Preparing for the Texas PreK-4 Teacher Certification

A Guide to the Comprehensive TExES Content Areas Exam

Edited by

Janice L. Nath
University of Houston–Downtown

John Ramsey
University of Houston

PEARSON

Boston   New York   San Francisco
Mexico City   Montreal   Toronto   London   Madrid   Munich   Paris
Hong Kong   Singapore   Tokyo   Cape Town   Sydney

Series Editor: Traci Mueller
Series Editorial Assistant: Krista E. Price
Marketing Manager: Elizabeth Fogarty
Senior Production Editor: Annette Pagliaro
Editorial Production: Walsh and Associates, Inc.
Composition Buyer: Linda Cox
Manufacturing Buyer: Andrew Turso
Cover Administrator: Joel Gendron
Text Design: Karen Mason
Electronic Composition: Galley Graphics

For related titles and support materials, visit our online catalog at www.ablongman.com.

Between the time Website information is gathered and then published, it is not unusual for some sites to have closed. Also, the transcription of URLs can result in unintentional typographical errors. The publisher would appreciate notification where these errors occur so that they may be corrected in subsequent editions.

Library of Congress Cataloging-in-Publication Data

Preparing for the Texas preK-4 teacher certification : a guide to the comprehensive TExES content areas exam / [edited by] Janice L. Nath, John M. Ramsey.
　　p. cm.
Includes bibliographical references and index.
ISBN 0-321-07676-1
　　1. Elementary school teachers—Certification—Texas.　2. Educational tests and measurements—Texas—Study guides.　I. Nath, Janice L.　II. Ramsey, John

LB1772.T4P74 2004
370′.76—dc21

　　　　　　　　　　　　　　　　　　　　　　　　　　　　2003052320

Printed in the United States of America
10 9 8 7 6 5 4 3 2　　　08　07　06　05　04

Contents

DOMAIN III   SOCIAL STUDIES

DOMAIN IV   SCIENCE

DOMAIN V   FINE ARTS, HEALTH, AND PHYSICAL EDUCATION

Preface

SETTING THE STAGE: WHO, WHAT, WHY, AND WHERE

Changing from ExCET to TExES

In the fall of 2002, the Texas State Board for Educator Certification (SBEC) implemented a new educator examination program that supplants the Examination for the Certification of Educators in Texas (ExCET), the educator certification program in place since 1986. The new program is called the Texas Examinations for Educator Standards (TExES).

This change is the result of the P–16 Initiative, a collaboration of SBEC, the Texas Education Agency, the regulator of elementary and secondary public education, and the Texas Higher Education Coordinating Board (the regulator of higher education). Their purpose was to establish a seamless, cohesive system of P–16 education that aligns educator certification with the mandated student curriculum, the Texas Essential Knowledge and Skills (TEKS). National Evaluation Systems (www.texes.nesinc.com) developed all the TExES under contract from SBEC.

This program is based on educator standards that defined the rigorous content and professional knowledge and skills that an entry-level educator should possess. This book is focused on preparing prospective teachers for one of the certification examinations, the Early Childhood to Grade Four Generalist (EC-4).

Who: The EC-4 Prospective Teacher Audience

This book is intended for those individuals seeking certification as teachers in early childhood through grade 4 classrooms in Texas. These prospective teachers must meet an array of quality and preparation criteria, including at least two state-administered examinations. This book addresses the standards, competencies, and associated content of the EC-4 Generalist examination. The Generalist standards and competencies require knowledge and skills associated with elementary curricular content and appropriate learning and assessment practices. The other examination required for certification is the EC-4 Pedagogy and Professional Responsibilities (PPR) examination. This second examination is specifically focused on the knowledge and skills associated with classroom pedagogy and professional ethics.

The What: EC-4 General Discipline Content

This book is a preparation resource that can be used as either a primary source text or a supplemental review guide for the EC-4 examination. Note that this book is not an SBEC publication; rather, it is an effort by experienced and dedicated educators to contribute to the certification process for the benefit of the state's prospective teachers and students. These educators are fully aware that passing this examination is not *all* that makes a good teacher, having seen numerous wonderful teacher candidates (who may not have easily passed the state examinations) teach excellent lessons with children. However, we do submit that this is excellent information for *any* EC-4 teacher to know.

The book's content focuses on the Texas standards, competencies, and allied content of seven areas of discipline knowledge (aligned with the TEKS, the mandated student curriculum of the state of Texas). The discipline areas, the basis of elementary curriculum, include reading/language arts, mathematics, science, social studies, fine arts, music, and health/physical education. A study skills chapter is also included to assist examination-takers in the preparation process.

Each content area chapter is organized around the pertinent standards. Each chapter first presents the Texas standards, a summary of the competencies with discussion, practice examination questions and discussion, and an overview of the related knowledge base (i.e., the facts, concepts, skills, and appropriate practice). However, due to the nature of each content area's standards and competencies, each chapter has its own unique organization. For example, some subject areas have more standards than competencies, while others have more competencies than standards. Thus, the length and organization of each chapter will vary.

Standards refer to broad, general goal statements related to each discipline area. They serve as an inclusive umbrella for a dimension of the discipline. Competencies are akin to objectives, operationalizing each standard into a number of more specific subcomponents of knowledge, skill, and appropriate practice. These competencies, however, have been paraphrased from the official text published by SBEC.

The examination questions use a multiple-choice format and are written at the comprehension and application level of Bloom's taxonomy. The discipline areas are not treated equally in terms of the number of questions for each. For example, the reading/language arts component of the examination represents about 40 percent of all examination questions. The math, social studies, science, and other combined (fine arts, physical education, and health) components on the other hand, each represent 15 percent of all examination questions.

Why: A Rationale for This Book

Prospective Texas teachers currently come from all over the United States and the world. Their educational experiences and cultural backgrounds vary to a significant extent in terms of quantity and quality. Their prior knowledge about U.S. public school curricula will also vary. However, Texas has mandated a statewide curricula. Texas history, for example, is a mandated curricular requirement, and Texas requires its EC-4 teachers to have appropriate knowledge of that subject regardless of their educational preparation and background. This book provides a resource tool for prospective Texas teachers to identify, review, and/or remediate the knowledge, skills, and appropriate practice required for this Texas Generalist examination.

Where: The Organization of the Book

This book is divided into eight chapters. Chapter 1 presents generic but relevant study skills and examination preparation guidelines. Chapter 2 deals with language arts and reading; Chapter 3 presents mathematics; Chapter 4 deals with social studies; Chapter 5 presents science; Chapter 6 presents art; Chapter 7 presents music; and Chapter 8 presents health and physical education. As noted, each chapter presents the standards, a summary of the related competencies with discussion, practice examination questions with discussion, and an overview of the related knowledge base (i.e., the facts, concepts, skills, and appropriate practice). Authors were tasked with offering as much as possible but were restricted by length limitations. We hope that you will continue to seek more theory and ideas for good teaching.

SBEC: Additional Background

If you've ever wondered who makes up the rules under which one becomes certified as a teacher, counselor, principal, superintendent, or any of the other professional roles in public schools, in Texas the answer is the State Board for Educator Certification. Since education is one of the powers reserved to the states under the Tenth Amendment to the United States Constitution, each state is really responsible for its own system of public education—including decisions about who is licensed to teach in that state.

The State Board for Educator Certification (SBEC) is the result of 1995 action by the Texas Legislature. Its purpose is "to recognize public school educators as professionals and grant educators the authority to govern the standards of their profession." The Board is responsible to the Legislature for overseeing all aspects of the preparation, certification, and standards of conduct of educators in the state's public schools.

In just a few years, SBEC has shown a willingness to be innovative. It has implemented an accountability system for entities that prepare educators (sixty-nine institutions of higher learning and seventeen additional alternative certification programs at this writing) that is unique in the nation. It is phasing out the historic practice of issuing lifetime certificates in favor of certificates that are renewable every five years and requiring professional development during the five-year life of the certificate to assure that educators stay current in their professional knowledge. Most recently, the Board is changing the classes of certificates to better meet the emerging needs of elementary and secondary schools in the state.

STRUCTURE. SBEC is currently composed of fifteen members appointed by the Governor to six-year terms. Of the total, twelve are voting members and three are participating, but nonvoting, members. The voting members currently comprise:

- Four classroom teachers
- One counselor
- Two school administrators
- Five citizens of the state not employed in public schools

The *non*voting members comprise:

- One dean of a Texas college of education
- One staff member of Texas Education Agency appointed by the Commissioner of Education
- One staff member of the Texas Higher Education Coordinating Board appointed by the Commissioner of Higher Education

MEMBERS. While members are appointed for six-year terms, as is usual with a group this size, individuals sometimes move or change positions so that they can no longer hold a certain seat (e.g., a classroom teacher becomes an assistant principal). To get the most up-to-date information on the current membership of the State Board for Educator Certification the best source is its website: www.sbec.state.tx.us.

This website contains a wealth of information on the Board, its current membership, scheduled meetings, agendas, minutes; information on requirements and standards that apply to various types of certificates; press releases and reports generated by the Board and its staff; information on investigations and enforcement of certification standards and the Code of Ethics. It is also an excellent source of information for individuals who are certified in another state and who wish to become certified in Texas.

Good luck to all prospective teachers! We hope that this information will help you pass the examination and also help you become an excellent and knowledgeable teacher. May you give your best to children each and everyday.

ABOUT THE EDITORS

DR. JANICE NATH is currently a faculty member in the Department of Urban Education at the University of Houston-Downtown. She is the co-editor of *Becoming a Teacher in Texas: A Course of Study for the Professional Development ExCET, Becoming an EC-4 Teacher in Texas:* A Guide for the Early Childhood through Fourth Grade (EC-4) PPR TExES, and *Forging Alliances in Community and Thought: Research in Professional Development Schools.* Dr. Nath headed a Professional Development School (PDS) site for many years and was Coordinator for Elementary Education at the University of Houston. She has also served as president of the AERA (American Educational Research Association) Professional Development School Research Special Interest Group (PDRS SIG) and of the Texas Coordinators for Teacher Certification Testing (TCTCT). She is currently a member of the CSOTTE Board (Consortium for Texas Teacher Educators). Her wish for readers is that they remember always that their knowledge and actions reflect upon all teachers.

JOHN RAMSEY, Ph.D., is Associate Professor of science education at the University of Houston. He has served as department chair, director of teacher education, doctoral and masters advisor, and principal investigator for funded projects. His professional experience includes more than thirty years in middle, secondary, and higher education. He has co-authored or co-edited nine books and published twenty-five refereed research articles. He has received the highest university teaching award granted at the University of Houston and was honored with the 2001 Research Excellence Award from the North American Association of Environmental Education. He has conducted more than 300 international and national professional development workshops and presentations and has served as a consultant for the United Nations, national and state agencies, international governments, nongovernment organizations, and businesses.

ACKNOWLEDGMENTS

We would like to thank Mary Seay and Charlotte Marrow of Schreiner University and Diann Rozell of North Texas State University for their assistance. We would also like to thank Allyn and Bacon reviewers—Gayle Allen (University of Texas) and Diana Allen (University of North Texas)—for their time and input.

Study Skills and Other Helpful Hints

Cynthia G. Henry

Janice L. Nath
University of Houston-Downtown

Studying early and studying smart for the EC-4 Generalist will pay off with a higher test score for you, the test taker. In fact, research suggests that good things happen to students who improve their study and test-taking skills. Students with strong study skills find it easier to study, consistently earn better grades and higher test scores, and become more successful in life. Therefore, we begin with this chapter to give you strategies and hints to help you study for and complete this examination with success. This chapter will be designed along a timeline and written in a question-and-answer format to facilitate your learning.

SEVERAL MONTHS BEFORE THE EC-4 GENERALIST

What should I do first?

Make sure that you have selected a good time to take the EC-4 Generalist and have begun the registration process properly (either through the state or through your teacher preparation entity). Late registration can cost you more money and may cost you a delayed test day. Some candidates can now register online, but you may still need a barcode or approval number if you are receiving certification training through a university or alternative certification program. Addresses can be found at the end of this chapter.

How should I begin preparing for the EC-4 Generalist?

Studying for this important exam can seem to be overwhelming. There is so much information to learn (the good news is that much of it will probably be a review). Therefore, it is necessary to break this task down into smaller, more manageable steps. The key is to get organized by developing time-management skills and material-management skills. Start to review and learn any new information early!

What time-management skills will I need and how do I develop them?

The primary time-management skills you will need to develop are to set manageable time goals and workload goals for each study session. For example, if you begin studying for the exam four months before the test date, plan to study about three days a week for approximately 30 to 60 minutes per session. This is a manageable and reasonable study schedule for most. However, if you begin preparing for the EC-4 Generalist one to two months before the test date, you will need to study more days during the week and spend more time in each study session to ensure that you sufficiently cover the materials on the test. Scheduling your study sessions by writing them on your calendar as you would an appointment with your doctor or dentist will emphasize the importance of this time for you. Also, try to schedule your study sessions for the same time of the day or evening. This will help you develop and stick to a study routine.

Did you know that our brains more easily remember the first and last items we read as compared to items in the middle of a passage or list? This is important, if you want to maximize the amount of material you can remember. Don't study continuously during your study sessions. It is better to take frequent study breaks to create as many beginnings and endings as possible without forfeiting any of those minutes you have set aside for your entire session. For example, each chapter of this book is divided into smaller sections to deal with separate indicators. Several concepts are often covered in each of these subdivisions. Try to concentrate on one of these concepts for a bit and then return to another. However, study breaks should not be long. A brief 2- to 5-minute mental vacation is all it takes to give your mind a rest while your mind absorbs the material you have just read. Some suggestions for brief study breaks include listening to a favorite song, stretching your muscles by doing a few exercises, getting a quick drink or snack, or simply closing your eyes for a few moments.

For each of your study sessions, you must also set a workload goal that can be accomplished within the time allotted to your study session. For example, a reasonable workload goal would be to read five to ten pages of content material from a textbook or study guide or to work through several practice questions and their correct answers. Setting small time goals and workload goals are powerful and effective ways to overcome most study blocks that can often make a longer study session seem overwhelming. As Henry Ford once said, "Nothing is particularly hard if you divide it into small jobs."

What material-management skills will I need and how do I develop them?

You may have many materials that help you study for this test besides this book. The material management skills you need include keeping your EC-4 study materials organized and accessible. If your study materials are scattered throughout your house, apartment, dorm room, or other locations, you will waste valuable time locating and organizing them before you can begin your study session. Find an easily accessible place such as a desk, bookcase, or filing cabinet and return all of your study materials to this location when you have finished using them.

HELPFUL HINT

Plan to do something fun after a study session. Studying for this examination requires hard work, commitment, and dedication on your part. Therefore, it is important to schedule an enjoyable activity with which to reward yourself after a study session.

Your materials should be organized in such a manner that you can quickly find the books, notebooks, note cards, or study guides that you need. Using different colored file folder or manila file folders with colored labels for each content area is an effective method of organizing a large body of study material. For example, if you place all of your mathematics materials in a red file folder, you will quickly be able to locate everything when you are ready to study that content area. Further organization of your materials may have to be done if the content areas contain multiple areas that you need to study and review separately. Some domains contain many subsections. Due to the breadth of these topics, several file folders of the same color should be labeled separately with each content title—but stored together in a box or desk drawer for easy access.

As well as material management skills, there are other methods for creating an optimal study environment. These methods include:

A. Keeping your study environment at approximately 68 degrees: Cooler temperatures help improve concentration and memory.
B. Studying facing a blank or neutral wall: Looking at a wall of eye-catching posters or pictures can be very distracting.

C. Ensuring your study environment is well lit with high-wattage, soft-light bulbs: Fluorescent or insufficient lighting quickly increases mental fatigue.

SEVERAL WEEKS BEFORE THE EC-4 GENERALIST

How should I spend my study time and on what should I concentrate when I have only several weeks before taking the EC-4 Generalist?

Organize a Study Group

At this point you should feel competent that you are covering new material and reviewing old material in an effective manner. If you have not begun to prepare for the EC-4 Generalist before this time, please read the information in the previous section to help you organize and begin your study process as quickly as possible. Select the main subject areas that you feel may be deficient and concentrate on those areas first. Also, remember that certain subjects (language arts/reading and mathematics) are weighted more heavily (followed by science and social studies) in this test, so focus on these areas if you do not have much time.

> **HELPFUL HINT**
>
> In addition to studying with this guide, attend a university, district, regional, school-sponsored, or commercial review seminar. A specially prepared review can be a worthwhile investment and can offer additional insights and guidance in your preparation process. Take advantage of this opportunity, particularly if you have previously not done well on this examination.

If you have been preparing on your own for a while, now is the time, if possible, to organize a study group for review sessions. Other students or teachers who are also preparing for this examination can often offer fresh insight into the content and help maintain motivation for your study sessions. Discussing terms and concepts with others requires you to become actively involved with the material, and one of the best ways to learn something new is to explain and teach it to someone else. Generating your own practice questions and answers and reviewing content material with a partner or a small group of other test takers is one of the most effective means of preparing for an important examination.

Use Your Senses

Successfully completing the EC-4 Generalist requires you to know and remember a large amount of information. Using numerous sensory channels to store information is a powerful way to remember and recall what you have learned. Try to use your senses of sight, hearing, and touch during each study session. Make it a habit to visualize, discuss, draw, diagram, and/or create a flash card for what you are reading and hearing. This strategy will help you make connections with the content material and, in turn, help you to recall the information you need when you take the examination. Memory models help as well. For example, you may have had such models such as "Please Excuse My Dear Aunt Sally" in mathematics to remember the order of operations, but you can create your own models to help you remember some of the information needed for this test, too.

Use Your Time Wisely

Using your time wisely is a critical component in getting the most out of each study session. If you focus your attention and concentration powers on the materials you are studying, you will be more likely to accomplish your goals. To help you focus and concentrate, try the following suggestions:

A. Alternate your activities. Use each study session to review two or more content areas. For example, do not spend an entire study session focusing only on basic science concepts or geography material. Changing topics within a content area or studying two completely different content areas during one session will help keep your mind fresh and more mentally alert.
B. Take notes or underline as you read. Using this strategy will help you focus on the most critical ideas and concepts in the material. You will be forced to think about the information being presented and what it means to you. Most importantly, this will stop you from getting to the end of a page or section and wondering what you have just read.
C. Begin and end on a positive note. Incorporating this strategy is a simple way to maintain your focus and motivation for studying. If you are not a person who enjoys studying for long and difficult examinations, end your study session at a point where it is easy and logical for you to pick up and begin again. Beginning and ending on a positive note will go a long way in keeping you motivated and helping you concentrate and focus.
D. Buy in! If you are going to be teaching young children in Texas, you really should know all this content information! It will be good for students and good for you as a professional, and it is expected to be a part of your professional knowledge. Buying in to this idea will help keep you motivated!

It is also important to remember that the number of indicators within each domain or content area reflects the percentage of the area covered on the EC-4 Generalist. The domains or content areas with more indicators will have more questions on the exam. You will need to spend a greater percentage of your study time reviewing the material in those areas—for example, language arts in the past has had over 30 percent of the test questions. Do not forget to look at the current information on these percentages by going to the website listed at the end of the chapter.

TWO WEEKS BEFORE THE EC-4 GENERALIST

How can I best spend my time two weeks before the EC-4 Generalist?

Playing Games

Continue to review your study materials both individually and with your study partner or study group, if possible. You should have a good review schedule in place by now that meets your study needs. Now is also the time to test yourself before you are tested. One way to test yourself is to make a set of flash cards. These should include important terms, concepts, and definitions. Use your flash cards to review key terms and definitions in a "memory game" format by placing the flashcards down and turning over two at a time try to make matches between the key terms and definitions, or use them in the more common manner of setting aside the ones you don't know for concentrated study. Carry these cards everywhere with you so that you can review a few minutes here and a few minutes there.

Another idea is to use the content material and practice questions in this book to help you make additional questions for each indicator. Creating your own questions will help you begin thinking like the test developers—you may be surprised at how closely your questions actually match the real test questions!

Preparing for Multiple Choice Exams

TEST HINTS. The EC-4 Generalist is written in a multiple-choice format. As explained in the Preparation Manual for this exam, available online, this test is designed to make you think by recalling factual information, analyzing information, comparing it with other knowledge you may have, or making decisions about information. You will be asked to answer each question by choosing one of several answers. Then you will mark your answer choice on a separate answer sheet (a scan-tron). The best way to answer multiple-choice questions is to narrow your answer options by using a process of elimination. Several helpful suggestions for narrowing your answer options include:

- Reading the question and the related paragraphs and other material carefully. As you read, underline key information and circle key words or phrases.
- Reading all answer choices before choosing an answer.

- Placing an "X" next to the answer choices you know are incorrect. You will probably be able to eliminate one or two choice immediately after using this strategy.
- Considering when two choices are similar to each other, one of them is usually the correct answer.
- Considering when two choices are exacts opposite of each other, one of them is usually the correct answer.
- Examining the root of the question and/or trying to determine exactly what the question is asking. After selecting an answer, then go back to see if the answer you selected really is a match for the question.
- Remembering your pedagogy. Do not answer in ways that go against good educational theory.
- Looking closely at the verbs. This can be a good indicator of the correct answer (for example, if a question contains the word *prepare*, the answer should indicate something that the teacher would do *prior* to or in preparation of . . .).
- Looking closely for words that would change the answer (*best, most, least, not*, etc.).
- Going with your first hunch when choosing an answer, as this will be correct more often than not. Mark your first choice on every question. If you have a concern about it, place a small question mark beside the number and come back if there is time. If not, at least you have given it your best shot. This is a long examination with considerable reading. If you have to come back to many questions left unanswered, you may run out of time.

ITEM FORMATS. You need to be familiar with several types of item formats found on the EC-4 Generalist. These item formats include single items, stimulus material items, clustered items, and, possibly, correct response set items. Knowing these formats will help you to be ready to answer. Each of these formats is described below:

Single item format: A problem or question is presented with four answer choices. You are required to choose the correct response or ending and mark this on your answer sheet.

Stimulus material item format: A question follows some type of stimulus material. The stimulus material may include charts, graphs, maps, and tables. The stimulus may also be a real-world classroom situation, a dialogue between a teacher and student, or examples of student work. When answering this type of question, be sure to read the stimulus very carefully.

Clustered item format: A group of questions or problems is related to a single stimulus. Again, consider the stimulus very carefully and remember to put

HELPFUL HINT

Try to visualize the classroom, if it is a scenario-based question. Try to see the teacher acting in ways that reflect the EC-4 Generalist standards. Cut to the chase of what it is you believe they are asking by ignoring nebulous details. Select your answer, and then go back to the question to double-check if your selection truly answers that particular question.

yourself in the described teacher's frame of mind when answering questions. Make sure that you are answering from the teacher's point of view given to you through the Texas standards, however. This test will have the same biases that the PPR (Professional Pedagogy and Responsibilities) TExES test does—student choice, authentic assessment, self-assessment, relevant instruction, age-appropriate instruction, use of technology as a resource, use of cooperative groups, higher-level thinking, and so forth. If you have a choice of which of the two required tests you take first, it may be worth your taking the PPR initially so that you have a clear understanding of these issues and can better apply the desired Texas pedagogy and philosophies to these content area questions.

Correct response set item format: A problem or question presented with a set of statements numbered with Roman numerals (I, II, III, IV). Below the Roman numeral statements are four answer choices labeled A, B, C, and D. You are expected to choose the Roman numeral statement or statements that correctly answer the question. You will find this answer in the A, B, C, or D answer choices and mark one of these as a choice. The important point of this format is that it allows you to choose more than one correct response to the question. At press, this format was under discussion for being reduced or removed in new tests.

ONE WEEK BEFORE THE EC-4 GENERALIST

HELPFUL HINT

Schedule your study sessions when you feel the most energetic and motivated. Understanding your patterns of mental energy and fatigue will help you get the most out of your study time.

With only one week to go, what can I do to best prepare for the EC-4 Generalist?

There are several important issues to consider in the week before you take the EC-4 Generalist. First, continue to review your study materials both individually and with a study partner or group (if possible). If you have been following a well-designed study schedule, this last week before the exam will be a review week for you. This is not the time to begin learning new content. At this point, you should feel confident with your knowledge base in almost all of the competencies, so spend your study time on the few competencies that you need to further practice and review.

Housekeeping

You also have a few housekeeping chores to complete this week. First, read your test admission ticket carefully. Your admission ticket provides you with important information such as the exam date, exam administration site, time of the exam, the exam for which you are registered, and what to bring to the exam. Remember that NES (National Evaluation Systems, Inc.) does not guarantee that you will have the time or the site that you originally requested. If you arrive at the wrong site or the wrong time, you will not be allowed to test. Mistakes are made in issuing the tickets, so also check the test for which you signed up. There are no extra tests brought to a site, so if your requested test was incorrectly marked and you did not catch it in time, again, you will not be allowed to test. If you are taking more than one exam on the same day (and we hope you are not), you will receive a separate admission ticket for each. Remember to take your admission ticket(s) with you to the exam site. You will not be allowed to enter the testing site without your ticket.

Make sure you know how to get to the test administration site easily. Although the directions will be printed on your test admission ticket, you may want to consult a road map and make a dry run to the site a few days before your exam. This will help you figure out how long it will take you to drive to the site on exam day and what traffic, road construction, and/or parking problems you may encounter along the way. Remember that if you are late to registration, you may be refused admission to the test that day and refused a refund for missing your exam. If you are driving to a testing site from out of town, you may want to request an afternoon testing time or make a hotel reservation to avoid driving in the early morning hours. Be sure to book early—others may have the same idea.

Additional information about testing requirements, registration, test results, and obtaining a teaching certificate can be found in the Registration Bulletin. It is always suggested to also check the SBEC website to find out the very latest information and possible changes.

Test Anxiety

This week you may be feeling some test anxiety about taking the EC-4 Generalist. Test anxiety is a psychological response to a perceived threatening situation. Most of your fellow test takers will also be feeling a little anxious and nervous. In fact, feeling this way before an important exam is perfectly normal and can be beneficial, as it helps increase your alertness and improves your attention to the task at hand. Many test takers who are too calm are not motivated to do their best work. Having "an edge" can be good, but feeling a great deal of anxiety and nervousness can interfere with your performance on the EC-4 Generalist. Test takers who experience a high level of test anxiety can lose their concentration, feel their hearts pounding, experience lightheadedness, break out in a cold sweat, and may be unable to recall simple information when completing the exam. Highly anxious test takers tend to score lower on tests than less anxious test takers. Implementing the following strategies can help you control test anxiety on this examination:

- Ensure that you are thoroughly prepared for the exam. Many times test takers will use test anxiety as an excuse for lack of studying for the exam. Overpreparation may be the best way to prevent test anxiety, because the better you know the material, the more confident you will be about taking the test.
- Simulate the testing situation multiple times so it is as close as possible to the real experience. This includes taking timed practice tests and completing chapter exercises that will help you visualize and experience what the real EC-4 Generalist is like. After completing the practice questions and exercises in this book, use them as a guide to help you generate additional questions for each competency.
- Register for only one test at a time. Many teacher preparation entities do not allow multiple tests on one day anyway, so be sure to plan testing in plenty of time as to be able to attain a passing score in order to maintain your teaching contract or other benchmarks. Many people put these tests off, then reach the time limit when they must pass on a particular testing date or lose their jobs. This anxiety can be extremely detrimental to test taking. Research is continuing to show that many who attempt to take more than one test do not do well on one or both. These tests are extremely long tests, and, at a certain point, anxiety and/or a loss of concentration can cause you to not be able to continue at your best.
- Do relaxation exercises and practice positive self-talk before and during the exam. Take several slow, deep breaths before beginning the exam and visualize yourself successfully completing the test. Throughout the exam, say to yourself, "I have studied hard, and I know this material" and "I am confident I am doing well."
- Reserve this day for this examination alone. Trying to catch a plane, be a member of a wedding party, or even having a "big date" later that day or evening can cause you to fret or lose concentration during the test. This is an expensive test that is not offered very often, so reserve this day for testing and focus on the test alone.
- Arrive early. Many test takers who have to drive a considerable distance begin to panic that they will not arrive in time for registration. Some sites have parking a considerable distance away, so those who arrive late may be rushing to get seated in time to begin. Both of these situations set up a negative beginning for the hours of testing to come.

Put yourself in the teacher's frame of mind described in the question, and answer the question from that point of view when taking the EC-4 Generalist. However, do not answer the question based on your personal classroom observations and teaching experiences *unless* these experiences match the same actions and philosophies found in the Texas materials for this examination and other tests involving professional development philosophies.

- If another test taker causes you to begin to lose attention or creates anxiety for any reason (tapping or making other noises, causing the table to move, etc.), ask your proctor to move you. Do not talk with another person about this, as your proctor could view it as cheating. That, in turn, could cause you to lose your test score for that day.

THE NIGHT BEFORE THE EC-4 GENERALIST

What should I do the night before the EC-4 Generalist?

You should spend the night before the EC-4 Generalist organizing for the exam the next day and doing a relaxing activity to take your mind off the task ahead. Read your admission ticket again to confirm you know where to go and what time you are expected to be there and seated. Also, collect all of the supplies you will need for the following day. These supplies include your valid admission ticket, two pieces of identification, sharpened pencils with erasers, an accurate watch that does not beep, a snack, and a lunch if you are taking more than one exam on the same day (and, again, we hope you are not). You may want to put an energy bar and/or a drink in your pocket or purse to give you a mid-test boost, as there may be no snack machines available at the test site. Only water bottles with twist-off and -on caps are officially allowed inside. The two pieces of identification you must bring are described as follows:

- One government-issued photo ID, in the name in which you are registered.
- One secondary ID with a signature. At the time of publication, a second picture was being discussed. Check the website or your current Registration Bulletin to see if this has been added.

In the Registration Bulletin you will find examples of acceptable forms of identification, what to do if you forget your required forms of identification, or what to do if you do not have photo identification with your current name, and so forth. Also, you will find a complete list of prohibited items. Many personal items are prohibited at the exam site, and you will be asked to store them at your own risk in a designated area if you should bring any of these with you. A list of items prohibited at this time is as follows:

briefcases	cellular phones	watches that	slide rules
backpacks	electronic pagers	that beep	calculators
packages	audiotapes	highlighters	calculator watches
textbooks	dictionaries	notebooks	any written or
spell checkers	photographic	scratch paper	unauthorized
	or recording		materials
	devices		

HELPFUL HINT

Remember that there is no penalty for incorrect answers on the EC-4 Generalist. Even if you do not know the answer for a question, it is to your advantage to guess rather than to not answer at all.

Talking on a cell phone may be seen as cheating. Leave your phone at home or in the car. Also, be aware that eating, drinking, and smoking are not permitted inside the testing room or areas, though you may do so if you briefly step out of the room. Visitors, including friends and relatives, must remain outside the test site. Remember to carefully read the most current Registration Bulletin to ensure you understand the most recent requirements of the EC-4 Generalist.

After organizing your supplies for the following day, you should plan to do a relaxing and enjoyable activity to help take your mind off the task ahead of you. If you do plan to review this evening, spend only about an hour going over your notes or flipping through your flash cards. Do not use this time as a long study session to cram for tomorrow's exam.

Most importantly, you should go to bed early and get a good night's sleep. Waking up feeling refreshed and well rested will go a long way in helping you feel confident about the task ahead. Sleeping is not a waste of time with a huge day in front of you.

THE DAY OF THE EC-4 GENERALIST

What should I do on the day of the EC-4 Generalist?

Before the Exam

When the big day is finally here, there are several things you can do to help yourself be as successful as possible on the EC-4 Generalist. First, eat a nutritious breakfast if you are scheduled to take the exam in the morning, or eat a healthy lunch if you are scheduled to take the exam in the afternoon. Nutritionists suggest that foods high in protein and low in carbohydrates can produce mental alertness. Based on this suggestion, you will want to eat brain foods such as lean meats and fish, leafy green vegetables, and peanuts, while avoiding cereals, pastas, potatoes, and breads. Also, don't overload on caffeine before taking the examination, as this can impair your ability to concentrate and focus. You want to be as calm and relaxed as possible, and this is very difficult to do if you have infused your body with too much coffee or cola. An added distraction is that you may find your concentration broken by having to leave the test for too many restrooms breaks.

HELPFUL HINT

A good backup for avoiding errors that have to do with being on one number on the test booklet and another on the scan-tron is to circle the answer you selected right in your examination booklet. That way, if you do have a mismatch with your scan-tron, you will not be forced to go back through the test and reread a number of questions to find out where your first mismatch occurred—you already have a record of the answers you selected in your booklet.

Second, dress in loose, comfortable clothing and don't forget any lucky charms, if they are a psychological boost to you. It is a good idea to dress in layers so that you can take off or put on a jacket or sweater if the room temperature feels hot or cold during the test. Feeling comfortable and relaxed will go a long way in helping you focus on the exam during the many hours of testing.

A third guideline to follow on test day is to arrive early at the test site and sit by yourself in the testing room. By arriving early (as discussed earlier), you will not feel rushed and will have time to relax and become comfortable with the testing environment. If you can separate yourself from your fellow test takers, you will be able to tune out their chatter about how difficult they think this test is going to be and how worried they are about failing. If you cannot choose your seat and other test takers are talking around you, use this time to focus on all of the hard work you have put into studying for this exam and how that effort will pay off for you. This is a great time to practice your positive self-talk and deep breathing exercises. When testing begins, however, be sure to be in your assigned seat, if applicable. You may not receive credit if you are not where you are assigned.

During the Exam

After the examination has been distributed, read the test directions very carefully. This is especially important when taking a multiple-choice test like the EC-4 Generalist because of the several types of item formats described in an earlier section. Test takers can also make serious mistakes when answers are required to be recorded on a separate scan-tron and scored by a test-scoring machine. Be sure to stop and check after every ten questions to make sure your scan-tron number matches the question number you are answering. If you do mismatch your answer sheet, it is much better to catch this early and correct it rather than realize what you have done at the end of the test or not catch it at all.

HELPFUL HINT

Since the EC-4 Generalist is very long and demanding, you may find it easier to take several short breaks during the testing session rather than working continuously through the exam. Try closing your eyes or putting your head on your desk or table for 15 seconds (being sure not to nod off!). If you feel yourself becoming tense, take a few deep breaths and practice positive self-talk, reminding yourself that you do know this material. Step outside for a moment and walk briskly or have that energy bar in your purse or pocket.

Time management is a big factor in your successful completion of the EC-4 Generalist. Remember that if you do not control your time, it will control you. Because the classroom in which you are testing may not have a clock, you may not be able to see a clock from where you are sitting, or the clock may not be accurate, make sure you have an accurate watch that does not beep. Since the EC-4 Generalist is a timed test, keeping track of the time you have left will help you budget your time during the test session. Use all of the time allotted for the testing session by pacing yourself through the exam. There are difficult questions on this test, so do not spend too much time on any one question. Mark your first inclination by putting a question mark beside it if you are uncertain, and then go on. When you are first given your test booklet, note how many questions your particular exam has and divide your time by the number of questions and factor in the number of minutes on breaks that you think that you will schedule. This will give you an idea of how many questions you have to answer per hour to finish—including brief breaks. Move at a consistent pace through the exam and monitor yourself to keep track of how much time you have left. Allow at least five minutes at the end of the test to thoroughly check your answer sheet, making sure that you have marked an answer for each question (even if you have to quickly just guess). It would be a shame to lose a point for an incomplete erasure or a mark made outside the guidelines. Clean up your scan-tron thoroughly.

There is a way to have your scan-tron rechecked, if you believe that you may have some stray marks AND if you are within a point or two of passing. Having your test rechecked is probably not worth it if you have under a score that is more that within two or three points of passing, but if your circumstances are such that you are out of time for your job, and you do feel that your scan-tron was a bit messy, directions for rechecking your score are found in the Registration Bulletin.

 ## SUMMARY

In conclusion, studying for and passing the EC-4 Generalist is an important component of your job as an effective Texas teacher. By following this schedule, organizing your time and materials, and using good study skills, you will have an excellent chance of being successful on this examination and entering the classroom as a competent and confident educator. If you have questions about registration bulletins, completing forms, test dates and registration deadlines, test cancellation, score reports, or other information regarding the EC-4 Generalist, please write, call, or email:

TExES Program
National Evaluation Systems, Inc.
P.O. Box 140467
Austin, TX 78714-0467
Telephone: (512) 927-5151
Telecommunications for the Deaf:
  (512) 926-1248

State Board of Educator Certification
Information and Support Center (SBEC ISC)
4616 Howard Lane
Austin, TX 78728
Telephone: (888) 863-5880 (toll free)
E-mail address: sbec@sbec.state.tx.us
Website: http://www.sbec.state.tx.us

If you have certification questions or questions about which tests you need, you may want to call or write the State Board of Educator Certification (SBEC).

Check with the website for a current address and possibly phone numbers if these should no longer be found.

ABOUT THE AUTHORS

CYNTHIA G. HENRY, Ed.D., is a preschool director in Atlanta, Georgia. She was formerly a professor in the Department of Curriculum and Instruction at the University of Houston and served as the Coordinator for the Teacher Internship Program. She was also actively involved in field-based teacher education there. Dr. Henry has been an elementary classroom teacher and has worked extensively with gifted and talented students and ESL students. She is co-editor of *Becoming a Teacher in Texas: A Course of Study for the Elementary and Secondary Professional Development ExCET.* Her research interests include teacher education, gifted and talented education, and parent involvement.

JANICE L. NATH, Ed.D., is a faculty member at the University of Houston-Downtown in the Urban Education Department. She is the co-editor of *Becoming a Teacher in Texas: A Course of Study for the Elementary and Secondary Professional Development ExCET* (for the former state competencies), *Becoming an EC-4 Teacher in Texas: A Course of Study for the Pedagogy and Professional Responsibilities (PPR) TExES,* and *Forging Alliances in Community and Thought: Research in Professional Development Schools.* Teacher education is her main area of interest along with technology in teacher education, action research, and others. She has been actively involved in field-based teacher education for many years. She has also served as the president of the AERA (American Educational Research Association) Professional Development School Research SIG and as president of the Texas Coordinators for Teacher Certification Testing (formerly, the ExCET Coordinators Association). Currently, she is a CSOTTE Board Member and officer.

Preparing to Teach Language Arts and Reading

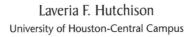

Laveria F. Hutchison
University of Houston-Central Campus

Eleanore S. Tyson
University of Houston-Central Campus

This chapter discusses the English Language Arts and Reading (Early Childhood–Grade 4) section of the *EC-4 Generalist.* It includes standards that discuss knowledge and classroom applications considered in literacy instruction and related areas such as oral language, phonemic awareness, comprehension, developmental writing, and assessment. In addition to a basic discussion of language arts and reading, other areas that support literacy have been added to provide a more complete overview of this section.

The authors of this chapter would like first to stress the importance of understanding as a test taker the components of each of these standards. As an example, let's consider *Standard VIII: Development of Written Communication*. First, the test taker needs to know the stages of the writing process, the meaning of each stage, and the relationship of each stage to the other English Language Arts and Reading standards and assessment procedures. Next, the test taker needs to understand the purpose and meaning of each test item that addresses this standard. Connections then need to be made to the meaning of key terms in the standard with the question and response choices. In this way, a test-taker determines the *best* answer that relates back to the standard. It is a circular process that goes from the standard to the purpose of the question and to the connection of response choices. As you study this chapter, you will be able to connect this information to your preparation for the Professional Roles and Responsibilities (PRR) TExES. There are questions that not only test content knowledge, but also your knowledge of best teaching practices as well. It takes practice in order to become a successful TExES question analyzer, but you can acquire this skill.

You are encouraged to read each standard, the definition of each standard, and each practice question. In addition, you should read the knowledge base that provides information related to the standard and critically analyze the application questions that follows. Also, it is important for you to read each knowledge-base section because standards often overlap. The English Language Arts and Reading (Early Childhood–Grade 4) section of the *EC-4 Generalist* consists of ten standards and provides test items for approximately 40 percent of the TExES test items. Additionally, these standards correlate with the Texas Essential Knowledge and Skills for English Language Arts and Reading (TEKS). The TEKS tells teachers what knowledge and skills children should gain at each grade level. Of course, that means that teachers must know that information in order to teach these skills, and they must also know the best ways to teach this information. Table 2.1 summarizes the instructional components of the TEKS for language arts and reading for pre-kindergarten through grade 4.

As you read the information about each standard, you will notice a relationship between the TEKS and TExES. Additionally, you can find a listing of the TEKS on the following website: http://www.tea.state.tx.us/teks.

STANDARD I (ORAL LANGUAGE)

Competency 001: Teachers of young children understand the importance of oral language, know the developmental processes of oral language, and provide a variety of instructional opportunities for young children to develop listening and speaking skills.

The teacher knows basic linguistic concepts, knows developmental stages in acquiring oral language, plans oral language instruction based on assessment procedures,

TABLE 2.1 Summary of Pre-Kindergarten–Grade 4 TEKS for Language Arts and Reading

Pre-kindergarten	Students interact with responsive adults and peers in a language- and print-rich instructional environment that provides opportunities for development in the following areas: 1. Listening comprehension 2. Phonological awareness 3. Functions of print 4. Letter knowledge
Kindergarten	Students engage in instructional activities that promote development of oral language usage, conceptual knowledge, narrative and expository print forms, alphabet usage, and letter formation.
Grade 1	Students engage in instructional activities that promote development of independent readers and writers by using various print forms, by providing reading materials that promote fluency and understanding, and by demonstrating the conventions of writing and spelling.
Grade 2	Students engage in instructional activities that promote development of independent readers by providing instruction that promotes sight vocabulary development, teaching and demonstrating a variety of word identification strategies, teaching comprehension skills, demonstrating graphic presentations, teaching note taking procedures, and teaching conventions of writing and spelling.
Grade 3	Students engage in instructional activities that promote structural analysis skills, glossary skills, elements of the writing process, independent reading activities, and activities that provide a transition from manuscript writing to cursive writing.
Grade 4	Students engage in instructional activities that demonstrate story structure analysis, produce narrative and expository writing products, practice the parts of speech in a variety of written forms, emphasize awareness of correct spelling and grammar, and demonstrate application of the elements of writing.

designs instructional practices that promote purposeful listening activities, provides various instructional activities that allow children to have opportunities to engage in oral language activities that involve adult and peer participation, and provides opportunities for children to evaluate the effectiveness of their own spoken language. The teacher needs to have an instructional environment that promotes discussions about books, objects, experiences, pictures, and other print and nonprint sources. Remember that the TEKS promotes oral language development and instruction.

Try this practice question.

Mr. Jones teaches a kindergarten class comprised of a diverse population of students with varying language proficiency levels. How can he encourage language development for all of his students?

A. Mr. Jones can facilitate a story writing activity where all students contribute to the story as he writes the class story on chart paper. Class members can then act out the story they created.

B. Students can memorize and chorally present a poem selected by the teacher to be shared with parents in a class presentation.

C. Mr. Jones can create language centers for students to work at during different times of the day that include a listening center, a puppet center, and a grocery story center.

D. A and C.

Response *A* incorporates and includes the language and voice of *all* the students in the classroom. Because students also see the teacher writing down what *they* say, children can understand how reading and writing are associated. Additional language use and oral expression are reinforced through the retelling and acting out of the story at the end. Response *B* does not promote language proficiency unless the students understand the words in the poem. There is an indication that, because it is a *teacher*-selected poem to present to parents, the message of the poem may have more meaning for the teacher and parents than for the students. Response *C* is also well rounded in the teacher's attempt to meet the language needs of *all* students whether they can or cannot recognize rhyming words or whether their language proficiency level is highly communicative or weak. The activities described in the centers would promote the language development of *all* students at any level of proficiency. Therefore, response *D* is correct.

Children come to school with a myriad of backgrounds and with varying degrees of language proficiency. Children's differences in language development are strongly shaped and influenced by language used in the home. Children fortunate enough to have had a rich literacy background at home are often confident and articulate. Their oral language is frequently quite advanced for their age. On the other hand, there are those children who, for a variety of reasons, are shy or reluctant to speak. Teachers must be aware of individual experiences with language to best meet the learning needs of their students. These children must feel comfortable speaking with another person at a personal and informal level before they will contribute to class discussions, speak out in a cooperative group, volunteer to take part in a skit, or give an oral report. When responding to questions about this standard, be aware that questions about students' language development will most likely focus on teacher awareness of individual students' background experiences with language and current language proficiency. The teacher's ability to meet students' learning needs with an appropriate instructional strategy (by considering individual students' learning and instructional levels, learning styles, personal backgrounds, and so forth) builds from students' present ability levels.

As the novice teacher begins to investigate the conceptual development of oral language, it is a good idea for him or her to review the features and stages of language development. A developed language base in young readers is important in learning to read. Although *learning theories* that explain the processes children follow in learning language are rather controversial, educators usually accept the following sequence (Jewell & Zintz, 1986):

1. Vocalizing sounds (crying or babbling) to obtain a response from a parent or caregiver.
2. Recognizing a stimulus-producing sound (hears a barking sound and looks at the family's dog).
3. Generalizing a word to identify an object (parent asks for the ball, and child responds by identifying the ball in a variety of ways such as looking at or touching the ball).
4. Speaking by age 3 years in phrases and sentences containing approximately four words; understanding the concept of "yes" and "no," asking and answering simple questions, and following directions such as "pick up the ball and give it to Mommy."
5. Developing language skills in preschoolers through focusing on using four to five words in a sentence, using a limited number of grammar rules, creating and orally presenting personal stories (about going to the zoo or to McDonald's), asking and answering questions, and describing objects and personal events.
6. Acquiring a speaking vocabulary of 2,000 to 3,000 words by kindergarten and continuing to develop oral language competencies.
7. Developing a continuous ability to produce words that includes use of social talk, correct grammar, and construction of oral and written complex sentences.

Basic related instructional components are generally apparent for the development of age-appropriate oral language skills. Early childhood teachers should foster a language-rich environment by displaying charts showing pictures of objects or actually displaying concrete objects being discussed in voice-recognition class, using picture books to enhance oral language development, providing technology using word walls that display high-frequency sight words, displaying items that identify colors, introducing symbols that explain directions, and so forth. Instructional practices that integrate language development usually provide expanded time-chunks for incorporating many or all of the entire language development components, hopefully engaging children in literacy as a whole. This intradisciplinary approach allows children to use a variety of cognitive resources such as predictable books, literature-based basal readers, trade books, computers, newsprint, visual media, peers, libraries, teachers, and other adults. The discussion of this standard highlights several components of linguistic concepts, then proceeds to discuss those that beginning teachers should recognize as part of the decoding process.

One concept that teachers should understand well is decoding. Numerous studies by educational researchers have provided information on the processes young children use in decoding words. As children attempt to pronounce a word, they gain information from the way a word is spelled (**orthography**), the way a word is pronounced (**phonology**), the way a word is defined (**semantics**), the recognition of the sounds heard in a word (**segmentation**), the sentence structure (**syntax**), and the meaning of a word in its contextual setting. This is a challenging process for teachers to convey to children and for children to apply to the many text forms or printed materials encountered in classrooms.

Another element for beginning teachers to consider is that classroom instruction needs to relate to students from cultural and linguistically diverse backgrounds. Diverse backgrounds include those students who speak Standard English, who speak nonstandard English, who are bilingual, who are emerging English speakers, and who speak no English at all. Linguistic considerations include the various dialects and languages present in classrooms. Let us investigate some strategies and terms that connect with these young learners.

The **language experience approach** (**LEA**) is an instructional method that incorporates the various components of language arts by using children's experience and backgrounds as the language structure for developing stories individually or in a heterogeneous group. These group or individually generated stories can discuss ideas about school activities, field trips, a trade book, observations, structured words, personal experiences, creative stories, or a variety of other topics. LEA is connected to *schema theory* by using students' experiences and backgrounds as a focus for developing stories. LEA allows children to observe the organization and mechanical functions of written language by observing the teacher print directionally from left to right and from top to bottom. Children also see printed word organization and spacing, punctuation, letter formation, and sentence structure (as the teacher writes down their stories, responses, etc.). Additionally, children with limited English proficiency (LEP) and with limited background experiences can benefit from LEA, because they are better able to comprehend reading material that they themselves dictate to the teacher.

As the connection of LEA and children with limited English proficiency is mentioned, there is the need to discuss **nonstandard dialects.** These are dialects used by children who speak only English, by bilingual students, and by multilingual students. It is important to note that Standard English is a dialect that is effectively used by many members of society (we might say "business" English). Nonstandard English is often connected to the usage of grammatical variations in language production. A dialect may belong to a cultural group, and usage in that group requires certain language rules just as with Standard English.

In relationship to LEA and how to most effectively use nonstandard English in classroom situations, consider the following conversational example between a student and a teacher:

Teacher: Have you decided on a title for your story?
Student: Yup. Me go write bout my cat are going to have kittens.
Teacher: Oh! I think that is a great idea. You are *going to write about how your cat is* going to have kittens. Let's get started.

The teacher accepts the child's idea that is stated in nonstandard English and models another way to restate the child's sentence using Standard English. Note that the teacher focuses on the ideas the child offers. The teacher is accepting and not critical of the child's language used to state the idea in this conversation. It is important to note that a child's personal usage of oral and written language has an important multicultural aspect, because not accepting a child's language production (especially when the language includes nonstandard English) could deter learning risks and language growth. However, teachers should always model many examples of correct and effective speech structures and writing examples in classroom situations, ask children to clarify their responses, and provide positive feedback that encourages Standard English. Many teachers feel that a goal for children is *bidialectism*. This means that children can feel less pressure using their home dialect as they learn to be successful in using Standard English in school and later in the business world.

It is important to state again that children enter school with oral and listening vocabularies that have been developing since they were born. These vocabularies have been shaped by children's cognitive, linguistic, cultural, and experiential backgrounds. A teacher's goal should be to promote children's development of reading and writing vocabularies that closely parallel these oral and listening vocabularies. Piaget's word *schema* reminds us that it is easier to learn if we can attach new knowledge to something already known.

Language interference is the use of sounds, syntax, and vocabulary of two languages simultaneously as a child participates in literacy activities. **Bilingual education** involves presenting reading and other subject area materials in the child's native language while gradually introducing English orally. **English-as-a-Second Language** (ESL) teachers may work with children from a variety of countries who speak a number of languages placed together in one class. As the beginning teacher instructs children who are in the instructional process of learning English (English Language Learners), it is important to explain the common meanings of English words before beginning instruction of multiple meanings of words and to use strategies such as LEA and restating discussed above.

In a language arts classroom, *listening* is another significant part of oral language learning. Students who become *active* listeners can remember important parts of a story, follow directions, respond to purpose-setting questions set by the teacher, participate in cooperative groups, and improve vocabulary development. As students learn to listen critically, the teacher should provide students with practice in building on prior knowledge, in learning to synthesize information from more than one source, and in solving problems. As students learn to listen for appreciation, the teacher should emphasize the understanding of mood and of the use of figurative language. Although there are a variety of instructional components that can be used, note taking and questioning are two that are important in this area.

Note taking is a selective listening activity that allows children to organize ideas, identify main ideas, and provide study points. Teachers can model *developmentally appropriate* note taking for students by presenting a graphic organizer such as a graphic mapping activity or an outline of the content (which may be partially filled in), narrative stories, picture books, and oral presentations. As children learn the process of identifying and recording important information, they can engage in cooperative groups to compare ideas. You will find additional information about note taking in the discussion of Standard VII.

Questioning is another area that promotes effective listening and higher level thinking. Teacher questioning should promote responses from children that help them comprehend literal, inferential, and appreciation comprehension ideas and meanings. You will find additional information about comprehension in the discussion of Standard VII.

Learning a language involves understanding how to analyze words. *Word analysis* is a strategy that includes three cueing systems that good readers develop and learn to use: **graphophonic** (sound/symbol relationships), **syntactic** (patterns of phrases, clauses, and sentences), and **semantics** (meaning of words and combinations of words). To become proficient in word analysis, children need to develop an effective sight vocabulary and know how to use contextual and structural analysis as well as phonics skills. All these are considered **facilitative** skills and are *not* considered reading. The actual understanding or comprehension of what has been read is the **functional** part of reading.

There are many strategies for developing and expanding vocabulary. Aside from using glossaries that are located in the back of textbooks, dictionaries, and thesauruses, students can use **word walls,** examine **homophones** and **homographs,** study **idioms, metaphors,** and **similes,** explore riddles and other word plays, engage in **word sorts,** and create semantic maps (word clusters) and semantic feature analysis grids. Below you will find descriptions of the highlighted words in this paragraph:

1. *Homographs.* Words spelled the same but have different pronunciations and meanings: for example, "She is wearing a red *bow.*" "She will *bow* to the queen."
2. *Homophones.* Words that sound the same but have different spellings and meanings: for example, "He is wearing a *red* shirt," "He *read* the book."

3. *Idioms.* Figurative sayings that have special meanings: as an example, *"Keep your shirt on!"* basically means "Don't get angry."
4. *Metaphors.* Comparison of two unlike things without using *as* or *like;* an example is *"The moon was a silver dollar against the night sky."*
5. *Semantic map (word cluster).* Writing a word or concept in the center circle of a cluster, drawing rays, writing information about the word or concept, and making connections between the word or concept and the related unit of study.
6. *Similes.* Comparisons between two things of a different kind or quality using *like* or *as.* An example is *"The rain came down like transparent sheets."*
7. *Word sorts.* Sorting a collection of words taken from a word wall or other source into two or more categories.
8. *Word wall.* A list of words children are learning or know posted on a poster (or an actual wall in a classroom) in a highly visible location.

A discussion of integrated language arts should include thematic learning units. **Thematic units** are used to connect the various components of language arts (speaking, reading, spelling, writing, and listening, etc.) with other content areas. Thematic units may have a focus in any content area (science, health, mathematics, etc.). Children enjoy units on, for example, butterflies, apples, shapes, cultures of other lands, and so forth. A first-grade thematic learning unit in social studies, for instance, could focus on "The Pilgrims Celebrating Thanksgiving at Plymouth in 1621." In this unit children might read, or their teacher can read to them, textbook information and **trade books** (trade books are children's literature sources that teachers sometimes use in instructional settings instead of basal readers or textbooks) about the topic. Additionally, children could research this period of history by investigating lifestyles, tasting foods the Pilgrims found in America, and focusing on significant people, types of transportation, and so forth. Children could examine a variety of sources, including computer-generated information, to collect information about the topic. It is important for teachers to consider instructional activities that include addressing children's interests. As an example, the teacher might encourage children to participate in writing and/or performing a short play that highlights this significant period. The unit might focus on games that children played during those times (both Pilgrim and Native American) compared to games children play now. Mathematics elements might compare the difference between how much things cost during that period and the present or measuring to determine how large the houses were in Plymouth colony. Counting songs (with lyrics dealing with a Thanksgiving theme) combine mathematics, reading, and music. Thematic units should contain a number of subject areas under the umbrella of one topic.

Another important language arts concept is *oral expression.* It takes practice and feedback to become adept in expressing oneself orally. Having a **conversation** with even one other person who is not a member of their own family may be a new experience for some children. A teacher's asking a child specific questions about his or her interests can help a child organize his or her thoughts and encourage the communication of information and ideas. Other informal speaking activities such as role-playing using a telephone encourage a child to adjust voice volume and wait for the other person's response. In this way, a child learns telephone etiquette as well as gains confidence. Textless, or wordless, picture books provide an opportunity for a young child to tell a story to the teacher. Because there is no text in these books, there is no correct way to relate the story, and the child has the freedom to interpret it any way he or she chooses. From this "reading," the teacher can assess a child's sense of story as well as vocabulary development and communication skills. **Show-and-tell** builds the speaker's confidence and stimulates conversation. It also provides an important link between home and school, because the child brings something from home that is special to him or her. Children are more articulate when they are talking about something that is well known and important to them. **Discussions** about special events or favorite books can also afford opportunities for oral language development. **Puppets** are confidence builders with many children, as noted earlier. Children who refrain from speaking in class will frequently feel comfortable talking to or through a puppet. The puppet becomes the center of attention, so the child feels less self-conscious and can therefore be more articulate. Other strategies for encouraging oral language development include *interviews, oral reports, debates,* and *dramatic presentations.* In a language arts classroom, *active speaking* is recognized as a critical component of learning. Noise levels vary because students are encouraged to work in pairs or in larger cooperative groups. These groups encourage discussions, reactions, and negotiations. Teachers can promote active speaking in classroom situations by implementing activities such as:

1. Rereading stories. Asking children to talk about their favorite parts of the story and their favorite characters in the story.
2. Retelling stories. Teachers may have children use props, puppets, dolls, etc., in the retelling process to encourage comprehension and fluency. (See discussion of story retelling under Standard VII.)
3. **Choral reading** and speaking that allows children to orally share written words. Choral delivery can also be used in a thematic unit as children orally deliver a poem or in a science class to read a section of print.
4. **Readers' theater,** which involves children's reading from a prepared script or from a script that children have written. Children learn to project the voice of characters, bring characters to life, and have eye contact with their audience. This activity incorporates reading and oral fluency skills by student performers and listening skills by the audience.
5. Social classroom talk, or conversation, that encourages informal discussions about characters in books or formal discussions about the procedure to solve a problem.

In a language arts classroom, students should have the opportunity to *actively read* from a variety of sources such as books, poems, magazines, computer screens, and other types of print. Students are encouraged to *actively write* and read aloud such products as poems, creative stories, journal entries, drafts and edited works, records of science experiments, and many other types of writing products. Very young children may begin to develop products such as shape books, picture books that show familiar objects, and letter books and be encouraged to read or explain them to others.

Effective assessment practices are important as teachers collect information for the purpose of making decisions about instructional practices. Teachers of young children usually collect instructional information by the use of observations of abilities, from parents during conferences, from informal conversations, and from formal and informal tests. Observational data can be recorded on checklists, in field notes, in notebooks, or in any form that will allow the teacher to organize and summarize collected data. Parental input is important because parents can provide information about the child's home environment. Additionally, parents can be encouraged to promote literacy activities in the home by (1) placing labels on objects/things that are in the home, such as *light, door, window,* or *bed;* (2) asking a variety of questions about favorite topics such as pets and toys; (3) rereading books or other materials children seem to love and enjoy; (4) helping children place cut-out magazine pictures into categories such as animals that bark, things that people eat, things that are green, etc.; (5) playing developmentally and age-appropriate games; (6) providing many opportunities for conversation; (7) reading predictable books; (8) going to the community library to select books to read and reread at home; and (9) encouraging and showcasing schoolwork and other beginning attempts of literacy activities in the home. Formal assessments used in early literacy settings usually measure knowledge of letters, oral vocabulary development, recognition of words, and visual and auditory discrimination ability (Barrett, 1965). The informal and formal assessment procedures that highlight different instructional practices will be discussed again in Standard X.

Try these practice questions.

Mrs. Parlez has several pre-kindergarten students in her class who are reluctant to speak in class. What activities might she use to stimulate the development of their oral language?

- **A.** Have students use puppets to tell a familiar story.
- **B.** Have students role-play telephone conversations.
- **C.** Have students "read" aloud textless, or wordless, books.
- **D.** All of the above.

Consider what activity might encourage a shy or reluctant child to speak in a class setting. With regard to Response *A,* young children will often speak using a puppet while they are too shy to speak face-to-face to an adult. Response *B,* role-play conversations using a play telephone, offers a familiar and comfortable way for a young child to express himself or herself. Response *C,* "read" aloud textless, or wordless, picture books affords a framework for oral storytelling. Since each of the above choices could be effectively used to promote oral language development, the correct answer is *D.* (It should be noted here that show-and-tell is often used with young children because it permits young children to talk about a topic or item that is important to them in a relaxed, accepting atmosphere.)

Mr. Cate, a fourth-grade teacher, has invited a guest speaker to discuss the important events related to the upcoming rodeo. Realizing that the speaker's main objective is to present a wide range of information over a 30-minute time period, which of the following would be the best listening practice or practices for Mr. Cate to implement for the children to use as they listen to the speaker?

    A. Provide a list of purpose-setting questions.
    B. Arrange the children into cooperative groups.
    C. Provide a summary of the speaker's discussion.
    D. Provide the children with an open note-taking sheet.

Remember that Mr. Cate is providing activities to support effective listening practices that would allow the children to have identified purposes for listening to the speaker. The use of cooperative grouping, recommended in Choice *B,* could be an effective practice for peer engagement to discuss aspects of the speaker's ideas after the speaker has finished. Providing the children with either a written or an oral summary of the speaker's ideas, recommended in Choice *C,* could provide ideas about the speaker's presentation afterwards. The note-taking sheet, recommended in Choice *D,* does not provide a purpose (giving the children questions/statements at different levels of comprehension to establish purposes/reasons to listen) for listening to the speaker. It is necessary to decide if identifying the purpose for listening to the speaker is most important. Does having a purpose to listen to the speaker assist the children in focusing on the content of the speaker's ideas, and does this knowledge allow them to have the information necessary to engage in other activities? Response *A* is the best response because this activity gives the children an effective method for gaining information by providing a rationale for collecting information about the speech.

Students in Miss Lucio's urban kindergarten class dictated a story about their field trip to the fire station. What should she *not* expect in the content of their oral delivery?

    A. Standard English.
    B. Inconsistent grammar structure.
    C. Details about the field trip.
    D. Events highlighting the field trip.

Actually, *B, C,* and *D* are components of the Language Experience Approach that are frequently found in dictated stories and that were discussed in Standard I; therefore, response *A* is what the teacher should not expect in a dictated story at this time in the young child's development. However, Standard English, or "business" English, is the target teachers try to reach.

Miss Chavez, a pre-kindergarten teacher, plans to provide a list of at-home activities for parents to use. Which parental activities should she suggest?

A. Allow your child to assist in planning family activities.
B. Read books to your child and allow your child to discuss the pictures.
C. Clip pictures from magazines that represent the color of the week.
D. All of the above.

In this situation, Miss Chavez could appropriately recommend each activity to parents as activities that could foster literacy concepts; therefore, *D* is the correct answer.

STANDARD II (PHONOLOGICAL AND PHONEMIC AWARENESS)

Competency 002:   Teachers of young children understand the components of phonological and phonemic awareness and utilize a variety of approaches to help young children develop this awareness and its relationship to written language.

The teacher understands the significance of phonological and phonemic awareness instruction to the reading process, adjusts instruction to meet the developmental needs of children, uses assessment practices to plan instruction, and designs a variety of age-appropriate instructional activities. Remember that beginning in pre-kindergarten and continuing through grade 4, TEKS objectives require using of a variety of print and nonprint language activities that expose children to phonemic awareness instruction.

Use this kindergarten teacher's instructional activity to answer the practice question that follows the activity.

Miss Fuentes, a kindergarten teacher, asks Alex, Mario, Mac, Armando, and Trenia to come to the literacy table. Miss Fuentes plans to use an oral activity to practice rhyming words. Below is the activity she uses with the children.
I am going to say two words together. After I say the words, I will call on one of you to tell me if the words rhyme. If the words rhyme, say "yes." If the words do not rhyme, say "no."

She uses the following list:

1. top/pop   **5.** sun/man
2. rag/big   **6.** make/take
3. sack/bat   **7.** pig/peg
4. look/book   **8.** could/should

Identify the prereading skill the kindergarten teacher is using:

A. Segmenting of rhyming sounds.
B. Auditory discrimination of rhyming pairs of words.
C. Visual discrimination of rhyming pairs of words.
D. Blending

Choice *B* is the correct response because the teacher is orally presenting pairs of words to the group of students for the purpose of orally identifying rhyming pairs. A description of segmenting and blending will be presented later in this section.

This standard highlights the concept of **phonological awareness** (the ability to use letter-sound knowledge to identify an unknown word) and **phonemic awareness** (the ability to recognize that spoken words are made up of a sequence of individual sounds that contributes to the young reader's ability to recognize and pronounce unknown words) (Rubin, 2000). As a teacher starts to develop instructional activities that demonstrate to the young reader that words are made up of a series of sounds, it is important to realize that several reading researchers have found that *phonemic awareness* abilities are strong indicators and predictors of successful reading development (Cunningham, Cunningham, Hoffman, & Yopp, 1998; Juel, 1988; Stanovich, 1994). Phonemic awareness is a necessary skill for the young reader to acquire in learning to read and spell. According to Adams (1990), young readers should be able to perform the following phonemic awareness tasks that relate to learning to read and spell.

1. *Rhyming and Alliteration.* Rhyming requires the young reader to recognize rhymes or to produce patterns of rhyming words. Rhyming is believed to be the least difficult phonemic awareness task to develop because young children have usually been exposed to oral productions of rhyming word patterns from books read to them, singing songs, adults' oral play language, and other auditory media sources. Rhyming, initially, is developed through listening. Later, the young reader learns to identify rhyming patterns in various types of printed materials. The following sentence is an example of rhyming: The girl saw a *hat* when she was sitting next to a *cat*. Alliteration requires the young reader to recognize words in a sentence or phrase that mostly begin with the same letter sound. The following sentence is an example of alliteration:

Tall Tella took tiny tots to town.

2. *Blending.* This task requires the young reader to blend a series of orally produced sounds to form a word. As an example, the teacher would produce the separate sounds of /t/, /o/, /p/ to the reader and expect the reader to say *top.*

3. *Segmenting beginning and ending sounds in words.* The young reader who has the ability to hear sounds in words should be able to hear and identify sounds at the beginning or end of a word. The teacher could ask the reader to identify the sound heard at the beginning of the word *top* and also the sound heard at the end.

As the young child develops phonemic awareness, he or she can recognize that words rhyme, that words can begin and end with either the same sound or a different sound, and that words are made of **phonemes** (the smallest unit of sound in a language that distinguishes one word from another word), which can be blended to form words.

It is important to mention that parents play a significant role in the development of children's phonemic awareness development by reading, saying, or singing rhymes together, playing oral language games, and encouraging early written expression by using scribbles and forms of **invented spelling.** Invented spelling is a written approximation based on how a child determines the spelling of a word. As an example, a kindergarten student might write the following sentence to describe his new puppy: M PUE ES QT AN VE TE (My puppy is cute and very tiny). The discussion of Standard VIII (Development of Written Communication) will provide additional information related to invented spelling. Early childhood teachers and early elementary school teachers should provide examples of reading materials and language activities that parents can use in the home to promote phonemic awareness. The home reinforces the work that teachers do at school. Young children need to be able to (1) associate sounds with letters in words; (2) learn the function of consonant sounds and letters in the initial, medial, and final position; and (3) see print in a variety of situations (big books, peer writing, word walls, trade books, basal readers, worksheets, charts, etc.).

Teachers of young children are encouraged to use *oral interaction* and *direct instruction* in demonstrating phonemic awareness patterns that show how sounds in words are manipulated. The following list provides an instructional structure for developing *phonemic awareness.*

1. *Promote language through different types of oral delivery.* Teachers of young children can use nursery rhymes, riddles, songs, read-aloud books, poems, and other creative ideas that provide sound production. Teachers can

demonstrate the same types of activities to parents during the annual Open House/Back to School Night, at parent–teacher conferences, through newsletters, on a website, and at various types of parental educational meetings. Children should be asked to respond to questions and statements related to reading selections in both narrative and expository print sources. The teacher and/or parent can ask questions such as "Which two words rhyme?" "Which two words begin with the same sound?" and "Identify the sounds that you hear at the end of the first two words in the following sentence." Rhyming words are used frequently as an instructional activity for young children, and the teacher should spend time demonstrating that rhyming words sound the same at the end of each word used in the rhyming pattern. Additionally, teachers should encourage children to make up their own rhyming word patterns.

2. *Create games and activities that develop an awareness of sounds in words.* As children begin to develop an understanding of the concept of phonemic awareness, the teacher can purchase or develop games and activities that practice sound patterns in words. As an example, teachers can say a word (or children's names, for example) and ask children to clap the number of syllables heard as the teacher repeats the word. The Elkonin box (1963) is frequently used to practice phonemic awareness by placing a picture on an overhead projector or worksheet and drawing the appropriate number of boxes needed to represent the sounds heard in the word. The teacher might have a picture of the word *hat* and three boxes under the picture (each box represents a sound heard in the word *hat*). Children then place some type of marker (paper chips, plastic counters, pennies, beans, etc.) in each box as the teacher pronounces a word with that sound. As children advance in their understanding of phonemic awareness, the teacher should ask the children to write the letter of each sound in the appropriate box. The teacher should have several examples of Elkonin boxes for the children to use. Another activity to help students delete or add phonemes to words is having an ending sound on tagboard (such as "at") with beginning sounds that can be flipped in front (c, f, m, etc.) or taken away. These flip charts can be teacher constructed on tagboard with the beginning phonemes on a binder ring. Technology programs abound for emerging readers, but a teacher must be sure that he or she uses a variety rather than *only* programs that are "worksheets" on the computer. One type of technology that helps students with difficulties in spelling in this area is recognition programs, where a computer "reports" in writing what a child says. The teacher must also make sure that *all* children are given appropriate grade-level reading activities and assignments.

3. *Design writing activities.* As children begin to develop an understanding of phonemic awareness, the teacher should provide classroom activities that allow children to experiment with language through writing words, phrases, sentences, paragraphs, and longer written segments. The more

opportunities children are given to write, the better they will become at understanding and hearing the sounds in words they can use to invent the spelling patterns used to produce a word. As children become capable of segmenting sounds used to spell words, the teacher should encourage children to approximate, or invent, the spelling of words based on the sounds heard in words. Teachers should then provide instruction in classroom settings that will enhance spelling patterns. Additionally, teachers can use classroom word walls to display spelling patterns used in words, sight words, and so forth. Teachers should remember to encourage children to use words from the word wall in both oral and written language formats.

In classroom settings, teachers can assess children's ability to use phonemic awareness through informal or formal means. Informal assessments that evaluate phonemic awareness include (1) teacher observations of students' completing phonemic awareness tasks that require students to complete written tasks and produce oral responses, (2) teacher use of rubrics and checklists that identify the level of performance students have acquired using phonemic awareness tasks, and (3) other teacher-generated products that provide evidence of students' growth using phonemic awareness tasks.

One formal assessment instrument is currently being used by teachers in Texas to determine children's ability to manipulate sounds in words and to determine how children understand these words. The *Texas Primary Reading Inventory* (TPRI). It is used in kindergarten through second grade, has been designed as an early reading assessment to determine young readers' early literacy and comprehension development (Carlson, Fletcher, Foorman, Francis, & Schat-

TABLE 2.2 Components of the *Texas Primary Reading Inventory*

Grade	Screening Section	Inventory Section
Kindergarten	Graphophonemic knowledge Phonemic awareness	Book and print awareness Phonemic awareness Graphophonemic knowledge Listening comprehension
Grade 1	Graphophonemic knowledge Word reading Phonemic awareness	Phonemic awareness Graphophonemic knowledge Reading accuracy and fluency Listening comprehension
Grade 2	Word reading	Graphophonemic knowledge Reading accuracy and fluency Reading comprehension

schneider, 2001). Table 2.2 shows the components of the TPRI's screening section and inventory section.

The *Yopp-Singer Test of Phonemic Segmentation* is another formal assessment used to measure children's ability to pronounce sounds in spoken words and to spell words. This is a 22-item assessment that requires children to respond to teacher-pronounced words by segmenting each pronounced word into separate sounds. This test allows teachers to identify students who need instruction and practice in phonemic awareness (Yopp, 1995).

Read this activity and respond to the question that follows.

Ms. Nguyen, a kindergarten teacher, asks students to "clap the number of syllables" heard in this list of words:

1. schoolhouse
2. building
3. pony
4. blue
5. Monday
6. hamburger
7. wagon
8. book

What is the purpose of this activity?

A. To determine the development of sight words.
B. To determine the ability to hear syllables.
C. To determine the readiness for teaching reading.
D. To determine the use of capital letters.

This activity allows Ms. Nguyen to determine how effectively her kindergarten children are hearing syllables in orally pronounced words. Therefore, Choice *B* is correct.

STANDARD III (ALPHABETIC PRINCIPLE)

Competency 003: Teachers of young children understand the importance of the alphabetic principle to reading English, know the elements of the alphabetic principle, and provide instruction that helps children understand that printed words consists of graphic representation that relates to the sounds of spoken language in conventional and unintentional ways.

The teacher knows the elements of the alphabetic principle, understands individual differences as related to the alphabetic principle, provides instructional activities that assist children in gaining competence in determining sound/letter relationships, and uses assessment practices that determine skill development. Remember that the TEKS promotes instruction that uses a variety of practices for developing print awareness, letter knowledge, word analysis strategies, and fluency development.

Read the following activity and respond to the practice question.

Have first-grade students name the letters of the alphabet. Have one sheet that lists the alphabet in sequence and one sheet that lists the alphabet in random order. Remember to present lowercase letters first in at least a 14-point print size. *You may repeat the same activity using uppercase letters.* What is the purpose of this activity?

    A. To determine alphabet letter recognition.
    B. To determine the use of uppercase and lowercase letter formation.
    C. To determine readiness for formal reading instruction.
    D. To determine alphabetizing.

The purpose of this instructional activity is to determine letter recognition of both upper and lower case letters in sequential and random order. Choice *A* is correct.

This standard focuses on elements of the **alphabetic principle,** which states that there is a one-to-one correspondence between alphabet letters (graphemes) and sounds (phonemes). The English language does not have a systematic alphabet system that has only one sound for each of the twenty-six letters of the alphabet because these twenty-six letters have approximately forty-four different sounds (phonemes). As an example, Tompkins (2001) states that "long *e,* for instance, is spelled fourteen different ways in common words. Consider, for example, *me, meat, feet, people, yield, baby,* and *cookie*" (p. 164). In addition to the alphabetic principle, it is important to state that **graphophonemic knowledge** is the understanding that written words are made up of systematic letter-patterns that represent sounds in pronounced words. This discussion will highlight instruction related to letter recognition, the relationship of letters in printed words to spoken language, and instructional activities used to enhance the development of letter recognition.

Letter naming, or *alphabetic recognition,* is an important skill to develop because children use this skill to acquire reading, spelling, and writing ability. It is important to mention that the alphabet is a series of abstract marks that must be assigned identities and sounds to promote usage in written context. As young children develop the skill of naming letters of the alphabet, they must learn to recognize the shapes of the uppercase manuscript letters, lowercase manuscript letters, uppercase cursive letters, and lowercase cursive letters. Additionally, young children need to identify letters based on formation, position on a line, length, and size. Children frequently have difficulty recognizing the difference between letters that look similar. As an example, the upper case letters *E* and *F* and the lower case letters *b* and *d* often confuse the young reader. Until recently, children who reversed or confused similarly formed letters (or words that contained similar letters) were considered to have learning deficits. However, today educators believe that constant exposure in a variety of instructional settings will assist children in developing the skills needed to overcome many of these somewhat common difficulties.

Many children enter school naming the letters of the alphabet by rote memory. However, teachers should realize that young children may not understand that these letter names connect to sound and writing. Children will need instruction in using the letters of the alphabet in random sequence and to learn, practice, and apply the basic sounds that each letter represents. According to Adams (1990), automatic and instant recognition of letters, presented in sequence and randomly, allow children to focus on learning and applying sound-symbol relationships.

Most educators agree that beginning teachers should come to their classrooms with a variety of instructional methods and activities to teach the young child to recognize and apply letter-name knowledge. As an example, Mr. Robinson may plan a lesson using sandpaper letters and other manipulatives, tactile activities, alphabet songs, and books that teach and practice the "letter of the day." Mrs. Jordon may use a multisensory (seeing, hearing, touching, and movement) approach to teach and practice forming the "letter of the day" by using paints, shaving cream, body-letter formation, different colored markers, and paper, clay, and sand. Both of these teachers understand that children should be encouraged to learn alphabet naming by direct instruction and through many types of exposure including visual, auditory, tactile, and kinesthetic. Additionally, teachers should use the consonant-vowel-consonant word pattern (C-V-C, e.g., *bat*) to model blending (see discussion of blending under Standard II). The teacher should use pictures to enhance the idea that letter naming connects to the reading of words. For example, as the teacher introduces the letter *h*, the teacher should show and pronounce the word *hat* and show a picture of a hat. Picture files of many things that relate to these sounds are valuable to show children (house, horse, hand, etc.) as they learn in this area.

It is also an effective practice for the teacher to adjust instructional pacing to meet the needs of children. As the beginning teacher considers ways to teach concepts that relate to the alphabetic principle, he or she may want to consider the following instructional sequence: (1) teach letter names in random sequence, (2) teach the formation and sounds of letters in random sequence, (3) teach lessons that highlight one letter at a time, (4) teach the likenesses and differences in letters based on formation and sound, (5) reteach difficult letters, and (6) provide skill lessons for students experiencing difficulty in learning letters.

As teachers consider ways to assess children's usage of the alphabetic principle, it is important to realize that assessment should be frequent so that teachers can address the instructional needs of learners. Teachers should initially assess children to determine their knowledge of the alphabet by asking them to name the written uppercase and lowercase letters of the alphabet presented in random order. This type of assessment allows the teacher to determine individual children's knowledge of letter names and to plan further instruction. Then the teacher should develop a variety of different assessments to use to determine children's growth and development in identifying letters of the alphabet. These assessments can also include activities such as asking a child to identify specific uppercase or lowercase manuscript letters of the alphabet by naming letters as the teacher points to specific letters, by pointing to specific letters as the teacher names a letter, or by matching uppercase and lowercase manuscript letters presented in columns.

Most educators agree that the beginning teacher should ask parents to become involved in the development of young children's emergent literacy. Teachers, with the permission of the school's administrative staff, could develop several of the following activities for the purpose of involving parents:

1. Design grade-level workshops to demonstrate ways to assist with decoding words, reading and asking questions, and homework assignments.
2. Develop take-home kits that include books for the child to read, practice worksheets that highlight a specific skill, fun activities, and additional suggestions for things to do in the home. Parent should be encouraged to play many sound games with their children, relating the sound to the letter, to words the child knows ("Brother is on his bike. What sound to you hear twice? That sound is a B.").
3. Produce a newsletter and a website that informs parents about classroom events, new skills that are being introduced, and other academic information. (Remember that English may not always be the language spoken at home.) Teacher-made VCR tapes can also be an effective way to reach parents.

Examine the following as an assessment activity. Then consider the question that follows.

Mr. Dwyer, a kindergarten teacher, places a teacher-made folder game in the literacy center. The directions ask students to match lowercase letters with the corresponding uppercase letters by pulling a length of yarn from one letter in the upper case column to its corresponding letter in the lowercase column. What is the purpose of this activity?

    A. To practice letter association.
    B. To play a game.
    C. To practice writing the alphabet.
    D. To practice writing conventions.

Choice *A* is correct because in this instructional situation Mr. Dwyer could use this activity to allow students to practice upper- and lowercase letter association. Then, following repeated instruction and practice (using games; computer activities; a variety of tactile products employing sandpaper letters, plastic letters, and other raised surfaces; books; and/or other literacy tools), he would use this as an assessment to determine students' growth in identifying upper- and lowercase letters.

STANDARD IV (LITERACY DEVELOPMENT AND PRACTICE)

Competency 004: Teachers of young children understand that literacy develops over time and progresses from emergent to proficient stages. Teachers use a variety of contexts to support the development of children's literacy.

The teacher understands literacy development from pre-kindergarten through conventional literacy acquisition, has an awareness of the different types of printed materials children use in instructional settings, and uses assessment practices in making decisions about instruction. Remember that the TEKS promotes knowing different types of print sources that teachers can use in instruction.

Try this practice question.

Which strategies should a teacher implement to foster students' enjoyment and appreciation of poetry?
  A. Reading poems, clapping out the rhyme in familiar rhymes, and recording a "top ten" set of poems for use in a listening center.
  B. Making personal collections of students' favorite poems, requiring memorization of poems, and dramatizing narrative poems.
  C. Illustrating Native American poetry, analyzing sections of poems, and sharing haiku with poetry pals in another classroom.
  D. Choral reading and peer editing.

First, consider which activity would lead to an enjoyment and appreciation of poetry. Since each item contains activities, you must decide if each of those activities leads to appreciation and enjoyment. Let us use the strategy of elimination on this item, so that if one choice does not promote enjoyment or appreciation, mark the entire item incorrect. For each suggested answer, underline or check those activities that would promote enjoyment and appreciation in poetry. In items *B, C,* and *D,* would each activity promote enjoyment? The activities in *A* would all promote appreciation of poetry; for younger children therefore, Option *A* is the correct choice.

This standard emphasizes instruction related to literacy development skills, or emergent literacy, and the use of a variety of text structures such as children's literature and expository text in instructional settings. Teachers should understand the developmental steps that children encounter in learning to become proficient readers in order to identify, diagnose, and prepare for effective instruction. **Emergent literacy** refers to reading and writing experiences that a child encounters before formal literacy instruction begins. These experiences occur in the home, social environments, and preschool settings. During the development of print association, children become aware of different types of print found in their environment. They begin to recognize that print is meaningful, develop the ability to rhyme, engage in reading environmental print (for example, reading McDonald's when passing the location in a car), and engage in story discussion during the reading of a favorite book. Children engaging in emergent literacy activities should receive meaningful direct guidance from an adult figure. Children should be allowed to develop language skills naturally; however, an adult can provide scaffolding to assist in gaining higher levels of understanding. *Scaffolding* refers to support for a learner as he or she enters a phase of readiness for a new skill. Educators believe that emergent literacy activities include prereading and prewriting activities that develop in a meaningful way. As an example, a young child may imitate an adult by writing a letter to an aunt or grandparent, even though that letter may contain scribbles that are only meaningful to the child. Also, the young child may learn to memorize a favorite book because a parent or teacher has read the same book to the child many times. It should also be stated that oral language develops in the young child from early developmental stages of babbling to developmental and mature speech. Often, teachers use a variety of children's text sources to enhance the development of literacy skills by using a pointer to demonstrate the left-to-right sequence for reading and by showing the parts of a book. Teachers can demonstrate these concepts by using "big books" and other types of narrative reading sources used in children's literature. As teachers assist children in developing literacy skills, it is important to realize that children are learning the alphabet in nonsequential order, acquiring phonemic awareness skills, developing a sight vocabulary, and learning to decode words that are encountered in isolated lists and in contextual settings. As elementary students develop into more proficient readers, they use a variety of decoding skills (e.g., phonics, context clues, and structural analysis), read with pitch and intonation, read with increased fluency and rate, develop orthographic awareness (correct spelling), recognize a greater number of sight words in both isolated lists and contextual text, and show an interest in a variety of text types. It is important to understand the stages that students experience in trying to become capable of reading various text types. Table 2.3 highlights literacy developmental stages in children from pre-kindergarten to grade *four.*

As you study Table 2.3, remember that the teacher should engage children in oral and written discussions of books, reread favorite stories to children, provide books on tape, provide games and activities that promote language development, model and instruct on strategies for determining the pronunciation of an unknown word, model comprehension strategies, provide opportunities for students to engage in higher-level thinking activities, teach and model

TABLE 2.3 Literacy Developmental Stages

Pre-kindergarten children begin to do the following:
- Become aware of environmental print
- Recognize signs (as an example, the STOP sign) seen frequently
- Recognize a limited number of letters and numbers
- Interpret forms of their writing that represent their written messages (a child could interpret a series of lines he or she made to mean "I have a new bike.")
- Actively participate in reading and writing activities
- Orally make rhyming word patterns
- Listen to short stories and retell their favorite parts
- Recognize the orientation of print (left-to-right, top-to-bottom, and print usage)

Kindergarten children begin to do the following:
- Retell information from narrative and expository text sources
- Write letters of the alphabet (in uppercase form) and numbers
- Recognize the sound that letters make in the initial position
- Make an association with onsets and rimes in one-syllable words
- Write a limited number of sight words
- Engage in invented spelling to communicate in printed form
- Use more descriptive words in oral expression

First-grade children begin to do the following:
- Read stories and discuss stories
- Write stories
- Develop comprehension strategies for getting the main idea, predicting outcomes, understanding sequence, using contextual clues, etc.
- Develop reading fluency
- Use word identification strategies to determine an unknown word
- Use limited punctuation marks
- Use appropriate capitalization in words such as their first name and the first word in a sentence
- Develop spelling techniques for writing words
- Develop sight words

Second-grade children begin to do the following:
- Increase sight word recognition
- Read a variety of text sources such as expository, poems, notes from peers, invitations, etc.
- Read for different purposes such as for information, fun, etc.
- Read with fluency
- Use effective comprehension strategies
- Use word identification strategies to determine the pronunciation of an unknown word
- Use an increasing number of punctuation marks in written products
- Use the elements of the writing process

(continued)

TABLE 2.3   Continued

Second-grade children begin to do the following (continued):
- Make the transition from invented spelling to correct spelling
- Use capitalization more extensively
- Engage in self-selected independent reading

Third-grade children begin to do the following:
- Increase sight word recognition
- Read with increased fluency, rate, and expression
- Use word identification strategies to determine the pronunciation and meaning of unknown words
- Use comprehension strategies to gain understanding of text sources
- Use reference sources to gain information
- Recognize the difference between narrative and expository text forms
- Write descriptively in different text forms such as expository paragraphs, stories, research reports, poems, letters, etc.
- Use effectively the elements of the writing process
- Proofread written products
- Develop and use an increased vocabulary
- Increase the ability to use correct spelling

Fourth-grade children begin to do the following:
- Increase sight word recognition that includes content area subjects
- Read a variety of text sources with increased understanding, fluency, rate, and expression
- Spell correctly in a variety of written forms such as paragraphs, poems, etc.
- Read longer text sources such as informational articles and trade books
- Produce effective written summaries
- Expand vocabulary usage
- Continue to use reference sources
- Use effective comprehension strategies to understand a variety of text sources
- Increase usage of punctuation

the writing process, and produce other effective ways to promote classroom literacy.

Teachers should be able to use different types of children's literature choices. **Genres,** or types, of children's literature include picture books, folk literature, realistic fiction, historical fiction, fantasy, science fiction, informational books, poetry, mysteries, and biographies. *Picture books* are those books in which the text and illustrations combine to form a meaningful whole. A special type of picture book is the *textless,* or *wordless,* picture book that relies solely on the illustrations to tell the story. Also included in the genre are alphabet books, counting books, and *concept books* (those that teach children about ideas such as shapes, colors, and feelings). Although we often consider picture books appropriate only for our youngest readers, there are many quality picture books that can be successfully used with upper elementary students. *Folk literature* (folklore) encompasses those tales that were originally told orally. Such styles as fairy tales, tall tales, fables, myths, legends, epics, ballads, and folk songs all are part of folk literature and often engage students in moral lessons about human nature. *Realistic fiction* stories are those that occur in contemporary times and are quite popular with children because they present characters and situations they can identify with. *Historical fiction* presents stories about characters and events of the past and can afford an effective way to introduce children to important periods in Texas, U.S., and world history. *Fantasy* and *science fiction,* stories in which anything can happen, can develop children's imagination as well as their creativity and sense of humor. *Expository text* (informational books), or nonfiction literature, can pique children's interest about specific topics and help answer many of their questions. *Biographies,* books about real people both past and present, introduce children to persons with interesting and often inspiring life stories.

Poetry is another major genre, or type, of children's literature. Teachers often do not include poetry in classroom instruction, either because they have negative poetry memories from their own school days or because they lack knowledge on how to select poetry for their children. Those memories might include being required to memorize poems and then listen to each classmate recite the same selection in front of the class, often reducing the enjoyment of poetry for many young readers, along with having to overanalyze and determine the "real" meaning of poems in the upper grades.

Poetry preference studies done over the past fifty years, in particular by Terry (1974) and Kutiper (1985), show that children have certain likes and dislikes regarding poetry. Children like poems to which they can relate—in other words, poems that deal with familiar experiences. They also like narrative poems, limericks, poems about animals, and poems with lots of sounds in them. When given the choice, children overwhelmingly prefer poems by contemporary writers to those by traditional writers. Sometimes young children do not like to read or hear haiku, though by fourth grade many begin to write, understand, and enjoy age-appropriate haiku.

Poetry is a genre that is meant to be heard. Children benefit from activities that promote listening to poetry or orally expressing poetry. Enjoyment comes from hearing favorite poems read or sung and by sharing them with others. This pleasure can then foster students' desire to create their own poems. Poem patterns such as couplets, triplets, biopoems, cinquains, and diamantes are both simple and fun for students to write. They can also feel a great sense of accomplishment when their poems are "published" or shared with others.

Teachers may use many of the genres discussed above to explore seven literary elements. These elements include: (1) setting, (2) character, (3) plot,

(4) style, (5) point of view, (6) mood or emotional tone, and (7) theme, or the "abstract statement about life or humanity reflected in a story or poem" (McGee & Richgels, 2000, p. 116). Older elementary children should be encouraged to include these elements in their writing.

The **basal reader** is another text source used to develop children's literacy skills. Basal readers are designed to provide a sequence of skills that are introduced, practiced, and applied by having students read narrative and expository text sources. After reading basal reader stories, teachers often have children use corresponding workbooks, skills sheets, and other types of supplementary instructional materials to reinforce skills introduced in each lesson. Most often basal readers and their accompanying materials, including a teacher's edition, are those "reading books" provided by schools.

Try this practice question.

Mr. Chaparral is about to introduce a unit on the westward movement to his fourth-grade students. Which of the following strategies would be most effective in immersing his students into this subject?

A. Have the students read the related chapter in their social studies textbook and answer the questions at the end of the chapter.
B. Organize the class into groups and let each group choose a novel.
C. Have the students read diaries, biographies, and nonfiction books about the westward movement and collaboratively create an illustrated timeline for the bulletin board.
D. Assign everyone to read, with the teacher's assistance, Laura Ingalls Wilder's *Little House on the Prairie.* Then have the students write a response to the story.

Consider which of the suggested activities would give students the most understanding of the westward movement. Response *A,* reading the chapter in the textbook, gives the students only one perspective on this historical period (the textbook author's perspective), and answering the questions at the end of the chapter is tedious, boring, and solitary. Response *B,* allowing groups of students to select a novel, does not provide a focus for a broader view of this lesson. Response *D,* assigning everyone to read the same book, does not take into consideration that fourth-grade boys and girls prefer to read about characters that are the same sex they are. Boys would probably prefer to read a book in which there was a male character. Response *C,* having students get into groups and choose their own book for reading and discussion, gives students the responsibility by allowing them to schedule their reading, conduct their discussion, and plan their final presentations to the class. Reading diaries, biographies, and other nonfiction literature pertaining to the historical period gives students a truer perspective of what life was like then. Allowing them to collaborate on a timeline lets children take responsibility for organizing and executing their work. Since this response involves a broad range of related literature, collaborative learning, and student decision making, the correct answer is *C.* The teacher must remember that books should be at the appropriate reading level for elementary children.

STANDARD V (WORD ANALYSIS AND DECODING)

Competency 005: Teachers understand the importance of word analysis and decoding to reading and provide many opportunities for children to improve their word analysis and decoding abilities.

The teacher knows that children develop word analysis and decoding skills in a predictable sequence, provides various instructional practices that allow children to develop skill in using word analysis and decoding strategies, uses a variety of assessment practices to determine children's word analysis and decoding development, exposes children to high-frequency sight words, and provides instruction in the relationship of word analysis to comprehension. Remember that the TEKS promotes instruction that emphasizes the introduction and independent usage of word analysis skills.

Try this practice question.

Mitch, a second grader, reads a word incorrectly in a sentence as he is reading orally to his teacher. After reading two more sentences, he goes back and corrects the error. What strategy did Mitch's teacher observe him using in determining his error?

A. Application of onsets and rimes.
B. Context clues.
C. Structural analysis.
D. Sight words.

Consider the approach Mitch used in determining the need to go back and reread the sentence. What clued him to the need to go back? Because Mitch is a second grader, he should have the ability to apply onsets (identification of the consonant at the beginning of a word) and rimes (identification of the consonants and vowels at the end of a syllable). However, it cannot be determined if he used this strategy because his self-correction was delayed until after reading two additional sentences. Therefore, Response A is not correct. We know that he made a miscue in reading, and we know that his teacher did not stop his reading. He pronounced a word incorrectly but continued to read two more sentences. It appears that the *contextual setting* gave him a clue that assisted in determining that a word had been pronounced incorrectly in a previous sentence. Therefore, it can be determined that Mitch used context clues in determining the need to go back to reread the sentence that contained the error. He did not use structural analysis and sight words in determining this error. Therefore, Response B would be correct.

Teachers and administrative educators frequently discuss the sequence in which word analysis and decoding skills should be introduced to the reader. According to Blevins (1998), the following sequence should be considered when teaching young children to read using word analysis skills.

1. Teachers should introduce consonants and short vowels in combination. The purpose of this combination is to develop decodable words that children will encounter in print and can transfer to spelling words (examples: *bat, pet, sip, hot,* and *cup*).
2. Teachers should introduce single consonants before introducing consonant blends or clusters.
3. Teachers should introduce consonants that have high utility. As an example, the letter *t* has a higher utility—that is, it is found in more words than the letter *z.*
4. Teachers should begin to introduce more complex letter combinations, such as consonant blends (example: *fl* in the word *flag*) and diagraphs (example: *oa* in the word *float*).

Teachers should know the definition of word recognition skills and how to apply these skills in instructional situations. The following list provides significant terms, definitions, and some examples.

1. **Affix.** A structural element added to the beginning or ending of a root or base word in order to alter the meaning, pronunciation, or function. Example: prefixes and suffixes such as *un-* (uncontrollable) or *-ness* (happiness).
2. **Alphabetic principle.** The idea that individual letters represent individual speech sounds; therefore, words may be read by saying the sounds represented by the letters, and words may be spelled by writing the letters that represent the sounds.
3. **Consonant blend or cluster.** Two or three letters in the same syllable that are blended or heard when pronounced. Example: "tr" in tree.
4. **Consonant digraph.** A combination of two or more letters that represent a sound that is different from the speech sound that the letters represent individually. Examples: "ch" in chop, "sh" in shop, "th" in thank, "wh" in whether, and "ph" in phone.
5. **Decode.** Associating printed letters with the speech sounds the letters make.
6. **Diphthong.** Two adjacent vowels in which each vowel is heard in the pronunciation. Examples: "ou" in house, "oi" in oil, "oy" in boy, and "ow" in brown.
7. **Explicit phonics instruction.** Providing children with direct phonics instruction that allows them to use decodable text-sources that are made up of words and sounds that have been previously taught.
8. **Grapheme.** A written or printed letter symbol used to represent a speech sound (phoneme).
9. **Grapheme-phoneme relationship.** The relationship between printed letters and the sounds they represent.

10. **Logographic awareness.** The first stage children experience when learning about words. Words are learned as whole units that are sometimes embedded in a logo such as a stop sign or the arches in the McDonald's sign.
11. **Morpheme.** The smallest meaningful unit of language. Example: "cat" is a morpheme whose pronunciation consists of three phonemes (c/a/t).
12. **Onsets and rimes.** *Onsets* are the consonants that come at the beginning of syllables in words. Example: the "bl" in the word *blend* is an onset. *Rimes* are vowels and consonants at the end of a syllable. Example: "end" in the word *blend* is a rime.
13. **Orthography.** Correct spelling.
14. **Phoneme.** The smallest unit of sound in a language that distinguishes one word from another word. Example: *cat* and *hat* are distinguished as sounding different by considering their beginning consonant phonemes /c/ and /h/.
15. **Phonemic awareness.** The knowledge or understanding that speech consists of a series of sounds and that individual words can be divided into phonemes.
16. **Phonic analysis.** The process of applying knowledge of letter-sound relationships to decoding texts. Teachers ask for this when they instruct children to "sound out" a word.
17. **Schwa sound.** In many words that are multisyllabic, one of the syllables receives less or diminished stress. The sound of the vowel in the syllable that receives the diminished stress has a softening of the vowel sound that is identified as a *schwa* sound and often pronounced as the "uh" sound. The word *about* contains the schwa sound.
18. **Sight vocabulary.** Any words a reader can recognize instantly without having to use any type of word recognition strategy. When a word cannot be taught with another word recognition strategies such as onsets and rimes, it is usually taught as a sight word.
19. **Syllable.** Divisions of speech sounds within words. Each **syllable** has one vowel sound. An open syllable ends in a vowel, and a closed syllable ends in a consonant. Teachers should teach the following rules:
    a. When there are two consonants between two vowels, teach students that the syllable is divided between the two consonants, unless the two consonants are a blend or a digraph. Example: *traf/fic* represents the V-C-C-V pattern where both consonants are the same and *pen/cil* represents the V-C-C-V pattern where the consonants are different.
    b. When vowel digraphs or diphthongs appear in a word, teach students not to divide between these vowel combinations. Example: *ea/ger* (*ea* represents a digraph) and *pow/der* (*ow* represents a diphthong).
    c. When there is a vowel-consonant-vowel pattern noticed in the middle or a word, divide into a syllable either before the consonant or after the consonant. If teachers instruct students to divide the word into a syllable

before the consonant, students should notice that the first vowel sound is long. Example: *mo/ment* represents the V-C-V pattern that shows a long sound pronunciation of the vowel. If teachers instruct students to divide the word into a syllable after the consonant, students should notice that the first vowel sound is short. Example: *sev/en* represents the V-C-V pattern that shows a short sound pronunciation of the vowel.

d. When there is a compound word, teach students to divide into syllables between the two words. Example: *seahorse* should be divided as *sea/horse*.

e. When a word has an affix (prefix or suffix), teach students to divide into syllables between the base word and the affix. Example: *remove* should be divided as *re/move*.

20. Vowel digraph. Two adjacent vowels that represent one speech sound. Examples: *ee* in *feet, oo* in *foot, ea* in *meat,* and *ai* in *sail.*

21. Word analysis. An inclusive term that refers to *all methods* of word recognition. Phonics is one such method. Other methods include *picture clues* (using pictures and graphic aids to assist in word pronunciation and meaning), *context clues* (using surrounding text to aid in word pronunciation and meaning), *sight words,* and *structural analysis* (which focuses on root words, base words, affixes, compound words, syllable division, and contractions).

In addition to becoming acquainted with these terms, beginning teachers should teach these skills directly and assist students in applying word recognition skills in a variety of literacy settings. For example, as students read various selections of print orally, they will frequently encounter words that they mispronounce in context. Encouraging students to reread the section of print where the mistake (or miscue) occurred will often produce the correct pronunciation (by using context clues that connect the word to background). As students advance, they should be able to use individual fix-up strategies to help with their comprehension. Although teachers should provide students with a wide variety of print sources, they should remember to suggest books that can be read independently and have words that are consistently pronounceable in approximately 95 percent of the text. Putting students in a position where they obtain overall success with a bit of a challenge is optimal (according to motivational theory). Always remember to apply the concept of the **zone of proximal development** in reading, which means discovering the place where children can be successful with some assistance from an adult or a capable peer. Teachers should allow time for students to discuss the main ideas presented by the author, other concepts, and the students' own purposes for reading. To further enhance fluency, teachers should encourage students to reread favorite sections of print. Word recognition skills are important; however, teachers should provide significant exposure to new words so that these words will become automatically pronounced as sight words.

Read the worksheet below and answer the four questions. (A third-grade student completed this worksheet.)

Name: _____**Maria Jones**_____   Date: _____**April 5, 200l**_____

Read the following passage and answer the questions.

Nicole is in a hurry this morning because Whitney's mother is picking her up at 10:00. The girls are going to the amusement park to spend the day. Since Nicole just moved to Simons two weeks ago, she has not been to this park. She hears the doorbell, runs to open the door, and sees Whitney. "Are you ready?" Whitney asks. "I am," replies Nicole.

    As Nicole enters the amusement park, she sees people who look as excited as she feels. She rides on the Big Blop, plays toss the ring and wins a stuffed rabbit, eats a hot dog, rides on the Turning Train, and goes to a puppet show. She tells Whitney's mother that this is the most fun she has had since coming to the new town. Whitney's mom tells the girls that it is time to go to the car for the ride home. As they leave the park, Nicole is sad because she is not ready to leave. Then she thinks, my mom can bring us the next time.

1. Describe the way Nicole feels when she woke up. Why did she feel this way?

    Happy. She is going to the park.

2. How long has Nicole lived in her new town?

    Two weeks.

3. List the things the girls do at the amusement park.

    rides, plays toss the ring, eats sees a show

4. How does Nicole probably feel as she leaves the amusement park?

    she is sad.

FIGURE 2.1

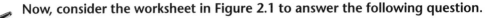 **Now, consider the worksheet in Figure 2.1 to answer the following question.**

Considering Maria's written responses on this worksheet, what assessment can the teacher make about her reading achievement?

    A. She can read words that contain consonant blends.
    B. She can read words that contain vowel digraphs.
    C. She can use structural analysis skills.
    D. All of the above.

As you think about the correct answer, you should consider that one function of this standard is to provide information connecting the reader, the text, and the context. So, does Maria seem to do this? Yes, because she basically answers the questions correctly. Nicole could have extended her response to Question 4 by indicating that she quickly began to feel happy because she thought of a way to come back to the amusement park. However, not including this extension does not make her response incorrect because the text states that Maria felt sad. The correct response is *D* because she reads several words that contain the following decoding elements:

    Consonant blends or clusters: *spend, blop, stuffed, train, bring, plays*

    Vowel digraphs: *train, feels, leave*

    Structural analysis: Example of a word from the story: compound word, *doorbell*

You should notice that Maria reads other words that are examples of several of the decoding terms included in the list of terms defined under this standard.

STANDARD VI (READING FLUENCY)

Competency 006:   Teachers understand the importance of fluency to reading comprehension and provide many opportunities for children to improve their reading fluency.

> *The teacher understands the relationship of reading fluency to comprehension, provides instructional practices that develop reading fluency, assesses reading fluency, and realizes that fluency involves rate, accuracy, and intonation. Remember that the TEKS promotes the usage of instructional strategies that enhance reading fluency.*

Try this practice question.

Ms. Routt, a first-grade teacher, has noticed that two students have limited knowledge and use of sight words. Which activity would *not* provide exposure to print?

    A. Provide students with a variety of books at their independent reading levels.

B. Ask the students not to reread their favorite part of a book but select something different to read.
C. Allow the students to look at the print as the teacher reads the book.
D. Have the students use taped versions of the books.

Each choice but one actually promotes literacy development. These children have had limited knowledge and use of sight words that could promote reading fluency. Therefore, they need to see and use print in a variety of ways and use stories of various types and in many different ways. This can be accomplished if Ms. Routt allows the children to actually see words in print and hear words that make up stories. Therefore, Response *B* correctly answers this question because the children are asked *not* to reread their favorite part of a book but to select something different. Rereading a motivating selection is an excellent way for students to gain word recognition. Additionally, big books, large print, colorful illustrations, and adequate spacing would be features that the teacher could use to assist the students in acquiring literacy development.

Reading fluency relates to a student's being able to (1) orally read a text source by using accuracy in pronouncing words, (2) comprehend effectively because attention is given to textual meaning, (3) provide expression that includes attention to punctuation, and (4) read with a rate that is appropriate for the purpose identified for reading the text source. Table 2.4 on page 50 provides an explanation of reading fluency components.

Children attending school often experience reading difficulties that alter fluency as it relates to comprehension. A discussion of the most common reading difficulties that influence reading fluency and instructional practices that address these difficulties follows.

1. *Word-by-word reading* is described as a student's pausing after each word in printed text. This type of reading is often caused by limited sight word knowledge and overdependence on the usage of phonics. As remediation practices, the teacher could:
   a. Assign reading materials at a lower level.
   b. Use familiar reading materials that contain known sight words.
   c. Have children dictate language experience stories that could be read aloud (review Standard I).
   d. Have children read along with taped text sources until fluency is reached.
   e. Provide opportunities for children to read at their independent level daily.
   f. Suggest reading materials for parents to have in the home that will allow children to practice using sight words and new exposure words.
2. *Insufficient knowledge of word recognition skills* refers to limited use of sight word knowledge, context clues, structural analysis, and other skills used to

TABLE 2.4   The Components of Reading Fluency

Read orally a text source by using accuracy in pronouncing words.
The student can recognize most of the words in the text with automatic and immediate recognition. Students may read text sources at the independent level, which means that approximately 95 percent to 100 percent of the words are recognized and pronounced correctly. However, many students need opportunities to engage in repeated readings of the same text sources before they reach this level of automatic and immediate word recognition.

Comprehend effectively because attention is given to textual meaning and not just to word identification.
The student can comprehend text if he or she does not need to spend a significant amount of time decoding words. The frequent pausing to figure out a word alters the flow of reading, thus causing comprehension to receive less attention on the part of the reader. Basically, fluency (continuous flow of word recognition) results in comprehension. *It is important to note that some students engage in effective word naming without effectively comprehending the text source.* Teachers should remember to evaluate comprehension by asking questions/statements at various levels, to allow students to retell sections of print, and to use other strategies as well.

Provide expression that includes attention to punctuation.
The student reads with attention to phrasing, appropriate breathing, voice intonation, tone, and attention to all punctuation marks. *Prosody* is the term frequently used to identify these reading considerations (Dowhower, 1991). Think about how you would expect a student to read this sentence: *I have a new puppy!*

Read with a rate that is appropriate for the purpose identified for reading the text source.

help in pronouncing an unknown word. As remediation practices, the teacher could:

a. Have children use sight words in isolation, phrases, and complete sentences.

b. Have children read a variety of print sources at the students' independent reading levels.

c. Have charts in the classroom that include onsets and rimes that appear in words that could be used in sentences. (A word wall could be used.)

d. Have available to children common affixes and words that contain the affixes written in complete sentences. (A word wall could be used.)

e. Have children continue to read text involving an unknown word. Have children consider the word's onset and the print following the unknown word.

3. *Ineffective comprehension* is recognized when a student is not able to tell about what has been read or is not able to respond to statements and questions posed about text that has been read. As remediation practices, the teacher could:

a. Develop questions and statements that encourage responses at different comprehension levels.

b. Encourage note taking and active listening.

c. Enhance word recognition knowledge.

d. Assign reading at appropriate levels.

e. Develop visual aids, such as pictures or felt-board figures, to show the sequence of a story that children are reading.

f. Explain the use of signal words and phrases, such as *first, also, on the other hand, in contrast, in comparison, next, then,* and *finally.*

g. Demonstrate the steps of the Question-Answer Relationships strategy (QARs) that are outlined in the discussion of Standard VII.

Many schools promote reading fluency in programs such as DEAR (Drop Everything and Read) or SSR (Sustained Silent Reading). Programs such as these often ask everyone in the school (including the teacher as a model) to select something from a large variety of reading material and read silently for a period of time—just for the enjoyment of it. Teachers have a part in guiding children to materials that will be interesting, exciting, and within their abilities.

Consider this practice question.

A second-grade teacher has noticed that Jamie is developing the reading behavior of a word-by-word reader, that is, she reads each word with a pause between it ("The . . . cat . . . ran . . . up . . . the . . . tree!"). Which strategy would be best for the teacher to use with this student?

A. Providing the student with books of interest.
B. Asking literal level questions.
C. Assigning reading material at a lower level of difficulty.
D. Encouraging the student to read orally in a small group.

Allowing a student to read books based on his or her interest (*A*) is an effective practice. However, these books may not promote fluency in reading orally because the books may not be written at the student's independent level. Asking literal questions (*B*) does allow the teacher to know if the student understands the stated concepts in a story, but this does not promote fluency. Assigning reading material at a lower level of difficulty allows the student to encounter known words. This practice, and the practice of allowing the student to reread favorite books at the independent level, would promote fluency. Encouraging students to read orally in a small group (*D*) often promotes anxiety. Therefore, Response *C* is the most effective practice for the teacher to use with Jamie.

STANDARD VII (READING COMPREHENSION)

Competencies 007 and 008:   Teachers understand the importance of reading for understanding, know the components of comprehension, and teach young children strategies for improving their comprehension.

The teacher knows the importance of reading for meaning, knows the levels of comprehension, provides effective strategies that enhance comprehension, uses a variety of assessment procedures, and instructs children on appropriate ways to gain information from expository text-sources. Remember that the TEKS promotes comprehension developmental instruction that allows children to engage in a variety of strategies. The teacher also understands the importance of research and comprehension skills to children's academic success and provides children with instruction that promotes their acquisition and effective use of these skills in the content areas.

Try this practice question.

Ms. Jones has decided to assign a series of expository paragraphs about "Early Days in San Antonio" to her fourth-grade social studies students to read during class. Which of the following would be *most* effective to use before having the students read this information?

   A. Summarize the paragraphs for students.
   B. Determine what students already know about the topic.
   C. Read a section to students to foster interest.
   D. Give students a series of questions to answer as they read.

Actually, each of these activities could be considered appropriate for Ms. Jones to use with her students. However, we are looking for the *most* effective method. It is always an effective practice to determine students' *background knowledge* about a new topic because it would be difficult for students to gain contextual meaning or, in this case, have an adequate background or understanding of this time in Texas history. By determining students' background knowledge, the teacher could then decide the amount of preparation necessary before the students could begin this learning activity. If the teacher determines that the students have either no background knowledge or limited background knowledge, she will realize that they are not yet ready for this activity. Instead, she would need to provide background knowledge so that they would be able to make connections and to comprehend this new information. Therefore, Response *B* is the most effective choice.

As a discussion of comprehension strategies is presented, it is important to identify and briefly explain literal, inferential, and evaluative comprehension. **Literal comprehension** requests readers to respond to questions and statements from stated text. A student, for example, could read, "The boy ran home from school." The teacher could ask this student to identify the specific details of where the boy had been and where the boy is going. This type of response does not require the student to incorporate any background experience or to consider thinking beyond print. Other literal comprehension categories that the elementary teacher should implement are (1) *identification of stated main ideas* in expository text structures (main ideas in narrative text structures are not usually stated directly for readers; instead, a sequential string of details are provided about characters, their problems, their solutions to the problems, and so on, that require the reader to identify a central theme or the general significance of the total narrative selection), (2) *identification of sequence of details,* (3) *identification of comparisons,* and (4) *identification of cause and effect relationships.* **Inferential comprehension** requests that readers use ideas and information that are directly stated in the text along with their intuition, background, and experiences to reach a conclusion or a hypothesis. As students make inferences, the teacher should assist them in examining their schema-based information to identify additional ideas needed to make responses. It should be expected and accepted that, as students make inferences, their responses may differ from other students' responses. Student responses should be accepted as long as they are connected to the literal meaning of the text. One category of inferential comprehension that teachers use in instruction is *predicting outcomes* or *ideas.* Teachers of young children can ask students to "predict what they think a story or textbook chapter is about by looking at pictures or reading the title of the chapter," or, as a story develops, "predict what will happen next." **Evaluative comprehension** requires that children compare information and ideas presented in the text with their own experiences, background, and values. These responses, given in their own words, might be about *reality versus fantasy, fact versus opinion,* and the *accuracy of information* that compares various written sources about the same topic. Comprehension can sometimes be a little tricky to teach, but teachers need to implement appropriate procedures for classroom usage that would assist students in effectively using text sources. It is also important for the teacher to develop and monitor comprehension before, during, and after the reading of a text source.

The *Directed Reading-Thinking Activity (DR-TA)* is a technique used to increase understanding of text structures. The DR-TA employs the following steps:

1. Assisting students in acquiring the skills needed during the reading of a text source. The teacher and students *survey* the material and *make predictions* from illustrations and other graphics. The teacher provides instruction by *introducing new technical terms* in isolation and in contextual settings, and the teacher assists students by providing teacher-directed and student-generated *questions* and statements to *provide purposes* for reading the selection.
2. Encouraging students to *write responses* to questions and statements as they read silently. Students should write their responses so that a discussion can be generated in the next step.

3. Continuing to develop comprehension by *discussing, clarifying responses,* and *redefining purposes* as students read orally and discuss sections of text that refer to the identified purpose-setting questions and statements.

4. *Rereading* the sections of the text silently and/or orally for continued instruction related to critical thinking (making inferences, drawing conclusions, identifying the main idea, making judgments, etc.). The teacher assists students in *applying* the textual information to *real-life situations* and in identifying additional instructional needs noticed during the discussion and reading of the text.

5. *Expanding instruction* to include the use of research skills, technology-based activities, related supplementary recreational reading from trade books and other sources, and group projects to develop additional cross-curricular cognitive ideas. (Stauffer 1969, pp. 14–15).

K-W-L is a strategy often used to promote comprehension and active learning of expository text sources. This strategy can also be used with narrative text sources. This strategy allows students to use their prior knowledge to identify what they already *know,* to have curiosity initiated by generating questions to show what they *want to know* about the topic, and to provide responses about what they *learned* about the topic after the lesson is concluded. Ogle (1992), the developer of K-W-L, recommends using the following diagram to record information (though there are a number of variations):

K—What I Know	W—What I Want to Know	L—What I Learned

Repeated story reading is a strategy that young children enjoy because they become so familiar with a text source that they can often read (or engage in pretend reading) on their own. Teachers should repeatedly read the story to children, encourage children to repeatedly read the same story, provide situations for children to discuss the story, provide props (costumes, dolls, puppets, sticks on characters, etc.) to retell or dramatize the story, and provide opportunities for children to engage in other literacy activities such as drawing and writing about the story.

Story retelling allows children to read or listen to a story that they will retell. This activity allows children to participate in language development, comprehension skill enhancement, and story structure awareness. Children have an opportunity to use their background and experiences in retelling and explaining the main ideas and supporting details of the story; to practice listening skills because the teacher should give children purposes to promote active listening; to practice the sequencing of what happened *first, second,* and *last* in the story; and to practice self-expression. Morrow (1989) recommends that when children experience difficulty in retelling a story, the teacher should ask about the story by using prompts such as:

1. What was the story about?
2. Who was the main character?
3. What was the main character's problem?
4. How did the character solve the problem?
5. How did the story end?
6. What was your favorite part?

It is important for teachers to remember that children can do story retellings in written form.

Summarizing is another skill area that needs to be considered as a significant comprehension strategy. In order to assist students in using summarizing effectively, teachers should (1) demonstrate to students how and why to omit noncontributing information from text sources, (2) explain what repeated details are and show why those details could be omitted in summarizing, and (3) continue to assist students in determining the author's stated main ideas or the overall general significance of a selection that could be used in a written summary. As teachers recognize that children are becoming proficient in developing effective summaries over smaller chunks of materials (paragraphs, subchapters, etc.), they usually begin to expose children to the skill of developing summaries over longer sections of print (summarizing a chapter, story, or novel). This process of combining extended sections to produce connected meanings and summaries can enhance understanding of the text.

The beginning teacher recognizes the importance of modeling and emphasizing strategies that are used to assist students in identifying concepts and information that they do and do not understand in their reading, writing, listening, and speaking activities. The teacher also recognizes that the cognitive concept of metacognition (metacognitive awareness, or self-regulation) is related to self-monitoring and provides instruction and activities that allow children to learn to self-monitor. This encourages children to assess their own cognitive growth, to identify inconsistent "missing areas," and to learn to match strategies that work best for themselves. As an example, Jody, a third grader, encounters an unknown geographical area that appears in the chapter of a social studies textbook. Jody realizes that ignoring the fact that she does not know anything about this area would alter comprehension; therefore, Jody could decide to seek the pronunciation of the geographic area and to determine the location of this area by looking at a map. The correct pronunciation and an understanding of the area's location provide additional background that can enhance comprehension. Additionally, the teacher frequently self-monitors him- or herself. This means he or she reflects on information delivered to children by asking them specific questions to determine if students are comprehending. This allows the teacher to make adjustments, if needed, by using different words to make the same statement, substituting words in oral delivery, and making directions clearer. In other words, the teacher is trying to make instruction more effective and meaningful for students.

In classrooms today, *listening* has become an important part of the daily routine. **Oracy** is the concept that identifies and describes the differences between the skills of listening and speaking from the skills of reading and writing. Oracy should be considered in classrooms in order to assist students in functioning in an active discussion-based environment (Wilkinson, 1974). Active listening is essential in classroom settings because speaking and reading are connected to purposeful listening.

Several factors that influence listening instruction should be considered as students become active listeners in school settings: (1) the student's background as related to experiences and to a cognitive knowledge base; (2) the level of language development; (3) the instructional level of the material being presented; (4) the speed, pitch, and intonation of the person providing the oral delivery of information; (5) the attention span of the listener; and (6) the instructional preparation of the listener, including having been given a purpose for listening, activities to organize the information, and activities that enhance memory for retaining the information that has been presented (Lundsteen, 1979).

This standard considers the use of listening activities as one way of assisting students in monitoring cognitive structures in classroom settings. It should be noted that effective listening needs instructional attention through various types of activities such as note taking, questioning, and listening-think-alouds.

Note Taking

Note taking, as mentioned earlier, is one of the most direct listening skills used in classrooms when seen as a teacher-produced method of delivering information to children in an oral form. Students must listen to succeed in this task. Note taking is also used when children use multiple sources such as encyclopedias, textbooks, interviews, charts, and narratives to collect information and record this information by making lists, answering questions, filling in note taking forms, and so forth. However, note taking is not stressed often enough in classroom situations. Let us examine a procedure that could be used to connect note taking, reading, and listening for elementary children. The teacher could begin the initial stage of note taking by providing a worksheet that outlines important points to be expanded upon by the teacher in oral delivery later. Let us consider the components of a teacher-delivered talk or mini-lecture in an elementary science class about "How Plants Grow." The teacher has developed a note-taking worksheet to be used by children to serve as purpose-setting points for effective listening. The following chart shows this type of example.

Topic: **How Plants Grow**	
Teacher provides questions for students.	Each student provides answers to questions.
1. How do plants start to grow?	Student provides a response.
2. What are the parts of a plant?	Student provides a response.
3. What does a plant need to grow?	Student provides a response.
4. Why are plants important to people?	Student provides a response.
Student summarizes information from the answer section. Student summary statements are based on information from the student's answers to the questions.	

When note taking children learn to differentiate significant details and main ideas from irrelevant information. This type of filtering of significant information helps children to determine the major points provided by the teacher. Allowing children to use sample notes developed by the teacher to compare notes taken in class by peers and make adjustments to individual notes provides children with an evaluation method. This type of self-assessment of the notes can often assist children in becoming more critical readers and listeners.

Other graphic organizers also help children organize information and read for a purpose. Concept mapping centers on a major focus and "radiates" related information or details. This helps students see main and subsidiary ideas very clearly. Other graphic organizers help students more easily comprehend visually areas such as cause-and-effect, storylines, timelines, and so forth.

Questioning

Questioning is one of the most used teaching strategies found in today's classrooms. Research indicates that many teachers ask questions only at the literal or knowledge level. This is *lower-level* thinking, according to Bloom's taxonomy (lower levels include knowledge, comprehension, and application; higher levels include analysis, synthesis, and evaluation). The first three levels provide basic thinking, but teachers' aims should always be to have children think at higher levels of comprehension. In language arts, for instance, teachers can pose questions and statements as a way of providing students with purposes for listening to orally delivered information and information found in text sources. These questions and statements should require responses that allow children to identify the main idea of a selection, determine details that discuss the main idea, and identify supporting details that further describe the initial details. The following are specific strategies that can be used by teachers to enhance questions and responses.

QUESTION-ANSWER RELATIONSHIPS (QARs). This is a directed-teaching strategy that develops students' awareness of the process used in answering questions by using the following steps:

1. Identifying *"right there"* questions that are literal and can be answered from information stated in the book and sometimes found in one sentence.
   a. Example question: What is Carmen's job?
   b. Answer that is stated in the text source: "Carmen has worked for the last ten years as a bus driver for elementary school students. She lives in Pasadena, but she works nearby in South Houston."
2. Identifying *"think and search"* questions requiring students to draw a conclusion. They are told that the information needed to determine the answer to the question can be found in the text source, but it will be in more than one sentence. Students are instructed on how to link this information by putting several ideas together to determine a response.
   a. An example question: How would you describe Emily?
   b. The answer would come from several sections of text that described Emily. The students would need to put the description together from the entire text source that describes her.
3. Identifying *"author and you"* questions requiring students to use text details plus their own background knowledge to make an inference. Children are instructed to determine answers by using text information and information they already know from their background. They must relate what they know to what is in their text source. Answers thus become more individualized rather than a single correct answer. As an example, children read a paragraph about "Going to the Zoo" on a very hot summer day. In the story a lady smiles and allows a little boy to go ahead of her on a ride. The children were asked to answer the following question: What type of person is the lady? The reader has to determine that the lady is probably a kind person because of her actions.
4. Identifying *"on your own"* questions connect evaluative responses, background consideration, and creative thoughts to determine an answer. Children, for example, having read about the life of Abraham Lincoln, could then be asked to identify the characteristics of a leader.

Another way to view this questioning is to look at the difference between *convergent questions* and *divergent questions*. Convergent question responses would allow students to use their text source to answer questions because there is one answer to a question. On the other hand, divergent question responses would require students to use the text source, their background knowledge, and their understanding of the information in the text to answer a question. In other words, the teacher could expect to hear a variety of individualized answers that are connected to the text sources.

RECIPROCAL QUESTIONING (ReQuest). Using ReQuest, students learn to pose their own questions and statements about content material being studied. Manzo (1969) recommends the following steps.

1. Teacher and students read the same passage silently.
2. Teacher closes the book and is questioned by students.
3. Roles change and the teacher begins to ask students questions.
4. Teacher assists students in developing logical responses to questions. When the teacher determines that children have an adequate knowledge of question-answer responses, the teacher then allows them to independently read to determine the answers to questions.
5. Teacher conducts a follow-up discussion. (pp. 124–125)

Listening-Thinking Strategy

The purpose of this strategy is to provide a format for teaching students how to develop predictive listening and comprehension. This strategy encourages students to make predictions as the teacher reads the title of a chapter or reads to an exciting point in a story. The teacher continues to read the selection and allows children to change or make new predictions. As the teacher reads to students, he or she uses pitch/intonation variations and storyline discussions to assist students in effectively listening to classroom discussions (Walker, 2000).

Many content areas utilize students' reading and writing skills in acquiring knowledge of concepts. It is important to understand that informational textbooks, or expository textbooks, contain such features as a preface, a table of contents, appendices, a glossary, and an index. In addition, each chapter within expository textbooks includes an introduction, headings, subheadings, graphics, purpose-setting questions, and a summary. Most expository textbooks are organized with the most important ideas stated first, with supporting ideas and descriptive details following in paragraph form. Students who understand this textbook structure often can distinguish the important/significant details from the less important details in reading material (Meyer, 1975). Additionally, authors of textbooks usually provide connective terms (such as *most important, however, because, after,* etc.) to help students connect one idea to another idea as they read information (Halliday & Hasan, 1976).

Content area teachers should identify specific strategies that can be embedded throughout lessons in social studies, science, health, and so forth. During pre-reading activities, the teacher introduces activities that activate schema and establishes purposes for reading. As students read silently, teachers provide them with activities that continuously monitor comprehension. After children finish reading, teachers should assist them in determining relevant applications of the new information, in building schema, and in extending comprehension skills by rereading portions of the textbook or other sources that supplement the chapter.

SQ3R (Survey, Question, Read, Recite, and Review)

In order to discuss Standard VII, which incorporates the structure of assisting young readers in becoming capable of learning to use expository text structures independently, an overview of *SQ3R* and its cognitive connections to other study strategies is needed. Also, it is necessary to indicate that this strategy is usually most effective with expository (informational-based) text-sources. In *SQ3R, S* means *survey,* Q means *question,* and *3R* means *read, recite,* and *review.* Let us discuss each separately and make connections with other study strategies, such as previewing, note taking, study guides, and test taking.

The *survey* step suggests that the reader, with the teacher's instructional guidance: (1) previews the reading selection and notices the title of the chapter and the titles of the subchapter headings; (2) notices new vocabulary; (3) reads the introduction and summary of the entire chapter; (4) reads the first sentence in each paragraph as each subheading is considered and reads both the questions at the end of each subsection and at the end of the chapter; (5) reads sections in bold or other types of selected print; (6) studies graphic and visual information such as maps, illustrations, graphs, etc., and becomes familiar with the purpose of this information; and (7) notices other relevant information. In using this step, readers will notice the structure of a chapter, thus allowing them to determine a framework for reading and comprehending the information. Additionally, Vacca and Vacca (1986) recommend that, as children preview a textbook (by examining the introduction, illustrations, new vocabulary terms, subchapters, the summary, etc.), they can often determine the amount of time it will take to complete the task and determine what they already know about the topic.

The *question* step recommends that the teacher aid readers in determining what questions about the reading material can be answered from the text source. These questions provide purposes for reading the selection, and are designed to assist readers in paying close attention to the information that is being read. Questions can be formulated in several ways; however, the most common way to formulate questions in this step is to change the stated subchapter headings into questions. As an example, a chapter in a third-grade social studies textbook might be titled "Living in China." In this chapter, students could probably expect to find a subchapter heading titled "The People of China" that could be changed by the student into a question that is "Who are the people living in China?" This can result in factual information about China but also a discussion on the differences among many Asian people (Japanese, Korean, Indian, Thai, etc.). Also, the teacher could prepare a study guide (study guides will be discussed later in this section), or a list of questions and statements that could be given to the students before beginning to read the text source.

The *read* step requires the student to answer the questions, or in some cases the statements, formulated in the question step. Opening the door to engage children in active reading through the use of questions and statements leads to connections of main idea information, details, and descriptive ideas. Imagine being given a reading assignment and being told that a test would follow on the next class day. Some children already have metacognitive strategies in place that would allow comprehension, but others would get very little from this assignment and would probably not earn a passing grade. One of the reasons that children might have difficulty passing such a test is that there was not a specific "road map" to follow to determine the understanding of the text material. As teachers, we do not want to always tell students exactly what they should learn as they read, but we do want to scaffold until they have acquired the metacognitive strategies that would allow independence in determining comprehension. For some students, this can be accomplished quickly, but for others it takes time to scaffold them on their way to becoming independent learners.

The *recite* step asks students to make either oral or written responses to the questions formulated in the question step. As students respond orally to answer these questions, teachers can additionally request readers to identify text locations that were used in making these responses, or children can provide written responses to the questions.

The *review* step allows pupils to evaluate the text information by rereading selected segments of the text so that they can verify their responses given during the recite step. Children can either read out loud or read silently the text sections that verify their answers. Remember, readers have had private time with the text source to answer the questions. After they have had an opportunity to read the text silently, it is instructionally appropriate to allow children to volunteer to read sections of the text orally that provide responses to questions generated in the question step. Because it is necessary to connect *why* it is appropriate to read silently before reading orally, let's review the components of DR-TA. This strategy encourages reading out loud to answer questions and to verify responses to answers. However, this oral reading comes *after* students have been given an opportunity to read the text source silently.

As we continue to discuss strategies that respond to this standard, the use of adjunct study materials such as study guides and graphic aids will be discussed in more detail. First, let us see exactly why adjunct study materials are important. According to Vacca and Vacca (1986), adjunct study materials add a way for children to interact and make connections with text material that is unfamiliar or difficult, analyze and discuss ideas and concepts found in text sources, and scaffold students in comprehending the text being read.

Study guides prepared by the teacher or commercially by the textbook authors benefit students during active silent and oral reading. Study guides usually provide a set of questions or statements for children to use as they study text materials. Although there are several types of study guides, three types will be discussed. The *interlocking study guide* is a type of guide that frames a group of literal questions, a group of interpretive questions, and a group of evaluative questions to be answered by readers. The *noninterlocking guide* arranges questions and statements in a nonordered fashion that does not group questions according to literal, interpretive, and evaluative levels, but intermingles questions between the three levels. As an example, the first question could be an evaluative question, the second question could be literal, the third question could be interpretive, and so forth. The last type of study guide to be discussed is the *Guide-O-Rama.* Teachers using this type of guide determine the purpose for reading the selection needed to answer specific questions. Teachers would not require students to read the sections of text that did not address the purpose for reading. However, the teacher determines and shows, by signaling, what parts of the text need to be used to complete the task. As an example, Mrs. Bell asks her children to read page 127, paragraph 4 to answer a question about a famous woman scientist. This type of signaling is done throughout the chapter to achieve gaining specific information that relates to content specific information.

Another study skill that needs discussion is the ability to *locate information.* The elementary teacher should assist students in learning to use an index. To assist children in learning to use an index, the teacher could design an activity in a fourth-grade social studies class that asks readers to identify headings that contain information about the production of oil. Students identify headings such as: oil, production of oil, types of oil products, procedure used in processing oil, sources of oil, and other topic choices that could be identified. After the list is formulated, children could use the textbook's index to determine if the headings are listed. Note that the skill of alphabetical sequencing is necessary to allow this activity to be effectively completed. Readers identify page references and use them to actually find the information in the textbook. When the concept of locating information using a book index has been mastered, the teacher should encourage readers to use index entries of other reference sources such as encyclopedias, almanacs, and atlases. Additionally, children should be taught to use the table of contents of text sources, to locate library sources, and to use computer technology to locate various types of information. Older elementary students can be taught to bookmark information and the rudimentary concepts of copyrighting and plagarism with technology.

Interpreting graphic information is important in increasing comprehension, but children may need special instruction in this area. Readers encounter maps, cartoons, charts, and other types of diagrams in textbooks. Usually there is text association that connects the graphics to the text, but children often do not include graphics in the process of completing the reading of the text information.

A map of the "Regions of Texas," for example, might be included in a fourth-grade social studies book and, to encourage children to interpret the information, the teacher could ask them to do the following on their own maps:

1. Outline the regions of Texas with yellow.
2. Color the water areas blue.
3. Trace the mountain range areas in brown.

This teacher-generated activity promotes graphic interpretation that allows students to make cognitive connections with print.

It is important for the elementary teacher to include test-taking strategies for elementary students. Teachers want to encourage readers to become effective test takers by encouraging them to consider doing the following:

1. Scan the entire test before answering test items to determine the test format, the type of test questions, and the points for each item to determine the approximate amount of time to consider spending on most test items.
2. Answer first the questions that you know.
3. Look for giveaway answers on objective tests and words that indicate extremes in the answer, such as *best, least, none, never,* and *always.*
4. Make an outline, list, or graphic structure to begin answering essay-type questions. Students should be encouraged to answer each part of an essay question.

Additionally, Carmen and Adams (1972) designed *SCORER* as a test-taking strategy. SCORER stands for and recommends the following: S stands for *schedule* and recommends that the test taker learns to predetermine the time they believe they will need to complete a test efficiently; C stands for *clue* and recommends that the test taker identify words that could assist in answering the question; O stands for *omit* and recommends that the test taker omit the hardest questions first and return to these difficult questions after known ones are answered; R stands for *read* and recommends that the test taker read each question carefully to determine if each part is fully understood (if taking an informal teacher-generated test, the test taker could seek clarification from the teacher); E stands for *estimate* and recommends that the test taker determine what should be included in a response (e.g., if taking an essay test, the test taker could make an outline of the information needed to complete the response); and R stands for *review* and recommends that the test-taker read over the test before finally submitting it to the teacher. This strategy allows the teacher to expect a degree of responsibility from students during test-taking situations. One instructional part of teaching in Texas involves preparing children for the TAKS test. Even if you do not teach at a TAKS grade level, you still have the responsibility of assisting teachers who do teach at TAKS grade levels by preparing children with test-taking skills. This is serious undertaking in Texas because of the amount of recognition and funding attached to test scores.

Consider the following practice questions that are related to comprehension.

Mr. Guntur, a third-grade teacher, reads a page of print from the science textbook to his students. Which of the following activities would be *most* effective in helping students organize the information?

    A. Have students take notes or fill in a graphic organizer.
    B. Give students a set of questions to consider.
    C. Have students determine the main idea.
    D. Give students study guide questions for homework.

The part that states "Mr. Guntur reads," cues us to consider that this relates to listening skills. We can then decide which activity promotes active listening. Having children take notes or fill in a graphic organizer as they listen to Mr. Guntur read (*A*) involves effective listening. Giving a set of questions to consider (*B*) is a good practice if questions are provided before reading or during reading. Giving students a study guide for homework (*D*) is also an effective practice as is determining the main idea (*C*), but they are not most effective for *active* listening. Therefore, response *A* is the best answer because it recommends that the children take notes or fill in a graphic organizer as they listen to their teacher read a page of print. Remember one test-taking strategy that is effective on the TExES is to watch for cue words such as *most*, as in this question.

Mrs. Jones's students have completed reading paragraphs on the "Battle of the Alamo." Now she wants to provide an opportunity to allow her children to extend their understanding of this topic. Which of the following would be the *most* effective practice that she could develop?

    A. Have students reread the paragraphs for determining a different purpose.
    B. Have students read information from different sources, such as trade books, computer-generated information, and magazines.
    C. Have students develop a dramatic play that identifies fictional and/or nonfictional characters who lived during the "Battle of the Alamo."
    D. Have students write a paragraph that identifies the major events of the "Battle of the Alamo."

Mrs. Jones has effective instructional choices, but which choice would promote an understanding of the topic that would allow children to read, develop purposes, and analyze the information? Each choice has fragments of knowledge extension; however, Response C promotes inferential comprehension. Having children develop a play would allow them to create characters based on their factual knowledge, and this activity would also promote an integrated usage of the levels of comprehension.

How can Miguel demonstrate that he can apply self-monitoring skills in his reading class to learn a concept?

A. By asking himself self-structured questions as he reads text silently.
B. By rereading a difficult sentence.
C. By asking his teacher a question.
D. All of the above.

Self-monitoring includes any technique that allows the learner to identify ways to completely understand a concept. Each of the choices could be considered a self-monitoring skill because it could be used by Miguel to determine a way to more effectively learn the concept. Therefore, *D* is the correct answer.

Tran, a third-grade student, is having difficulty understanding the main idea of sections of text. Which of the following activities would be most appropriate for the teacher to suggest that Tran use to become more effective in determining the main idea?

A. Show an example of a summarized paragraph.
B. Have the student paraphrase major facts and ideas after each paragraph in a section.
C. Teach the student underlining and note-taking strategies.
D. Provide an outline prepared by the teacher.

The best choice is *B* because the student needs a procedure that can assist in developing a system for learning to determine the main idea of a selection. Although paraphrasing after each paragraph is time-consuming, this strategy allows the reader to use purpose-setting questions or statements to guide in determining main idea choices.

A first-grade teacher, Mrs. Beck, read a story to her students. Which of the following activities would help the teacher best determine if her students comprehended the story?

A. Have students tell their favorite part of the story.
B. Have students write about their favorite character.
C. Have students illustrate the main parts of the story.
D. Have students identify the setting of the story.

Consider which activity would give Mrs. Beck the *best* assessment of how well her students comprehended the story. Since each choice contains an activity, you must decide which is *best* for understanding the elements of the *entire* story. In Response *A*, children are being asked to consider only their favorite part of the story. Response *B* asks pupils to write about a part of the story; whereas in *C*, they are required to illustrate the main parts of the story. This illustration would allow the teacher to assess students' understanding of the whole story rather than just one segment of the story. Response *D*, again, asks students for one specific element of the story. Therefore, Response *C* is the correct choice.

A first-grade social studies teacher's most effective practice in getting students prepared to either read a chapter or to listen to the teacher read (with a purpose) a chapter on "Community Helpers in the United States" would be to:

A. Have students brainstorm and write (or draw) things they know about "Community Helpers in the United States."

B. Have students define community helpers by using their textbook's picture and word glossary.

C. Distribute a mapping activity and have students attempt to fill in information about community helpers.

D. Have students view a film on community helpers.

This teacher is showing evidence that he or she knows ways to incorporate reading skills in other content areas. Decades ago, a social studies teacher probably would have assigned the reading without any initial preparation. However, today teachers use a variety of strategies to enhance decoding and comprehension. Let's look at the choices. Response *A* is an effective practice because it investigates students' background knowledge and encourages them to write about, or to draw about, what they know. Response *B* is not an effective practice because students have not discussed this topic; therefore, they may not select the best definition for the term as it relates to their social studies textbook. Response *C* is not effective because students have not yet been given the type of instruction that would prepare them to fill in a mapping activity. Response *D could be* effective if the teacher had given students a purpose for viewing a film or if a film had been used as an extension to the lesson. Therefore, *A* is the most effective practice.

Mrs. Torres has found that her second-grade students experience difficulty comprehending their science textbook. Much of the difficulty appears related to new vocabulary and terminology presented in chapter discussions. Which of the following language arts strategies could she use to increase understanding of concepts presented in the science textbook?

A. Students chorally read the text aloud and stop on each page to discuss words that they cannot pronounce.

B. Students, individually or in pairs, are assigned a vocabulary word from the textbook. They are to paraphrase, or write in their own words, a definition of the vocabulary word.

C. The teacher writes a synopsis, or summary, of each chapter in the textbook at a lower reading level to increase student comprehension of the text material.

D. All of the above.

Response *A* does not present a language arts skill that improves *comprehension* and learning of science *concepts*. The activity described only promotes phonics knowledge (and possibly not that effectively either). Response *C* does not teach a language arts skill because students are not involved in lowering the reading level of the text source. Response *B* empowers students to use their own language to create meaning of new vocabulary terms and concept knowledge in the science content area. Response *B* is the correct answer.

Mr. Campo, a fourth-grade teacher, has assigned students to read a science chapter for homework. Identify the *most* effective procedure Mr. Campo could recommend that students use to begin the assignment.

  A. Take thirty minutes to read the chapter.
  B. Preview the chapter before beginning to read.
  C. Identify a website that might have additional information about the chapter that they could access at home.
  D. Read the introduction to the chapter.

Remember that children are preparing to read the chapter as a homework assignment, and this means that Mr. Campo is recommending startups to assist in reading the assigned text. In this case, he would not suggest a time frame for completing the reading assignment (A) because students read at different rates. A website (C) would provide additional background information for the students. However, the website would probably be most effective in the extension section of the lesson because this question does not indicate that the teacher has established the level of students' background knowledge. Also, remember technology bias from your Pedagogy and Professional Responsibilities TExES because many lower socioeconomic status families may not have easy access to technology at home. An effective practice the teacher could recommend would be for the students to preview the chapter before beginning to read (B). The preview would allow students to notice new vocabulary terms, graphic aids, questions, and other features related to the chapter. Choice (D) may not be as inclusive of these types of items. Another consideration would be for Mr. Campo to preview the chapter with children before assigning it as homework. Mr. Campo might find that students need assistance with skills such as the pronunciation of several words encountered during the preview. Therefore, B would be the best answer.

Mr. Baco, a second-grade teacher, has his students gather information about Native Americans from a social studies textbook, a trade book, a website, and field trip to a museum. Mr. Baco assigns students to work in cooperative groups to synthesize information found in each source. What is a purpose of this assignment?

  A. To illustrate how people dressed during this time.
  B. To notice how different sources describe a topic.
  C. To develop a paragraph.
  D. To practice reading from a variety of sources.

Mr. Baco obviously intends for the students to gain insight into the topic by using a variety of sources, and it is important to understand that he wants students to synthesize information found in different sources. Therefore, B is the correct response because students can see how different sources discuss and describe Native Americans.

STANDARD VIII (DEVELOPMENT OF WRITTEN COMMUNICATION)

Competency 010:   Teachers understand that writing to communicate is a developmental process and provide instruction that helps young children develop competence in written communication.

> *The teacher understands the emergent and developing stages of literacy that include writing styles, provides instruction that incorporates the elements of the writing process, uses instructional practices that provide opportunities for children to write in a variety of forms, and monitors children's writing development. Remember that the TEKS promotes using strategies that emphasize developmental writing and elements of the writing process. Additionally, the TEKS recommends that beginning teachers provide examples of the different types of writing selections.*

Answer the practice question that relates to a classroom situation.

Ms. Keith, a fourth-grade social studies teacher, has made the following assignment.

You are to interview a relative or friend who has fought in a war. Use the following as discussion areas during your interview: which country started the conflict, location of the war, time of the war, the causes of the conflict, when and where the major battles were located, the results of the peace agreement, and the role that the relative played. Ms. Keith asks the students to bring their notes to class in one week.

Sidney is excited about this assignment, understands the purpose of the assignment, interviews his aunt who served in the Gulf War, and brings his notes to Ms. Keith early. Ms. Keith notices the following about Sidney's notes: The notes are incomplete in content, words are spelled correctly, and punctuation and other mechanics are basically correct.

How can Ms. Keith best assist Sidney in producing notes that are more complete in content?

   A. Have Sidney read examples of interview notes from his language arts textbook.
   B. Encourage Sidney to prepare a draft of the notes.
   C. Have Sidney reread his notes.
   D. Have Sidney explain the purpose of the assignment.

Test taker 1 selected *A*, believing that looking at examples from a commercial textbook and allowing Sidney to compare his notes would be adequate. Test taker 2 selected *C* because Sidney seemed to skip the initial phases of the writing process, and test taker 3 selected *D* because the teacher engaged Sidney in an oral activity. To answer this question effectively, knowledge of the phases of the writing process would be helpful. However, the logic of the other test takers includes the usage of examples from textbooks and teacher connection with a student's product. But do these ideas address the writing process? It is important for the test taker to consider each choice, but the most effective response is *B*.

This standard addresses the developmental process that young children use to learn to communicate in written form. Baghban (1984) suggests that children learn to write in stages that are scaffolded, or supported, by teachers. The *emergent stage,* which usually begins before kindergarten, allows the child to produce print in a variety of forms such as scribbling, drawing, and a combination of letter formations and drawings. Teachers of young children should encourage the practice of these beginning efforts in forming letters as it strengthens the connections of letter recognition in beginning to read, too. Children in the emergent stage should have a number of activities that help them recognize and form letter shapes. As mentioned earlier, these might include having students touch sandpaper letters, make letters out of clay, draw letters in sand trays or on their desks with shaving cream, as well as more traditional methods. Teachers will know if students are able to distinguish shapes through letter matching activities. Children will read their drawings in a story format as if they constructed a written source, often reading from left to right and top to bottom because they have observed adults reading to them. In this stage, the child may write his or her first name and may try to produce other words that are often spelled in invented spelling forms (an example of invented spelling would be **gone** spelled as **gon** because of the way the child perceives how the word sounds). They may also write using the name of the letter to communicate (I LVV U or U C ME). The beginning writing stage, which usually starts in first grade, allows the child to continue to use invented spelling to label pictures and to write sentences and short stories. The teacher will notice that children begin to write sentences that describe personal items, show a developing awareness of correct spelling patterns (word walls are often used to show spelling pattern examples that could be used in both spelling and word pronunciation), and use a story form that shows a description of a beginning and an ending of a story. The *developing writing stage* begins to show a process for writing that is explained in the following section. Teachers need to assess students' writing by using writing products to look for development in **mechanics** (correct formation and use of lower- and uppercase letters, directionality from left to right, use of punctuation, etc.) and for development in spelling (review Standard IX for information about spelling development). It is useful to remember that children's fine motor skills may not match their knowledge. Teachers who provide a number of materials with which to write (crayons, markers, chalk, dry-erase boards, paints, etc.) may be able to assess children much better. Children who feel frustrated with a traditional pencil and paper may be much more comfortable and skillful with other writing instruments.

This standard addresses the writing process that is used in the integrated language arts classroom. It should be noted that more than ten years ago teachers approached the process of writing in a much different way. At that time, teachers basically focused on having students produce papers that contained spelling or grammar errors and that could easily be assigned a letter grade. Currently, teachers are focusing on the components of the writing process by using models that scaffold and encourage students to use different genres such as creative stories, poetry, content-specific expository products, and other types of narrative products (Ziegler, 1981). They basically want children to enjoy producing ideas on paper first without being punished for mechanics. (As an aside, in management, teachers should avoid associating writing with punishment in assigning "lines" when children misbehave.) Teachers understand that students basically follow a process that is sequential. Most teachers assist children in understanding the phases of the writing process. Therefore, it is important to identify and discuss the following phases of the writing process.

Phase 1: Prewriting

This phase allows students to explore topics for consideration, identify ways to gather information about the topic, determine (with their teacher's help) the purpose for the writing assignment, determine the intended audience, and select the format of the product (that is, if the product will be a poem, a creative story, an expository response, etc.). Many teachers find that this is often the most difficult phase because students often cannot begin to get their ideas into written form.

Phase 2: Drafting

The students have gathered information about the topic. Therefore, during this phase students begin to write about the things they have learned. Students are encouraged to write and not be too concerned about mechanics such as spelling, grammar, and punctuation until revisions are made.

Phase 3: Revising

The teacher encourages children to be concerned with revising the content of their writing assignment but not yet consider correcting mechanics such as spelling and punctuation. Students are encouraged to consider their audience by selecting the most effective wording to convey clear meaning, provide supporting details, and present descriptive meaning. During the revision phase, teachers often encourage children to discuss their products with peers and to conference with the teacher. This exchange with peers and the teacher will often suggest more effective ways to revise their writing. This phase also fosters repeated exchange because students continue to redevelop their content by considering comments from peers and from the teacher.

Phase 4: Editing

During the editing phase, the teacher encourages students to proofread their content by looking for mechanical errors such as misspelled words and incorrect punctuation. Teachers encourage children to collaborate with their peers for the purpose of assisting in proofreading to identify errors. Additionally, the teacher will often act as a proofreader.

Phase 5: Publishing

As noted in Phase 1, an important consideration for a writer is the audience who will read the content of the product. The writing products can be shared through books, verbal sharing, collections of stories and poems bound by the teacher in book form, reports, or other of types of oral and written forms. Children should also be encouraged to self-assess their progress by looking back at their work over time.

The previous steps are often part of a *writing workshop* that last over several days. The teacher may use a routine format that includes: (1) a minilesson on a strategy that supports the writing experience (i.e., sequencing, techniques for getting ideas, etc.) for about 10 minutes; (2) a statement of purpose for three or four minutes in which students give their goals for the day; (3) a twenty- to thirty-minute sustained writing block where the teacher pulls out students for conferences; and (4) a five- to ten-minute sharing time (Duthie, 1996).

As teachers help young children develop writing skills, the teacher should allow children to connect reading and writing (by either narrative or expository selections that students read themselves or that the teacher reads to the children). Teachers can accomplish this skill by asking children to reflect on ideas from various types of text sources. As an example, children may be asked "What if . . ." questions to promote children's thinking about text sources. The "What if . . ." responses can be used as a writing activity. Teachers should encourage written text to include words from word walls and from phonemic awareness instruction (review Standards II, III, and IV to connect the usage of word recognition discussions).

Children must have a variety of situations that encourage writing. They should be encouraged to electronically mail (e-mail) to pen pals who live in various parts of their state, the United States, and the world. Journal writing provides a way for children to express their literary experiences. They can participate by writing in various types of journals, such as those that center on describing a character from a story and those that have a short "story starter." It is important for the teacher of young children to model effective writing forms by responding to children's writing activities and by assisting them in using the phases discussed above in the writing process. Many examples of the types of writing selections that students are encouraged to use should be provided. Table 2.5 on page 72 provides a list, with suggested content, of these writing selections.

Children should always be encouraged to write for meaningfulness. When children see a direct link with the real world and writing communication, they

TABLE 2.5 Content for Writing Selections

A summary paragraph should include:
- An accurate restatement, written in your own words, of the main ideas of the text
- A restatement of supporting details
- Omission of unimportant details

A narrative paragraph should include:
- Descriptive details to develop the characters, setting, and plot
- A clear beginning, middle, and ending
- A logical organization, with clues and transitions, to help the reader understand the order of events (examples of transitions would be *first, but, last, also,* and *next*)
- A consistent tone and point of view
- Language that is appropriate for the audience
- An explanation of the importance of the events and ideas

A compare-and-contrast paragraph should include:
- The subject being compared and contrasted (a Venn diagram is an appropriate graphic aid to use)
- Specific and relevant details
- Transitional words and phrases that signal similarities and differences
- A conclusion

A conclusion paragraph should include:
- A summary of the main points
- A description of personal feelings about the topic
- A brief restatement of the thesis
- A provocative question or call for some type of action

A cause-and-effect paragraph should include:
- A statement that includes the cause-and-effect relationship being examined
- A connection between causes and effects
- Facts, examples, and other details to illustrate each cause and effect

A problem-solving paragraph should include:
- A concise explanation of the problem and its significance
- A workable solution and details that explain and support the solution
- A conclusion that restates the problem

are more motivated to learn (rather than filling out a worksheet). Letters that are really sent to friends, relatives, or guest speakers requesting for or explaining something, communicating with technology, entertainment, and so forth make writing more valuable.

Try this practice question.

Students in Ms. Mitza's second-grade science class have been writing descriptive expository paragraphs about "Ocean Life," and the students are using the computer lab to do the assignment. As Ms. Mitza observes her students, she notices that they are composing their paragraphs, frequently doing a word count, and checking their spelling. She wants her students to use a variety of text sources to locate information and organize their paragraphs around main ideas as they revise.

Which of the following instructional strategies would be most effective in achieving this goal?

A. Providing a variety of text sources.
B. Modeling paragraph construction.
C. Asking children if they have described main points. *Paragraphs*
D. Encouraging students to graphically organize their paragraphs before beginning to write information.

Response C is correct because the teacher wants her students to construct paragraphs that contain information related to their main topic. It is an effective practice to have a variety of text sources available and to encourage children to develop their own graphics as they construct their paragraphs. However, it is also important to remember that, in the revision phase, children are constructing text without being concerned about editing.

STANDARD IX (WRITING CONVENTIONS)

Competency 009:   Teachers understand how young children use writing conventions and how to help children develop proficiency in using writing conventions.

The teacher understands the stages children use in acquiring writing conventions, knows the stages of spelling development, uses systemic spelling instruction to teach letter patterns in words, and applies assessment practices to enhance instruction. Remember that the TEKS promotes developmental application of the writing conventions.

Use the chart on page 75 to answer the practice question.

A third-grade teacher has just opened Devin's portfolio. The teacher notices four writing samples (pre-kindergarten, kindergarten, grade 1, and grade 2) that are a part of Devin's portfolio. What can the teacher determine about Devin's writing products?

A. His writing in Samples 1 through 3 shows little use of writing conventions.
B. His writing in Samples 1 through 4 shows development in spelling.

C. His writing in Sample 4 shows development in letter formation and punctuation but also shows errors in spelling.

D. His writing in Sample 3 shows that he understands the formation of only uppercase letters.

Think about all you know about children and their developmental stages for writing, spelling, punctuation, etc. Actually, Devin shows literacy development and progress with each of his portfolio products. So, let's think about each of the answer choices. Choice A does not give Devin credit for many things he does effectively. For example, in Sample 1, Devin uses spacing of scribbles to communicate his thoughts. In Sample 2, he is beginning to use uppercase letter formation and number formation, and he continues to demonstrate usage of spacing. In Sample 3, he is beginning to show usage of letter-sound association and punctuation. Choice B gives Devin credit for showing developmental spelling patterns. Choice C does give Devin credit for development in letter formation and punctuation, but sufficient credit regarding spelling is not given. Actually, he misspells two words (he writes *an* instead of *and*, and he writes *kat* instead of *cat*). But credit should be given for letter-sound association. Choice D indicates that Devin knows the formation of only uppercase letters. However, he is showing development in spelling and punctuation. Therefore, Choice B is the best answer.

It is important for the teacher of young children to understand that writing is an exciting activity that comes in a variety of forms (scribbles, drawings, and letter or number formations) that often will produce reversals, words, and sentences. Parents and teachers who encourage very young children "to write" strengthen the process of understanding that writing is an important activity and the ability of students to recognize the shape of writing that will be required later on. Young children often write from the bottom up (not from the top down), write from right to left (not from left to right), and mix a variety of written forms to spell or invent the spelling of a word. Most young children have some exposure to print and have had the opportunity to observe the conventions of print (parents have read books to them, preschool and kindergarten teachers have used a variety of "big books," and they have had access to books for examination or reading). In order for the teacher to explain the importance of becoming aware of conventions used in writing, it is important to identify the types of conventions that could be used with young children. Spandel and Stiggins (1997) have identified several conventions that teachers should model and include in instruction. They recommend that teachers demonstrate: (1) left-to-right direction of print normally by pointing as they read orally; (2) the idea that people read/write from the top to the bottom of a page; (3) that space should be left on both sides of a word to show division; (4) that culmination pronunciation marks should be used; (5) awareness of the proper usage of lowercase and capital letters; (6) awareness and growth of correct spelling; (7) usage of left and right margins, neatness, developmental

Devin's Portfolio Samples

(child's scribble writing)	Sample 1 Pre-kindergarten (I have a kite.)
(child's scribble writing)	Sample 2 Kindergarten (I am four.)
I HV A PPE.	Sample 3 Grade 1 (I have a puppy.)
I like My dog an Kat. My dog is big.	Sample 4 Grade 2 (I like my dog and cat. My dog is big.)

grammar usage; and (8) the awareness of a storyline. Teachers are encouraged to observe growth patterns and to collect samples of writing that document this growth over time.

As you recall from the discussion of Standard VIII (Development of Written Communication), children go through a developmental process in learning to construct meaning by using print. Students who are learning to spell go through a developmental process by using scribbles to indicate spelling approximations. Table 2.6 summarizes the stages of spelling development.

Try this practice question.

Why do you think the teacher wrote "excellent" on this first-grade student's story?

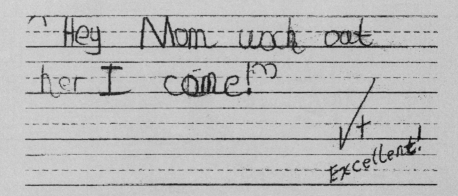

FIGURE 2.2

    A. The student used more than one type of punctuation mark.
    B. The student used left-to-right orientation.
    C. The student illustrated the story.
    D. All of the above.

This student correctly used several writing conventions (punctuation marks, left-to-right orientation, spacing, directionality, and capital letters). The child also included an illustration. Therefore, *D* is correct. It is important to remember to provide a variety of writing examples to use in classroom settings. As an example, use word walls to display descriptive and other types of words, provide topics for students to use during writing sessions, have a variety of writing products available for students to access, and provide feedback to students for the purpose of developmental growth.

TABLE 2.6 Stages of Spelling Development

Prephonetic (pre-kindergarten to beginning/middle of kindergarten)
Students use scribbles that show a sense of directionality, symbols, and other forms to present written language. Students often understand the purpose of written forms of language because they see print in books, on signs, and on different items in their environment. However, students do not understand yet the concept of using letters to produce words.

Prephonetic/Semiphonetic (end of kindergarten to middle of grade 1)
Students are aware of some of the sounds of the alphabet. They begin to realize that letters of the alphabet stand for sounds they hear in a word.

Phonetic (middle of grade 1)
Students understand the regular sounds of the alphabet and begin to use invented spelling. In most cases, words they spell can be interpreted (or read) by others because they spell by using the sounds in a word (for example, a student could spell *BOOKS* as *BOCZ*).

Transitional (end of grade 1 to beginning of grade 2)
Students begin to spell words based on how words sound. They are beginning to spell words based on how words look because they are experiencing more words in printed form. Usually students place a vowel in each syllable they write, and they are beginning to use limited structural analysis (prefixes, suffixes, and inflectional endings). They continue to use invented spelling, but it is used with some correct spelling. The student might spell *BOOKS* as *BOKS*.

Conventional (grade 2 through grade 4)
Students begin to spell more words consistently correctly and seem to understand the meaning of more words. They spell correctly one-syllable words that have a short vowel sound, and they understand and correctly use verb past tense. They have difficulty with dividing words into syllables and spelling words that have double consonants. At this point, the student should be able to spell *BOOKS* correctly.

Source: Adapted from Gentry, 1981.

STANDARD X (ASSESSMENT AND INSTRUCTION OF DEVELOPING LITERACY)

Competency 011 (Assessment of Developing Literacy): Teachers understand the basic principles of literacy assessment and use a variety of assessments to plan and implement literacy instruction.

The teacher uses a variety of formal and informal assessment techniques, analyzes children's reading and writing performance for instructional purposes, knows the procedure for determining children's reading levels, uses assessment practices for the purpose of preparing lessons, and communicates children's progress in literacy development to parents and other professionals. Remember that the TEKS promotes systematic assessment for the purpose of effective on-grade-level instruction.

Try this practice question.

During an informal assessment, Ms. Enzo recorded the way a first-grade student, Corbin, read the following sentence:

The boy likes to play baseball.

"She ba   base."

Based on this sample, where should Mrs. Enzo focus *initial* reading instruction?

    A. Automatic sight word recognition.
    B. Picture clues.
    C. Compound words.
    D. Syllable division.

Ms. Enzo should provide instruction on sight word recognition so that textual meaning can be emphasized. Picture or illustration clues could be helpful, but the test item does not provide a picture for Corbin to use. Although baseball is a compound word and can be applied to syllable division, she would help Corbin *initially* by using instruction that focuses on sight word recognition. Therefore, Response *A* is correct.

In today's classroom settings, assessment can usually be viewed as either formal or informal. Formal assessment often centers on norm-referenced standardized tests. Formal tests are published tests "for which norms based on the performances of large numbers of students have been developed" (McCormick, 1999, p. 80). Norms provide information for educators to compare the test performance of students with other students in a sample group. For example, in many Texas elementary schools, the Iowa Test of Basic Skills is administered to students. Their scores are then compared to what seems "normal" for a great number of test-takers at that level (e.g., students in your school in Texas would be compared to students in the same grade in Georgia). Additionally, *criterion-referenced* tests should be discussed. These are published tests, less formal than standardized tests, that provide information about the types of skills students have either mastered or not mastered. Criterion-referenced tests can be standardized, but the results are not used for comparison, so this type of test is usually not "normed." Scores are not compared to other students but to how well a student knows particular concepts. The TExES test is an example of a criterion-referenced test because scores will reflect a percentage of how many questions were answered correctly by a test-taker. A criterion is the level of performance used to determine if a student has or has not mastered a task level, and criterion-referenced tests are based on specific objectives. As an example, a social studies objective might be stated: The student will demonstrate mastery by correctly identifying and describing five (5) rivers found in Texas.

The *Reading Miscue Inventory* helps teachers determine if students' reading miscues (words read differently from what is actually written) prevent them from obtaining correct information from the passage. This assessment assists in determining if children are using background and context clues to assist in reading. The Reading Miscue Inventory stresses that (1) reading is the ability to obtain meaning, (2) reading is not an absolute process because effective readers often substitute words, and (3) teachers should not treat all miscues the same way. Let's look at an example of a miscue that does not basically change the meaning of a sentence: The boy saw a red *automobile* is read aloud by a child as The boy saw a red *car*. The teacher decides if the student has altered a word in a sentence significantly enough to change the meaning of the sentence, and, in this case, he has not. However, if the child had substituted *hat* for *automobile*, then the teacher would have realized that this miscue changed the entire meaning of the sentence and would signal serious difficulties in analyzing words.

Informal assessment (see additional information in Standard II) is a nonstandardized measure that could be an observation, a checklist, a teacher-generated test, an interest inventory, an interview, a portfolio, an informal reading inventory, a reading miscue inventory, or another type of measure that would give a teacher insight into student performance. Most informal assessments and the implementation processes have been a part of your schooling for years and are clearly understood. However, several need additional discussion.

Teachers use a **running record** to identify the number of correct words a student pronounced in lines of print. To conduct a running record, the teacher would use a blank sheet of paper to place check marks, or ticks, that represent each correctly pronounced word. The teacher would mark, or record, miscues and errors by using the same criteria used in marking informal reading inventory responses and miscues (Clay, 1985).

Portfolio assessment has become a much discussed concept in education. A **portfolio** is a collection of student-generated products that show growth, progress, or improvement over a period of time. Calfee and Perfumo (1993) suggest that the portfolio could include the following student-generated products identified by the teacher and/or by the student for their importance and usage in a particular area of reading/writing: rough, final, and published drafts; content-entry journals; tests and quizzes; illustrations; independent and group-generated projects; and other types of literacy products. Each item should be carefully selected by the teacher and/or the student. The length of portfolios can vary in length from long and involved to rather brief. Additionally, teachers' written comments should be maintained over time to document children's academic achievement history. Portfolio collections provide a meaningful picture for parents during conferences and for students to self-assess their own progress.

Another type of assessment is an **Informal Reading Inventory (IRI),** which contains a series of graded paragraphs followed by a comprehension analysis. Teachers have many types of commercially prepared IRIs from which to select. Most contain the following components: (1) a graded word list to determine the starting paragraph level and basic information about a child's sight word vocabulary, (2) two sets of paragraphs with one to be read orally and the other to be read silently, and (3) a series of comprehension checks at different levels. The basic purpose of the IRI is to determine a child's (1) independent level (students can read at school or at home without assistance), (2) instructional level (students are challenged and require instruction from the teacher), (3) frustration level (students are experiencing material that is too difficult to read), and (4) listening capacity level (students can benefit from hearing the teacher read text aloud that will be followed by questions). It is important to remember the following criteria for determining reading levels as structured by an informal reading inventory (see Table 2.7).

Capacity level (also called hearing or listening level) is tested by the examiner reading to a child at the next level beyond his or her determined frustration level. The comprehension checks are administered until the child scores below 70 percent on questions related to the paragraphs that are read aloud to the child. The purpose of the capacity level, which measures listening comprehension, is to determine the level of reading material children could understand if they could read the material themselves (Spring & French, 1990).

Most educators agree that instruction is a cycle that should lead from lesson objectives to effective instructional activities to assessment and back to new objectives that target what the teacher noted during assessment. Let's look at how a first-grade teacher could assess the following written product to plan instructional activities and additional *authentic assessment* activities (see Figure 2.3).

TABLE 2.7   Reading Levels of an Informal Reading Inventory

Level	Word Recognition Accuracy Percentage	Comprehension Percentage
Independent	95 to 100% correct	90 to 100% correct
Instructional	90 to 94% correct	70 to 89% correct
Frustration	Below 90% correct	Below 70% correct

The Three Littl bear
porrage and went
for a Littl wake and
wen They came bake
Thre porrige wose gon

FIGURE 2.3

Let's assume that Mrs. Kumar has read *The Three Little Bears* to her class and has asked Emily to do a written retelling of the story (see Standard VII to review the components of story retelling). The teacher should note that Emily understood the following: (1) the family structure of the bears, (2) the name of the food they were going to eat, (3) what they did, and (4) what had happened to their food when they returned. Mrs. Kumar should assess the written retelling to determine instructional strategies that could be used to help Emily orally retell omitted details about the story. For example, Mrs. Kumar could ask Emily to tell about other characters in the story, other things that happened in the story, where the story took place, the main problem and how it was solved, and so forth. Additionally, Mrs. Kumar should assess Emily's writing conventions (see Standard IX to review writing conventions) and determine further activities that could be used in instruction. A teacher might plan an additional lesson on using punctuation at the end of a sentence, in which several activities would give the child practice in using an appropriate punctuation mark at the end of several different sentences. This brief discussion highlights that assessment and instructional practices should be used daily to make instructional decisions.

Try these practice questions.

Mr. Orion provides the following information about Patrick's reading performance during a parental conference:

"Patrick reads slightly above grade level. He enjoys reading orally in class and has a positive attitude about learning. There is some concern about the usage of miscues during oral reading. This is causing Patrick to make some comprehension mistakes. This is not necessarily a habit yet, but strategies that will assist Patrick in being more accurate in oral reading should be provided."

Which instructional practice/s would be effective to use?

   A. Establishing strategies that would allow Patrick to use his own background knowledge to determine word selection during oral and silent reading.
   B. Instructing Patrick on how to use metacognitive strategies to ask questions about the material being read.
   C. Instructing him to use context clues to determine unknown words.
   D. All of the above.

Actually, Patrick should have grade-appropriate sight word recognition. However, it would also be an appropriate practice to encourage him to use his own background in determining word choices, to use self-determined questions (using a metacognitive strategy) to assist in meaning, and to use context clues to determine unknown words. Therefore, Response *D* would be correct.

Students in Mr. Canto's third-grade mathematics class have been writing journal entries to describe the process used in solving math problems. Mr. Canto has just requested that his students give him journal entries submitted over the last five Mondays. Which type of assessment best describes Mr. Canto's request?

   A. Portfolio assessment
   B. Informal reading inventory
   C. Criterion-referenced testing
   D. Norm-referenced testing

Mr. Canto is using portfolio assessment considerations in his request to see a rather specific collection of student-generated products that could indicate a pattern of academic or nonacademic growth. Therefore, *A* is the correct response.

SUMMARY

This chapter has discussed the instructional importance of acquiring knowledge about the concepts to be tested in the ten standards of English Language Arts and Reading in Early Childhood-Grade 4 TExES examination. This chapter should serve as a review of information you have studied in coursework and applied in different types of instructional settings. As you connect this information to your current knowledge base, you will notice an increase in basic information that will assist you in preparing for the TExES examination. In addition to acquiring a cognitive knowledge base needed to be successful when taking this examination, it is necessary to properly apply this information to successfully teach children in classroom settings. The importance of designing effective language arts and reading lessons cannot be overstated. Planning this type of instruction requires the

development and use of activities that are meaningful and interesting so that all children can participate in an effective learner-centered classroom environment. Therefore, educators who understand the process and reasons for designing and conducting effective instruction for reading and language arts will be able to identify and meet the needs of *all* children.

 GLOSSARY

You should become familiar with the following terms so that you can establish an effective knowledge base. This knowledge base will provide you with more information when considering the most effective response to questions on the TExES.

Affix. A structural element added to the beginning or ending of a word in order to alter the meaning, pronunciation, or function (e.g., prefixes and suffixes).

Alphabetic principle. The idea that individual letters represent individual speech sounds; therefore, words may be read by saying the sounds represented by the letters, and words may be spelled by writing the letters that represent the sounds.

Alphabetic recognition. The ability to name letters of the alphabet.

Balanced approach to reading. The use of different strategies and approaches to teach reading.

Basal reader. A collection of stories that match the instructional level of children.

Bilingual education. Instruction that involves presenting reading and other subject area materials in the child's native language while gradually introducing English orally.

Choral reading. Oral reading, often of poetry, involving more than one reader.

Consonant blend or cluster. Two or three letters in the same syllable that are blended or heard when pronounced (e.g., "*tr*" in *tree*).

Consonant digraph. A combination of two or more letters that represent a sound that is different

from the speech sound that the letters represent individually (e.g., *ch* in *chop*).

Conversation. In formal speaking activity involving two or more persons taking turns talking about a subject.

Debate. A discussion involving varying viewpoints on a central topic, where sides are supported.

Decode. Associating printed letters with the speech sounds the letters make.

Dialect. A linguistic change or variation in speech pronunciation that is different from the standard, or original, pronunciation.

Diphthong. Two adjacent vowels in which each vowel is heard in the pronunciation (e.g., "*ou*" in *house*).

Discussion. Focused conversations about a specific topic.

Emergent literacy. Children's reading and writing development before formal instruction in classroom settings.

English as a Second Language (ESL). An instructional program that teaches English to students whose native language is not English.

Evaluative comprehension. Level of comprehension that requires children to compare information and ideas presented in the text with their own experiences, background, and values.

Facilitative. Skills such as word analysis that enable a reader to identify words.

Functional. The actual understanding or comprehension of what has been read.

Genre. A description of the type of text being read (e.g., poetry, biography, mystery, fantasy).

Grapheme. A printed letter symbol used to represent a speech sound (phoneme).

Graphophonemic knowledge. Written words are made up of systematic letter patterns that represent sounds in pronounced words.

Graphophonic. Sound/symbol relationship.

Homographs. Words spelled the same but having different pronunciations and meanings; for example: "She is wearing a red *bow*," and "She will *bow* to the queen."

Homophones. Words that sound the same but have different spellings and meanings; for example: "He is wearing a *red* shirt." "He *read* the book."

Idioms. Figurative sayings that have special meanings; for example, "*Keep your shirt on!*" basically means "*Don't get angry.*"

Inferential comprehension. Level of comprehension that requires children to respond to questions and statements based on ideas and information that are directly stated in the text along with the use of their intuition, background, and experiences to reach a conclusion or a hypothesis.

Informal reading inventory (IRI). A series of graded paragraphs followed by a comprehension analysis used to determine a child's independent, instructional, and frustration level for reading.

Interview. One person asking another individual questions and recording the person's responses.

Invented spelling. Temporary spelling patterns young children use to approximate the spelling of words (e.g., a young child might write "*It wus a preti da*" instead of "*It was a pretty day.*"

Language experience approach (LEA). An instructional method that incorporates children's experiences and background as a means of developing instructional reading stories.

Language interference. The use of sounds, syntax, and vocabulary of two languages simultaneously as a child participates in literacy activities.

Literal comprehension. Level of comprehension that requires children to respond to questions and statements that relate directly to stated text.

Logographic awareness. The first stage children experience when learning about words. Words that are learned as whole units are sometimes embedded in a logo such as a stop sign or the arches in the McDonald's sign.

Metaphor. Comparison of two unlike things without using *as* or *like* (e.g., "The moon was an orange floating on the silver platter of the sea.").

Morpheme. The smallest meaningful unit of language (e.g., *cat* is a morpheme whose pronunciation consists of three phonemes, c/a/t).

Nonstandard dialect. Grammatical variations in a language most often associated with a cultural group.

Onsets and rimes. *Onsets* are the consonants that come at the beginning of syllables in words—for example, the "*bl*" in the word *blend* is the onset. *Rimes* are vowels and consonants at the end of a syllable—for example, the "*end*" in the word *blend* is the rime.

Oracy. The concept that identifies and describes the differences between the skills of listening and speaking from the skills of reading and writing.

Oral reports. Individual or group reports delivered orally to an audience.

Orthography. Correct spelling.

Phoneme. The smallest unit of sound in a language that distinguishes one word from another word. Example: *cat* and *hat* are distinguished as sounding different by considering their beginning consonant phonemes /c/ and /h/.

Phonic analysis. The process of applying knowledge of letter-sound relationships to decoding texts. Teachers ask for this when they instruct children to "sound out" a word.

Phonemic awareness. The knowledge or understanding that speech consists of a series of sounds and that individual words can be divided into phonemes.

Phonics. Using letters and the sounds of letters to determine the pronunciation of a word.

Phonological awareness. The ability to use letter-sound knowledge to identify an unknown word.

Phonology. The way a word is defined.

Portfolio. A collection of student-generated products that show growth, progress, or improvement over a period of time.

Puppets. Animal or human characters made from a variety of materials to be held or slipped over the hand and used in dramatic play.

Readers' theater. The oral presentation of drama by two or more readers using a printed script. Normally used to create motivation and oral fluency.

Running record. An informal assessment that provides a record of a child's oral reading development and behavior.

Semantic feature analysis. Constructing a grid for a concept (example: mammals) where examples of the concept are listed vertically (example: cow, bat, squirrel) and features are listed horizontally (example: has fur, swims, flies). Students then decide which feature matches each word.

Sematic or concept map (word cluster). Writing a word or concept in the center circle of a cluster, drawing rays, writing information about the word or concept, and making connections between the word or concept and the related unit of study or details from readings.

Scaffolding. Support for a learner as he or she enters a phase of readiness for a new skill.

Schwa sound. In many words that have more than one syllable, one of the syllables receives less or diminished stress. The sound of the vowel in the syllable that receives the diminished stress has a softening of the vowel sound that is identified as a schwa sound and often pronounced as the "uh" sound. The word *about* contains the schwa sound.

Segmentation. The recognition of the sounds heard in a word.

Semantics. The way a word is defined.

Show-and-tell. A traditional informal speaking activity in which a child brings something from home that is special to him or her and tells the class about it.

Sight vocabulary. Any words a reader can recognize instantly without having to use a word recognition strategy. Many teachers have children personalize a word bank of the sight words they can read.

Similes. Comparison between two things of a different kind or quality using *like* or *as*. An example: "*The rain came down like transparent sheets.*"

Syllable. Divisions of speech sounds within words.

Syntactic. Patterns of phrases, clauses, and sentences.

Syntax. The sentence structure.

Textless books (also known as **wordless books**). A picture book with few or no words in which the illustrations convey the story.

Thematic units. Instructionally generated learning activities that center on a topic of interest such as a variety of content areas discussing "Butterflies."

Trade books. Children's literature sources that teachers sometimes use in instructional settings instead of textbooks.

Vowel digraph. Two adjacent vowels that represent one speech sound (e.g., "*ee*" in *feet*).

Word analysis. An inclusive term that refers to *all methods* of word recognition. Phonics is one such method. Other methods include *picture clues* (using pictures and graphic aids to assist in word pronunciation and meaning), *context clues* (using surrounding text to aid in word pronunciation and meaning), *sight words,* and *structural analysis* (which focuses on root words, base words, affixes, compound words, syllable division, and contractions).

Word sorts. Sorting a collection of words taken from a word wall or other sources into two or more categories.

Word wall. A list of words children are learning or know posted on a poster (or an actual wall in a classroom) in a highly visible location.

Zone of proximal development. Children learn within their instructional level or just beyond their instructional level with scaffolding from an adult or from a capable peer.

 # REFERENCES

Adams, M. J. (1990). *Beginning to read: Thinking and learning about print.* Cambridge, MA: Massachusetts Institute of Technology.

Baghban, M. (1984). *Our daughter learns to read and write: A case study from birth to three.* Newark, DE: International Reading Association.

Barrett, T. C. (1965). The relationship between measures of prereading visual discrimination and first grade reading achievement: A review of the literature. *Reading Research Quarterly, 1,* 51–76.

Blevins, W. (1998). *Phonics from a to z: A practical guide.* New York: Scholastic Professional Books.

Calfee, R. C., & Perfumo, P. (1993). Student portfolios: Opportunities for a revolution in assessment. *The Reading Teacher, 46,* 532–537.

Carlson, C., Fletcher, J., Foorman, B., Francis, D., & Schatschneider, C. (2001). *Texas primary reading inventory (TPRI) teacher's guide.* Austin: Texas Education Agency.

Carmen, R., & Adams, W. (1972). *Study skills: A student's guide to survival.* New York: Wiley.

Clay, M. M. (1985). *The early detection of reading difficulties: A diagnostic survey with recovery procedures.* Portsmouth, NH: Heinemann.

Cunningham, J. W., Cunningham, P. M., Hoffman, J. V., & Yopp, H. R. (1998). *Phonemic awareness and the teaching of reading: A position statement from the board of directors of the International Reading Association.* Newark, DE: International Reading Association.

Dowhower, S. L. (1991). Speaking of prosody: Fluency's unattended bedfellow. *Theory into Practice, 30,* 165–175.

Duthie, C. (1996). *True stories: Nonfiction literacy in the primary classroom.* York, ME: Stenhouse.

Elkonin, D. B. (1963). The psychology of mastering elements of reading. In B. Simon & J. Simon (Eds.), *Educational psychology in the U.S.S.R.* (pp. 165–179). London: Routledge and Kegan Paul.

Gentry, J. R. (1981). Learning to spell developmentally. *The Reading Teacher, 34,* 378–381.

Halliday, M., & Hasan, R. (1976). *Cohesion in English.* London: Longman.

Jewell, M., & Zintz, M. F. (1986). *Learning to read and write naturally.* Dubuque, IA: Kendall-Hunt.

Juel, C. (1988). Learning to read and write: A longitudinal study of fifty-four children from first through fourth grade. *Journal of Educational Psychology, 80,* 437–447.

Kutiper, K. (1985). *A survey of the adolescent poetry preferences of seventh, eighth, and ninth graders.* Unpublished doctoral dissertation, University of Houston, Houston, Texas.

Lundsteen, S. W. (1979). *Listening: Its impact at all levels on reading and the other language arts.* Urbana, IL: ERIC Clearinghouse on Reading and Communication Skills and the National Council of Teachers of English.

Manzo, A. V. (1969). The request procedure. *Journal of Reading, 13,* 123–126.

McCormick, S. (1999). *Instructing students who have literacy problems.* (3rd ed.) Upper Saddle River, NJ: Prentice-Hall.

McGee, L., & Richgels, D. (2000). *Literacy's beginnings: Supporting young readers and writers.* Boston: Allyn and Bacon.

Meyer, B. (1975). *The organization of prose and its effect on memory.* Amsterdam: North-Holland.

Morrow, L. M. (1989). Using story retelling to develop comprehension. In K. D. Muth (Ed.), *Children's comprehension of text: Research into practice* (pp. 37–58). Newark, DE: International Reading Association.

Ogle, D. M. (1992). KWL in action: Secondary teachers find applications that work. In E. K. Dishner. T. W. Bean, J. E. Readence, & D. W. Moore (Eds.), *Reading in the content areas: Improving classroom instruction* (3rd ed., pp. 270–281). Dubuque, IA: Kendall-Hunt.

Rubin, D. (2000). *Teaching elementary language arts.* Boston: Allyn and Bacon.

Spandel, V., & Stiggins, R. (1997). *Creating writers: Linking writing assessment and instruction.* New York: Addison Wesley Longman.

Spring, C., & French, L. (1990). Identifying children with specific reading disabilities from listening and reading discrepancy scores. *Journal of Learning Disabilities, 23,* 53–58.

Stanovich, K. E. (1994). Romance and reality. *The Reading Teacher, 47,* 280–291.

Stauffer, R. G. (1969). *Teaching reading as a teaching process.* New York: Harper and Row.

Terry, C. A. (1974). *Children's poetry preferences: A national survey of upper elementary grades.* Urbana, IL: National Council of Teachers of English.

Tompkins, G. E. (2001). *Literacy for the 21st century: A balanced approach* (2nd ed.). Upper Saddle River, NJ: Prentice-Hall.

Vacca, R., & Vacca, J. A. (1986). *Content area reading.* Boston: Little, Brown and Company.

Walker, B. J. (2000). *Diagnostic teaching of reading.* New Jersey: Merrill.

Wilkinson, A. (1974). Oracy in English teaching. In H. DeStefana & S. Fox (Eds.), *Language and the language arts* (pp. 64–71). Boston: Little, Brown and Company.

Yopp, H. K. (1995). A test for assessing phonemic awareness in young children. *The Reading Teacher, 49,* 20–29.

Ziegler, A. (1981). *The writing workshop, Vol. 1.* New York: Teachers and Writers Collaborate.

ABOUT THE AUTHORS

LAVERIA F. HUTCHISON, Ed.D., is an associate professor at the University of Houston-Central Campus in Houston, Texas. She teaches undergraduate and graduate literacy courses and coordinates the Secondary Education Program Area. She serves as an editorial advisor for the National Reading Conference and serves on the Print and Media Awards Committee for the International Reading Association. Dr. Hutchison received her doctoral degree from Ball State University in Muncie, Indiana.

ELEANORE S. TYSON, Ed.D., is a clinical associate professor at the University of Houston-Central Campus in Houston, Texas. She teaches undergraduate and graduate literacy courses in the teacher preparation program. Among her favorite courses to teach are those in children's literature. She designs web-based lessons related to children's trade books. Dr. Tyson received her doctoral degree from the University of Houston.

Preparing to Teach Mathematics

Norene Vail Lowery
University of Houston

Rena M. Schull
Rockhurst University

Charles E. Lamb
Texas A&M University

This chapter presents three sections for test takers who will teach mathematics in EC-4 classrooms. The first section highlights the current emphases on the teaching and learning of mathematics. This overview describes the move from traditional mathematics teaching to elementary mathematics classrooms of today. The second section presents standards and competencies for the TExES with a brief elaboration. Sample question items that correspond to each area are given along with information for successful completion of the mathematics portion of the TExES Generalist exam. A snapshot teaching scenario follows this section with more practice questions and information addressing mathematics such as manipulatives, formulas, and other vital information for EC-4 mathematics. A glossary is found at the conclusion of the chapter.

AN OVERVIEW OF MATHEMATICS TODAY

The current vision of the EC-4 mathematics learning environment is probably not the same as most adults have experienced. Traditional classrooms adhered strictly to curricular activities that were presented part-to-whole with emphasis on basic skills, memorization, textbook problems, and drill sheets as students worked individually at their seats. Learning was teacher centered and teacher directed, and mathematical concepts were presented in a didactic manner. Having a correct answer was the singlemost way to have one's work evaluated, and assessment was separate from ongoing instruction. This description of a traditional classroom contradicts much of what cognitive research findings are discovering concerning human learning (Brooks & Brooks, 1993).

Reform efforts in mathematics education call for new ways of teaching and learning mathematics. The advances in cognitive psychology and the emergence of the constructivist approach to teaching and learning promote new methods of addressing mathematics in the classroom (Davis, Maher, & Noddings, 1990). Goals for mathematics education that affect curricular content, instructional strategies, the classroom learning environment, and the assessment of knowledge have been established by the National Council of Teachers of Mathematics (NCTM). Mathematics education should reflect these goals by helping students: (a) learn to value mathematics, (b) become confident in their own abilities, (c) become mathematical problem solvers, (d) learn to communicate mathematically, and (e) learn to reason mathematically (NCTM, 1989). The overall goal is to have students become mathematically literate.

National Standards (NCTM, 1989, 1991, 1995, 1998, 2000) for mathematics, the Texas Essential Knowledge and Skills (TEKS), and the Texas Assessment of Knowledge and Skills (TAKS) all promote *active* learning environments that are *learner centered.* Within this type of classroom, teachers seek to understand students' prior knowledge and connect it to current concepts. Questioning strategies aim to develop higher-order thinking skills in children, and cognitive terminology such as classify, analyze, predict, create, and justify is used in learning interactions. While manipulatives are used to assist children in "seeing," "reflecting," and "thinking" to provide a concrete basis for abstract concepts, learning centers are used to provide relevant, exploratory, and interactive contexts for learning mathematics both for individual students and small groups. Opportunities are created that address diversities in learning styles, gender, culture, multiple intelligences, and ability. Learners in these classrooms are not passive but *active* in all aspects.

Other strategies have changed as well. The incorporation of mathematical representations (models, tables, graphs, etc.) is promoted for children to develop better conceptual understanding of mathematical concepts. Elementary mathematics learning has moved beyond basic facts and procedures. The NCTM

Principles and Standards for School Mathematics (2000) and the organization's website (www.nctm.org) provide teachers with developmentally appropriate, grade-level visions of teaching and learning mathematical content and process skills. Mathematics in today's classrooms should come alive through experiences that inform children of the value and utility of mathematics through historical aspects, present-day professions, and everyday living. The mathematical content and processes emphasize reasoning and authentic problem solving. Lessons connect mathematical ideas to other subject areas in interdisciplinary instruction and join together other mathematical concepts. Real-world contexts and applications also help children to value mathematics and see its relevance. Instructional materials involve using the textbook as only *one* source of many, and children utilize primary sources of data with manipulatives and physical materials. As technology advances, its uses in mathematics classes are also evolving. The use of calculators and computers support instruction. Assessment is not just the end of the chapter test but is ongoing (formative) and interwoven with teaching by placing a focus on learning processes. Alternative forms of assessment (e.g., observations, checklists, interviews, performance tasks, journals, and portfolios) are incorporated in the assessment process.

The picture of a perfect mathematics classroom continues. A traditional teaching approach with rows of desks and individual seatwork gives way to an active mathematical learning environment with small groups of students problem-solving collaboratively. Children are encouraged to talk about mathematics as they work cooperatively to solve problems. Children become motivated to learn and discuss mathematics (content and processes) in an interactive, hands-on, minds-on approach. Reasoning and communicating are highly valued components in this classroom, and the classroom is a safe learning environment that is an active community of problem solvers (including the teacher as a co-learner and investigator). This creates a new role for the teacher as facilitator to children constructing their own knowledge.

INTRODUCTION TO THE MATHEMATICS STANDARDS

There are eight elementary mathematics standards and four competencies. Within each of these is embedded the vision for improving teaching and learning mathematics. Each standard is designed and correlated with the TEKS (Texas Essential Knowledge and Skills) and the TAKS (Texas Assessment of Knowledge and Skills) that tests students on the TEKS. The first part of this section presents the Texas Education Commissioner's guidelines for pre-kindergarten curriculum; the second part presents the introductory information from the TEKS for the early childhood grades. As there is at the time of this publication no state-required pre-kindergarten curriculum, use of these guidelines is recommended. The third part of this section presents the mathematics standards and competencies with sample questions and discussion.

Pre-Kindergarten Curriculum Guidelines

Mathematics learning builds on children's curiosity and enthusiasm and challenges children to explore ideas about patterns and relationships, order and predictability, and logic and meaning. Consequently, quality instruction occurs in environments that are rich in language, encourage children's thinking, and nurture children's explorations and ideas. These ideas include the concepts of number pattern, measurement, shape, space, and classification.

1. **Number and Operations:** Understanding the concept of number is fundamental to mathematics. Children come to school with rich and varied informal knowledge of number. A major goal is to build on this informal base toward more thorough understanding and skills. Children move from beginning to develop basic counting techniques in pre-kindergarten to later understanding number size, relationships, and operations.
   The child:
   - arranges sets of concrete objects in one-to-one correspondence
   - counts by ones to 10 or higher
   - counts concrete objects to 5 or higher
   - begins to compare the numbers of concrete objects using language (e.g., *same* or *equal, one more, more than,* or *less than*)
   - begins to name *how many* are in a group of up to three (or more) objects without counting (e.g., recognizing two or three crayons in a box)
   - recognizes and describes the concept of zero (meaning there are none)
   - begins to demonstrate part of and whole with real objects (e.g., an orange)
   - begins to identify first and last in a series
   - combines, separates, and names "how many" concrete objects

2. **Patterns:** Recognizing patterns and relationships among objects is an important component in children's intellectual development. Children learn to organize their world by recognizing patterns and gradually begin to use patterns as a strategy for problem solving, forming generalizations, and developing the concepts of number, operation, shape, and space. Pattern recognition is the first step in the development of algebraic thinking.
   The child:
   - imitates pattern sounds and physical movements (e.g., clap, stomp, clap, stomp, . . .)
   - recognizes and reproduces simple patterns of concrete objects (e.g., a string of beads that are yellow, blue, blue, yellow, blue, blue)
   - begins to recognize patterns in their environment (e.g., day follows night, repeated phrases in storybooks, patterns in carpeting or clothing)
   - begins to predict what comes next when patterns are extended

3. **Geometry and Spatial Sense:** Geometry helps children systematically represent and describe their world. Children learn to name and recognize the properties of various shapes and figures, use words that indicate direc-

tion, and use spatial reasoning to analyze and solve problems.
The child:

- begins to recognize, describe, and name shapes (e.g., circles, triangles, rectangles—including squares)
- begins to use words that indicate where things are in space (e.g., *beside, inside, behind, above, below*)
- begins to recognize when a shape's position or orientation has changed
- begins to investigate and predict the results of putting together two or more shapes
- puts together puzzles of increasing complexity

4. **Measurement:** Measurement is one of the most widely used applications of mathematics. Early learning experiences with measurement should focus on direct comparisons of objects. Children make decisions about size by looking, touching, and comparing objects directly while building language to express the size relationships.
The child:

- covers an area with shapes (e.g., tiles)
- fills a shape with solids or liquids (e.g., ice cubes, water)
- begins to make size comparisons between objects (e.g., *taller than, smaller than*)
- begins to use tools to imitate measuring
- begins to categorize time intervals and uses language associated with time in everyday situations (e.g., *in the morning, after snack*)
- begins to order two or three objects by size (seriation) (e.g., largest to smallest)

5. **Classification and Data Collection:** Children use sorting to organize their world. As children recognize similarities and differences, they begin to recognize patterns that lead them to form generalizations. As they begin to use language to describe similarities and differences, they begin sharing their ideas and their mathematical thinking. Children can be actively involved in collecting, sorting, organizing, and communicating information.
The child:

- matches objects that are alike
- describes similarities and differences between objects
- sorts objects into groups by an attribute and begins to explain how the grouping was done
- participates in creating and using real and pictorial graphs

TEKS for PreK-4

An understanding of the expectations for student achievement as given by Texas Education Agency (TEA) helps readers to approach the TExES in a competent and confident manner, ready to teach young children. For all grades preK through 4 the introduction to the TEKS expectations in achieving mathematical learning states:

> *Problem solving, language and communication, connections within and outside mathematics, and formal and informal reasoning underlie all content areas in mathematics and that students use these processes together with technology and other mathematical tools such as manipulative materials to develop conceptual understanding and solve problems as they do mathematics. (TEA, 1997, p. A-1)*

> *Throughout mathematics in grades kindergarten through 2 students build a foundation of basic understanding in number, operation, and quantitative reasoning: patterns, relationships, and algebraic thinking; geometry and spatial reasoning; and measurement and probability and statistics. Students use numbers in ordering, labeling, and expressing quantities and relationships to solve problems and translate informal language into mathematical symbols. Students use patterns to describe objects, express relationships, make predictions, and solve problems as they build an understanding of number, operation, shape, and space. Students use informal language and observation of geometric properties to describe shapes, solids, and locations in the physical world and begin to develop measurement concepts as they identify and compare attributes of objects and situations. Students collect, organize, and display data and use information from graphs to answer questions, make summary statements, and make informal predictions based on their experiences. (TEA, 1997, p. A-1)*

> *Throughout mathematics in grades 3 through 5 students build a foundation of basic understandings in number, operation, and quantitative reasoning: patterns, relationships, and algebraic thinking; geometry and spatial reasoning; measurement; and probability and statistics. Students use algorithms for addition, subtraction, multiplication, and division as generalizations connected to concrete experiences; and they concretely develop basic concepts of fractions and decimals. Students use appropriate language and organizational structures such as tables and charts to represent and communicate relationships, make predictions, and solve problems. Students select and use formal language to describe their reasoning as they identify, compare, and classify shapes and solids; and they use numbers, standard units, and measurement tools to describe and compare objects, make estimates, and solve application problems. Students organize data, choose an appropriate method to display the data and interpret the data to make decisions and predictions and solve problems. (TEA, 1997, p. A-13)*

The curriculum and the learning expectations are presented in a spiraling effect. This means that each previous year provides a foundational basis for further concept development and elaboration for the following year.

Mathematics Standards and Sample Questions with Discussions

The standards and competencies to which they relate are initially stated with a brief elaboration that enhances the view of the role of the EC-4 teacher. Following each are sample questions for readers. Each section gives further elaboration in the light of current relevant literature and research. Because some areas of the standards and competencies are very broad, every sample item attempts to capture the essence of the standard to its broadest scope and to assess the most important aspects of each standard.

STANDARDS I (NUMBER CONCEPTS), VII (MATHEMATICAL LEARNING AND INSTRUCTION, AND VIII (ASSESSMENT)

The mathematics teacher understands and uses numbers, number systems, and their structure, operations and algorithms, quantitative reasoning, and technology appropriate to teach the statewide curriculum (Texas Essential Knowledge and Skills [TEKS]) in order to prepare students to use mathematics (Standard I). The mathematics teacher understands how children learn and develop mathematical skills, procedures, and concepts; knows typical errors students make, and uses this knowledge to plan, organize, and implement instruction; to meet curriculum goals; and to teach all students to understand and use mathematics (Standard VII). The mathematics teacher understands assessment and uses a variety of formal and informal assessment techniques appropriate to the learner on an ongoing basis to monitor and guide instruction and to evaluate and report student progress (Standard VIII).

Competency 012 (Mathematics Instruction): The teacher understands how children learn mathematical skills and uses this knowledge to plan, organize, and implement instruction and assess learning.

The EC-4 teacher plans appropriate activities for all children based on research and principles of learning mathematics. Instructional strategies that build on the linguistic, cultural, and socioeconomic diversity of children and that relate to children's lives and communities are employed. Developmentally appropriate instruction along a continuum from concrete to abstract and instruction that builds on strengths that address needs of the child is provided by the teacher. The teacher knows how mathematical learning may be assisted through the appropriate use of manipulatives and technological tools. It is important to motivate children and actively engage them in the learning process by using a variety of interesting, challenging, and worthwhile mathematical tasks and by providing instruction in individual, small-group, and large-group settings. Mathematics instruction uses a variety of tools (e.g., counters, standard and nonstandard units of measure, rulers, protractors, scales, stopwatches, measuring containers, money, calculators, software) to strengthen children's mathematical understanding. Appropriate learning goals based on the Texas Essential Knowledge and Skills (TEKS) in mathematics are developed while using these learning goals as a basis for instruction. The teacher helps children make connections between mathematics, the real world, and other disciplines. Various questioning strategies encourage mathematical discourse and help children analyze and evaluate their mathematical thinking. The teacher uses a variety of formal and informal assessments and scoring procedures to evaluate mathematical understanding, common misconceptions, and error patterns. It is important that the teacher understands the reciprocal nature of assessment and instruction and knows how to use assessment results to design, monitor, and modify instruction to improve mathematical learning for individual children, including English Language Learners. The teacher understands how mathematics is used in a variety of careers and professions and plans instruction that demonstrates how mathematics is used in the workplace.

Consider the following question:

Mrs. Jones was teaching her prekindergarten class about volume, but she could not get students to understand that the liquid in a cup was the same as when she poured the liquid into a flat bowl. What was happening? Select the best answer.

A. The children are in the preoperational stage and do not have the ability to conserve yet.

B. The children are in the preoperational stage and do not have the ability to transform yet.

C. The children are in the preoperational stage and do not have the ability to classify yet.

D. The children are in the preoperational stage and do not have the ability to seriate yet.

It is true that children are normally in the preoperational stage at this age. *Transformation* (B) refers to the ability to record a process of change. Even though children see a transformation occur (such as a line of coins, where the teacher moves or lengthens the row but does not add to the number of coins), they are unable to understand. The preoperational child will say that the lengthened row is a different row now rather than one that has been changed or transformed. *B is correct. Reversibility* refers to the inability to mentally cancel a change. *C is also correct. Seriation* refers to the ability to order things in a series according to increase or decrease in length, weight, or volume, so this would not be the right answer. This ability usually appears in the concrete operational level (7–11 years). *Classification* is the ability to group on the basis of common characteristics or attributes. This allows a child to master ordering more than one object ($A < B < C$). This also appears at this age (7 to 11 years), though children in prekindergarten and kindergarten can form simple groups, usually on the basis of one attribute. The best answer, however, would be *A*. Children below the approximate age of 7 in the preoperational stages do not have the ability to *conserve* or see that the amount of something stays the same regardless of its shape or container (a clay ball flattened into a pancake). The ability to conserve also makes it difficult for young children to see that the amount of something is the same no matter of the number of pieces into which it is divided (a candy bar divided into halves). The more that children work with materials such as water, sand, clay, rice, beans, paints, etc., the more they will understand conservation, reversibility, more/less, bigger/smaller, and the structures and meaning of numbers.

Teachers of young children must have a thorough understanding of intellectual growth expectations. Piaget believed that cognitive growth occurs as a progressive construction of logical structures that are constantly modified and combined into more powerful logical structures. To the teacher this means that each and every child is on an individually developing continuum in that classroom. As children interact with their environment, they create internal representations that work to accommodate new experiences. It is the role of the teacher to plan and teach learning experiences that are appropriate for the developing stages of children. By observing and talking with children, teachers are better able to plan appropriate mathematical tasks that encourage progression along this developing continuum for individuals.

A brief review of Piaget's stages of cognitive development will help teachers understand mathematics educational theory for young children much more clearly. In the Sensorimotor stage (birth to age 2), children are egocentric and not aware of things outside their immediate environment. Learning involves pulling, pushing, turning, twisting, rolling, poking, and interacting with many different properties of objects. Children at this level require a rich environment with many stimuli. In the Preoperational stage (ages 2–6) children realize that objects exist outside the immediate environment. Learning involves discovering distinct properties and functions of objects as they compare, sort, stack, roll, distinguish triangles from squares, and begin to use abstractions to communicate (*That is a red square; The cat is under the table,* etc.). The ability to conserve often begins toward the closing of this stage as students engage in a number of "dump-and-fill" play activities. These include exploration of space (going under chairs, into cabinets, etc.) and emptying and filling matrials from areas such as cabinets and boxes. Children at this level should interact with a wide variety of objects, items, and materials (buckets, shovels, funnels, sand, water, etc.) to practice describing sorting, reversibility, and finding patterns based on attributes. During the Concrete Operational stage (ages 6–12), children complete the ability to conserve, begin to use symbols, and to classify with multiple attributes. They require experiences with touching, smelling, seeing, hearing, and performing. They begin to label and use symbols to describe and communicate as a form of internal representation. They must use hands-on tools to investigate. Children are progressing to abstraction, although moving to the Formal Operational stage (ages 12 and over) is not a guaranteed progression by a specific age (as is the case in any of Piaget's stages). The use of symbols and logical systems to build new knowledge is required. At this upper level they can interpret ideas, think independently, and combine new abstractions to create new ideas. Piaget suggests that there are four broad factors that are necessary and that affect the progression through these stages of cognitive development. They are (1) maturation, (2) physical experience, (3) social interaction, and (4) equilibration. Clearly, learning experiences for children through the age of 12 must involve objects, tools, interaction, reflection, and social interaction with materials for optimal cognitive growth. The EC-4 teacher knows that mathematical concepts are best learned by children by manipulating materials and observing what happened—individually and collaboratively. A key to EC-4 mathematics is planning *concrete* experiences that facilitate learning. A sound mathematics classroom learning environment and curriculum reflect this cognitive approach to learning.

Consider the following question:

Ms. Mehrman wishes to foster critical thinking skills in her first-grade students. Using overhead attribute blocks, Ms. Mehrman places an attribute block on the overhead and has her students identify the four attributes (size, shape, color, thickness) of the block. She then asks the students to select a block that is "one different" from the beginning block (that is, it has only one attribute different from the original one). She places the new block next to the first one and begins to form a "train." The class identifies the four attributes of this new block and justifies that it is "one different" from the first block. The students are now asked to find a block that is one different from this second block, and the process continues. This activity would be most appropriate for developing students' understanding that:

    A. There can be more than one answer to a question.
    B. It is necessary to recognize the four attributes of each block.
    C. The size of the attribute blocks may be large or small.
    D. The thickness of the block is very important.

Students need to identify the attribute, but this activity requires a deeper level of understanding that fosters the development of critical thinking skills. Size is only *one* of the attributes. Thickness is only *one* of the attributes. Therefore, if Mrs. Mehrman puts up a large red block, students could select "one away" that was a blue, yellow, smaller, thicker, etc., block. The correct response is *A*. This activity will help students understand that there can be many correct answers to a question. This question requires children to engage in higher-order thinking. Too often, children think that there is only one right answer. This activity requires children to characterize each attribute block and consider which attribute block has only one attribute "different" from the block just played. There are many "correct" answers from which to choose.

Asking good questions is imperative for the teaching and learning of mathematics. Questions should pose thoughtful response and reflection. Those types of questions move children from the knowledge and comprehension levels of Bloom's taxonomy upward to application, analysis, synthesis, and evaluation. Children should develop thinking that enhances their abilities to analyze, solve, and expand upon problem situations. Learning explorations and environments should provide many opportunities for learners to be safely challenged. In mathematics, "there should be explorations that have no answers, no precise answers, or that have many answers" (Troutman & Lichtenberg, 1999, p. 386). Timing is also a factor in better questioning. Asking thought-provoking questions, using appropriate wait time that promotes children's reflective thought, and asking children to elaborate and justify their responses helps encourage higher-order thinking.

Answering questions is not enough. It is through communication that mathematical ideas are organized, extended, clarified, and realized. Teachers should guide children in learning how to talk about mathematics in the classroom, and children should become comfortable and competent in expressing their mathematical ideas. "Students who are involved in active discussions in which they justify solutions—especially in the face of disagreement—will gain better mathematical understanding." (Cobb & Lampert, 1998, p. 85)

Thus it is through interaction that children begin to express ideas to peers, teachers, and others as well as reflect on their own and others' responses. This can only occur in a risk-free learning environment where a teacher builds a sense of community through careful and reflective planning, questioning, and listening. Communicating mathematically allows teachers to informally and formally assess understanding and progress. As children communicate mathematically, they better understand and self-assess their own abilities.

Consider the following question:

Ms. Ismail asks her fourth-grade students to discuss then package color tiles into individual bags. There are 420 color tiles in the class set, and 24 students in her class. How many color tiles will be in each student's bag? How many are left over?

The students decide to divide 420 by 24 and get an answer of 17.5. They are not sure what the answer means. The best response for Ms. Ismail would be to:

A. Have the students recheck their answers.
B. Ask students to discuss why they divided and what 17.5 means to this answer.
C. Cut some color tiles in half.
D. Ask students to round their answers.

Having students recheck their computations could improve computational accuracy but would not foster higher-order thinking. Having students use concrete objects to replicate the problem might cause a deeper understanding, but without the teacher guiding the activity, students might not connect. Rounding the answer has no application to this question. The teacher is asking students to assess their understanding of division and what the remainder means. She is encouraging students not just to give a set answer but to continue to question what that answer might mean to a real-life problem when something cannot be divided. The best response is *B*.

Situations such as this one are important to address in the classroom. This provides the teacher with opportunities to informally assess the understanding of mathematical learning by allowing children to talk through their understanding. Children need activities that challenge their thinking and afford them experiences that help them to make sense of the mathematics that they are learning.

As with the vision of teaching and learning mathematics in today's classroom, assessment is changing. Strict use of pencil-and-paper testing is no longer sufficient for mathematics. A variety of approaches to assessment are being implemented in the classroom setting, particularly more alternative forms of assessment to provide a more complete and thorough picture of a child's level of mathematical understanding. Because children enter school with different levels of understanding and experiences with mathematics, assessment should be used to adapt instruction to children's needs. Interviews, checklists, and observations are more appropriate for assessing very young children. Writing and drawing in mathematics journals provides children with time for reflecting on the mathematics that they are learning and provides teachers with insight into children's thinking. Performance tasks that challenge children to perform or to apply their learning to new situations or events are used to reveal how children are learning and applying that learning to become successful problem solvers.

It is important to remember in assessment that in early childhood classrooms, children may often have difficulty manipulating objects physically (the use of fine and gross motor skills). For example, a teacher may believe that a child really does understand a particular mathematics concept, yet an assigned task (e.g., cutting and pasting paper objects) was completed incorrectly. The EC-4 teacher must be aware that younger children cannot physically complete some types of tasks easily, yet they can understand the concept. Knowing about the mental/physical gap helps a teacher to better assess the child's true understanding by using an informal approach to assessment (such as questioning or interviewing) rather than always relying on a set product. Mrs. Kay, for example, sits with her individual children at times and says, "Okay, I'm going to be the one with the pencil this time and you are going to tell me what to do." At other times, she asks partners to show each other how to work problems as one watches (Ashlock, 1990). Encouraging many forms of representations that reveal children's understanding of mathematics is important. Checklists, open-ended question responses, the use of rubrics, portfolios, student self-assessment, peer evaluation, and, as mentioned earlier, interviews and observations should all be a part of mathematics assessment.

Observation of children's learning mathematics informally provides teachers with unforeseen opportunities (teachable moments) to engage in questioning and probing into the child's thinking. These offer opportunities for meaningful learning. Teachers should not limit assessment to determining children's computation abilities or problem-solving skills. Teachers must also assess the child's attitude and mathematical thinking as applied to everyday problems. Much research has been shown that attitudes and anxiety play a part in success. This seems to be more true for mathematics than many other subjects. Games that identify the strongest and weakest math students, for example, should be avoided with young children who are learning. Mathematics teaching, learning, and assessment must be inclusive of children of diversity, both genders, poverty, and those with special needs. For example, the female early childhood student must be observed in the block's center as much as the family center. The most important type of assessment to determine and diagnose error patterns challenges the child to do a problem as teacher observes the problem solving strategies used by the child.

Consider the following question:

Ms. Baumbach is working with the entire first-grade class. She says, "I have put some pennies, nickels, and dimes in my pocket." She places her hand in her pocket. "I have put three of these coins in my hand. How much money do you think I have in my hand?" *Many children are confused and begin voicing guesses. In order to facilitate problem solving in this situation, the teacher should:*

 A. Suggest an approach using trial and error.
 B. Suggest an approach that uses real coins.
 C. Allow students to verify their guesses.
 D. All of the above.

The teacher wants her students to develop problem-solving skills. Trial and error allows students to explore different possible solutions. These explorations foster development and logical reasoning and applying this reasoning to real-life situations. Using real coins helps students to connect the problem to the real world. Students value money and want to become accurate when dealing with money. The use of actual coins makes the problem more pertinent to their everyday lives. Students need to verify their guesses and this problem helps them develop understanding of the possible answers. This problem should help students realize that there are many possible and correct responses. The correct response is all of the above (D) because it includes all the previous responses. Students need to develop several strategies to become good problem solvers.

Along with more realistic or authentic lessons, another area of major importance is problem solving.

> *Problem-solving means engaging in a task for which the solution method is not known in advance . . . problem-solving is an integral part of all mathematics learning, not an isolated part of the mathematics program. Students should have frequent opportunities to formulate, grapple with, solve complex problems that require a significant amount of effort. (NCTM, 1998, p. 76)*

Teachers should carefully and reflectively select and plan learning experiences that are relevant and grade appropriate. Relevant problems are created that focus and motivate children to want to solve the problem because they can see a need or interest in their own lives and believe that they have or can acquire the skills to solve it. Young children should be introduced to problem solving in play. Ms. Clemens, for example, notices Shak and Brandy playing in the sandbox with cars. "Hm-m-m," she says. "It looks like it might be difficult to drive over to this side because your car might get stuck in the 'river.' What could you do?" Teachers select grade-appropriate problem-solving challenges through the expectations of the TEKS. NCTM (1989) notes the importance of problem solving in mathematics by stating that it "should be the central focus of the mathematics curriculum. As such, it is a primary goal of all mathematics instruction and an integral part of all mathematical activity" (p. 23). However, problem solving is not just the traditional "story or word" problems at the end of the chapter in the textbook. Problem solving is a designated *process standard* (NCTM, 2000). Process standards are specific skills and strategies that are used to acquire and use mathematics content knowledge. As such, problem solving is not a separate entity but is viewed as a *skill* and an *attitude* that infiltrates the mathematics learning environment. Teachers who encourage their students to solve problems, offer opportunities to apply strategies, who make students think, and who ask carefully worded questions (rather than simple recall questions) will provide their students with a rich problem-solving experience.

The NCTM Standards (1989) recommend that students develop and apply a variety of strategies to solve multistep and nonroutine problems. These strategies should include situations where students "model situations using verbal, written, concrete, pictorial, graphical, and algebraic methods, reflecting on and clarifying their own thinking about mathematical ideas" (NCTM, 1989, p. 78). Additional recommendations include learning experiences that emphasize deductive and inductive reasoning methods, real-world relevancy, and the use of patterns and relationships to recognize, describe, analyze, and extend mathematical situations (NCTM, 1989). Teacher must teach these strategies such as drawing a picture, looking for a pattern, systematically guessing and checking (trial and error), acting problems out, etc., so that children will be able to apply them independently.

It is the teacher who determines the learning environment in a mathematics classroom. This section reminds us that it is the role of the teacher to be the facilitator, resource person, and to provide opportunities to solve relevant problems through meaningful, concrete exploration and to encourage children to consistently gain new strategies in order to problem solve.

STANDARDS I (NUMBER CONCEPTS) AND II (PATTERNS AND ALGEBRA)

Standard I also overlaps with the competency below. The mathematics teacher understands and uses numbers, number systems and their structure, operations and algorithms, quantitative reasoning, and technology appropriate to teach the statewide curriculum (Texas Essential Knowledge and Skills [TEKS]). The mathematics teacher understands and uses patterns, relations, functions, algebraic reasoning, analysis, and technology appropriate to teach the statewide curriculum in order to prepare students to use mathematics (Standard II).

Competency 013 (Number Concepts, Patterns, and Algebra): The teacher understands concepts related to numbers and number systems and demonstrates knowledge of patterns, relations, functions, and algebraic reasoning.

The EC-4 teacher analyzes, explains, and describes number concepts (e.g., odd, even, prime), operations and algorithms, the properties of numbers, and models the four basic operations with whole numbers, integers, and rational numbers. Numbers are used to describe and quantify phenomena such as time, temperature, and money. The teacher applies knowledge of place value and other number properties to perform mental mathematics and computational estimation. The teacher illustrates relations and functions using concrete models, tables, graphs, and symbolic expressions. An understanding of how to use algebraic concepts and reasoning to investigate patterns, make generalizations, formulate mathematical models, make predictions, and validate results should be taught to students at this level. The EC-4 teacher knows how to identify, extend, and create patterns using concrete models, figures, numbers, and algebraic expressions and uses properties, graphs, and applications of relations and functions to analyze, model, and solve problems in mathematical and real-world situations. The teacher is able to translate problem-solving situations into expressions and equations involving variables and unknowns and models and solves problems, including proportion problems, using concrete, numeric, tabular, graphic, and algebraic methods.

Consider the following question:

Ms. Bell's first-grade class has surveyed the students at Washington Elementary School about their favorite soft drink from a list of Pepsi, Coke, Mountain Dew, and Sprite. A total of 42 students participated in their survey. Which would be the most appropriate graph to use to display this data?

A. A bar graph.
B. A line graph.
C. A circle graph.
D. A pictograph.

A line graph (*B*) is used to represent continuous data points. However, this problem deals with discrete and separate objects that have no connection. Each drink is a separate item that is not related or connected to any other drink. A circle graph (*C*) involves the understanding and application of degrees, ratios, and the use of protractors. These topics are covered in subsequent grade levels. Pictographs (*D*) are introduced later as another way to represent data. Students are then developmentally ready to code the data. Bar graphs are appropriate for primary grades. The correct response is A. As an aside, when students are engaging with these types of activities, the teacher must include possible rationales for them (other than "isn't this fun to know" or "isn't this a fun activity?") For example, fast-food restaurants clearly would be able to use this type of data to match customer preference; the school carnival committee could use this to provide drinks that people prefer; and so forth.

Students should develop organizational skills needed to properly handle larger quantities of data. Choosing an appropriate graphical representation is a fundamental requirement that children need to present data in an accurate manner. Not only is it imperative for the teacher to model mathematical terminology, symbols, and communication, it is necessary for the teacher to provide active opportunities for children to do so.

Consider the following question:

Mr. Batiste distributes color tiles to each student in his kindergarten class. He asks the students to sort the tiles by color. Mr. Batiste sorts his set of color tiles on the overhead. When the students have completed the task, Mr. Batiste asks kindergartners to describe the data. Which of the following is the *best* description of Mr. Batiste's teaching objective?

A. He wants to assess his students' knowledge of color.
B. He wants to assess his students' ability to classify the color tiles.
C. He wants his students to be able to discuss and explain the results of the sorting.
D. He wants his students to work independently.

Color recognition is an important concept for kindergarten students to learn (A). However, it is not the best response. Sorting by color (B) is an important process for kindergarten students to learn. The ability to work alone is an important learning activity (D). However, this answer is also not the best answer. The best response is C. Mr. Batiste is encouraging his students to develop and use accurate mathematics vocabulary to synthesize the results of their sorting activity.

Let's try another question:

Ms. Ketkar has been working with her fourth-grade class on ordering decimals. To help students develop an understanding of the "size" of decimal values and to better help them "see" the decimals, Ms. Ketkar should use which of the following representations:

A. An egg carton.
B. Cuisenaire rods.
C. Dot paper.
D. Centimeter grid paper.

An egg carton (A) has 12 sections and would not be appropriate for fostering the development of the understanding of decimals that are based on powers of 10. Cuisenaire rods (B) are generally used when comparing and relating lengths. They are often used with fractions, area, and perimeter. Dot paper (C) is often used to help students develop spatial abilities. It is useful when asking students to do pictorial presentations of a concrete shape. The centimeter grid paper is based on 100 units, 10 rows and 10 columns (D). It provides a visual means of developing decimal notations. This is the correct response.

The development of number and numeration concepts must include the understanding of numbers, ways of representing numbers, relationships among numbers, and number systems. Providing a visual picture of the size of a number enables students to have a concrete method to show the ordering of decimals. The knowledge and skills associated with number and numeration concepts is necessary for all students. Without a strong foundation in these areas, children will not achieve success and thrive in everyday mathematical situations. Children learn names of numbers first before ever understanding that a number symbolizes an amount. After learning the names and order of numbers, young children move to understanding one-on-one correspondence by using every opportunity in the classroom to touch and count. Mr. Jenson lines up students to go to lunch by touching them and counting, "One, two, three . . ." He also asks students to put away materials by counting, for example "One block, two blocks, . . ." as appropriate. Children must also learn to recognize and form the shape of numbers, or to write the name of numbers. As discussed with distinguishing and writing letters in the previous chapter, children should be given tactile experiences such as touching sandpaper numbers, stamping numbers, forming numbers in sand, shaving cream, or with clay, and so forth, remembering that some children do not develop fine motor skills with a pencil for some time. From this basis, children must have learning experiences that foster the development of the meaning of operations and how they relate to each other along with the use of computational tools, strategies, and estimation abilities.

Howden (1989) believes good intuition about numbers and their relationships (number sense) may be developed by children through carefully planned learning experiences. Teachers who encourage good number sense teach common sense about numbers. It is not assumed that some children are good at mathematics and that some are not but that *all* children are capable of learning mathematics. Number sense strategies are taught and enhanced through activities that are logical, relevant, and set in real-world contexts. Estimation skills help children think about the correctness of their mathematics. Children are constantly challenged to think about numbers: "Does this answer make sense? If so, why?" "Is this amount larger or smaller? If so, why?" Good number sense provides a foundation for developing all other areas of mathematics.

"Some surveys of adults reveal that mental computation and estimation are used as opposed to traditional computation" in everyday living (Carlton, 1980; Fitzgerald, 1985). As the use of technology as a mathematics tool advances, the importance of estimation as a basic skill is even more critical because users must have an idea if their technological computations are "in the ball park." In the real world, a bank teller (or customer) who uses a calculator to quickly add deposits of $525.00 and $280.00 should know to recheck the figures if the calculator answer displays and answer of $1505.00. Children should be experienced with the use, development, and application of estimation skills. NCTM (1989) states:

. . . (students) should be able to decide when they need to calculate and whether they require an exact or approximate answer. They should be able to select and use the most appropriate tool. Students should have a balanced approach to calculation, be able to choose appropriate procedures, find answers, and judge the validity of those answers. (p. 8)

For her first lesson on estimation Ms. Babinoux filled a glass jar with huge candy balls. She told children that the person who came closest to guessing the correct amount in the jar would win a prize. Children were excited to guess. Some children guessed a thousand and some children guessed ten. The closest person guessed 100 (there were 90 in the jar). She awarded the prize and then moved to some problems on the board. This focus was:

A. Appropriate because it was relevant in showing students the value of estimation.
B. Appropriate because it motivated students to use mathematics to get the prize.
C. Inappropriate because students had no estimation tools, so their answers were just "shots in the dark."
D. Inappropriate because it is not age-appropriate to ask children to estimate.

It is certainly appropriate to have children begin to think of the logic of their answer through estimation, so the answer is not *D*. The focus did motivate the students, but they did not use correct estimation skills to get the prize (*B*). This focus began the process of showing a rationale for having tools to estimate. It would have been very relevant had Ms. Babinoux immediately tied this to how and why we need to have estimation tools or some ways to estimate in cases like this one (such as estimating how many candy balls are on the top row and how many possible rows there are in the jar and multiplying). Unfortunately, she did not use it in that manner. The correct answer is *C*.

By having a solid personal understanding of number and numeration concepts, teachers will be better prepared for planning appropriate learning experiences for students. Understanding number and numeration concepts means that teachers of children EC-4 should be competent in mathematics by having or developing a solid foundation of number sense and of basic computation of numbers themselves. Teachers may also review and test on mathematical content by taking released TAAS/TAKS tests online. Any of the grade-level tests are good reviews. Readers are encouraged to seek additional resources at http://www.tea.state.tx.us/student.assessment/resources/release/index.html.

1. http://www.tea.state.tx.us/student.assessment/taks/index.html
   This website highlights the new student testing, TAKS, and provides a clear picture of what mathematics concepts should be taught and assessed at each grade level.

2. http://www.tea.state.tx.us/teks/teksfaq/ch111.html
This website highlights the student TEKS.

Consider the following question:

To aid her second-grade students in comparing fractions, which manipulative should Ms. Asif use to help her students "see" the size of the fractions?

A. Fraction strips.
B. Base ten blocks.
C. Egg cartons.
D. Attribute blocks.

Base ten blocks (*B*) would be more appropriate in activities involving place value or decimals. Egg cartons (*C*) would be appropriate for use with fractions with 12 as a denominator. Attribute blocks (*D*) would be appropriate manipulatives to use in activities that involve sorting and classifying. The fraction strips could be used with all fractions (*A*). This is the correct response. (Fraction strips are a set of paper strips that are cut and shaded to represent the relation between and among wholes, halves, thirds, fourths, and other fractional parts of a whole.)

Consider another question:

Ms. Garcia has been working with her kindergarten class on pattern recognition. To assess her students' understanding of patterns, she asks them the following question: "What would be the next number in this pattern? 1, 1, 2, 2, 3, 3, 4,"

A. 5
B. 3
C. 4
D. 6

5 (*A*) is not in the pattern. 3 (*B*) is not in the pattern. 6 (*D*) is not in the pattern. 4 is the correct response (*C*). The pattern begins with repeating sequential counting numbers.

To analyze data and to make accurate predictions, strategies are necessary. Activities should be selected to promote logical reasoning and the relationship between terms in a sequence. For the elementary teacher it is imperative that children have opportunities to learn basic concepts of patterns and relationships to build on as they advance in study. In some subject areas, information can be learned in isolation, but mathematics is forever built upon a foundation of basics. Early experiences with patterns, functions, and relationships provide a foundational basis for later development of algebra and the study of solutions to equations. In later study, students begin to understand functions, reasoning about abstract objects, generalizations, and symbolic notation. These concepts underlie all areas of mathematics and the basis of mathematical communication. This is expressed in the following statement:

> The search for and analysis of patterns and order are an integral part of doing mathematics, whether it is developing a computational algorithm, exploring properties of shapes, or figuring the solution to a probability problem. Children can learn the processes of doing mathematics as they learn mathematics content. However, the ability to reason is so important in this science of pattern and order that attention should be given explicitly to helping children develop their reasoning skills. (Van de Walle, 1998, p. 392)

Patterns are a way of helping children organize and order the world. Sorting, classifying and ordering objects help with patterns, geometric shapes, and data. Young children are able to identify patterns in their environment. Teachers encourage making generalizations about patterns. "Tell me about that pattern on your sweater." "How do you know that it is a pattern?" "What is a missing part of a pattern?" "How would you make a pattern longer/different?" Children should be encouraged to explore and model relationships using language and, later, notation describing their observations.

Many types of activities involving patterns (including echo patterns, stamping, stringing various objects, gluing or drawing patterned art projects, etc.) help to build logic and reasoning abilities in students. The early childhood class, for example, provides opportunities to string bead patterns, make trains, get in line in certain patterns, and so forth. Planning learning experiences that foster student growth in these areas are crucial building blocks to achieving success in mathematics. The early childhood teacher uses calendar time to show patterns of repeating days of the week. Older children keep weather patterns data or event patterns that lead into cause-and-effect or logical decision making. For example, "I predict that it may be cold again tomorrow, so I will need to bring my jacket." Pattern recognition also helps young children understand human behavior. ("Kevin is always talkative and lively, but today he is quiet, and when approached, snaps a bit. There is something different in his behavior pattern. Let's see if he is feeling bad.)

Consider the following question:

Second-grade students are studying patterns. They notice that the sequence 2, 4, 6, 8, . . . has a pattern and that the values are increasing by 2. The sequence 5, 10, 15, 20, . . . is increasing by 5. These patterns help build the foundation for which math concept?

A. Addition.
B. Fractions.
C. Algebraic thinking.
D. Subtraction.

Addition (*A*) is not appropriate; no computation is required. Fractions (*B*) could be any number representing a part of a whole, without a pattern. Subtraction (*D*) is not appropriate; no computation is required. The correct response is C. This question demonstrates the importance of building a foundation for algebraic reasoning.

Two components of algebraic thinking for young children are (a) making generalizations and using symbols to represent mathematical ideas and (b) representing and solving problems. Learning experiences where children are making generalizations from observations about number and operations develop a foundation of algebraic thinking. The use of terminology such as associative and commutative are not necessary at this stage, but teachers should be aware of the algebraic properties used by young children and begin to draw attention to the concept. Studying patterns, functions, and algebra is the beginning of learning about the various uses of variables and how to solve equations.

STANDARDS III (GEOMETRY AND MEASUREMENT) AND IV (PROBABILITY AND STATISTICS)

The mathematics teacher understands and uses geometry, spatial reasoning, measurement concepts and principles, and technology appropriate to teach the statewide curriculum (Texas Essential Knowledge and Skills [TEKS]) in order to prepare students to use mathematics (Standard III). The mathematics teacher understands and uses probability and statistics, their applications, and technology appropriate to teach the statewide curriculum (Standard IV).

Competency 014 (Geometry, Measurement, Probability, and Statistics): The teacher understands concepts and principles of geometry and measurement and demonstrates knowledge of probability and statistics and their applications (TEKS) in order to prepare students to use mathematics.

The EC-4 teacher applies knowledge of spatial concepts such as direction, shape, and structure and identifies and uses formulas to find lengths, perimeters, areas, and volumes of basic geometrical figures. Mathematical reasoning is used to prove geometric relationships, and the teacher uses translations, rotations, reflections, dilations, and contractions to illustrate similarities, congruencies, and symmetries of figures. Knowing measurement as a process, methods of approximation and estimation, and the effects of error on measurement are necessary. The teacher understands the use of numbers and units of measurement for quantities related to temperature, money, percents, and speed. The teacher has knowledge of conversions within and between different measurement systems. The use of graphical and numerical techniques to explore data, characterize patterns, and describe departure from patterns is known by the teacher. The theory of probability and its relationship to sampling and statistical inference and how statistical inference is used in making and evaluating predictions is important. The EC-4 teacher supports arguments, makes predictions, and draws conclusions using summary statistics and graphs to analyze and interpret one-variable data, knows how to generate and use probability models to represent situations, and uses the graph of the normal distribution as a basis for making inferences about a population.

Consider the following question:

Ms. Fischer plans to introduce the concept of volume to her second-grade class. She wants her children to understand volume through exploration. Which would be the most appropriate for her to use?

A. Color tiles.
B. A measuring cup. *3 dimensional*
C. Pattern blocks.
D. Attribute blocks.

Color tiles (*A*) are used to represent two-dimensional situations. They are often used for perimeter, area, and multiplication arrays. Pattern blocks (*C*) are often used for two-dimensional activities such as tessellations and area. They also can be used effectively with fractions. Attribute blocks (*D*) are designed for activities using sorting and classifying. The best response is *B*. Volume is a three-dimensional quantity and the measuring cup is the only three-dimensional object presented as a choice.

The application of mathematics to other curriculum areas and to the real world is a necessary and important component of the mathematics classroom. The value of connecting what children are learning in the classroom to its application in real-life situations cannot be overstated ("Why is it important, boys and girls, to have a correct lunch count? On a field trip we have 18 children who are on the bus. There are 21 children in our class. Should I tell the bus driver to leave now? Why or why not?"). ". . . (S)tudents should not only learn mathematics, they should also learn the utility of mathematics and the interrelatedness of mathematical ideas" (NCTM, 1998, p. 90). Most content areas have components or concepts that can be related to mathematics in some way. Teachers who focus upon these relationships use them to enhance mathematical appreciation and student growth. When mathematics is integrated with other subject areas, its value, understanding, and relevance are extended. Dump-and-fill activities, comparison books, and others where students have an opportunity to see differences prior to formal instruction help young children begin to understand more/less, bigger/smaller, greater than/less than, and so forth. Setting up a class store is another easy way to do this. This may also fit with a token economy management system, where children need to have so many play dollars or tokens to "purchase" a variety of reward items ($10 for 10 minutes of free time on the computer, $50 for being able to eat lunch with friends in the classroom on Friday, etc.).

A close interdisciplinary relationship exists between mathematics and science. Science often uses mathematics to explain and extend concepts. This link is through content and process. For example, much of science relies on patterns of data and measurement. Another example is the use of data and statistics that help students clarify issues related to health issues in their personal lives and as consumers. Using survey data, children can link data analysis and statistics to learn more about social studies. Map skills also require working with numbers. In turn, the use of ratio, proportion, and percents extends children's understanding of mathematics. Mathematical connections abound in other areas such as in music (patterns in rhythms and fractions) and in sports (measurement, geometry, data analysis and statistics, and much more). There is an abundance of literary connections, including wonderful children's books about numbers and other mathematical concepts, available for teachers. Using a literature focus can help motivate and stimulate student interest in mathematics. Counting and shape books, rhymes, songs, and fingerplays complement learning mathematics. There are numerous books, for example, that lend a great focus for mathematics.

Let us look at some examples. Dinosaur books such as *How Big Were the Dinosaurs* or *The Littlest Dinosaur* might introduce a lesson on size or measurement, for example. Children are motivated and interested when a story gives life to the mathematics they are learning. A teacher may want to take a digital photo of something a child has created in the block center so that the child can describe it and/or tell a story about it ("This is my tower. I built it with cubes. Lots of people live here. There are some offices here, too."). Children who create a class survey, then write their own "story" about it are extending mathematics into language arts. For example, after graphing class shoes, Sara wrote, "There were fifteen kids who had tennis shoes on. Four had those kind of shoes with straps. They were girls. I think kids like tennis shoes best. People who make shoes ought to make mostly tennis shoes. I like tennis shoes best, too!" Using mathematics in applied situations leads to deeper understanding. Making tally charts and asking young children to explain them is also a way to have children understand the concept of one-to-one correspondence in naming numbers. At snack time groups in Mrs. Barton's PreK class tallied choices of snacks to determine which was more popular, noting, "Ten like cookies best."

Consider the following question:

Which of the following activities would provide the best opportunity for fourth-grade students to apply measurement skills to a science context?

A. Investigating the habitat of butterflies.
B. Determining the melting point of an ice cube.
C. Exploring the properties of water.
D. Investigating the properties of rocks and minerals.

The investigation of the habitat of butterflies (*A*) would increase students' knowledge of butterflies but would not be a measurement activity. Learning about the properties of water (*C*) would not necessarily be a measurement activity but could be associated with volume. However, this is not the best answer. Determining the properties of rocks and minerals (*D*) is not necessarily a measurement activity, but could be associated with volume. However, this is not the best answer. *B* is the best response. In order to determine the melting point, students would need to measure and record the temperatures preceding the melting point.

And this additional question:

Margie grouped her third-grade students in groups of four and gave each group a piece of yarn. She asked the students to make different closed figures with the yarn and to describe what they thought was happening to the area and perimeter of the shapes. She hoped that the students would discover which property (area or perimeter) remained the same, regardless of the shape.

A. The area of the figure. → L × W
B. The perimeter of the figure. → L + W + L + W. length of yarn remains =
C. The length of the figure.
D. The width of the figure.

Area is the product of length times width ($a = l \times w$). As either the length or width is changed, the area (*A*), the space inside, will be different. Since the yarn is being used to make different shapes, the length and width of the figure will change as the figure is changed. The width of the figure (*D*) will vary as the yarn is being moved to create new figures. The correct response is *B*. The perimeter is the distance around the figure. Although the yarn may change shape, the total length of the yarn (representing the figure's perimeter) remains constant.

Geometry helps students understand the three-dimensional world in which they live. Through the study of geometry, teachers must offer students ways to interpret and reflect on the physical environment with real and abstract methods. Learning activities should promote interaction with physical models, drawings, and software. These are exceptionally effective in helping children visualize geometric concepts.

> *Geometry and spatial sense are fundamental components of mathematics education. . . . Geometric representations can help students make sense of area and fractions; histograms and scatterplots can lead to insights about data; and coordinating graphs can be used to analyze and understand functions. Spatial reasoning is helpful in using maps, planning routes, designing floor plans, and creating art. (NCTM, 1998, pp. 61–62)*

Students must be encouraged to use geometric ideas in representing and solving problems in a variety of contexts. Geometric puzzles, geoboards, and blocks help children understand many-sided figures and circles. Geometry for young children should focus on manipulation. Primary children can construct many plane and solid figures from blocks, dominos, and even marshmallows or gumdrops and toothpicks. When children manipulate these objects, they see relationships much easier (two right triangles make a square, etc.). Hands-on and interactive experiences are the best ways to help children learn concepts and techniques that help them interpret their physical world. Children through fourth grade should be able to identify basic geometric shapes such as the circle, square, rectangle, triangle, quadrilaterals, pentagon (a 5-sided polygon), hexagon (a 6-sided polygon), octagon (an 8-sided polygon), and solid figures such as the cube, cone, pyramid, and so forth. When children are introduced to shapes in school, "bombardment" is the best instructional policy. The teacher, for example, may put on her hat with a circular brim and her apron with huge circles, while children work with paper plates, make circles from various materials in centers. Students come to the circle to sing a "circle song" and are served snacks that are circular (cross cuts of fruit, etc.). Basic concepts addressing symmetry, rotation, reflection, and transformation are also learned. Finding the perimeter (distance around) of figures and some area (surface measurement) measurements are taught in the primary grades.

Consider the following question:

Ms. Oar divided her first-grade students into groups of two. She asked each student to fold a piece of construction paper in half. On one-half of the paper each student was asked to construct a design using pattern blocks. When the students had finished their designs, the students switched places with their partner and were asked to replicate their partner's design on the other side of the paper. This activity would be most appropriate for:

A. Development of skills needed for repetition.
B. Understanding that different students will have different designs.
C. Development of spatial ability and awareness.
D. Recognition of properties of polygons.

This activity only helps students learn to duplicate and does not address higher-order thinking. This would not necessarily foster geometric understanding. This activity would help students notice polygons and their properties but would be more appropriate for development of spatial skills. The correct response is C. This activity would help students foster spatial skills and awareness.

Let's try another question:

Ms. Shanar wanted her first-grade class to develop an understanding of *nonstandard* measurement. She asked her children to measure the distance from the bottom of the classroom door to the doorknob. An appropriate tool to use is:

A. A paper clip.
B. A pencil.
C. A hula hoop.
D. A color tile.

A paper clip (*A*) would be too small and too difficult for first-grade students to try to use to measure a vertical distance. The hula hoop (*C*) is round and would not be appropriate for measuring a linear length. The color tile (*D*) is small. It would be very difficult for students to estimate the vertical distance using the color tile. A pencil would be the most appropriate item to use of the choices presented (*B*). It is longer than the paper clip or color tile and would be easier for the students to use to estimate the distance.

Measurement concepts include length, time, area, mass, and volume or capacity. Please refer to the appendices (beginning on page 140) to review measurement units, if needed, for more information. Measurement is used every day by children as they explore their environment and ask questions. "How tall am I?" "How long will it take to get there?" "How much longer till lunch?" "How much do I need?" "How far is it to my house?" Students need many experiences using standard and nonstandard measurement to foster their understanding of the physical aspects of the real world. A *nonstandard measurement* is any item that is used to measure other items. This might be a child's finger, a shoe, a book, a paper clip, and more. Using such a nonstandard unit to measure another item, such as the length of a table, allows the child to grasp the concept using a repeated movement or a repetition of that unit. In other words, for the question "How long is the table?" children can use a book, placing the book on the table, making a mark and counting, "One." Then they can slide the book further along the table, make a mark and count, then repeat the procedure the length of the table while recording or counting the number of book lengths that are used to measure the table. While nonstandard measurement helps young children grasp the concept of repeated measurement, it also increases understanding of estimation skills.

The study of measurement is necessary for everyday life as well as for connecting other mathematical concepts and other content areas. It includes number operations, geometric ideas, statistical concepts, and notions of function (NCTM, 1998). Learning experiences should provide students with ample opportunities for selecting units and understanding appropriate measurement units and understanding the techniques, tools, and formulas of measurement. Other components of measurement study should include selecting and using benchmarks to estimate measurement (such as an inch is about as wide as an adult thumb) and scaling (making an object smaller/larger or drawing to scale). Older children will select and apply appropriate standard units and tools to measure length, area, volume, weight, time, temperatures, and the size of angles.

Teachers select learning experiences that foster student understanding of measurement and all associated aspects of applying measurement, including understanding that measurements can be approximations and that different units affect precision of measurement. Learning to select and use the most reasonable and appropriate unit of measurement is vital for understanding and application (e.g., "just a couple of blocks down the street," in reality, turns into a mile walk). The study of measurement is most effectively taught with the use of concrete materials. Children must have opportunities to handle measurement tools and apply concept knowledge to real-world, relevant situations (e.g., taking a teaspoon rather than a tablespoon of medicine). Children who measure the pet gerbil's cage for paper or the goldfish bowl for water, the bulletin board to put up new borders, space for a new center, and milk and cocoa in a kitchen center for chocolate milk, for example, are learning mathematics for everyday situations. Measurement is a fundamental concept for connecting mathematics with itself and to other content areas such as social studies, science, art, health, and physical education.

As mentioned, measurement concepts should first be taught with nonstandard units in order for children to grasp the concept. The second step is to introduce standard measurement units and scales that are used in everyday life such as inches, feet, yards, centimeters, meters, quarts, gallons, and so on. From this basic understanding, children should be able to understand the need for measuring with standard units and become familiar with standard units in the customary and metric systems. The third step in learning measurement is to carry out simple conversions such as from inches to feet or centimeters to meters within a measurement system. Most importantly, children should be able to understand such attributes as length, area, weight, volume, and size of angle and select the appropriate type of unit for measuring each attribute (see pages 140–141 for review if needed). Providing a way for children to experiment with a measuring is important for all grades and can be part of a kitchen, shop, garden, science, social studies, or growth center. Older elementary children will develop, understand, use formulas, and develop strategies for determining area, surface area, and volume of rectangular solids.

Consider the following question:

Mr. Kurz is interested in having his second-grade class understand problem solving in real-world situations (determining the amount of decorative wall border needed for putting up a place for students' work). The children are asked to measure the width of their classroom using nonstandard measures. Stephen finds that the classroom is 36 shoes wide. Amy finds the classroom is 9 jump ropes wide. Which mathematical concept will the children apply to convert from one nonstandard measure to the other?

A. Metric measurement.
B. Absolute value.

C. Area and perimeter.
D. Ratio and proportion.

Response A implies the use of the metric measurement system with no connection to other types of measurement. Absolute value (B) applies to the distance from the origin and would be used if *direction* from the origin was being considered. Area and perimeter (C) relate to attributes of geometric shapes. Ratio and proportion (D) would provide a method of converting from one measurement system to another and is the correct response.

Consider also the following question:

Ms. Rubalcava has placed 10 color tiles, 8 green color tiles and 2 yellow color tiles, into a paper bag. She tells her students that there are 10 color tiles in the bag and some are yellow and some are green. She shakes the paper bag and, without looking, picks one color tile from the bag. It is green. She asks the students to guess which color the tile in her hand is. She then opens her hand and shows the class the color tile. Ms. Rubalcava asks a student to record the color on the board with a tally mark. She places the color tile back in the bag and repeats the process 10 times. Her first-grade students help her tally her results. After the tenth pick, the tally is 7 green and 3 yellow. She asks the students to guess how many green tiles and how many yellow tiles are in the bag. She repeats the experiment and this time the tally is 9 green and 1 yellow. She repeats the process several more times and the students tally the data. Her purpose in this experiment is:

A. To help her students count.
B. To show the students that it is impossible to know how many green tiles and yellow color tiles there are without opening the bag.
C. To help students learn to organize and interpret data.
D. To better understand the concept of addition.

Even though the students do count the number of green tiles and yellow tiles (A), the object of this lesson is to develop an understanding of predicting how many tiles of each color are in the bag. Although the students will not know for certain how many green tiles and yellow tiles are in the bag (B) until all the tiles are shown, the students can learn how to give accurate predictions based on several repetitions. The object of the lesson is not to have students count the green tiles and yellow tiles (D) but to understand the concept of probability. The students will develop an understanding of how to collect data and why it is important to conduct several experiments in order to make a prediction. C is the correct response.

It is possible to help children to develop understanding of unknown situations. They can learn to form a rational basis to forecast accurate predictions when absolute certainty is not possible but when other necessary information is presented.

Probability and prediction is connected to data collection. Children are often interested in questions such as, "What is your favorite color?" "What kind of candy do you like the most?" and so forth. Inquiries such as these may be used to interest children in collecting information (data) and in developing how to best represent the findings of that data (graphing, charting, making a table). Teachers model these procedures with very young children as a class effort and gradually build a foundation of understanding. Older children enjoy conducting surveys that are part of their everyday lives. For example, they may wish to find out how many children prefer hamburgers or pizza in the lunchroom and how the cafeteria personnel use such data to plan for these preferences.

Consider the following question:

Mr. Webb's fourth-grade class has completed a unit on statistics. Frank, one of his students, wants to attain a 92 average for the five tests given each quarter. If Frank scored an 86 on his first test, a 96 on his second test, a 94 on his third test, and a 90 on his fourth test, what grade must Frank earn on his fifth test for a 92 test average?

    A. 92
    B. 93
    C. 90
    D. 94

For the goal average, there must be 460 grade points accumulated ($92 \times 5 = 460$). Frank must determine his current grade point by adding the four test sources ($86 + 96 + 94 + 90 = 366$). The difference will result in the needed test score of 94 ($460 - 366 = 94$). To check this, the sum of the five test scores, divided by 5, would result in an average of 92. The correct response is *D*.

In an increasingly technological world, it is imperative that students have experiences with concepts concerning data, statistics, and probability. Beginning in the primary grades, learning activities should include organizing data into categories, sorting experiences, and other informal activities that encourage refining questions and decision making. "Students can pose questions to investigate, organize the responses, and create representations of their data" (NCTM, 1998, p. 103). Building a foundation in the early grades with these types of activities allows students to further their understanding by interpreting data using methods of exploratory data analysis. Young children can question and gather data about themselves and their surroundings; sort and classify objects by attributes; represent data using concrete objects, pictures, and graphs; and discuss events related to their own experiences as likely or unlikely to happen (NCTM, 2000). Children might ask, "How many of us are wearing tee shirts today?" The results may be tallied, put into a chart, or a class picture graph may be created using a tee shirt as the displayed icon. Predicting what are the chances of an event can be done with young children. "Do you think at least five people will make

100 on our spelling test on Friday? Why or why not?" Learning experiences based on data can help students to develop and evaluate inferences, make predictions, create representations, and stimulate communication. Along with these experiences, children need to understand and apply basic notions of chance and probability. The goal of a mathematics curriculum such as this is to produce students who are prepared for informed decision making. It is the responsibility of the teacher to provide such a learning environment that encourages and nurtures questions, interpretation, inference, and probability. Only through these efforts will mathematical literacy be achieved.

STANDARDS V (MATHEMATICAL PROCESSES) AND VI (MATHEMATICAL PERSPECTIVES)

The mathematics teacher understands and uses mathematical processes to reason mathematically, to solve mathematical problems, to make mathematical connections within and outside of mathematical problems, and to communicate mathematically (Standard V). The mathematics teacher understands the historical development of mathematical ideas, the interrelationship between society and mathematics, the structure of mathematics, and the evolving nature of mathematics and mathematical knowledge (Standard VI).

Competency 015 (Mathematical Process): The teacher understands mathematical processes and knows how to reason mathematically, solve mathematical problems, and make mathematical connections within and outside of mathematics.

The EC-4 teacher understands the role of logical reasoning in mathematics, knows methods, and uses of informal and formal reasoning, and applies correct mathematical reasoning to derive valid conclusions from a set of premises. The teacher applies principles of inductive reasoning to make conjectures and uses deductive methods to evaluate the validity of conjectures. Mathematical arguments and examples of fallacious reasoning are evaluated and recognized. The teacher understands connections among concepts, procedures, and equivalent representations in areas of mathematics (e.g., algebra, geometry) and understands how mathematics is used in other disciplines and in daily living. Manipulatives and a wide range of appropriate technological tools are known and used to develop and explore mathematical concepts and ideas. The teacher demonstrates knowledge of the history, the evolution of mathematical concepts, procedures, and ideas, and recognizes the contributions that different cultures have made to the field of mathematics and the impact of mathematics on society and cultures.

Consider the following question:

The students in Ms. O'Shea's fourth-grade class have completed studying addition, subtraction, multiplication, and division of whole numbers. To assess their understanding of whole number operations, Ms. O'Shea asks her students to mentally estimate the answer to the following question: 36×98

1. A number slightly less than 3600.
2. A number a lot less than 3600.
3. A number slightly more than 3600.
4. A number a lot more than 3600.

This question will help Ms. O'Shea assess her students' understanding of:

A. Multiplying a whole number by 100.
B. Multiplication is the inverse of division.
C. When you multiply, the product is always larger than the factors.
D. Multiplication is a shortcut for repeated addition.

To obtain a product much smaller than the whole number multiplied by 100, the value of the factor must be closer to one. To obtain a product slightly larger than the whole number multiplied by 100, the factor has to be slightly larger than 100. To obtain a product a lot larger than the whole number multiplied by 100, the factor has to be considerably larger than 100. The correct response is A. When a whole number is multiplied by a number slightly less than 100, the product will be smaller than the whole number multiplied by 100. The closer the value approaches 100, the closer the product will be to that product.

Students need to be provided opportunities to assess their own understanding of mathematical operations. Various activities should be used that present applications of the mathematical operators in many contexts. Mathematical concepts should be explored in a holistic manner. Because a goal of mathematics instruction is computational fluency, children should have opportunities to master basic facts and operations and apply relevant experiences to real-world situations. Rarely does someone approach you in a conversation and ask, for example, for 21 to be divided by 7. Mathematics is normally based in some type of context. Understanding the meaning of arithmetic operations and how they are related is important.

"Children should be able to decide which mathematical operations (addition, subtraction, multiplication, division) should be used for a particular problem, how the same operation can be applied to other situations, how operations relate to one another, and what results to expect" (NCTM, 1998, p. 53). The meanings of addition and subtraction are the focus of preK–2, while the meaning of multiplication and division is the focus of grades 3 through 5. Mental math skills are required learning experiences, though drilling students over and over again to memorize facts creates boredom rather than understanding. Although NCTM advocates the appropriate use of calculators and computers, "when the instructional focus is on developing student-generated or conventional computational algorithms, the calculator should be set aside to allow for this focus" (NCTM, 1998, p. 51).

Consider the following question:

Ms. Ashman is teaching her class to do long division. This algorithm was introduced as follows:

```
16 ⌐ 89
  −16   |
   73
  −16   ||
   57
  −16   |||
   41
  −16   ||||
   25
  −16   ℍℍ
    9
```

FIGURE 3.1

What teaching approach emphasizing the product of division is this?

    A. The quotient of the dividend and the divisor.
    B. Multiplication by the reciprocal of the divisor.
    C. The inverse operation of multiplication.
    D. Multiple subtractions of the divisor from the dividend.

The response *A* would use the standard algorithm for long division. Response *B* has no relevance to the question; it would apply to division with fractions. Division is the inverse of multiplication and could be used to check the solution. However, *D* is the correct response: Division is a shortcut for repeated subtraction. Groups of 16 are being removed from the original large group. Each tally mark represents the formation of a group of 16. *(89 is the dividend; 16 is the divisor, the answer is the quotient, and the leftover is the remainder.)*

Consider the following question:

Ms. Sikes wants to incorporate calculators into her third-grade mathematics curriculum. She distributes calculators to each student. She asks students to enter the number 6734 into their calculators. She then asks her students, in only one step, to have the number 6704 show on their calculator display. Ms. Sikes uses this activity to develop her students understanding that:

    A. Calculators provide correct solutions.
    B. Calculators can be used for guess-and-check problem-solving strategies.

C. Calculators can be used when an answer is needed quickly.

D. Calculators can be used to help understand place value.

Using calculators to check answers will not help to develop higher-order thinking skills. Having the students skip count by 5s could help students recognize the pattern in a guess-and-check situation, but this is not relevant to this activity. Using the calculator to add the numbers would be using the calculator as a computation tool. This question assesses students' understanding of place value. *D* is the correct response. The calculator would allow students the freedom to explore and to verify when they found the correct solution.

Texas strongly believes that technology needs to be incorporated into the mathematics classroom. Calculators provide a means for students to develop higher-order thinking skills in a noncomputational setting, because they allow children to focus on logic, reasoning, and estimation, rather than becoming bogged down by procedural computation. This may be doubly so for children with learning disabilities, since calculators may allow them to function very well in problem solving. Computers also provide motivating ways to reach children, although teachers should be aware that many programs offer only "worksheets on a screen." In contrast, Driscoll and Nagel (2002) describe a CD-ROM program that asks teams of children to express their categorization and classification strategies by putting together "things that go together" by clicking on them. Two trees (one big, one small) and three fish (one big, two small) are presented. At first the partners discuss the trees as one group and the fish as another, then the idea of *big versus small* categories emerge. These types of computer programs and many others add much to the mathematics classroom or a math center.

Teachers of mathematics maintain professionalism by staying knowledge-able and informed about current developments in the field of mathematics education such as new mathematical principles and standards, recent theories on learning and mathematics, instructional strategies, technology, and effective ways in which to implement these concepts. Workshops, journals, and the Internet help (NCTM website: www.nctm.org). By participating in professional development activities and using reflection, teachers are better able to gain ideas for interesting lessons and plan worthwhile mathematical tasks.

Consider the following question:

All fourth-grade classrooms are having a pet show next week. Mr. Messick is in charge of the show and needs to know about how many entry forms to print to send home. Mr. Messick gives his fourth-grade class the following problem to help solve this problem.

Seven children have pets at home. The *mean* number of pets per child is 2. How many pets does each child have? If there are 124 fourth-grade students, how many entry forms will need to be printed? Write several sentences explaining your answer.

National curriculum standards recommend open-ended problems like this. Which of these statements explains why?

A. Problems of this type are best solved by applying algebraic principles (solving for unknowns) to real-world contexts.

B. Open-ended problems like this allow for a variety of solutions and explanations and promote inquiry, reasoning, and communication.

C. In dealing with uncertainty, students have opportunities to collect and analyze data.

D. The teacher can use this problem for an easy assessment of the students' reasoning process and correct any misconceptions as there is only one correct answer.

Algebraic applications (*A*) would not be appropriate, as it is beyond the needs of this situation. This situation does provide an opportunity to collect and analyze data (*C*). It also provides for teacher assessment and methods of communication and verification. *B*, however, is the best response. The question provides children with an opportunity to apply classroom knowledge to real-life contexts. This is a major focus for student learning today. It is important that children learn mathematics with relevant, real-world application and contexts. In this situation, some children may have one pet, no pet, three pets, and so on. There is uncertainty of the exact number as in real life. Open-ended situations such as this model real-life situations and decisions that are

It is very difficult to teach something that you may not remember or understand well yourself. Teachers must have achieved a level of competence and confidence in mathematics to successfully instruct their students. Obtaining a fourth-grade mathematics book or workbook and working all of the problems will help you assess any areas that may need review or refer to the websites previously mentioned for review for a particular grade level.

DISCUSSION

In traditional mathematics instructional programs teachers taught by telling, and students learned by watching and listening to the teacher. Drill-and-practice followed direct instruction to determine if students could do what had been taught. Students were expected to replicate what they had seen the teacher do. This is not the view of mathematics instruction envisioned by mathematics education reform efforts. Reflected throughout the NCTM standards (1989, 1991, 1995, 2000) is a common theme—the learner is *active* and *interactive*. More hands-on, minds-on activities and lessons are promoted to accommodate and incorporate cognitive learning theories where children use exploration to build their own knowledge. A developmental or constructivist view of learning mathematics requires a significant change in how mathematics should best be taught and learned. Constructivism suggests that students begin learning with *doing*—"trying to make sense of unfamiliar situations, testing new ideas and conjectures, and even posing their own questions to answer" (Van de Walle, 1998, p. 39).

In the Texas classroom and on the TExES, the learner must be seen as *active*. The following is a list originating from the *Curriculum and Evaluation Standards for School Mathematics* document (NCTM, 1989) and discussed in Van de Walle (1998). These verbs reflect a more appropriate view of mathematics objectives in an active manner rather than a traditional view that encouraged passive learners:

explore	predict	justify
formulate	solve	investigate
develop	verify	discover
construct	explain	describe
represent	conjecture	use (p. 13)

Classrooms that encourage the use of these terms will foster student achievement. The role of such a learning environment is to provide an exploratory setting, pose challenges, and offer the support that will encourage mathematical construction. Mathematics educators that subscribe to the constructivist view of teaching and learning mathematics acknowledge that learners must be actively engaged in activities that promote this role for the learner.

In 2000, NCTM produced a document that incorporated all three of its previous documents (NCTM, 2000). Two of its principles warrant special notice within this summary and discussion: the Teaching Principle and the Learning Principle. Let us review what we have learned in this chapter through these principles.

THE TEACHING PRINCIPLE

Effective mathematics teaching requires understanding what students know and need to learn and then challenging and supporting them to learn it well. (NCTM, 2000, p. 16)

"More than any other single factor, teachers influence what mathematics students learn and how well they learn it. Students' mathematical knowledge, their abilities to reason and solve problems, and their self-confidence and dispositions toward mathematics all are shaped by teachers' mathematical and pedagogical decisions" (NCTM, 1998, p. 30). This statement has serious implications and designated responsibilities for the classroom teacher. These components include *analysis of* and *reflection on*

teaching and learning, *worthwhile mathematical tasks, the learning environment,* and *classroom discourse.*

Only through *thoughtful analysis* and *reflection* can teachers make the myriad of decisions surrounding successful teaching. Teachers must use their knowledge of mathematics, pedagogy, student learning, questioning, instructional strategies, and more to plan, teach, and assess the learning environment. Teachers apply all knowledge into practice within the classroom to determine a *learning environment* (Ball, 1993) for learning mathematics. Teachers who hold high expectations that all their children can learn mathematics (along with searching for exciting mathematics lessons) will have children who enjoy math with a high sense of self-efficacy.

Using pedagogical content knowledge allows teachers to draw upon previous experiences and successes to apply to new situations such as determining *worthwhile* tasks (Shulman, 1986). Other factors, including *curriculum* and *learning goals,* help to shape the mathematical environment with the teacher as a co-learner (a vital role in constructivism). A crucial factor in the learning environment is the teacher's dispositions toward mathematics, learners, and mathematics education. Even young learners can "read" messages that teachers are not approaching a subject wholeheartedly either because they don't like it or are unsure of math concepts themselves. There must be a risk-free atmosphere that encourages student interaction and discourse. The TExES mathematics class may remember Vygotsky's theory in which learning is enhanced through dialogue and social interaction. Teachers must also have knowledge of resources (curricular frameworks and guides, instructional materials, lesson plans, etc.) to help inform decision making and planning.

Teachers can provide classrooms that promote thinking, but it takes much more than worthwhile mathematical tasks and commitment to discourse. It takes deep insight about mathematics, about teaching, and about learners, coupled with a sound and robust mathematics curriculum and thoughtful reflection and planning. (NCTM, 1998 p. 33)

Teaching in the real world means being knowledgeable about many things. Children come to the classroom with diversity in prior learning: special needs; special talents; differences in culture, gender, socioeconomic backgrounds; and more. Each has his or her own perspective of the world, needs that he or she is seeking to be met, and informal experiences with mathematics. Awareness of each individual child's background and needs is crucial. The teacher must take responsibility for making sure that children who are differently abled have access to materials to help understand and the time to explore those materials—adapting instruction to the individual child. Mathematical challenges must be created for gifted and talented children. Diversities and multicultural perspectives are celebrated. Teachers must accommodate learning for all children through planning, questioning, teaching, and assessing. Mathematics for young children is a natural way of beginning to explore their world. It is at the early childhood level that the playing field of diversities can best be addressed before the disparities widen. Girls, minorities, and children in poverty still often are not reaching their potential in mathematics due to bias. Teachers must provide learning experiences that give *all* children equal mathematical tools. Assessment in the classroom must focus on the child's understanding, thought processes, and attitudes about learning mathematics. Developing and modeling a positive attitude toward the teaching and learning of mathematics in the classroom helps to promote and foster learning for all children. The following resources appropriately address this vision of teaching and learning in the Texas classroom (but should not be limited to these alone): the TEKS, the TAKS objectives, the NCTM Principles and Standards for School Mathematics (NCTM, 2000), selected district textbooks and developed curricula guidelines, other valuable website resources as listed in the appendices of this chapter, veteran colleagues

and administrators, quality programs of inservice and workshops (many of which are offered in Texas through Regional Service Centers), and reputable computer mathematics software and commercial learning programs, and activity sources that are learner centered.

THE LEARNING PRINCIPLE

Students must learn mathematics with understanding, actively building new knowledge from experiences and prior knowledge. (NCTM, 2000, p. 20)

This second vital principle involves learning. Learning mathematics is viewed differently today than previously. It is believed that networks of knowledge create a structure of conceptual organization in learning. Old and new knowledge are connected and children's *prior knowledge* and experiences effect new knowledge (Noddings, 1990). EC-4 teachers must consider this view in two ways. First, children may come to their class with rich and varied prior knowledge and experiences in mathematics or very little to no mathematical background. Second, teachers have a responsibility to each child to provide all the experiences and knowledge established by the TEKS in their grade level so that children can successfully move through the Texas curriculum.

The sense of a *mathematical community* is another perspective on learning mathematics (Lave, 1991). These perspectives blend to help create an active *community of learners* in the classroom where conceptual understanding thrives and procedural proficiency is present. Children must have opportunities to develop an appreciation and value for the usefulness of mathematics. In other words, students should (a) develop a disposition to see mathematical power, (b) become autonomous learners that analyze and reflect, and (c) develop the ability to communicate mathematically. "To understand what they learn, [students] must enact for themselves verbs that permeate the mathematics curriculum: examine, represent, transform, solve, apply, prove, communicate" (National Research Council, 1989, pp. 58–59).

Children learn better through learning activities that are motivating and challenging within relevant, real-world contexts. This can be achieved through the use of manipulatives, technology and other mathematical tools, active discourse, and group collaboration. In order for teachers to be able to provide such a learning environment, Van de Walle (1998) presents seven strategies for effective teaching of mathematics.

1. Create a mathematical environment.
2. Pose worthwhile mathematical tasks.
3. Use cooperative learning groups.

4. Use models and calculators as thinking tools.
5. Encourage discourse and writing.
6. Require justification of student responses.
7. Listen actively. (p. 34)

The teaching and learning of elementary school mathematics now has a different profile. The roles of the teacher and the learner are different. It is now believed that teachers and students together share responsibility for mathematics learning (NCTM, 1998). Through careful, reflective planning teachers are able to create learning environments that are challenging, motivating, and active communities of mathematical learning.

SUMMARY

Mathematics means much more than arithmetic. Most of us experienced mathematics learning in a much different way than we expect teachers to teach today. It is more than practicing arithmetic, working addition, subtraction, and multiplication and division problems on worksheets. Teaching and learning mathematics today is providing children with many varied opportunities to construct their own concepts of mathematics across all grade levels. For young children, each learner constructs knowledge based on experimentation and observations with real-world materials and situations. The role of the EC-4 teacher is to provide a learning environment that fosters these experiences. Teachers support the language for the concepts that children are learning by using the correct terminology from the start and provide the time and materials that best represent a concept available for manipulation. There must be time for hands-on manipulation for learners, and symbols should be introduced only after concepts are well understood by the children.

Early childhood is a perfect time for children to become interested in counting, sorting, building shapes, finding patterns, measuring, and estimating. Good mathematics instruction invites children to experience mathematics as they play, describe, and think about their world. Teachers have a duty to think carefully about how and what children will learn about mathematics in the lessons and centers they provide and a duty to monitor this learning carefully. Minority and low-income groups often have difficulty in school with mathematics. However, early experiences such as these help these children to better achieve. Many of young children come to school with informal mathematical abilities that should be nurtured in a safe learning environment, and motivation occurs when they can explore patterns, shapes, measurement, what numbers mean, and how they work. However, children need proper guidance to maintain this level of motivation and interest by effective EC-4 teachers. These teachers interpret what children are doing and thinking and attempt to see mathematics from the children's point of view. EC-4 teachers decide which concepts children are able to learn or abstract from their experiences, as lessons are planned that are developmentally appropriate and culturally considerate. Lessons that promote intellectual, social, emotional, and physical development encourage mathematical understanding in children. This type of teaching helps children to be self-motivated, self-directed problem solvers as they develop their first mathematics attitudes and abilities.

Teachers must create learning environments that encourage and motivate children to want to do mathematics and challenge them to represent and reflect on their mathematical thinking. This environment must be exploratory with plenty of learning centers that offer children experiences with blocks, shapes, real-world items (such as items for shopping, money, sand and water for measurement), blocks for construction, and other manipulatives that encourage experimentation. Learning centers are designated areas of a classroom where the teacher has strategically provided opportunities for children to explore and experience mathematics, as well as other content areas, through different contexts, materials, and events. These are selected based on the teacher's goals for student learning and grade level appropriateness. Learning centers are effective across all grade levels. Through informal observations of children at play, teachers are capable of gaining much insight into the levels of the mathematical understanding. Other learning centers for exploration and lessons are planned by the EC-4 teacher that are developmentally appropriate based on these observations. Questions to ask children working with materials might include, "How tall is it? How much bigger is it? How do you know? Can you show me another way to do this? How are those shapes different?" Mathematics in early childhood cuts across many daily activities. Doing the daily calendar, talking about the weather, dividing items for tasting, playing in the kitchen center all offer learning opportunities for young children. Playing with the sand and water tables, sorting as children are putting away toys, or learning about exchange in playing shopping or pretending to order and pay for items in a "restaurant" are important learning situations. In these early grades mathematics should be seen as how we use it in the real world, not as a separate subject or entity.

It is important to continue to encourage this attitude of utility of mathematics. Using mathematics is apparent in daily activities as well as in other subject areas. If the class is studying shells or leaves, this is a perfect opportunity for the children to practice classifying, seriation, graphing, counting, measuring, and patterning. Classification skills develop from observation, reflection, and practice, and discussion of different characteristics and attributes of objects. Children are able to distinguish shape, size, color, texture, and so on. *Seriation* requires keeping in mind the characteristics on one element while comparing it to another element. Children compare objects very naturally: "Mine is bigger," "This is heavier," or "Yours is taller than mine." Graphing with EC-4 develops from using pictographs to more sophisticated use of the coordinate system. Counting progresses through developmental stages for children. First, a child knows that each object must have a name (counting word); then the child knows that the list of names have an order; and then the child makes the connection between counting and number. Teachers encourage counting events at all times: "I have four children who are ready to go to lunch. Who will be number 5?" and so forth. Measuring is based on the ability to *conserve*. Using the child's natural interest in size and shape to develop measurement concepts is important for the teacher. Patterns are visual, auditory, spatial, numerical, or combinations of these. Skip counting is encouraged as children begin to count by twos, threes, fives, and so on. Children can make patterns with beads, blocks, tiles, pattern blocks, pieces of paper, shoes, their bodies, leaves, shells, flowers, seed, and many other items. They can recognize patterns on the calendar, in blocks, games, in the classroom, and in other contexts, materials, and events. Building on these experiences, *functions* are the patterns created when certain actions are performed on objects or numbers. These are the building blocks for developing algebraic concepts. This type of thinking is encouraged by activities such as, if one child has two feet, two children have four feet, three children have six feet, and so on as the pattern becomes a function. Providing children with experiences where they use blocks to construct sets of objects and then think about the relationships that exist between the sets helps encourage the development of the concept of one-to-one correspondence. (This is the concept that one object can be related to another object.) Technology also offers a multitude of software choices outside drill activities that may be selected for use in the classroom to support instruction and encourage exploration and practice for developing children's understanding of mathematics.

Successful EC-4 teachers build on children's everyday activities, incorporate their cultural origins, languages, technology, and mathematical concepts and strategies. They use a variety of instructional strategies, create meaningful contexts, and provide for active participation to help children learn, develop, and appreciate mathematics in their world. The NCTM Principles and Standards for School Mathematics and the TEKS for Texas schools offer guidelines for what mathematics is to be learned at different levels and the progression of that learning. Effective teachers remember that how mathematics is taught is just as important as what mathematics is taught.

A SNAPSHOT OF TEACH-ING MATHEMATICS IN THE ELEMENTARY CLASSROOM

Classroom Scenario

The scenario exemplifies the vision of teaching elementary mathematics in the classroom according to national standards and state guidelines. Highlights of the scenario are represented in italics within parentheses. These comments explain why and how this type of lesson represents the "best" in teaching mathematics.

This third-grade class has been working on problems that involve separating or dividing. The teacher, Mr. Kaster, is attempting to provide the class with some early involvement with multiplicative situations (using multiplication). Simultaneously, Mr. Kaster wants to include experiences with contexts for deepening their knowledge of and skill with addition and subtraction. This third-grade class has the knowledge and skill for performing addition and subtraction, but their understanding of multiplication and division is still quite informal. There has been some development of the concept of fractions that connects to their ideas about division. The class has

not yet learned the division algorithm (the conventional procedure for dividing).

The twenty-five students in Mr. Kaster's third-grade classroom are planning to share a class treat.

(Mr. Kaster seized this "teachable moment" to engage the students in real-world, relevant problem solving.)

The class treat involves 48 chocolate-iced cupcakes that were provided by a local bakery as a treat associated with the class field trip the previous day. Mr. Kaster has given the class the following problem:

If there are 48 cupcakes for our class treat, how many can each child have?

(Mr. Kaster knows that this problem will most likely elicit alternative representations and solution strategies as well as different answers. This provides a wonderful opportunity for mathematics learning. It should additionally help the students develop their ideas about division, fractions, and the connections between them.)

The students are encouraged to think about the problem individually. After about 5 minutes, Mr. Kaster allows the students to form their problem-solving groups.

(To promote collaboration and problem solving, Mr. Kaster has the students work in small groups of three and four to discuss their ideas about the problem. This is a routine practice for this class.)

(Adapted from NCTM Professional Standards for Teaching Mathematics, 1991, pp. 58–59)

While the students are working in small groups, Mr. Kaster walks around the room informally eavesdropping on the small group discussions.

(This is an extremely valuable method of informal assessment.)

While walking around the room of small groups working together, Mr. Kaster notices that one group immediately decides to represent the problem with mathematics manipulatives.

(Mr. Kaster always has various manipulatives available at the small group tables as well as all the full complement of manipulatives that are displayed in the math center of the classroom.)

Two groups chose color tiles to be cupcakes and began to represent the problem. Another follows, but selects pattern blocks. A fourth group begins to draw pictures of cupcakes. Group 5 works with paper and pencil and then sees that other groups have chosen different ways of representing the problem. They, too, select pattern blocks. After much discourse, group 6 scans the other groups to see what they are doing. This group decides to use pattern blocks. As one of the students is about to choose pattern blocks from the mathematics center, another student rushes over and whispers in her ear. She then selects to use fraction circles.

As Mr. Kaster continues to facilitate the small group work. The leader of one group raises his hand.

(This is the system that Mr. Kaster has in place addressing small group discussions. Each member of the group has a role to fulfill. Roles are rotated periodically. Questions that arise must first be addressed in small group discussion. When there is a consensus that no solution is agreeable, only then and only the group leader may raise his or her hand to ask for help. This promotes cooperative collaboration and learning within the groups as well as facilitating discourse and problem solving skills.)

The student asks if they should include Mr. Kaster in the number of people having a cupcake. The other groups overhead this and readily agree that Mr. Kaster should have a treat, too. They agree to change the number of people from 25 to 26 to include Mr. Kaster.

After the groups have worked for about 20 minutes, Mr. Kaster asks if the children are ready to discuss the problem in the whole group. The groups seem to agree. Mr. Kaster asks who would like to begin.

(The teacher allows time for the children to develop their solutions independently, with a few others, and then involves the whole group. By asking who would like to share their solution, he encourages the students to take intellectual risks.)

Two boys, Juan and Mark, come to the front of the class. Using the overhead projector, they write:

$$\begin{array}{r} 48 \\ -26 \\ \hline 24 \end{array}$$

One explains, "There are 25 kids in our class plus Mr. Kaster makes 26, and so if we pass out 1 cupcake to each child, we will have 24 cupcakes left, and that is not enough for each of us to have a second cupcake, so there will be some leftover ones."

(Students are expected to justify their solutions, not just to give answers.)

Mr. Kaster and the students reflect on this solution that was presented. Mr. Kaster scans the class and asks if anyone has a comment or a question about this solution.

(The teacher solicits other students' comments about the boys' solution without labeling it right or wrong. As members of a learning community, Mr. Kaster expects the students to decide if an idea makes sense mathematically.)

One girl, Amanda, says that she thinks that solution makes sense, but that "8 minus 6 is 2, not 4, so the answer should be 22, not 24." She demonstrates by pointing at the number line above the chalkboard. Starting at 8, she counts back 6 from 8 to get 2 using a pointer. The two boys reflect on this information for a moment. The class is quiet.

Mr. Kaster waits.

Then Juan says, "We revise that. Eight minus 6 is 2."

Mr. Kaster listens closely but does not jump into the interactive discourse.

(The mathematical learning environment should be established as a "risk-free" atmosphere. Students should be encouraged to respectfully another's ideas. The boys "revise" ~ation because they have been convinced by girls' explanation. There is no sense here that being wrong is shameful.)

Another student remarks that their group had the same solution as the first one shared—one cupcake.

"Ashley?" asks Mr. Kaster, after pausing for a moment to look over the classroom of students. Mr. Kaster remembers that this group had a different approach.

Ashley states that her group may have found a way to give each student in the class more than one cupcake. Ashley coaxes another group member, Sam, to go to the overhead with her.

Using overhead small colored tiles, the students demonstrate that each tile would represent a whole cupcake. The students proceed to divide the entire group of 48 cupcakes into two groups. One group represents the one student—one cupcake idea (26), while the other group (22) represents the leftover cupcakes.

(These actions demonstrate the same subtraction problem of the previous two boys that used the conventional representation of the problem.)

Ashley, "If we could cut these tiles in half, then each of us would get one whole cupcake and half of another one, we think." Sam and the rest of that group agree, "Each of us would get one and a half cupcakes."

Another student, Tom, suggests that since the colored tiles cannot be cut in half, that they try to use the pattern blocks like his group had tried. The class agrees that this would be a good idea.

Tom joins Ashley and Sam at the front of the room. Using pattern blocks, the students demonstrate how 48 cupcakes minus 26 cupcakes leaves 22 remaining cupcakes to divide in half. Using the blocks by exchanging whole blocks (hexagon) for two pieces (trapezoids), they represent the 22 cupcakes as 44 half cupcakes. The group then proceeds to assign each of the 26 people with half a cupcake.

Mr. Kaster asks, "Do you have any leftovers?"

(The students work together to solve the problem. Sometimes they build on the solutions offered by classmates. Mr. Kaster gathers insights about students through close listening and observation [informal assessment].)

At times, Mr. Kaster takes the responsibility for pushing (facilitating) students' thinking forward.

"There are still 18 half cupcakes or 9 whole cupcakes leftover," replies Steve.

"What do the rest of you think about this?" asks Mr. Kaster.

(Mr. Kaster expects the students to reason mathematically.)

Several students give explanations in support for Steve's solution.

"I think that does make sense," says Mary, "but I had another solution. I think the answer is 1 plus one-half plus one-fourth." Mary is a member of the group that chose to use fraction circles to help in their small group discussion of the original problem.

(Students seem willing to take risks by bring up different ideas.)

After waiting for the class to have a time of reflection on Mary's comments, the teacher continues.

"I don't understand," Mr. Kaster says. "Could you show what you mean?"

(Mr. Kaster seizes the opportunity to extend the class's thinking about fractions through this real-world problem that has motivated and engaged all of the students into actively thinking mathematically using many approaches and representations of their thinking. This has been done throughout the use of manipulatives, conventional procedures, collaboration, and classroom discourse within a community of learners in a risk-free environment.)

This scenario is just one snapshot of the many ways that teachers of mathematics are able to develop rich mathematical learning environments in their classrooms. This exemplifies a learner-centered classroom. Teaching in this manner helps the teacher facilitate student understanding of mathematics. The use of *manipu-*

latives, small and large group collaborative discourse, and active hands-on, minds-on learning experiences help students to value mathematics as well as to develop conceptual understanding of mathematics. This empowers the student to become mathematically literate and leads to successful student achievement and progress.

APPENDIX 3.1
More Practice Questions

Select the best response to each of the following questions.

1. Mr. Morales asked his fourth-grade students to choose their favorite color from a list of red, blue, green, and yellow. After the students had made their selections, the class tallied their data. Which type of graph would be the most appropriate to use to use for this information?
   A. A circle graph.
   B. A line graph.
   C. Box and whiskers plot.
   D. A scatter plot.

2. Ms. Maxwell wanted to help her second-grade students better understand place value. A good manipulative to use would be:
   A. Cuisenaire rods.
   B. Color tiles.
   C. Base ten blocks.
   D. Attribute blocks.

3. How many lines of symmetry does a rectangle have?
   A. One.
   B. Two.
   C. Four.
   D. Six.

4. Ms. Miller is using base ten blocks with her first-grade class to solve addition and subtraction problems. She asks her students to "show" her, using the blocks, the number 34. A possible solution is:
   A. 3 flats; 4 longs.
   B. 3 flats; 4 units.

C. 2 longs; 14 units.
D. 1 long; 14 units.

5. Alex spends approximately 45 minutes each school day on homework. If Alex continues to spend 45 minutes a school day on homework, how much time will Alex have spent after 15 days of school?
   A. 6.75 hours.
   B. 10 hours, 25 minutes.
   C. 11 hours, 15 minutes.
   D. 11 hours, 45 minutes.

6. Using the metric system, Mr. Coulter asks his class to estimate the length of their desk top. A "reasonable" estimate could be:
   A. 60 cm.
   B. 60 mm.
   C. 60 m.
   D. 60 km.

7. Use the problem below to answer the question that follows:

$$+ \frac{\overline{\rule{1cm}{0pt}} \quad \overline{\rule{1cm}{0pt}} \quad \overline{\rule{1cm}{0pt}}}{\overline{\rule{3cm}{0pt}}}$$

$$\overline{\rule{1cm}{0pt}} \quad \overline{\rule{1cm}{0pt}} \quad \overline{\rule{1cm}{0pt}}$$

Use each numeral 0, 1, 2, 3, 4, and 5 exactly once. Place a digit in each box so that you will have the largest sum possible.

This problem would be most appropriate for providing students an opportunity to use which problem-solving strategy?
   A. Working backwards.
   B. Extending the problem.
   C. Looking for a pattern.
   D. Drawing a diagram.

8. Before going on a field trip, Ms. Jurca must decide how many buses to request for all fourth-grade classes with a total enrollment of 315. She orders enough buses to transport all of the students. If each bus carries 60 students, how many empty seats will there be? *A calculator is chosen by a fourth grade student to help solve this problem. The student divides 315 by 60 for a solution of 5.25. The student is confused and asks Ms. Jurca for help. The teacher's best initial response might be:*
   A. Ask the student to explain why he or she divided 315 by 60 and what that answer represents.
   B. Suggest that the student use paper-and-pencil to check the answer.
   C. Suggest that the next step should be to multiply and then subtract.
   D. Explain that the answer 5.25 means that 6 buses will be needed to transport all of the students.

9. Children in Ms. Baker's fourth-grade class were asked to find the number of cats and dogs owned by the class. There was a total of 12 dogs and 9 cats for the class. Ms. Baker wanted her students to use a pictograph to represent the data. If a square represented 3 dogs and a triangle represented 3 cats, how many triangles should the students use to graph the data?
   A. 4.
   B. 3.
   C. 7.
   D. 2.

10. Ms. Martin is using rocker scales in her second-grade classroom. She has her students place objects of different weights on the scales. This activity could best be used to foster her students' understanding of:
   A. How to weigh objects accurately.
   B. How to predict which object is heavier.
   C. How to find the total weight of objects.
   D. How to better understand the concepts of less than and greater than.

11. The first step for the teacher to do when developing students' prenumber concepts is:
   A. Spend class time working with concrete objects.
   B. Spend class time working with pictorial objects.
   C. Spend class time having students write their numbers.
   D. Spend class time having students recognize the words for the numbers.

A third-grade student is given 12 colored tiles and is asked to create as many differently shaped rectangles as possible for each number from 1 to 12. Ms. Longino models these directions with six tiles, making two rectangles, as is shown below. Use this information to answer questions 12 through 14.

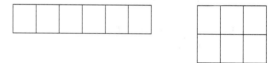

12. Ms. Longino has chosen this activity to help develop the student's understanding of which of the following number concepts?
   A. Percentages of whole numbers.
   B. Least common multiples.
   C. Factors of whole numbers.
   D. Numeration systems other than base 10.

13. If during the activity, a student asks why a 4×3 rectangle and a 3×4 rectangle have the same shape, Ms. Longino may use this opportunity for a lesson on which of the following geometrical concepts?
   A. Right angles and perpendicular lines.
   B. Properties of congruent figures.
   C. Properties of similar figures.
   D. Area and perimeter.

14. Ms. Longino wants to encourage the application of higher-order thinking skills. Of the following questions, which would be the best question to ask at the end of this activity?
   A. How many more rectangles could you make with 15 colored tiles?
   B. Which number from 1 to 12 made the most rectangles?
   C. For any given number of colored tiles, how could you determine how many rectangles can be made?
   D. For any given rectangle, how can you determine the perimeter of the rectangles?

15. Ms. Jacob divided her second-grade students into groups of four and gave each group a copy of a grocery store advertisement. Students were asked to work as a group and plan a meal for four people that contained one item from each food group. Students were asked to ensure that the meal was nutritious and the least expensive meal they could plan. Ms. Jacob's objective for this activity is:
   A. Help students learn the food groups.
   B. Connect mathematics to real-world situations.
   C. Help students develop communication skills.
   D. Foster collaborative working groups.

16. Ms. DeVillier placed 60 color tiles in a bag: 20 red, 10 blue, 10 yellow, 20 green. She asked her third-grade students to construct a graph to accurately represent the ratios of the color tiles. The ratio of the area for the green tiles to the area of all the tiles should be:
   A. 2:4.
   B. 1:2.
   C. 1:3.
   D. 3:1.

Best Answers to Practice Test Questions Representing the Standards Listed

Be sure to look at the information that follows this section if you are unclear about these terms (for example, attribute blocks are described in Table 3.1, Common Mathematics Manipulations, found on page 132). Other terms are described in the glossary on page 141.

1. A. *Circle graph:* This is the best answer to represent this type of data. A *line graph* indicates continuous data. A box and whiskers plot shows the shape of a data set. A scatterplot graph shows paired data values.

2. C. *Base ten blocks:* These are the best manipulatives for place value concepts. Cuisenaire rods may be used with fractions, ratio and proportion, measuring, and more. Color tiles may be used for counting, probability, fractions, and some place value. Attribute blocks would be used for sorting, classifying, and other activities.

3. B. *Two: Lines of symmetry divide the shape into mirror images.* A rectangle has two: one from side to side in the middle and the other drawn from end to end in the middle. Lines of symmetry may be formed when a shape is folded. From corner to corner would be a diagonal, not a line of symmetry.

4. C. *2 longs; 14 units.* This is the best answer. A long has a value of 10 units. Two longs would represent 20 units. Add the 14 units and the total number represented is 34. A flat has the value of 100 units.

5. C. *11 hours, 15 minutes.* The answer may be found by multiplying 45 minutes by 15 days and converting the total number of minutes to hours and minutes. This is done by dividing the product of 45 × 15 by 60 (minutes in an hour). The remainder is indicated as minutes leftover after making as many hours as possible.

6. A. *60 cm (centimeters).* This is the most reasonable answer. Millimeters are too small. A centimeter is about the width of

TABLE 3.1 Common Mathematics Manipulatives

Name	Description	Concept Usage
Attribute blocks	color, shape, size, and thickness; five shapes, three colors—yellow-red-blue, large and small in size	classification, grouping prenumber activities, symmetry, measurement, problem solving
Base ten blocks	wooden/plastic pregrouped/trading models	help to create mental images and understandings of place value, operations, geometry, measurement
Calculators		problem solving, checking solutions, place value, number magnitude
Chips, trading	colored chips with assigned values—groupable place value—two-sided, colored	place value, for regrouping in carrying and renaming, fractions, number sense for decimals and operations, links blocks to algorithms
Counters/Tiles	many varieties such as plastic bears, frogs, chips, beans	prenumber activities, number sense, numeration
Cubes • Unifix • Multilink • Wooden	—one side connects —all sides connect —do not link	can be used to develop one-to-one correspondence, counting, sorting, basic operations, geometry, spatial sense, albegra groupable place value
Cuisenaire rods	colored and length determine value	fractions, basic operations, logic, problem solving, area, perimeter, and more
Geoboards	square board with pegs—rubber bands used	area, logical thinking number concepts geometric figures, shapes, angles
Miras	reflective surfaces	symmetry, rotation, flips, and more
Paper folding	any area of paper	fractions, symmetry, recognizing polygons and more
Pattern blocks	many shapes and colors—squares, triangles, rectangles, trapezoids, rhombuses, hexagons	fraction concepts, counting, sorting, matching, logical thinking, problem solving, symmetry
Pentominoes	12 puzzle pieces	logic
Spinners, dice, money, clocks, number lines	varied	varied
Tangrams	square made of seven shapes: five triangles, square, parallelogram	problem solving, geometry, directions, symmetry, congruence

TABLE 3.2 Mathematics in Learning Centers

Center or Play Area	Mathematics Concepts	Manipulatives/Representations
Games, puzzles, and regular daily items	Grouping, counting, matching, patterning, ordering	Classification, numeral identification, logic, geometric forms
Housekeeping/Kitchens	Counting, measuring, one-to-one correspondence, estimation	Play money, numerals, labels
Water play/Sand table	Measuring, counting, conservation, estimation, positioning	Can draw numerals in sand, use measuring tools
Music/Puppets	Counting, one-to-one correspondence, patterning, classification	Create patterns with music, role play
Painting	Grouping, measuring, patterning, classification	Numeral writing, geometric designs
Woodworking	Measuring, counting, patterning, comparing size and shape, classification	Numeral writing, geometric designs, patterns
Block building	Counting, comparing size, one-to-one correspondence, classification, patterning, geometric shapes, positioning, estimation	Blocks as symbols, labels, can be used as many different representations

the human little finger. A meter is comparable to a yard, and a kilometer is closest to a mile (though less than a full mile). Meters and kilometers are too large. (An inch is approximately 2.54 cm.)

7. *C. Looking for a pattern.* This is the best strategy to apply in a problem such as this. The other strategies are more appropriate when there is more information available. For example, if a few digits were placed in the problem, the work backwards would be appropriate. Extending the problem is not a good choice because there is not enough information provided. Drawing a diagram is not appropriate in this case.

8. *A. Ask the student to explain why he or she divided 315 by 60 and what that answer represents.* This teacher response exemplifies the constructivist approach to teaching

mathematics. It allows children to reflect and justify their responses in order to make sense of the problem at hand. The other response choices here are not appropriate for a learner-centered mathematics classroom.

9. *B. 3. This answer is best as there are 9 cats.* The triangle represents 3 cats, so 9 divided by 3 = 3 triangles needed for the graph.

10. *D. How to better understand the concept of less than and greater than.* This activity is asking children in general to measure the differences in objects in relation to each other. Understanding the concept of less than and greater than is very well represented in this activity for second grade. Children are able to compare without using a specific measuring scale. The next step would be to ask children to "predict" which is heavier.

11. *A. Spend class time working with concrete objects.* Children are better able to understand mathematical concepts by first using concrete objects to manipulate. From there, learning progresses to pictorial or graphic, symbolic, and abstract.

12. *C. Factors of whole numbers.* As children work with the 12 tiles to make different rectangles, the results create rectangles of different dimensions that are multiplication arrays (1×12, 12×1, 2×6, 6×2, 3×4, 4×3). These represent the factors of 12.

13. *B. Properties of congruent figures.* By definition, congruent figures have the same size and same shape. Thus, 4×3 and 3×4 are congruent figures.

14. *C. For any given number of colored tiles, how could you determine how many rectangles can be made?* This question is the best answer as it challenges children to reflect, evaluate, and generalize the concept to another situation that allows many differ-ent responses. This has the children thinking beyond the usual recall of information.

15. *B. Connect mathematics to real-world situations.* It is extremely important that children learn and apply mathematics to real-world contexts to provide relevancy and to motivate children's problem-solving thinking.

16. *C. 1:3.* Students need to develop organizational skills needed to properly handle large quantities of data. Choosing an appropriate graphical representation is a fundamental requirement that students need to present data in an accurate manner. This response gives the ratio of the area of all of tiles to the area of the green color tiles. This is the correct response: There are 60 color tiles total and 20 of the 60 are green. (In this case, the ratio of the green tiles [20] to the entire group of tiles [60] is written 20/60. This simplifies to 1/3 and is written in ratio form of 1:3.)

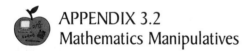

APPENDIX 3.2
Mathematics Manipulatives

Guidelines for Children Using Manipulatives in the Teaching and Learning of Mathematics

Active, "hands-on, minds-on" learning involves the use of manipulatives. Manipulatives provide a concrete basis for understanding abstract concepts and are very effective teaching tools for all students. Most educators support the use of manipulatives to help students' conceptual understanding by aiding better internalization and visualization of concepts and ideas. The guidelines below offer some suggestions for management of materials appropriate for all levels of learning and interactions.

- Free time for exploration is necessary whenever a new material or manipulative is introduced. This is also appropriate for learning centers, as well as several moments prior to beginning a lesson.

- Arrange and prepare the materials beforehand according to the purpose of the lesson.

- Clear expectations must be provided for lesson goals and the use of materials.

- Specific directions concerning the purposes in using the manipulatives is imperative. Teachers and students must understand the purpose of the materials related to the lesson in order to make the connections from models to an internalized idea.

- Explicit guidelines must be established for what is acceptable and not acceptable behavior for using manipulatives.

- Teachers should model the use of materials and "think aloud" about what they represent.

Recommended Minimum Manipulative Materials

Kindergarten (Early Childhood)
Interlocking counting cubes (1,000)
Attribute blocks (four sets—60 each)
Pattern blocks (four sets—250 each with two mirrors)
Buttons, shells, keys, and other familiar objects for counting/sorting
Measuring instruments for time (demonstration clock)
Play money

Grade 1
Interlocking counting cubes (1,000)
Attribute blocks (four sets—60 each)
Pattern blocks (four sets—250 each with two mirrors)
Measuring instruments (to measure length, volume, mass, temperature, and time)
Play money

Grade 2
Interlocking counting cubes (1,000)
Base ten blocks (ones, tens, and hundreds for each child)
Attribute blocks (four sets—60 each)
Pattern blocks (four sets—250 each with two mirrors)
Measuring instruments, both metric and customary (to measure length, volume, mass, temperature, and time)
Play money
Two- and three-dimensional geometric models (two sets of common shapes and solids)

Grade 3
Interlocking counting cubes (1,000)
Base ten blocks (ones, tens, and hundreds for each child, one thousand block for each four children)
Pattern blocks (four sets—250 each with two mirrors)
Fraction models—circles, squares, bars, and/or rods

*Manipulatives introduced in earlier grade levels may continue to be used through fourth grade.

Measuring instruments, both metric and customary (to measure length, volume, mass, temperature, and time)
Play money
Two- and three-dimensional geometric models (two sets of common shapes and solids)

Grade 4
Base ten blocks or other place value models (ones, tens, and hundreds for each child, one thousand-block for each four children)
Decimal models
Fraction models—circles, squares, bars, and/or rods
Measuring instruments, both metric and customary (to measure length, volume, mass, temperature)
Interlocking centimeter cubes (2,000)
Tangrams—one per child
Two- and three-dimensional geometric models (two sets of common shapes and solids)
Geoboards—one per child and one for teacher demonstration

Common Mathematical Difficulties for Children
Most difficulties that children have with arithmetic stem from a lack of understanding of important place-value concepts.

Place-Value Difficulties
- Associating place-value models with numerals
- Using zero when writing numerals
- Using regrouping concepts to represent numeral
- Naming place-value positions in a numeral
- Giving nonstandard place-value representations for a numeral

Addition and Subtraction Difficulties
- Identifying addition or subtraction situations
- Using counting to find basic addition facts
- With zeros in computations
- Using counting to find differences that are related to addition facts
- Regrouping when computing sums and differences

- When the two numerals in an exercise have a different number of digits
- A sum involving several addends or when a sum or difference involves large numbers

Multiplication and Division

- Identifying multiplication and division situations
- Determining the basic facts
- Using the basic multiplication facts to find related quotients
- Applying place-value concepts and basic facts to obtain products and quotients of multiples of ten
- Using zeros in a product or quotient
- Using the distributive property of multiplication over addition when computing products
- Regrouping when computing products and quotients
- Aligning partial products
- Solving word problems "when"

Rational Numbers
Difficulties associated with fractions.

- Associating meaning with a fraction
- Using the equivalent fraction rule
- Applying appropriate uses of a common denominator
- Making appropriate interpretations for mixed numerals such as 2-2/3 or 5-3/8
- With the meaning of the operations

Difficulties associated with decimals.

- Associating meaning with a decimal

- With place value and with the equivalent fraction rule
- With place value an with common denominators in addition and subtraction
- With the meaning of the operations and in distinguishing between various rules for the operations

Reading and Writing Difficulties

- Mathematical terms and symbols that are based on precise definitions are not generally learned in out-of-school environments.
- Sometimes words that have precise mathematical meaning are used ambiguously in everyday conversations.
- Mathematical words have other meanings in ordinary usage.
- Words are used inappropriately in mathematical context.
- The names and meaning of many mathematical symbols cannot be determined by looking at the symbols.
- Sometimes inappropriate or misleading visual models are given to illustrate the meaning of mathematical terms and ideas.
- Mathematical language is more concise than ordinary language.
- The organization of mathematical communications differs from the organization of ordinary reading materials.

(Adapted from Troutman & Lichtenberg (1999))

APPENDIX 3.3
Content Practice Test

This section includes problems addressing various mathematical concepts to help refresh some basic mathematical thinking and procedures. Answer the questions below and check your responses with the answers. (For further review visit the websites previously listed and/or locate some mathematics textbooks to study.)

1. Which number is a prime number: 9, 21, (41), or 36?
2. Complete. $\underline{3.2}$ kg = 3,200 g
3. There are 32 employees at the office. Of the employees, 20 are women. What percent of the employees are women?

4. Multiply: $-5.2 \times +2.6 = \underline{\quad ? \quad}$
5. Write in exponent form: $4 \times 4 \times 4 \times 4 \times 4$
   4^5
6. Divide. _____

   $0.02 \mid 1.576$

7. What are the coordinates of point *A*?

3,-2

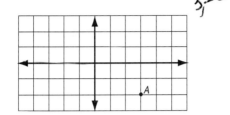

8. What is the LCM of 12 and 15?
9. Rosa spends 1/3 of her allowance on lunch and 1/4 of her allowance on entertainment. How much of her allowance is left?
10. What percent of 40 is 35?
11. Find the circumference.

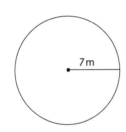

7 m

12. Find the volume.

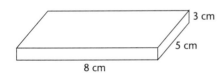

3 cm
5 cm
8 cm

13. A sweater that usually sells for $29.00 is on sale for $26.10. What is the percent of decrease?
14. How tall is the house?

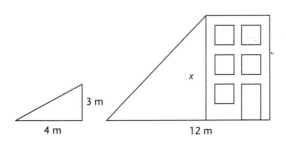

3 m
4 m
x
12 m

15. Subtract.

    6 yd 1 ft
    −3 yd 2 ft

16. What is the surface area?

3 cm
4 cm
5 cm

17. Solve for *n*. $5n - 14 = -19$
18. Add.

$$5\frac{1}{6}$$
$$+ 6\frac{5}{8}$$

19. Round 68.0719 to the nearest tenth.
20. Jamyce has received grades of 89, 92, and 85 on 3 tests. What grade must she get on the next test in order to have an average of 90?
21. Subtract: $-6 - -5 =$ ___?___
22. Find the perimeter.

7 cm
5 cm
12 cm

23. Which line is perpendicular to line *AB*?

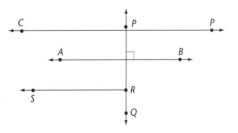

C
P
P
A
B
S
R
Q

Use the Venn diagram on page 138 to answer questions 24–27.

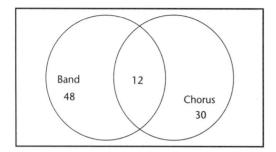

Band
48

12

Chorus
30

24. How many students are in the band?
25. How many students are in the chorus?
26. How many students are in the band and the chorus?
27. How many students are in the band but not in the chorus?
28. How many square meters of carpeting are needed to carpet a room that measures 12 meters by 19 meters?
29. Which ratio is equal to the ratio 3:4?
   A. 4:3
   B. 6:7
   C. 15:20
   D. 20:15
30. Write as a percent: 3/8

Use the spinner to answer questions 31–34. You spin the spinner. Find each probability.

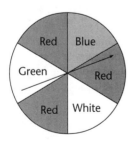

Red   Blue

Green

Red

Red   White

31. P (red) (probability of hitting a red section).
32. P (not blue) (probability of *not* hitting a blue section).

   You toss a coin and then spin the spinner above. Find each probability.
33. P (head, red)
34. P (tail, red)

Find the permutation.

35. There are 4 students and 4 chairs in a room. How many different possible seating arrangements are there?
36. Carrie used a 3-meter-long leash to tie her dog to a tree. What is the area of the circular region in which Carrie's dog can play?

Using the data below to answer questions 37–40.

85	75	70	70	70
100	90	85	90	65
70	90	80	65	85
75	100	75	95	95
65	90	90	85	90

37. The mode is _____ .
38. The range is _____ .
39. The median is _____ .
40. The mean is _____ .
41. Solve: $(6 \times 4) - (18 \div 3)$
42. Solve: $6(4 + 5)$

Answers with Procedural Rationale

1. *41.* A prime number has only 1 and itself as a factor.
2. *3.2.* 1000 g in one kg.
3. *62.5%.* 20 is what part of the total, 32? Divide 20 by 32 for the decimal, 625. Change into a percent.
4. *–13.52.* The product in multiplication of a positive and a negative number will be a negative number.
5. *4^5.* The number of times the number is used as a factor determines the exponent.
6. *78.8.* The decimal point in the divisor and the dividend is moved two places to the left to make the divisor a whole number. Then division procedures are followed.
7. *(3, –2).* The first number in a coordinate pair represents the x-axis (horizontal) value, the second number is the y-axis (vertical) value.
8. *60.* The LCM is the least common multiple and is found by listing the multiples of 12

and listing the multiples of 15. Find the common multiple from the list that is the least in number.

9. *5/12.* Change 1/3 and 1/4 to have a common denominator of 12 (4/12 + 3/12), add to obtain 7/12. That subtracted from 1 (the allowance) (12/12 – 7/12) will be 5/12.

10. *87.5%.* To find a percent of a number, divide 35 by 40. The decimal answer is then changed to a percent (.875 becomes 87.5%).

11. *43.96 m.* C = 2πr; π = approximately 3.14.

12. *120 cubic cm.* The volume is found by multiplying the measurement of each of the edges (8 × 5 × 3).

13. *10%.* Subtract the sale price from the original price ($2.90). Find what percent that is of the original $29.00 (Divide $2.90 by $29.00 to get .10, to become 10%.)

14. *9 m.* This is a proportion problem. The small triangle is *similar* to the triangle drawn from the building. *Similar* figures have angles and sides that are in proportion . The given ratios may be determined to be 3:4 and x (the unknown) is to 12. 3:4 as x is to 12. Cross products may be used to solve. (4x = 3 times 12 or 36). Solve for x.

15. *2 yd 2 ft.* The 6 yd 1 ft must be renamed as 5 yd 4 ft, as 1 yd is renamed (3 ft) and added to the already 1 ft. Subtract.

16. *88 square cm.* Surface area is the sum of all the areas of each face of the figure. In this case there are 6 faces. Each is a rectangle. A = lw. (4 × 1, 4 × 1, 8 × 4, 8 × 4, 8 × 1, 8 × 1)

17. *–1.* Add 14 to both sides of the equation. 5n = –5. Divide both sides by 5; n = –1.

18. $11\frac{19}{24}$. To add unlike fractions, determine the least common denominator (24), then add. ($5\frac{4}{24} + 6\frac{15}{24} = 11\frac{19}{24}$).

19. *Zero is in the tenths place.* The 7 in the hundredths place determines that the zero be rounded up to 1. 68.1 is the answer.

20. *To obtain an average of 90 from four tests, a student would need a total of 360 grade points.* Add the first three scores to total, 266. Subtract this from 360 to get 94.

21. *–11.* To subtract –5 from –6 use the inverse of –5 which is a +5. Another traditional saying is to change the sign of the second number and add, when subtracting like signed numbers. To begin to teach students this concept, use a number line or use 2 color counters and teach making zero pairs (pairing a negative to a positive to make zero).

22. *38 cm.* Add the length of all four sides to determine the perimeter.

23. *Line PQ.* Perpendicular lines form a right angle at the point of intersection.

24. *60 (45 + 12).* This represents only the band members' set.

25. *42.* This set includes those that are members of the chorus and the band and only the chorus. (30 + 12)

26. *12.* This set is only those members that are in the band and the chorus.

27. *48.* This set represents the total of 60 minus those that are in both (12) totaling 48.

28. *228 square m.* To find the area for a rectangle, multiply the length by the width.

29. *15:20.* Two equivalent ratios make a proportion.

30. *37.5%.* 3 represents what percent of 8. 3 is divided by 8. That decimal quotient is changed to a percent.

31. *1/2.* There are three red sections on the spinner out of a total of 6 sections. 3/6 becomes 1/2 in its simplest form.

32. *5/6.* There is only one blue section of the spinner and five that are not blue. 5 out of 6.

33. *1/4.* The probability of spinning a red is 1 out of 2 (3/6), for tossing a head is 1/2. Multiply the two probabilities: 1/2 × 1/2 = 1/4.

34. *1/4.* Same as above.

35. *There are 4 choices for the first student. Once he sits down, there are only 3 choices for the second student. The third student has two choices. The last student has only 1 choice.* Mathematically this is represented as 4 × 3 × 2 × 1 = 24.

36. *28.26 square m.* The leash represents the radius of a circle. To find the area of a circle, multiply pi (3.14) times the radius squared.

37. *90.* The mode is the most often occurring number.

38. *35.* The range is the difference of the largest and the smallest number.

39. *85.* The median is the middle number. It is the average of the two middle numbers when the numbers are arranged in order.

40. *82.* The mean is the average. Total all numbers and divide by the number of numbers.

41. *18.* PEMDAS (Please Excuse My Dear Aunt Sally) This phrase represents the order of operations. Perform operations in parentheses first, then exponents, multiplication, division, addition, subtraction.

42. *54.* Same as above.

 APPENDIX 3.4

Geometric Formulas and Measurement Units

P = Perimeter   A = Area   Volume = Volume   SA - Surface Area
(b = base, l = length, w = width, h = height)

Rectangle	P = 2l + 2w	A = lw
Square	P = 4s	A = s^2
Parallelogram	P = sum of all sides	A = bh
Triangle	P = sum of all sides	A = 1/2 bh
Trapezoid	P = sum of all sides	A = 1/2 h (b1 + b2)
Polygon	P = sum of all sides	A = depends on shape
Circle	C = 2πr or πd	A = $2πr^2$
Prism	V = Bh	SA = the sum of the area of each face
Cylinder	V = $πr^2h$	SA = $2πrh + 2π^2$

Measurement Units

Customary	Metric
Length	**Length**
12 inches (in) = 1 foot (ft)	1000 meters (m) = 1 kilometer (km)
3 ft = 1 yard (yd)	100 centimeters (cm) = 1 m
36 in = 1 yd	10 decimeters (dm) = 1 m
5,280 ft = 1 mile	1000 millimeters (mm) = 1 m
1,760 yd = 1 mile	10 cm = 1 dm
	10 mm = 1 cm
Area	**Area**
144 square in = 1 square foot	100 square mm = 1 square cm
9 square ft = 1 square yd	10,000 square cm = 1 square m
43,560 square ft = 1 acre (A)	10,000 square m = 1 hectare (ha)
Volume	**Volume**
1,728 cubic inches (cu in) = 1 cubic foot (cu ft)	1000 cubic mm = 1 cubic cm
27 cu ft = 1 cubic yard (cu yd)	1000 cubic cm = 1 cubic dm
	1,000,000 cubic cm = 1 cubic m

Measurement Units Continued

Customary	Metric

Capacity
8 fluid ounces (fl oz) = 1 cup (c)
2 c = 1 pint (pt)
2 pt = 1 quart (qt)
4 qt = 1 gallon (gal)

Capacity
1000 milliliter (mL) = 1 liter (L)
1000 L = 1 kiloliter (kL)

Weight
16 ounces (oz) = 1 pound
2000 lb = 1 ton (T)

Mass
1000 kilograms (kg) = 1 metric ton
1000 grams (g) = 1 kg
1000 milligrams (mg) = 1 g

Temperature
32 degrees F = freezing point of water
98.6 degrees F = normal body temperature
212 degrees F = boiling point of water

Temperature
0 degrees C = freezing point of water
37 degrees C = normal body temperature
100 degrees C = boiling point of water

Time
60 seconds (sec) = 1 minute (min)
60 min = 1 hour (hr)
24 hr = 1 day (da)
7 da = 1 week (wk)
4 wk = 1 month (mth)
12 mths = 1 year (yr)
52 wk = 1 yr
365 da = 1 yr

APPENDIX 3.5
Terminology

Acute angle. An angle that measures greater than 0 degrees and less than 90 degrees.

Acute triangle. A triangle that contains an acute angle.

Addend. A number that is added. In 5 + 8 = 13, the addends are 5 and 8.

Adjacent angles. Two angles with a common vertex, a common ray, and no common interior points.

Algebra. A branch of mathematics in which arithmetic relations are explored using letter symbols to represent numbers.

Algorithm. A step-by-step procedure used to find a solution.

Angle. Two rays with the same endpoint. The endpoint is called the vertex of the angle.

Arc. Part of the circumference of a circle.

Area. The number of square units needed to cover a surface.

Associative property of addition. The sum is always the same when the addends are grouped differently. (2 + 3) + 4 = 2 + (3 + 4).

Associative property of multiplication. The product is always the same when the factors are grouped differently. (2 x 3) x 4 = 2 x (3 x 4)

Average. A number obtained by dividing the sum of two or more addends by the number of addends.

Bar graph. A graph using vertical or horizontal bars to display numerical information.

Basic fact. A number sentence that has at least two one-digit numbers. Examples are: $7 + 1 = 8$, $15 - 8 = 7$, $9 \times 2 = 18$, $8 \div 4 = 2$

Bisect. To divide into two congruent parts.

Box and whiskers. A graph showing the shape of a data set.

Capacity. The volume of a figure, given in terms of liquid measure.

Circle. A plane figure with all of its points the same distance from a given point called the center.

Circle graph. A round graph that uses different-sized wedges to show how portions of a set of data compare with the whole set.

Circumference. The distance around a circle.

Commutative property of addition. Two numbers can be added in either order. The sums are the same.

Commutative property of multiplication. Two numbers can be multiplied in either order. The products are are the same.

Common denominator. A common multiple of two or more denominators. For 1/6 and 5/8, it would be 24.

Common factor. A number that is a factor of two or more numbers. A common factor of 9 and 6 is 3.

Common multiple. A number that is a multiple of two or more numbers. A common multiple of 2 and 3 is 6.

Complementary angles. Two angles whose measures add up to 90 degrees.

Composite number. A whole number greater than 1 that is not prime.

Cone. A solid with a circular base and one vertex.

Congruent. Having the same size and the same shape, as in a congruent figure.

Congruent angles. Two angles that have the same measure.

Conjecture. A well-thought out guess, prediction, or estimate.

Coordinate system. A graph with a horizontal number line (x-axis) and a vertical number line (y-axis) that are perpendicular to each other. The point of intersection is called the origin and labeled 0 on the graph. An ordered pair (x, y) is used to name a point on a coordinate system.

Counting. 1, 2, 3, 4 (naming sequence of numbers).

Cube. A rectangular solid with six congruent square faces.

Cylinder. A solid with two bases that are congruent circles.

Decimal. A number that uses place value and a decimal point to show tenths, hundredths, thousandths, and so on.

Dependent events. Events such that the outcome of the first event affects the outcome of the second event.

Denominator. The bottom number of a fraction, telling in how many parts the whole is divided.

Diagonal. In a polygon, a segment that connects one vertex to another vertex but is not a side of the polygon.

Diameter. In a circle, a segment that passes through the center and has its endpoints on the circle.

Difference. The answer for subtraction. In $16 - 9 = 7$, 7 is the difference.

Distributive property of multiplication over addition. The product of a number and the sum of two numbers equals the sum of the two products. $3 \times (4 + 2) = (3 \times 4) + (3 \times 2)$.

Dividend. A number that is divided by another number. For example, in $36 \div 4 = 9$, the 36 is the dividend.

Divisible. When one number is divided by another and the remainder is 0, the first number is divisible by the second number.

Division. An operation on two numbers that results in a quotient and a possible remainder.

Divisor. A number that divides another number. In the example $36 \div 4 = 9$, the 4 is the divisor.

Endpoint. The point at the end of a line segment.

Equally likely outcomes. Outcomes that have the same chance of occurring in a probability experiment.

Equation. A mathematical sentence that uses the = symbol.

Equilateral triangle. A triangle with three congruent sides.

Equivalent fractions. Fractions that name the same fraction (1/2 = 2/4 = 4/8).

Even number. A whole number that is a multiple of 2.

Event. The particular outcome one is looking at in a probability experiment.

Expanded form. Expressing a number as factors. 325 = (3 × 100) + (2 × 10) + (5 × 1).

Exponent. A number that tells how many times the base is to be used as a factor. (In 2^3, 2 is the base, 3 is the exponent.)

Face. A flat surface of a solid figure.

Fact families. The related number sentences for addition and subtraction or multiplication and division that contain all the same numbers (for example, 2 + 3 = 5, 3 + 2 = 5, 5 − 3 = 2, and 5 − 2 = 3).

Factor. A number to be multiplied or a number that divides evenly into a given second number is a factor of that number. (2 × 3 = 6, 2 and 3 are factors of 6.)

Factor tree. A diagram showing how a composite number breaks down into its prime factors.

Factorization. Writing a whole number as a product of factors. (The factorization of 12 would be 2 × 2 × 3 = 12.)

Frequency. The number of times a score appears in a list of data.

Function. For every input value there is one and only one output value.

Greatest common factor (GCF). The greatest whole number that divides two whole numbers. (The GCF of 24 and 32 is 4 evenly.)

Greatest possible error (GPE). The GPE of a measurement is equal to one-half the unit of measure.

Height of a triangle. The perpendicular distance from a vertex to the opposite side, or base.

Hexagon. A polygon with six sides.

Independent events. If two events A and B are independent, then the probability that both will happen is P(A) × P(B).

Integers. The whole numbers and their opposites. . . . −2, -1, 0, 1, 2 . . .

Inverse operations. Operations that "undo" each other. Addition and subtraction are inverse operations. Multiplication and division are inverse operations.

Isosceles triangle. A triangle with two congruent sides.

Least common denominator (LCD). The least common multiple (LCM) of two denominators. (30 is the LCM of 1/6 and 1/15.)

Least common multiple (LCM). The smallest number that is a common multiple of two given numbers. (The LCM of 3 and 4 is 12.)

Line. A straight path that extends forever in both directions.

Line graph. A graph in which a line shows changes in data, often over time.

Line of symmetry. A fold line of a figure that makes the two parts of the figure match exactly.

Line segment. Part of a line with two endpoints.

Mass. The amount of matter that something contains.

Mean. The average of a set of numbers; the sum of the numbers divided by the number of numbers.

Median. The middle number of a set of numbers after they have been placed in numerical order. If there are an even number of numbers, the median is the average of the two "middle" numbers.

Minuend. The number from which another number is subtracted. (For example, 14 − 8 = 6, 14 is the minuend.)

Mode. The number that occurs the most frequently in a set of data.

Multiple. A multiple of a number is the product of that number and a whole number. Some multiples of 2 are 4, 6, and 8.

Multiplicand/multiplier. A number that is multiplied by another number. (In 7 × 4 = 28, the multiplicand is 7; the multiplier is 4.)

Numerator. The top number in a fraction, telling how many parts of the whole are being named.

Obtuse angle. An angle that measures greater than 90 degrees and less than 180 degrees.

Obtuse triangle. A triangle that contains an obtuse angle.

Octagon. A polygon with eight sides.

Odd number. A whole number that is not a multiple of 2.

Order of operations. When there is more than one operation and parentheses are used, first do what is inside the parentheses. Next, multiply or divide from left to right. Then add or subtract from left to right (PEMDAS).

Ordered pair. A number pair, such as (2, 3), in which the 2 (x-axis) is the first number and the 3 is the second number (y-axis).

Outcome. Any possible result in a probability experiment.

Parallel lines. Lines in the same plane that do not intersect.

Parallelogram. A quadrilateral (any four-sided polygon) with opposite sides parallel and congruent.

Pentagon. A five-sided polygon.

Perimeter. The sum of the lengths of the sides of a polygon.

Perpendicular lines. Lines that intersect at right angles.

Pi. The number obtained by dividing the circumference of any circle by its diameter. A common approximation for π is 3.14.

Pictograph. A visual representation used to make comparisons. A key always appears at the bottom of a pictograph or picture graph showing how many each object represents.

Plane. A flat surface that extends indefinitely in both directions.

Plane figures. Two-dimensional figures with flat surfaces such as squares, rectangles, hexagons, triangles, pentagons, quadrilaterals.

Point. A location in space.

Polygon. A simple closed figure (square, triangle, hexagon, etc.).

Polyhedron. A space figure with all flat surfaces (faces).

Power of a number. A number found by multiplying the number by itself one or more times.

Prime factor. A factor that is a prime number. (Prime factors of 15 are 3 and 5.)

Prime factorization. A composite number expressed as a product of primes. ($24 = 2 \times 2 \times 2 \times 3$ or $2^3 \times 3$).

Prime number. A whole number greater than 1 with exactly two whole positive factors: 1 and itself.

Probability. The chance that an event will occur.

Product. The answer in a multiplication problem.

Proportion. An equality of ratios. (1/2 = 4/8)

Quotient. The answer in a division problem.

Radius. In a circle it is a line segment that connects the center of the circle with a point on the circle.

Range. The difference between the highest and lowest values in a data set.

Ratio. A comparison of two or more values. 1/2, 4/6; or 1:2, 4:6; or 1 is to 2, 4 is to 6.

Rational counting. The ability to order and enumerate objects in sets.

Rational number. Any number that can be expressed as a fraction a/b, where a and b are integers and b ≠ 0. Examples are: 3 as 3/1, 1/4, .34, 56%, and so on.

Ray. Part of a line that has one endpoint and goes on and on in one direction.

Reciprocals. Two numbers whose product is 1. 2/3 × 3/2 = 1

Rectangle. A parallelogram with four right angles.

Reflection. The mirror images of a figure that has been "flipped" over a line.

Remainder. The amount left over after a division problem. 18/4 = 4r2

Rhombus. A parallelogram with four congruent sides.

Right angle. An angle that measures 90 degrees.

Right triangle. A triangle that contains a right angle.

Rotation. The image of a figure that has been turned, as if on a wheel.

Rote counting. The naming of numbers in order without making any connection between numbers and sets of real-life objects.

Rounding. Expressing a number to the nearest thousandth, hundredth, tenth, one, ten, hundred, thousand, and so on as directed.

Scalene triangle. A triangle with no congruent sides.

Scatter plot. A graph showing paired data values.

Segment. Part of a line including two endpoints.

Similar figures Figures with the same shape but not necessarily the same size.

Slide. See *Translation*.

Solid figures. Three-dimensional figures such as cones, spheres, cylinders, cubes, prisms, pyramids.

Sphere. A solid with all points an equal distance from the center.

Square. A rectangle with four congruent sides.

Statistics. A branch of mathematics that deals with the organization, description, and analysis of data.

Subtrahend. A number to be subtracted from another number. (In $15 - 8 = 7$, the 8 is the subtrahend.)

Sum. The answer in an addition problem.

Surface area. The sum of the areas of all the surfaces of a space figure.

Symmetry. A figure has line symmetry if it can be folded on a line so that the two halves of the figure are congruent. The fold line is called the line of symmetry.

Translation. The image of a figure that has been slid to a new position without flipping or turning.

Trapezoid. A quadrilateral with one pair of parallel sides. These sides are called the upper and lower bases.

Tree diagram. A diagram used to find the total number of outcomes in a probability experiment.

Triangle. A polygon with three sides.

Unit price. The ratio of the total cost to the number of units.

Variable. A symbol, usually a letter, that stands for an unknown quantity.

Venn diagram. A diagram that uses regions to show relationships between sets of things.

Vertex. The common endpoint of two rays that form an angle, or the point of intersection of two sides of a polygon or polyhedron.

Volume. The number of cubic units needed to fill a figure.

Weight. A measure of the force that gravity exerts on a body.

Whole number. Any one of the numbers 0, 1, 2, 3, . . . There is no largest whole number. The smallest whole number is zero.

Zero property for addition and subtraction. For any number n, $n + 0 = n$ and $n - 0 = n$. Zero is the additive identity for addition.

Zero property for multiplication. For any number n, $n \times 0 = 0$.

 REFERENCES

Ashlock, R. (1990). *Error patterns in computation on semi-programmed approach* (5th ed.). New York: Macmillan.

Ball, D. L. (1993). With an eye on the mathematical horizon: Dilemmas of teaching elementary school mathematics. *Elementary School Journal, 93*(4), 373–397.

Brooks, J. G., & Brooks, M. G. (1993*). In search of understanding: The case for the constructivist classroom.* Alexandria, VA: Association for Supervision and Curriculum Development.

Carlton, R. A. (1980, May). *Basic skills in the changing work world.* Monograph. Ontario, Canada: University of Guelph.

Cobb, P., & Lampert, M. (1998). *Communication.* Paper prepared for the National Council of Teachers of Mathematics. Reston, VA: NCTM.

Davis, R. B., Maher, C. A., & Noddings, N., (1990). Suggestions for the improvement of mathematics education. In R. B. Davis, C. A. Maher, &

N. Noddings (Eds.), *Constructivist views on the teaching and learning of mathematics.* [Monograph Number 4]. *Journal for Research in Mathematics Education,* 187–191. Reston, VA: NCTM.

Driscoll, A., & Nagel, N. G. (2002). *Early childhood education, birth-8: The world of children, families, and educators.* Boston: Allyn and Bacon.

Fitzgerald, A. (1985). *New technology and mathematics in employment.* Birmingha, AL: University of Birmingham, Department of Curriculum and Instruction.

Howden, H. (1989). Teaching number sense. *The Arithmetic Teacher. 36*(6), 6–11.

Lave, J. (1991). Situated learning in communities of practice. In L. B. Resnick, J. M. Levine, & S. D. Teasley (Eds.), *Perspectives on socially shared cognition* (pp. 63–82). Washington, DC: American Psychological Association.

National Council of Teachers of Mathematics. (1989). *Curriculum and evaluation standards for school mathematics.* Reston, VA: Author.

National Council of Teachers of Mathematics. (1991). *Professional standards for teaching school mathematics.* Reston, VA: Author.

National Council of Teachers of Mathematics. (1995). *Assessment Standards for school mathematics.* Reston, VA: Author.

National Council of Teachers of Mathematics. (1998). *Principles and standards for school mathematics: Discussion Draft. Standards 2000.* Reston, VA: Author.

National Council of Teachers of Mathematics. (2000). *Principles and standards for school mathematics.* Reston, VA: Author.

National Research Council. (1989). *Everybody counts.* Washington, DC: National Academy Press.

Noddings, N. (1990). Constructivism in mathematics education. In B. Davis, C. Maher, & N. Noddings (Eds.), *Constructivist views on the teaching and learning of mathematics.* [Monograph Number 4]. *Journal of Research in Mathematics Education,* 7–18.

Shulman, L. (1986). Paradigms and research programs in the study of teaching. A contemporary perspective. In M. Wittrock (Ed.), *Handbook of research on teaching* (3rd ed., pp. 3–36). New York: Macmillan.

State Board for Educator Certification (SBEC). (2001). Certification strand for generalist early childhood fourth-grade. http://www.sbec.state.tx.us/certstand/genec_4.htm (May 22, 2001).

Texas Education Agency. (1997). *Texas essential knowledge and skills for mathematics.* Austin, TX: Author.

Texas Education Agency. (1998). *Texas assessment of academic skills mathematics objectives.* Austin, TX: Author.

Texas Education Agency. (2001). Curriculum guidelines for early childhood. http://www.tea.state.tx.us/curriculum/early/prekguide.html (May 22, 2001).

Troutman, A. P., & Lichtenberg, B. K. (1999). *Mathematics, a good beginning.* New York: Brooks/Cole Publishing Company.

Van de Walle, J. (1998). *Elementary and middle school mathematics, teaching developmentally* (3rd ed.). New York: Longman.

RESOURCES

Artzt, A. F., & Newman, C. M. (1990). *How to use cooperative learning in the mathematics classroom.* Reston, VA: NCTM.

Baroody, A. J. (1993). *Problem solving, reasoning, and communicating (K–8): Helping children think mathematically.* Columbus, OH: Merrill.

Burns, M. (1985, February). The role of questioning. *The Arithmetic Teacher,* 14–16.

Burns, M. (1992). *About teaching mathematics: A K–8 resource.* White Plains, NY: Cuisenaire.

Carpenter, T. P., Carey, D. A., & Kouba, V. L. (1990). A problem-solving approach to the operations. In J. N. Payne (Ed.), *Mathematics for the young child* (pp. 111–113). Reston, VA: NCTM.

Eisenhower National Clearinghouse for Math and Science Education (http://www.enc.org/). This site offers mathematics and science Internet links for teachers, stories, and ideas about mathematics and science teachers.

Fennema, E. (1973, May). Manipulatives in the classroom. *The Arithmetic Teacher,* 350–352.

Hart, L. C., Schultz, K., Najee-ullah, D., & Nash, L. (1992). The role of reflection in teaching. *Arithmetic Teacher, 1,* 40–42.

Hope, J. (1989). Promoting number sense in school. *The Arithmetic Teacher, 39*(6), 12–16.

Kamii, C., & Lewis, B. A. (1990, September). Research into practice: Constructivist learning and teaching. *The Arithmetic Teacher, 38*(1), 34–35.

Math Forum (http://www.forum.swarthmore.edu/). This site includes classroom materials, online mathematics activities, software, articles, and more.

Mathematics Lessons Database (http://www.mste.uiuc.edu/mathed/queryform.html). This lesson in mathematics and programs related to teaching mathematics.

National Council of Teachers of Mathematics (http://www.nctm.org). This is the national organization responsible for the creation and publication of the mathematics standards.

Stenmark, J. K. (Ed.). (1991). *Mathematics assessment: Myths, models, good questions, and practical suggestions.* Reston, VA: Author.

Texas Education Agency. (1998). *TAAS Mathematics objectives and measurement specifications and the mathematics update 1998–1999: A guide to TAAS and the Texas Essential Knowledge and Skills (TEKS).* Austin, TX: Author.

Thornton, C. A. (1990). Strategies for the basic facts. In J. N. Payne (Ed.), *Mathematics for the young child* (pp. 133–151). Reston, VA: NCTM.

Teachers are encouraged to seek additional resources for review at the following websites:

http://www.tea.state.tx.us/student.assessment/ resources/release/index.html. Teachers may review and test on mathematical content by taking released TAAS tests online. Any of the grade-level tests are good reviews.

http://www.tea.state.tx.us/student.assessment/taks/ index.html. This website highlights the new student testing, TAKS.

http://www.tea.state.tx.us/teks/teksfaq/ch111.html. This website highlights the student TEKS.

ABOUT THE AUTHORS

NORENE VAIL LOWERY, Ph.D., is Assistant Professor of Mathematics Education in the Curriculum and Instruction Department of the College of Education at the University of Houston, Houston, Texas. Research interests include elementary and middle school mathematics education, preservice and inservice teacher education, assessment, and the integration of literature and mathematics.

RENA M. SHULL, Ph.D., is a Visiting Assistant Professor in the Department of Mathematics, Physics and Computer Science for Rockhurst University, Kansas City, Missouri. Dr. Shull headed a Professional Development School (PDS) site and taught elementary mathematics methods for many years at the University of Houston. Her research interests are technology in the mathematics classroom and number sense.

CHARLES E. LAMB, Ed.D., was a faculty member at the University of Texas at Austin from 1975–1994. He served as a faculty member at Texas A&M University from 1994 to 2001. As Professor Emeritus, he continues to teach part-time, as well as serve on graduate committees. He frequently speaks at conferences and does educational consulting.

Preparing to Teach Social Studies

Trenia L. Walker
University of Pittsburgh

The National Council for the Social Studies (NCSS) established a Task Force on Standards that defined social studies as:

> the integrated study of the social sciences and humanities to promote civic competence . . . The primary purpose of social studies is to help young people develop the ability to make informed and reasoned decisions for the public good as citizens of a culturally diverse, democratic society in an interdependent world. (1994, p. 3)

This was the guiding definition of social studies for the team who developed the TEKS (Texas Essential Knowledge and Skills) for Social Studies (Social Studies Center, 2000). Mike Moses, Commissioner of Education in Texas states, "Although all of public education prepares students for the responsibilities of citizenship, we know that the goal of providing students with the knowledge and skills necessary to assume their roles as leaders in our state and nation in the twenty-first century rests primary with the social studies" (available online http://www.tea.state.tx.us/resources/ssced/index.htm). The basic purpose of social studies is to produce good citizens. In our classrooms and in the world beyond, we want people to learn to live and work responsibly together. Social studies instruction is critical, both to prepare students to become responsible, thoughtful, participating citizens and to provide students with the basic skills they need to function in our society. Often mathematics and reading programs are considered the basics in EC-4 education; however, social studies is also basic. As Farris (2001) points out, teachers

> cannot wait until children are in fourth grade to begin teaching social studies for the same reasons they would not wait until then to teach mathematics or literacy. Fourth grade is too late; children's basic attitudes and concepts are formed by then. Lessons in which 25 percent of the curriculum content comes from social studies will help shape the citizens of tomorrow. (p. 80)

Social studies advocates know that not every child will not choose to become a space engineer or a brain surgeon, but certainly *every* one of them will be a citizen of our country and the world and, hopefully, a thoughtful one who contributes positively to society. For this reason, it is vital that EC-4 teachers devote instructional time to social studies. A good social studies program will also integrate opportunities to develop students' skills in other subjects including reading, writing, and mathematics (Chapin & Messick, 2002).

There are several ways of viewing social studies knowledge and skills for the EC-4 teacher and for students. Table 4.1 on page 150 compares teacher standards, TExES test framework, and the TEKS strands for students. Notice the overlap in what teachers should know (and on what they are tested) and what children should know.

It is beyond the scope of this chapter to provide all the knowledge, skills, and values-development information necessary in social studies for the EC-4 teacher. However, every attempt will be made to connect the EC-4 social studies teaching standards with the competencies covered on the Texas Examinations of Educator Standards (TExES), Texas Essential Knowledge and Skills (TEKS) for social studies, and the social studies scope and sequence for Texas schools. The social studies test framework for the Generalist EC-4 certification (as seen in Table 4.1) is made up of four competencies (numbers 16–19): social science instruction; history; geography and culture; and government, citizenship, and economics.

TABLE 4.1　A Comparison of Knowledge and Skills for Teachers and Students

Teacher Standards (What teachers should know and be able to apply)	TExES Framework (What test takers should know and be able to apply)	TEKS Strands (What EC-4 students should know and do)
Knowledge	Social science instruction	**Knowledge**
History	History	History
Geography	Geography and culture	Geography
Economics	Government, citizenship,	Economics
Government	and economics	Government
		Culture
Values		
Citizenship		**Values**
Culture		Citizenship
		Science, technology, and
Skills		society
Research		
Intra- and interdisciplinary		**Skills** (based on the strands
teaching		above)
Recent issues and develop-		
ments in the field		

The State Board for Educator Certification (SBEC) defines each of these competencies:

Social science instruction: The teacher uses social science knowledge and skills to plan, organize, and implement instruction and assess learning.

History: The teacher demonstrates knowledge of significant historical events and developments and applies social science skills to historical information, ideas, and issues.

Geography and culture: The teacher demonstrates knowledge of geographic relationships among people, places, and environments in Texas, the United States, and the world; understands the concept of culture and how cultures develop and adapt; and applies social science skills to geographic and cultural information, ideas, and issues.

Government, citizenship, and economics: The teacher understands concepts and processes of government and the responsibilities of citizenship; knows how people organize economic systems to produce, distribute, and consume goods and services; and applies social science skills to information, ideas, and issues related to government and economics.

The Texas Social Studies Center (SSC, 2000) believes that a comprehensive social studies program depends on the integration of the eight strands of the TEKS to ensure that students become responsible citizens in the twenty-first century and that they possess factual and conceptual knowledge, intellectual skills, and basic democratic values.

In the text that follows, each of the competencies that make up Domain III (the social studies component) for EC-4 educators will be introduced with a statement that broadly defines what an entry-level EC-4 educator needs to know and be able to do. A descriptive statement follows that describes in more detail the type of knowledge and skills covered by the standard. For each indicator, there is a section that indicates how the content can be taught in appropriate ways for EC-4 students. A sample question of the kind that might be found on the TExES precedes a detailed explanation of the standard. Another sample question concludes each section. These questions should be used to organize your reading and review of the content in each of the standards. Because the knowledge standards (history, geography, economics, and government) contain so much information, they have been broken down into smaller, more manageable units. Each of these smaller units begins with a key question related to the information it contains. These questions should be used to guide your reading, further study, and review of the material in each section.

STANDARDS I, II, AND III

The social studies teacher has a comprehensive knowledge of the social sciences and recognizes the value of the social sciences. The social studies teacher effectively integrates the various social science disciplines. The social studies teacher uses knowledge and skills of social studies, as defined by the Texas Essential Knowledge and Skills (TEKS), to plan and implement effective curriculum, instruction, assessment, and evaluation.

Competency 016 (Social Science Instruction): The teacher uses social science knowledge and skills to plan, organize, and implement instruction and access learning.

The beginning teacher: knows state content and performance standards for social studies that comprise the Texas Essential Knowledge and Skills (TEKS) and understands the vertical alignment of the social sciences in the TEKS from grade level, including prerequisite knowledge and skills; understands the implications of stages of child growth and development for designing and implementing effective learning experiences in the social sciences (e.g., knowledge of and respect for self, families, and communities; sharing; following routines; working cooperatively in groups); selects effective, developmentally appropriate instructional practices, activities, technologies, and materials to promote children's knowledge and skills in the social sciences; selects and uses appropriate technology as a tool for learning and communicating social studies concepts; selects and uses instructional strategies, materials, and activities, including appropriate technology, to promote children's use of social sciences skills and research tools; provides instruction that relates skills, concepts, and ideas in different social science disciplines; helps children make connections between knowledge and methods in the social sciences and in other content areas; uses a variety of formal and informal assessments and knowledge of the TEKS to determine children's progress and needs and to help plan instruction for individual children, including English Language Learners.

Consider the following practice question:

Which of the following instructional techniques would teachers who adhere to the principles of multicultural education most likely choose?

   A. Lecture.
   B. Inquiry.
   C. Cooperative groups.
   D. Independent study.

Although you might have said that inquiry is a worthy part of social studies instruction, one would want to use cooperative groups (C) to teach the principles of multiculturalism. This is particularly appropriate in diverse classroom settings. Manning and Baruth (2000) state that research on cooperative learning and intergroup relationships has shown that students in cooperative-learning situations develop great appreciation for cooperative-learning classmates (p. 236).

Intra- and Interdisciplinary Issues

Traditional education programs emphasize the teaching of individual subjects—language arts, mathematics, science, and social studies. These subjects are separated into blocks of instruction time with very little connection to one another. The limited number of hours in the school day precludes all subjects from receiving equal instruction time, causing social studies teachers to be particularly concerned. Along with science, social studies has become one of the subjects most likely to be preempted, postponed, or ignored altogether. Maxim (1999) observes: "If social studies is somehow squeezed into the day's schedule, children are often led through a quick oral reading of a textbook section and a brief question-answer recitation period . . ." (p. 23). To remedy these practices, teachers seek themes to integrate EC-4 school subject areas. These themes cut across all disciplines, allowing for learning opportunities that are *deeper*, not *wider*.

The National Council for the Social Studies (1994) has identified five key factors of teaching and learning that make for powerful social studies teaching and learning. Social studies teaching and learning must be meaningful, integrative, value based, challenging, and active (pp. 11–12). When social studies is integrative in its treatment of topics, it cuts across the disciplinary boundaries (both intradisciplinary [overlapping lessons within the social studies areas] and interdisciplinary [overlapping lessons between social studies and other subject areas]); spans time and space; and integrates knowledge, beliefs, values, and attitudes to action. All of this is to develop a working knowledge of the evolution of the human condition through time, its current variations across locations and cultures, and an appreciation of the potential implications for this knowledge for social and civic decision making (NCSS, 1994).

Traditionally, EC-4 social studies programs have sequenced content in a pattern of outwardly expanding environments. In Texas, the focus by grade level is generally:

PreK and K: Self, home, family, and classroom
    1: Student's relationship to the classroom, school, and community
    2: Local community and impact of individuals and events on the history of the community, state, and nation
    3: How individuals have changed their communities and world
    4: History of Texas

There are six disciplines of social studies commonly found at the EC-4 levels: geography, anthropology, sociology, history, economics, and political science. Pursuing these themes generally means that the social studies subjects will be integrated across the entire discipline. For example, a mock trial can follow the reading of the *Real Story of the Three Little Pigs,* or fairy tales with similar plots and themes can be compared across cultures. Themes around books such as *Everybody Eats Rice* (or bread) invite reading, tasting, and geographical curiosity.

Interdisciplinary education's greatest strength is its potential for helping children go beyond superficial knowledge. It enables them to develop an in-depth, multidimensional understanding of a topic. For example, why separate many topics into distinct subjects when they can be multiple dimensions of the same topic in many ways?

Thematic units make it easy to integrate other subjects with social studies and to integrate the various strands of social studies shown in Table 4.1. For example, in a unit on homes, young children can orally describe, write about, and draw their own homes and those they find in their neighborhoods. They can then investigate shelter that is located in other parts of the world and discover why others have created different types of homes or shelters to match various conditions and environments. They can also investigate building homes using spatial skills in a block center. By looking back at the homes and shelters of the past, they can focus upon inventions that make our homes more comfortable now.

Maxim (1999) writes that "social studies appears to be the major area for blending subjects previously taught separately" (p. 24). Berg (1988) answers the question of where social studies fits in the integration of subjects:

Right in the middle! A major goal of the social studies is to help students understand the myriad interactions of people on this planet—past, present, and future. Making

*sense of the world requires using skills that allow one to read about the many people
and places that are scattered about the globe; to use literature to understand the
richness of past events and the people who are a part of them; to apply math concepts
to more fully understand how numbers have enabled people to numerically manage
the complexity of their world. The story of humankind well told requires drawing
from all the areas of the curriculum. (unnumbered pullout section)*

By integrating subjects through themes, students become involved in activities
that are ultimately more meaningful and *powerful*.

Engaging *All* Students

Teachers need to have more than knowledge of the subject matter; they must also
have an understanding of their students. The four commonplaces of education
are learners and learning, content, teachers and teaching, and classroom environment (Grant & Vansledright, 2001). These topics provide a useful framework
for examining social studies classrooms. Increasingly, teachers are confronted
with a wide variety of students in their classrooms. Among today's students there
is growing ethnic diversity, as well as a wide range of socioeconomic backgrounds
and intellectual abilities. One of the biggest challenges for teachers is to design
quality, thought-provoking, and engaging learning opportunities for *all* students.

The world inside classrooms reflects today's world. The current inclusion
movement seeks to integrate all types of learners into the classroom. There are
many who disagree with this idea; however, advocates "strongly believe that
students with learning disabilities increasingly benefit both academically and
socially from placement in the regular classroom" (Farris, 2001, p. 328). Depending on the school district, inclusion might also extend to students identified as
gifted. The classroom teacher has the task of reaching and teaching students along
this "extensive continuum of skills and abilities" (Farris, 2001, p. 329). In a social
studies classroom that reflects a wide range of student abilities, teachers often
must change their focus. Instead of focusing on skills development and memorizing facts, teachers should "refocus on interdisciplinary teaching and theme-
based units, student portfolios, and cross-grade grouping whenever possible
while continually keeping the individual child in mind" (Farris, 2001, p. 330).
Learning should center on inquiry-based activities that would help develop
higher-level thinking skills.

Critical thinking has a perfect place in the social studies classroom as young
students begin to compare and contrast and ask questions about the way we and
others live. Research has shown that students from about the age of 5 with both
low and high abilities can learn skills associated with critical thinking (Swartz &
Perkins, 1990). These researchers found that students with both low- to medium-
ability thinking can be improved in all subject areas, whereas the thinking of
high-ability students can be improved in particular subject areas. According to
Johnson (2000), thinking skills instruction should be "embedded within the

current curriculum" and used to "help students learn more and learn more deeply" (p. 15).

Another consideration for teachers is that teaching must always be about teaching "something." There are many areas where social studies overlaps with other subjects. Farris (2001) suggests that to "overcome flagging motivation often attributed to the student with learning disabilities, to challenge the gifted readers, and to hook the child with ADD [Attention Deficient Disorder], lively children's literature books are the answer" (p. 333). Reading quality children's literature enhances a child's understanding of social studies. McGowan and Guzzetti (1991) note:

> Literary works are packed with conceptual knowledge about the human condition and can supply meaningful content for skill-building experiences. . . . Perhaps more completely and certainly more intensely than with textbooks, a creative teacher can use trade books to engage students in the pursuit of such citizenship competencies as processing information, examining other points of view, separating fact from opinion, and solving problems. (p. 18)

Student motivation may be increased to a greater degree through the use of children's books with social studies themes and content than with a social studies textbook alone. Textbooks are primarily concerned with facts, whereas literature is primarily concerned with feelings: compassion, humanness, misfortune, happiness, awe, and grief (Maxim, 1999). Unfortunately, social studies teaching and learning—more than any other subject—is dominated by textbooks (Loewen, 1995). Most of the criticisms aimed at textbooks (physical size and weight; prose style that is bland and voiceless; and excessive coverage of information that makes them boring) should really be about targeting the ways teachers use them (Maxim, 1999). Texts are not meant to be the entire social studies curriculum, only a single resource.

Other subjects besides language arts have the potential for connecting to social studies. For example, environmental studies combines the subjects of science and social studies. This is true for most of the *people-related* topics in social studies. However, social studies does make a unique contribution in the curriculum by

- Providing a forum for children to learn about and practice democracy.
- Helping children to explain their world.
- Assisting children in positive self-development.
- Helping children acquire a foundational understanding of history, geography, biography, and the social sciences.
- Promoting a genuine sense of the social fabric.

Above all, social studies is the only curriculum subject with people constantly at the center of the subject matter (Ellis, 2002).

Implication of Child Development in Social Studies

As in other subject areas, age and developmental levels play a part in effective teaching and learning. This is particularly true in social studies, where children need a wealth of concrete and visual items to enhance development of spatial skills. The level of development of social skills and values is also of concern. Teachers of very young children provide experiences that both tie children together as a group with commonalities and help them identify traits that make them unique as individuals. Activities that feature name games, focus on physical similarities and differences, and family-based themes are all a part of a good developmental social studies program.

Constantly creating situations where social skills are enhanced is also an important social studies developmental process. It is difficult to have a country in which values are a part of one's life, yet where there have been few opportunities while growing up to express one self, feel empathy, belong to a group, and practice other social skills. It is difficult to have democracy in a place where only authoritarianism has been seen and where children have few choices and feel powerless. Small activities such as voting on tomorrow's snack from a menu of items, sharing in a core group, or choosing a center or project increase social studies elements in the classroom daily. Providing time for young children to *play* in social situations is also a huge step in this direction, as is directed or creative dramatics (e.g., phone conversations, pretending to be at the store, doing chores, etc.). Role play is also a part of communication, particularly with issues that involve the emotions, empathy, and decision making. A teacher may ask for scenarios such as, "Let's pretend that Roberto accidentally tore Janna's paper. How would Roberto feel? What could he say? What could Janna say?"

Reflective Teaching

As a *people-centered* subject, social studies teachers must tackle controversial, often contradictory, issues such as conflict and respect. Savage and Armstrong (1996) write, "Teaching social studies is not for cowards" (p. 8). Social studies teachers "tend to be thoughtful people who have a point of view and who are willing to stand up for their commitments" (p. 9). These are important qualities and actions to model for students. Along with modeling appropriate behaviors, social studies teachers must make many decisions daily regarding instruction. Essentially, they decide what role they and the students will play during an activity. For example, teachers will be *experts* during direct instruction lessons, *consultants* or *facilitators* during cooperative group events, and *coaches* during inquiry and problem-solving activities. Despite the role changes, all teaching methods have some common elements. All require teacher direction of the student thinking processes, preparation, concern with motivation, setting up of the learning experience, and the creation of some evaluative technique. There are many factors to consider when choosing a particular teaching method. Not all students learn in the same way or have the same skill level, so teaching successes may vary. Also, some methods may be more appropriate for certain topics than for others.

Teaching decisions require reflective practice. The most effective teachers are those who regularly examine their own teaching. Grant and Vansledright (2001) believe that teachers should perform "regular examinations of and introspection into what, who, and how you're teaching, and why you choose to do what you do" (p. 265). They must consider how their beliefs and actions will influence their students and the subject(s) they teach. This is particularly true in social studies, where teachers may have strong beliefs and values that affect what occurs in the classroom.

Teachers should engage in professional growth with regard to social studies. Teaching and learning within a particular discipline such as social studies is not static but rather in a state of flux. Texts are adopted for a number of years, so information can become outdated quickly; teachers should be sure to present current knowledge and to make use of current events that touch the lives of their children. Teachers also cannot become complacent in their thinking about what, who, and how they teach, and they should update their methods to match children's needs.

Teachers are professional educators and should make connections with others in their field. Professional organizations offer opportunities to interact with colleagues and gain insights into current research on teaching and learning strategies. It is imperative that teachers keep up to date with the latest issues and trends in their fields. Social studies teachers have numerous resources. For example, they can consult the monthly and quarterly journals published by the National Council for the Social Studies (NCSS)—*Social Education* and *Social Studies and the Young Learner*. The NCSS also publishes a monthly newsletter for members and maintains an online site at http://www.ncss.org that contains a great deal of information. There are also links to listservs maintained by NCSS members where social studies educators may freely exchange information and ideas. There are a number of state and regional organizations that also provide professional development opportunities for social studies educators.

Technology as a Teaching Tool

One of the most important issues in social studies education today is the role of technology in teaching and learning. Technology has played a leading role in connecting the world in unprecedented ways. Instantaneous communication, access to media and popular culture, and globalization have contributed to this interconnectedness of the world. Educators need to understand the role of technology in the world of today and the possibilities for the future. Clearly, technology has a role to play in contemporary social studies education.

There are many technologies that might be incorporated into the classroom: television, videos, audio recordings, CD-ROMs, computers, and other tools. Many wonderful CDs, television programs (taped by a media specialist), or videos offer windows to the world and its people to children. Teachers should be sure to view these before class presentation to ensure that they are age-appropriate in content, interest, and presentation. Computers have been placed in some elementary schools since the late 1970s. During those early days they were primarily used to provide drill-and-practice opportunities for students. Students were presented problems and entered their responses; the computer would send a graphic grade—a smily face for correct or an explosion for incorrect. Clearly, this use concerned those educators who came to view computers as centers of busy work with the same limitations as regular worksheets. While many of these drill-and-practice computer programs remain, computer software that seeks to develop higher-level thinking skills in social studies is increasingly important. Some of these software applications are:

1. **Tutorial software:** These programs display information step-by-step and organize questions and answers. Unlike the older drill-and-practice programs, tutorial programs focus on the presentation of new knowledge and skills rather than review and reinforcement of previously acquired information. A popular tutorial program for children 7 and up is Weekly Reader Map Skills, designed to develop children's basic map skills.

2. **Problem-solving software:** These programs present complex situations in which students face a dilemma, choose from a number of possible alternatives, and arrive at a solution. These programs encourage active exploration and discovery. One of the most popular problem-solving programs for children in grades 3 through 8 is *Where in the World is Carmen Sandiego?*

3. **Simulation software:** These programs place students into situations that are as authentic as possible. One of the most popular simulations is *The Oregon Trail*. It presents a series of decisions that pioneers faced in 1847 as they set out in wagon trains to find new homes in the Oregon Territory. For example, if a student decides to hunt or stop at a fort, he or she loses time and may fail to pass through the mountains before the winter snows begin. This could lead to illness or not having enough food. With each decision, children are shown the consequences of their choices. Other popular simulation programs are *SimAnt, SimCity, SimSafari,* and *SimEarth*. In each of these simulations, children are placed into setting where they describe, create, and control a system.

4. **Word processing, database, and spreadsheet software:** These programs are designed to facilitate the efficient collecting, revising, storing, and printing of text. Word processing programs enable students to prepare neat, well-edited written pieces, as well as other products such as signs, banners, brochures, and newspapers with the desktop publishing features found in many word-processing programs. Databases are simply collections of data. These database programs allow a level of organization never before possible.

Students can enter, store, and compare information about nearly any social studies topic. Primary children can facilitate mathematical calculations and social studies questions with simple spreadsheets such as developing a budget for a school project; comparing popular and electoral votes by state in a national election.

5. **Hypermedia presentation software:** These programs are communication tools that combine video, graphics, animation, and text. These "authoring" programs enable students to organize and communicate information in more aesthetically innovative ways. Some of the most popular presentation software titles for students are *PowerPoint, HyperStudio, ClarisWorks,* and *KidPix.* Social studies is a perfect place for students to begin class, small group, or individual presentations through these tools.

6. **Information gathering software:** CD-ROMs and the Internet offer exciting maps, news articles, ready-made databases, and virtual tours to areas, including countries, museums, and other interesting places. Encyclopedias and search engines help students find information on a wealth of social studies topics.

6. **Telecommunications software:** Classroom connections to the Internet are becoming increasingly common. With these connections, the following areas of cyberspace are accessible by students:
The World Wide Web
Electronic mail (e-mail)
Newsgroups and listservs

Children can "chat" with other students in many places in their school, city, state, country, and the world and participate in joint social study projects with other classrooms in their school or afar. E-mails can be written to support their beliefs on issues to guide children in showing their responsibilities to let other know their feelings on issues. They can scan photos and write join newspapers, books, and reports. Access to the Internet can, and should, do more than merely provide more information to students. The Internet should allow children to open the doors of their classroom and interact with people all over the world.

Consider the following practice question:

Children normally learn best when social studies is:

- **A.** Separated from other subjects.
- **B.** Integrated across the disciplines according to a common theme.
- **C.** Taught only from the textbook.
- **D.** Taught by an expert academic specialist in social studies.

Students should be given opportunities to make deeper connections with topics so lessons will become more meaningful. The best answer is *B.*

STANDARDS IV (HISTORY) AND X (SCIENCE, TECHNOLOGY, AND SOCIETY)

The social studies teacher applies knowledge of significant historical events and developments, as well as of multiple historical interpretations and ideas, in order to facilitate student understanding of relationships between the past, the present, and the future. The social studies teacher understands developments in science and technology, and uses this knowledge to facilitate student understanding of the social and environmental consequences of scientific discovery and technological innovation.

Competency 017 (History): The teacher demonstrates knowledge of significant historical events and developments and applies social science skills to historical information, ideas, and issues.

The beginning teacher: knows traditional points of reference in the history of Texas, the United States, and the world; demonstrates knowledge of the individuals, events, and issues that shaped the history of Texas; understands similarities and differences among Native American groups in Texas and the Western Hemisphere before European colonization; understands the causes and effects of European exploration and colonization of Texas, the United States, and the Western Hemisphere; knows how geographic contexts and processes of spatial exchange (diffusion) have influenced events in the past and helped to shape the present; demonstrates knowledge of the origins and diffusion of major scientific, mathematical, and technological discoveries and the effects of discoveries throughout history; relates historical information and ideas to information and ideas in other social sciences and in other disciplines; knows how to formulate historical research questions and use appropriate procedures to reach supportable judgments and conclusions; understands historical research and knows how historians locate, gather, organize, analyze, and report information using standard research methodologies; knows characteristics and uses of primary and secondary sources used for historical research (e.g., databases, maps, photographs, media services, the Internet, biographies, interviews, questionnaires, artifacts); analyzes historical information from primary and secondary sources; and evaluates information in relation to bias, propaganda, point of view, and frame of reference; applies evaluative, problem-solving, and decision-making skills to historical information, ideas, and issues; knows how to communicate and interpret historical information and ideas in written and graphic forms; analyzes historical data (e.g., population statistics, patterns of migration, voting trends and patterns) using appropriate analytical methods.

Consider the following practice question:

Mrs. Scott is teaching her third-grade students about the Underground Railroad. She wants to make sure the lesson is meaningful, so she plans to bring in a primary source. Which of the following would be considered a primary source?

A. A biography of Harriet Tubman.
B. A wanted poster of Harriet Tubman from those times.
C. *Follow the Drinking Gourd,* a book by Jeanette Winter.
D. The textbook chapter on the Underground Railroad.

Choices *A, C,* and *D* are all examples of secondary sources since they report information second-hand. The best answer is *B* because this poster was a "witness to the events" of the times. *this would have been better!*

Teaching History *→should be ONE subject only!*

History has long been dominant in the social studies curriculum at all levels. The topics of history are similar across grade levels, although teaching methods and objectives may vary. For example, a third-grade class studying the community may use a computer to create a database of historical places in their community. These might include historic buildings, old homes, and other places of historical interest. Second-grade students may study older forms of transportation used in their communities (walking, horses, trains, and so on) and compare these to newer forms (cars and planes). They, too, could create a database for their information. This would allow children to categorize, arrange, sort, select, and display their information. These examples demonstrate how EC-4 students could meet history standards in different ways.

Unfortunately, most social studies teaching does not encourage students to connect their newly learned concepts with their lived experiences. Most classroom experiences are determined by the content of textbooks rather than the pursuit of meaningful knowledge. According to Levstik and Barton (2001), history for primary grade-level students rarely amounts to more than learning a few isolated facts about famous people connected to major holidays. In fact, when asked why they think history is a subject at school or how it might help them, students sometimes can think of little except that it might be useful is they were ever on "Jeopardy!" They do not see it as patterns of human behavior from which we can learn. To get more understanding from history, teachers must begin with the concerns and interests of students and must help them find answers to questions that grow out of those concerns and interests (p. 14). History must be made to seem alive! The National Standards for History (National Center for History in the Schools, 1996) stress that teachers should bring history alive by using "stories, myths, legends, and biographies that capture children's imaginations and immerse them in times and cultures of the recent and long-ago past" (p. 3). Documents, witnesses, and physical remains (artifacts) offer students clues to historical mysteries. Social studies teachers need to provide students opportunities to apply critical thinking skills to organize and use information acquired from all these resources. *myths & legends should NOT be part of history!!*

One way of understanding social questions involves organizing and judging information from primary and secondary sources such as computer software, interviews, biographies, and artifacts. *Primary sources* are first-hand sources; *secondary sources* use primary sources to deliver information at a later time. It is "second-hand" information. For example, suppose a car accident occurred in which a car hit another from behind. A description of the accident that a witness gives to the police is a primary source because it comes from someone actually there at the time. The story in the newspaper the next day is a secondary source because the reporter who wrote the story did not actually witness it. The reporter is presenting a way of understanding the accident or an *interpretation*. Students should be able to locate each of these types of sources, use them, and also understand that both can contain biased viewpoints, particularly secondary sources. In the example above, the eyewitness may himself have been hit in the past and embellished the story a bit because he or she is in sympathy with the driver who was hit, as could be the reporter. Social students teachers must teach children to analyze all such data for "spin," or bias of some kind. Children need to be able to carry out investigations just like real historians.

Social scientists gather a great deal of facts and figures about people's activities. By organizing these data in different ways, they may observe certain patterns and relationships that will lead to useful conclusions. Statistics are numerical data that represent information about a given subject. There are many ways to display statistics, and these can be used in all areas of the social sciences. Graphs are a convenient way of organizing data. An economist could use a *line graph* to show the change in oil production over time. A political scientist might present statistics in a *bar graph*. A *circle graph,* or pie chart, is an easy way to show the parts, or percentages, into which a total amount is divided. The full circle represents 100 percent, a half circle is 50 percent, and so on. Circle graphs are useful for showing the percentage of the population of a large city represented by each of its ethnic groups. For young children, graphing may begin with percentages of each type of pet they have at home, type of lunch desired each day (and the importance of ordering correctly), or type of shoes worn. *Charts* and *tables* are also important means for organizing and displaying information. Children should be taught to read and interpret this information and to construct these types of graphs using keys. Again, social studies teachers should always remember to establish a rationale for collecting and using data (rather than, "Isn't this interesting?"). For example, a local grocery store might want to stock gerbil food and shavings for cages when data shows local households have a number of these animals as pets.

Other visual means are also effective in EC-4 social studies teaching and learning. *Timelines,* for example, are graphic representations of a succession of historical events, constructed by dividing a unit of time into proportional segments. A timeline is an effective method of illustrating time spans between events. As children study the past, timelines help them put events into perspective by allowing them to "see" when important things happened (Maxim, 1999).

Because young children relate to time as it is meaningful to them, their first experiences in grasping prehistory experience is focusing on routines. Calendar time helps bring attention to the day of the week, yesterday, tomorrow, the seasons, and the routine of the day (in terms of teaching *after* and *before* and to sequence events). To help young children understand how things change with time, teachers can measure children throughout the year, keep a lost-tooth chart, photo board, and so forth. Maxim recommends that, for the very youngest students, teachers construct timelines on topics of immediate experience. Routines of the daily schedule can be illustrated on a beginning timeline. Older children can create a timeline for their school year or neighborhood to reinforce the concept of change and cycles. When students have some experience with constructing timelines around events close to them, teachers should expand students' experiences by sequencing major events over a period of time. For instance, children can use clothespins to clip cutouts of symbols for major holidays in the United States in sequence of the year. The students must decide which symbol comes first, second, and so on as they place the cutouts in proper sequence. Children can also construct a timeline of important events of their lives by illustrating these on a long strip of adding machine tape. They make decisions about what events to include (birth of a sibling, first time to ride a bike, etc.).

Maps are another visual means of representing information. Maps are used to show distances, strategic locations, boundaries, physical features, resources, climate, and so on. In order to use maps effectively, students must learn to "read" them. Learning to read maps is similar to learning to read the printed word. Children must learn to associate arbitrary symbols with something real in the environment. The "actual symbolic representation on maps is too abstract for kindergarten and early primary-grade children to use," notes Maxim (1999, p. 369). However, this does not mean that young children are incapable of using symbols of any kind (as parents realize when they are passing the "Golden Arches").

There are a variety of activities that will help students discover relationships between some physical aspect of their environment and its symbol. For example, children can informally play with blocks and other building materials. Playing with blocks will help children conceptualize space as they construct environments that simulate real locations ("In the Block Center today, boys and girls, I want you to try to build our classroom"). Teachers might also take students on a class trip to take pictures around the school or neighborhood. These pictures can then be mounted on blocks of wood and children can be encouraged to play with them as they would their regular blocks and reconstruct their neighborhood. *Photographs* can be used to present visual data, and a number of schools are acquiring digital cameras that enhance technology connections. Teachers first take pictures of children to show them that familiar things can be represented by *scale* models. They point out to them that their picture is small while they are really much bigger. Taking pictures of many of the things in the classroom and asking children to point to the real object leads children to understand that real things can be represented in much smaller ways. *Cartoons* are also a way to develop symbolic understandings. Cartoons may be used to depict real people and to express all sorts of ideas and opinions. It is important to remind children that hurtful or otherwise inappropriate images or expressions should never be used. The most important thing to remember is to begin with symbols that are familiar to students or are seen often (the heart symbol in "I [heart] Texas"; the international symbol for men's or women's restrooms; the symbol for "don't walk"; and so forth.

EC-4 social studies teachers help students understand the concept of historical time, investigate their personal and family histories, and examine other sources of historical data. Personal involvement will help students acquire a more balanced sense of history—it is not only something one *knows* but also something that one *lives*. Children must be given opportunities to *explore* social studies rather than simply be *exposed* to it. These standards ask that teachers not only know facts and provide meaningful activities but that they also know and have students involved in the methods of historians. Seefeldt (1997) gives these methods as: (1) problem identification [i.e., investigators perceive that a problem is meaningful to them in some way], (2) the ability to gather information from the past, (3) the ability to observe data carefully, (4) the ability to analyze data and make inferences, and (5) the ability to draw conclusions.

According to Maxim (1999), to develop our students' interests in history we must have a firm grasp of not only how to teach but also what to teach. Successful history teaching requires that EC-4 teachers develop their knowledge of people, ideas, and events in the past. Knowledge of history will ultimately provide both teachers and students some insight for a better understanding of current problems and conflicts.

History Content

Given the extensive nature of the information that this standard covers, it will be broken down into the following headings and subheadings:

United States History and International Relations
Exploration and settlement
National unity
Regional differences
Industrial growth
Reform movements
International affairs
International relations between the superpowers
The present

Texas History
Earliest inhabitants
Early European exploration and development
Revolution, republic, and statehood

Each subheading will begin with a key question dealing with the information contained within that topic. It is advisable to use these questions as a guide for your reading, as well as a review mechanism for each section. The organizing questions may also provide possible themes for developing history learning opportunities for your students.

United States History and International Relations

I. Exploration and Settlement
Key question: *How did a desire for freedom influence daily life and government in early America?*

- From the fifteenth through the seventeenth centuries, European nations explored and settled large parts of the New World. The Spaniards, landing first in the West Indies, established colonies in South America and Mexico. Later, in 1565, they explored Florida and founded a settlement at **St. Augustine.** Their explorations were motivated by the search for gold, the desire for territory, and the wish to convert native populations to Roman Catholicism.

- In the 1600s, the French and the English explored the wilderness lands of North America. The French founded colonies in Canada and along the Mississippi River. They were more interested in staking claims to land and trading in furs and fish than in developing permanent settlements.

- The English settled along the eastern coast, founding their first permanent colony in 1607, in **Jamestown,** Virginia. During the early years the majority of settlers died of starvation, various diseases, or hostile action by Native Americans. From 1608 to 1609, the strong leadership of **John Smith** kept the colony from collapsing. When Smith returned to England in 1609, the conditions in the colony became critical again. In 1612, John Rolfe discovered a new type of tobacco in Virginia, which became the first cash crop in the New World. Harsh conditions, coupled with poor relations with the Native Americans resulted in decreasing numbers of English immigrants to the colony. In 1619, the need for workers brought the first Africans to Virginia. At first they were treated as **indentured servants** rather than slaves. An indentured servant was a person who agreed to work several years for a person or company in return for passage to America. Trade was also important to the English settlers, who began to export tobacco, cotton, fur, and timber.

- The desire for political and religious freedom brought many colonists to the New World. Puritans, Catholics, Quakers, and Pilgrims sought the right to worship without government interference.

- In 1620 the **Pilgrims,** a small group of religious separatists led by **William Bradford,** came to America on the **Mayflower.** Prior to coming ashore they drafted an agreement, the **Mayflower Compact,** committing these settlers of the **Plymouth Colony** in Massachusetts to self-government and majority rule. Thus, the Compact outlined the first form of **democracy** in America. This settlement marked the beginning of permanence and expansion on the North American continent.

- In 1629 **Puritans,** a larger group than the Pilgrims, led by **John Winthrop,** formed a joint-stock company they called the Massachusetts Bay Company. A **joint-stock company** raises capital by the sale of stocks. English King Charles I, happy to be rid of the Puritans, granted the group a charter to found a colony in the New World. Winthrop wanted to create a colony that would be a "city on a hill," to model for the world what a Christian community ought to be. The Puritans organized carefully prior to their journey, which meant that the **Massachusetts Bay Colony** never went through the "starving years" that other new colonies had during their first years. Other also settled parts of the colonies because of religious tolerance—William Penn founded Pennsylvania for the Quakers and George Calvert, Lord Baltimore, was given Maryland for Catholic settlement.

- In 1692 Puritans in Massachusetts were shaken by the accusations of young girls in **Salem** that they were being tormented by several witches who lived in the village. The **Witch Trials** resulted in 20 executions, 19 by hanging and one crushed by rocks.

- By the 1700s, town meetings were conducted throughout the New England colonies. People voted, created their own laws, and sent representatives to colonial assemblies.

- By the eighteenth century, **individualism,** the belief in the dignity and worth of each person, had a firm religious and political base in the British colonies.

- Colonial economies experienced rapid growth as settlers worked to establish their own farms and businesses. Differing geographical and economic conditions led to three distinctive groups of colonies: New England, Middle, and Southern.

- The **New England colonies** of Massachusetts, New Hampshire, Rhode Island, and Connecticut, which had poor soil, generally developed fishing, trading, and shipbuilding industries.

- The **Middle colonies** of New York, New Jersey, Pennsylvania, and Delaware grew large quantities of grain on family-sized farms.

- The **Southern colonies** of Maryland, Virginia, North Carolina, South Carolina, and Georgia had a climate and soil that favored the development of large plantations on which tobacco, indigo, and rice were grown.

II. National Unity
Key question: *What led the states to adopt a central government in 1790?*

- During the first half of the eighteenth century, England pursued a policy of **salutary neglect** and did not attempt to exercise much economic or political control over its North American colonies.

- In 1763, however, as a result of enormous debts arising from the **French and Indian War,** England decided to levy taxes on the prospering colonies.

- The **Stamp Act of 1763** placed a tax on newspapers and legal documents. Following colonial protests, this tax was repealed.

- In 1767, England imposed the **Townsend Acts,** which required new taxes on tea, glass, paint, and paper. Most colonial legislatures sent protests to the British Parliament. The British initially responded by increasing the number of troops stationed in America. By 1770, tensions between colonists and soldiers ran high. In Boston, the friction between the two groups led to an incident in which five colonists were killed. Samuel Adams labeled the incident the **Boston Massacre.** In 1770 Parliament, under a new prime minister, repealed all the taxes except the one on tea. Angry colonists threw all the tea from English cargo ships into Boston Harbor. In response to the **Boston Tea Party,** England closed the port of Boston and severely limited self-government in Massachusetts. The fundamental disagreement was over England's taxation of the colonists without colonial representation in the decision-making process: **taxation without representation.**

- The British government passed four acts, collectively known by the colonists as the **Intolerable Acts,** in response to the dumping of the tea. The port of Boston was closed until the tea was paid for; the Massachusetts royal governor was given greater authority over the colonial legislature; royal officials accused of a crime could be tried elsewhere; and the Quartering Act required American colonists to house British troops.

- In 1774, Americans formed the **First Continental Congress** in response to the Intolerable Acts. They met in Philadelphia and their first act was to draft a petition to the British Parliament to protest the Intolerable Acts. The colonists protested to England and began to organize a militia to protect themselves.

- Initially, the British government paid little attention to the First Continental Congress. By 1775 the British sent more troops to Massachusetts to arrest the leaders of the rebellion. **General Gage** led 700 British soldiers to Concord on a mission to search for and destroy a reported stockpile of colonial arms and ammunition. The Americans tracked the British troop movements and sent two riders, **Paul Revere** and **William Dawes,** to alert the countryside.

- When the British got to Lexington they found a group of 70 American **Minutemen,** militiamen ready at a moment's notice, waiting for them on the village green. A British officer ordered the men to drop their weapons and disperse. The Minutemen held on to their weapons but did begin to leave the green. At the same time, a shot was fired. This was *the shot heard 'round the world,* marking the beginning of the Revolutionary War. The American **Minutemen** drove the British from **Concord** and **Lexington.**

- In June 1775, at the **Battle of Bunker Hill,** the Americans were driven back, but they inflicted huge losses on the British.

- In 1776, Thomas Paine published *Common Sense,* which gave reasons why it was foolish to believe that Americans could reconcile with England.

- The colonists issued the **Declaration of Independence in 1776,** in which the basic principles of the United States government were set forth.

- **George Washington** led the American army. The Continental Army spent one very hard winter at Valley Forge, Pennsylvania. Washington led a surprise attack on the British by sneaking the army across the Delaware River in the middle of winter, showing the British their resolve.

- In October 1781, the **Battle of Yorktown** was the last major battle of the revolution. The British forces, under the leadership of **Cornwallis,** surrendered to the joint forces of the Americans under Washington and the French under **Rochambeau.**

- In 1783, the signing of the **Treaty of Paris** meant that the colonies had won their freedom from England.

- After the Revolutionary War, the colonies became independent states, joined together in an association under the **Articles of Confederation,** which were ratified in 1781.

- The Articles established a weak central government with a Congress that could declare war but was not allowed to recruit an army. There were no central courts. States taxed each other's goods and used different currencies.

- **Shays' Rebellion,** an uprising of debtor farmers in Massachusetts, showed the states how inadequate the Articles of Confederation were. The central government did not have the authority to put down the rebellion.

- Recognizing the Articles' many weaknesses, 55 delegates, the **Founding Fathers,** from the various states met in Philadelphia and eventually drafted the **Constitution,** which was adopted in 1790.

- The Constitution was a result of a series of *compromises.* Among the most important were those concerning representation in the legislature and the method of electing the president, the debate over ratification divided the nation into **Federalists,** who supported the Constitution, and **anti-Federalists** who feared a strong central government might abuse its power and the liberties of the people and the states.

- The promise of a **Bill of Rights** led the anti-Federalists to accept the new government. These are the first ten amendments to the Constitution. Anti-Federalists wanted to guarantee that citizens would be protected from the new government so they wanted many rights specified: freedom of religion, speech, press, assembly, and government petition; to bear arms; against unreasonable search and seizure; speedy and public trial; and no self-incrimination, excessive bail, or cruel and unusual punishment.

III. Regional Differences

Key question: *How did the territorial and economic growth of the country lead to the War between the States?*

- During the first half of the nineteenth century, the United States acquired through wars, treaties, and purchases more and more land west of the original thirteen colonies.
- In 1803, **President Thomas Jefferson** bought territory from the French, the **Louisiana Purchase,** which nearly doubled the size of the United States.
- Southern colonies who depended on agriculture increasingly used slave labor brought from Africa.
- Protected from Europe by an ocean, U.S. leaders continued to encourage territorial expansion and adopted a policy of neutrality toward foreign powers.
- In 1823, **President James Monroe** restated this policy of noninterference in the **Monroe Doctrine** to warn European nations against intervening in the Western Hemisphere.
- By the 1840s, people began to believe in **manifest destiny,** the idea that the United States was destined to expand from ocean to ocean.
- In 1848, when gold was discovered in California at **Sutter's Mill** (near present-day Sacramento) the question of slavery in the Western territories became more critical. The **"forty-niners"** were a rough group, and California became a wild and lawless place. As a result, many of the fortune seekers had been too afraid to bring their valuable slaves to the area. Therefore, in 1849, California sought statehood as a free state. This posed a significant threat to the balance of free states and slave states in the United States.
- As the country grew and prospered, regional differences became more pronounced. The Northeast developed an industrial and trading economy, while the South became more dependent on exporting cash agricultural crops to Europe. In the West, cheap land encouraged smaller family farms, which sent food to Northeastern cities.
- Regional differences led to **sectionalism,** with Americans looking at issues increasingly in terms of what would benefit their region. Northerners favored **tariffs** on imported goods to protect their industries. Southerners, who imported more goods, opposed tariffs. Northerners favored the **National Bank,** which gave them a stable currency and investment funds. Westerners and Southerners favored state banks, which would give them easier credit. Westerners wanted federal funds for the construction of roads and canals so they could get their produce to market. Southerners favored the extension of slavery to new territories, something Northerners and Westerners both opposed. Growing sectionalism meant that Northerners and Westerners came to view the further extension of slavery as empowering the South at their expense.

- With the 1828 election of **Andrew Jackson,** sectional issues dominated national politics. A Westerner, Jackson antagonized Southerners by enforcing tariffs and alienated Northerners by dismantling the National Bank.

- Sectional disputes further intensified when the Supreme Court, in the **Dred Scott** case, invalidated compromises over the issues of extending slavery into new territories. The gap between the industrial North and agricultural South widened as both sought to control the central government.

- When **Abraham Lincoln** was elected president in 1860, the Southern states felt that their interests were no longer represented by the federal government and seceded from the Union.

- Under the leadership of **Jefferson Davis,** eleven states formed the **Confederate States of America** (the **Confederacy**). The Confederate States were: South Carolina, Mississippi, Florida, Alabama, Georgia, Louisiana, **Texas,** Virginia, Arkansas, Tennessee, and North Carolina. The four slaveholding border states—Maryland, Delaware, Kentucky, and Missouri—and nineteen free states remained in the **Union.**

- The **Civil War** began in 1861 when Confederate soldiers fired on federal troops at **Fort Sumter** in South Carolina.

- The **Union** had a decided advantage over the Confederacy, with twice the population of the South and three-quarters of the nation's wealth. In addition, it had more factories and railroads.

- In July 1862, the first major battle of the war, the **First Battle of Bull Run** resulted in a victory for the Southern forces. General "Stonewall" Jackson led the Confederate troops against the poorly trained Union troops under the command of **General Irvin McDowell.** This led to a shakeup in command in the Northern forces. Lincoln had great difficulty finding someone to command the Union army. From 1862 to 1864 the succession of men Lincoln tried as commander of the Union army was: **General George McClellan, General Ambrose Burnside, General Joseph "Fighting Joe" Hooker, General George Meade,** and finally **General Ulysses Grant.** With Grant, Lincoln found a general who would be capable of winning the war.

- Naval engagements were an important aspect of the Civil War. Early in the conflict, the Confederate navy achieved supremacy with its **ironclad** vessel, the **Merrimack.** Originally, the Northern navy had only wooden ships that could not compete with the iron-plated ship. In 1862, the South's naval supremacy was ended by the Northern ironclad ship, the **Monitor.**

- In September 1862, the **Battle of Antietam,** technically a Northern victory, resulted in the single bloodiest engagement of entire war. At the end of the single day of fighting, 22,726 lay dead, dying, or wounded.

- The most celebrated battle of the Civil War took place July 1 through 3, 1863, at the small town of Gettysburg, Pennsylvania. In the **Battle of Gettysburg** Meade led 90,000 Union soldiers against Lee's smaller Confederate contingent of 75,000 soldiers. Meade was severely criticized for allowing Lee to retreat with his remaining army back into the Confederacy. Critics said that Meade had missed a chance to end the war. However, the battle so weakened the Southern army that Lee never again attempted a serious invasion of the North.

- The Battle of Gettysburg was one of the costliest battles in history. When the fighting ended on July 3, there were 50,000 fallen bodies on the battlefield. The battlefield cemetery was officially dedicated on November 19, 1863. President Abraham Lincoln delivered the dedication. In his relatively short speech, later referred to as the **Gettysburg Address,** he memorialized the Union dead and emphasized the power of their sacrifice. He placed the common soldier at the center for the struggle for equality as he reminded the audience of the higher purpose for which their blood had been shed.

- On January 1, 1863, Lincoln issued the **Emancipation Proclamation,** freeing the slaves in the Confederacy. Immediately, it freed only a few slaves, but it clearly established for the North that this was a war being fought not only to preserve the Union but also to eliminate slavery.

- By 1865, the Confederacy was defeated. Confederate General **Robert E. Lee** formally surrendered to Union general **Ulysses S. Grant** at **Appomattox,** Virginia, and the nation began the hard task of recovery.

- More than 618,000 Americans died in the course of the Civil War, more than have died in all American wars combined.

IV. Industrial Growth

Key question: *What were the effects of industrial growth on farms and cities?*

- Reconstruction hit the South very hard economically, as the North sought to punish it for the war. Many lost their land because of the inability to pay taxes and produce crops (lost of life, limb, and workers), so that even agriculture was depressed.

- In the South, during the Civil War and **Reconstruction,** Blacks were given constitutional guarantees of freedom and protection through the **Emancipation Proclamation** and the **Civil War amendments to the Constitution** (Thirteenth, Fourteenth, and Fifteenth).

- As a result of these protections, Southern states passed **Jim Crow laws,** which legalized **segregation** and other laws that denied Blacks the right to vote.

- Most Blacks became sharecroppers, who farmed other people's land in exchange for a portion of their crops.

- Unlike Southern sharecroppers, Western and Midwestern farmers benefited from the rapid industrialization of the period. As agriculture became more mechanized, they were freed from backbreaking labor. However, they felt they were denied their fair share of the nation's wealth. Farmers often went into debt to purchase new equipment. Railroads charged them exorbitant rates to transport produce to markets, and middlemen siphoned off much of their profits. Farmers therefore demanded government regulation of railroad rates and cheap loans to ease their debts. They joined the **Grange,** a movement pressing their demands for reform and also formed the backbone of the **Greenback** and **Populist** parties.

- In 1880, only one-quarter of the population of the United States lived in cities, but by 1910, that figure had almost doubled. Rapid technological advances of the industrial revolution fostered the development and expansion of industries. Scientific production techniques, such as the **assembly line**, transformed U.S. industry, the economy, and society. Henry Ford's use of the assembly line to produce automobiles saw the United States go from four cars on the roads in 1895 to nearly five million by 1917. In 1916, while Ford was putting more cars on the road, the **Federal Aid Roads Act** established the framework for constructing a national network of highways. Americans became more mobile than ever before.

- Between 1880 and 1910, immigrants as well as farmers flocked to U.S. cities to take jobs in the factories. They received low wages and worked under hazardous conditions. In 1911, a fire at the **Triangle Shirtwaist Factory** focused national attention on unsafe working conditions. One hundred forty-six people, mainly women, died because exit doors had been locked by management in order to keep out union organizers.

- To help workers, the **Knights of Labor** and other unions were started. **Samuel Gompers** founded the **American Federation of Labor (AFL)** in 1886.

- At the same time, industrial leaders, such as **Andrew Carnegie** and **Cornelius Vanderbilt,** created **trusts** to consolidate their control over steel and railroad companies. They virtually eliminated competition (created **monopolies**) so that they could set high prices and control the market for their products. They became active in state and national politics in order to impede attempts to regulate their industries.

V. Reform Movements
Key question: *How did reforms improve the life of Americans in the first half of the twentieth century?*

- From the turn of the century until the First World War, members of the **Progressive Movement** sponsored legislation to improve the quality of U.S. life.

- Reformers enacted pure food and drugs laws to protect consumers.

- Reformers supported women's efforts to gain the right to vote, which was finally granted in the **Nineteenth Amendment.**

- Child labor was outlawed, and children were guaranteed schooling under compulsory education laws.

- With the passage of **antitrust laws** to eliminate monopolies and other unfair trade practices and the creation of the **Federal Reserve System,** government took on a greater role in regulating the economy.

- After World War I, Americans grew tired of reforms and wanted a Return to Normalcy, an era in which government would play a less important role in people's lives.

- In the "Roaring" 1920s, the economy boomed, and Americans devoted themselves to the making and spending of money. Sports and film stars attracted national attention. Jazz music gained popularity. The novel *The Great Gatsby* (1925), by F. Scott Fitzgerald, came to symbolize the entire era.

- On "Black Tuesday," October 29, 1929, the **stock market crash** brought national prosperity and good times to a sudden and violent end. Stock prices fell rapidly, thousands of people lost their investments, and businesses and banks closed. The nation was soon in the grip of the **Great Depression,** with millions of people unemployed. Families looked for public relief and charitable assistance. In the cities, "soup kitchens" and "bread lines" formed to feed hungry families.

- Rural areas were also hard hit during the Depression. One of the worst droughts in U.S. history began in 1930. The region, stretching north from Texas into the Dakotas, came to be known as "**The Dust Bowl.**" A steady decline in rainfall and an accompanying increase in heat turned fertile farm regions into virtual deserts. Many farmers left their land in search of work. One of the classic portrayals of this period is John Steinbeck's novel *The Grapes of Wrath* (1939).

- **President Franklin Roosevelt (FDR)** proposed a **New Deal** to combat the effects of the depression. He proposed legislation to offer relief to the unemployed, to prevent economic abuses, and to reconstruct the economy. Although FDR's legislative proposals eased some suffering, the Great Depression did not end until the country **mobilized** for war. U.S. industry returned to full strength to manufacture the military machinery necessary for our entry into World War II.

- The **Social Security Act** provided social insurance for the elderly and the unemployed.

- The **Security Exchange Commission (SEC)** was set up to regulate the stock market.

- The **Works Progress Administration (WPA)** gave jobs to the unemployed.

- The **Tennessee Valley Authority (TVA)** put people to work building a series of dams that provided electricity to one of the most depressed rural areas in the nation.

VI. International Affairs

Key question: *What was U.S. foreign policy during the first half of the twentieth century?*

- From the 1890s to the 1940s, U.S. foreign policy alternated between **isolationism** (retreat from international concerns) and **internationalism** (active involvement in world affairs).

- In the late 1890s, the United States adopted an activist foreign policy toward the Caribbean and the Pacific. It began to pursue a policy of **imperialism,** the political and economic control of other territories for purposes of prestige, power, and wealth.

- In 1898 the United States went to war to free Cuba from Spanish rule to protect U.S. trading interests. As a result of the **Spanish-American War,** the United States gained control of Puerto Rico, Guam, and the Philippines. Cuba was liberated but soon became a U.S. protectorate.

- At the same time, the United States annexed the Hawaiian Islands.

- In 1903, the U.S. government gained control of a ten-mile strip of land across which the **Panama Canal** was built.

- In 1914, with the assassination of **Archduke Franz Ferdinand,** European nations took sides and formed powerful alliances. As a result, this local controversy escalated into **World War I.**

- The United States maintained a policy of **neutrality** until 1917, when Germany resumed submarine warfare and sank unarmed U.S. merchant ships and unarmed ships with U.S. passengers aboard such as the *Lusitania.*

- The United States joined the **Allied Powers**—Great Britain, France, and Russia, among others—in fighting the **Central Powers**—Germany, the Austro-Hungarian Empire, and their allies.

- Several new weapons of war were tested during the **trench warfare** of World War I. Poison gas, rapid-fire machine guns, and the airplane are just a few of these weapons of devastation. The war became a virtual **stalemate,** with neither side gaining ground, until the United States entered the war.

- The **American Expeditionary Force (AEF),** under the command of **General John J. "Black Jack" Pershing,** entered the war in the spring of 1918. He gained the nickname "Black Jack" when he led African American troops during his regular army days. Pershing eventually became the highest ranking general in United States history.

- The first major battle in which the AEF participated saw the defeat of the Germans at **Belleau Wood** (June 1918). The entry of the United States into the war was seen to turn the tide in favor of the Allies.

- When Germany accepted defeat in November 1918 both sides signed an **armistice.**

- In early 1918, Russia signed a separate peace agreement with the Central Powers and left the war. This was a result of the October 1917 **Bolshevik Revolution** in which the communists led, by V. I. **Lenin,** took control of Russia.

- During the treaty making at the French palace at **Versailles,** President Woodrow Wilson's idealist **Fourteen Points** to foster world trade and fair territorial settlements were ignored by the European powers. The United States never ratified the Treaty of Versailles due to Wilson's political miscalculations and subsequent stroke.

- Disillusioned with the peace-making process, Americans returned to an isolationist policy and rejected United States membership in the **League of Nations,** an international organization intended to settle international disputes peaceably.

- Without the U.S. influence in the peace process, the Allied powers sought to punish Germany. **Reparations,** or payment for damages, became the central focus of the Treaty. Almost immediately, Germans began to experience devastating economic hardships. It was not long until a charismatic leader, **Adolf Hitler,** emerged to rally the German people into "fighting back" against the people who were opposing them.

- With the rise of militaristic governments—**Adolf Hitler** and the **Nazis** in Germany, **Benito Mussolini** and the **Fascists** in Italy, and the **Emperor Hirohito** and **Admiral Hideki Tojo** in Japan—the postwar settlements did not last long. In the 1930s, these **Axis** powers sought to absorb neighboring countries, and Britain declared a policy of **appeasement** (giving in to keep the peace) in response.

- **World War II** erupted in 1939 when German troops marched into Poland, violating its independence. The United States began by supplying the **Allies,** including France, Great Britain, and the Soviet Union, against the **Axis** powers (Germany, Italy, and Japan), though remaining militarily neutral.

- At 7:55 A.M. the Japanese bombed **Pearl Harbor** in Hawaii. In a little over an hour, Japanese planes surprised and sunk eight battleships and three cruisers, killing more than 2,400 sailors. **President Franklin Delano Roosevelt (FDR)** declared that the United States would enter the war.

- U.S. forces fought the war in both Europe, mainly on land, and the Pacific, mainly on the seas. The chief military planner for the United States was Chief of Staff **George C. Marshall.**

- In 1942–1943 the tide of battle in Europe shifted when the German offensive on the **Eastern Front** was stopped at **Stalingrad** by the Russian forces, and the Americans and Allied forces, under the leadership of **General George Patton,** recaptured North Africa.

- Hitler's **Final Solution** had called for the extermination of the Jews (and other "unsuitables" not of the "master race") of Europe. German Jews were the first be sent to concentration camps. As Germany occupied other countries, the Jewish citizens were identified and sent to concentration camps in southern and central Germany, Poland, and Austria. These camps, originally built to house German political prisoners, became death camps. The **Holocaust** claimed the lives of 6 million Jews, almost two-thirds of Europe's Jewish population.

- On June 6, 1944, the commander of U.S. military forces in Europe, **General Dwight D. Eisenhower,** launched the Allied invasion to liberate France from the Germans—**D-Day.** The Germans had expected the invasion to come at the narrowest part of the English Channel and had not prepared extensive defenses on the beaches of Normandy where the almost 3 million Allied troops came ashore. The D-Day invasion proved to be one of the turning points of the war.

- The land war ended in Europe on May 8, 1945 (VE-Day, Victory in Europe Day), but continued in the Pacific against Japan.

- U.S. strategy in the Pacific could be considered "island hopping." The U.S. Navy and the Marines battled the Japanese on island after island as they moved across the Pacific Ocean toward Japan. There were two separate U.S. operations on the Pacific front: **General Douglas MacArthur,** based in Australia, moved from New Guinea to the Philippines, and **Admiral Chester Nimitz,** in Hawaii, directed U.S. attacks on key Japanese-held islands. Primarily, the Pacific Campaign was waged by forces from the United States, Australia, and New Zealand.

- By 1942, U.S. fear and mistrust of the Japanese increased, particularly for those who were living along the Pacific Coast. FDR authorized **relocation camps** in the interior of the United States to intern all U.S. citizens of Japanese ancestry who were living in California. More than 100,000 people were identified, told to dispose of their possessions (which often meant abandoning them), and taken to these centers. In 1944 their internment was upheld by the Supreme Court. Although most were released in 1945, few were ever compensated for their financial losses.

- In June 1942, Japan lost four aircraft carriers compared to one U.S. carrier in the **Battle of Midway.** This was the first defeat the modern Japanese navy had ever suffered, and it left the United States in control of the Central Pacific.

- Island fighting intensified as U.S. forces advanced toward Japan. Week after week, the Japanese sent *kamikaze* (suicide) planes against the U.S. ships, sacrificing some 3,500 of them while inflicting great damage.

- In February 1945, the **Battle of Iwo Jima,** only 750 miles from Tokyo, was the costliest battle in the history of the Marine Corps. Twenty-six thousand U.S. Marines were killed in this battle.

- The **Battle for Okinawa,** 350 miles south of Japan, was another victory for U.S. forces. The United States and its allies suffered nearly 50,000 casualties on land and sea before Okinawa was taken. Over 100,000 Japanese died in the battle.

- On April 15, 1945, President Roosevelt died during his third term in office. He was succeeded by his vice president, **Harry S Truman.**

- In May 1945, U.S. forces began a firebombing campaign on Tokyo itself. Some 80,000 civilians lost their lives from the firestorms started by the napalm dropped on the city by U.S. bombers. Japan still did not surrender.

- In order to end the war, President Truman made the decision to use two nuclear weapons against Japan. On August 6, 1945, a U.S. B-29, the *Enola Gay,* dropped an atomic bomb on the city of **Hiroshima.** The explosion incinerated 4 square miles of the city, instantly killing more than 80,000 people. Many more survived to suffer the effects of radioactive fallout or pass the effects on to their children in the form of birth defects. A second bomb was dropped on **Nagasaki** on August 9, 1945, inflicting another 100,000 deaths.

- Emperor Hirohito persuaded his ministers to surrender unconditionally on August 14, 1945. On September 2, 1945, on board the U.S. battleship *Missouri* anchored in Tokyo Bay, Japanese officials signed the articles of surrender.

- Over 14 million combatants, not including civilians, lost their lives in World War II.

VII. International Relations between the Superpowers

Key question: *How did the United States react to Soviet expansion after World War II?*

- Since World War II, relations between the Soviet Union and the United States have dominated world affairs. The two nations, along with their allies, kept their wartime pledge to create an international organization, the **United Nations**, to replace the disbanded League of Nations.

- In the late 1940s, the Soviet Union gained control of the governments of Poland, Hungary, Bulgaria, East Germany, Rumania, and Czechoslovakia, later known as the countries behind the **Iron Curtain.**

- The United States responded with the **containment** doctrine to block further Soviet expansion and with the **Truman Doctrine** to provide military and economic aid to countries threatened by **communism.**

- In 1947, the U.S. government offered the **Marshall Plan** to all European nations requiring assistance to rebuild their economies after World War II.

- In 1949, the United States and its Western allies formed the **North Atlantic Treaty Organization** (NATO) to provide for a common military defense against the Soviet Union and its allies.

- In 1955, the Soviet Union responded by creating an alliance of its own—**The Warsaw Pact**—with the communist governments in Eastern Europe.

- The relationship between the two superpowers, particularly during the late 1940s and early 1950s, has been characterized as a **cold war,** a state of tension and hostility just short of declared war.

- The superpowers have also experienced periods of **detente,** or a relaxation of tensions. During such periods, summit conferences, cultural exchanges, and agreements such as the **Limited Nuclear Test Ban Treaty,** the **Helsinki Accords,** and the **Strategic Arms Limitations Treaties** (SALT) have taken place.

- Perceiving Soviet threats to the **Third World** (the underdeveloped nations of Asia, Africa, and Latin America), the United States undertook policies of military alliances and economic and technical aid to prevent a domino effect (the fall of one country to communism leads to the fall of all the neighboring countries) by **containing** communism.

- In Asia, relations between the superpowers were severely strained when Communist forces under the leadership of **Mao Tse-tung** won the civil war in China in 1949. The exiled Chinese government of **Chiang Kai-shek** established their government in Taiwan (Formosa). The United States recognized the Chinese government in Taiwan and refused to recognize the existence of the mainland (Communist) Chinese government until 1979.

- In 1950, the United States fought the **Korean War** to prevent the further expansion of communism. The war ended with an agreement to divide Korea at the 38th parallel. Currently, there are two separate countries on the Korean peninsula: North Korea, which is communist controlled, and South Korea, which is democratic. The United States still maintains a military presence at the 38th parallel to enforce the division.

- The U.S. fought Communist forces in Southeast Asia for more than ten years. By 1954, the United States was paying a major portion of the French war costs in Vietnam. When the French suffered their ultimate defeat in 1954 at **Dien Bien Phu,** President Eisenhower was not prepared to commit U.S. forces to fight in **Vietnam.** An international conference held at Geneva divided the country at the 17th parallel. **Ho Chi Minh** gained control of the North Vietnam, and the French continued to rule in the South. The agreement also stated that an election would be held within two years to decide the unification of the country. That election was never held. Instead, the United States took over for the French and installed a new leader in the South, **Ngo Dinh Diem.**

- In 1960, President Kennedy sent the first U.S. military advisors to Vietnam. The United States was there merely to advise the South Vietnamese military in its fight against the Communists in North Vietnam.

- On August 2, 1964, a U.S. destroyer, the *Maddox,* was fired on by North Vietnamese torpedo boats in the Gulf of Tonkin. On August 4, the U.S. Navy sent another destroyer, the *C. Turner Joy,* into the Gulf of Tonkin with orders to fire at the North Vietnamese torpedo boats if they were fired upon. President Johnson also ordered retaliatory air strikes on North Vietnamese naval bases.

- On August 5, 1964, President Johnson asked Congress to pass a resolution allowing him to take "all necessary measures to repel any armed attack against the forces of the United States and to prevent any further aggression." The resulting **Gulf of Tonkin Resolution** meant that the United States would become an active participant in the conflict. U.S. combat forces in South Vietnam rose from 16,000 in 1963 to 500,000 in 1968.

- In 1968, the Vietnamese launched the **Tet Offensive,** a surprise attack from the North on a major Vietnamese holiday. The U.S. public, watching much of the bloody conflict on the nightly television news, began to doubt whether the United States should remain in the war in Vietnam.

- Richard Nixon, running on an anti war platform, won the election of 1968. Nixon announced that *Vietnamization* of the war would begin immediately. Withdrawals of U.S. troops began in June 1969. This did briefly quiet public protests against the war. However, in April 1970, Nixon ordered the secret bombing of Cambodia, in effect widening the war in Indochina. News of the bombing led to widespread protests across the United States. On May 4, 1970, at Kent State in Ohio, members of the National Guard killed four students and injured nine others as they were protesting the war. Ten days later, police killed two Black students at Jackson State University in Mississippi during a demonstration.

- The growing antiwar sentiment caused Congress to withdraw the **Gulf of Tonkin Resolution** in December 1970. Nixon, however, ignored the action. Then, in June 1971, the *New York Times* published a front-page story on the history of the U.S. war in Vietnam. The feature was based on the findings of a top-secret Defense Department study—**The Pentagon Papers.** The report confirmed what the public had believed for a long time: The government had been dishonest, both in reporting the military progress of the war and in explaining its own motives for U.S. involvement. The Nixon Administration went to court to suppress the documents but the Supreme Court ruled that the press had the right to publish them.

- During this period, the morale and discipline among U.S. troops in Vietnam was rapidly deteriorating. The trial and conviction of **Lieutenant William Calley,** who was charged with overseeing the massacre of over 100 unarmed South Vietnamese civilians in the village of **My Lai,** attracted widespread attention to the dehumanizing effects the war was having on those who fought it.

- Many Americans remain concerned about the thousands of soldiers who never returned from Vietnam. In 1995, the Pentagon reported that there are still 2,202 U.S. soldiers missing in action (MIA) in Southeast Asia—1,618 in Vietnam. Far more Americans are still listed as missing from the Korean War (8,170) and World War II (78,750), but those missing in Vietnam seem particularly significant. This is partly due to the belief of many Americans that U.S. soldiers could be still alive and could be held as prisoners.

- In 1973, the United States and Vietnam signed an agreement to end the war. U.S. involvement in Vietnam was officially over, leaving South Vietnam to its fate.

- In January 1975, forces from North Vietnam invade South Vietnam. **President Gerald Ford** asked Congress for emergency aid to South Vietnam, but the request was refused. In April, the army of North Vietnam marched into Saigon and the South fell.

- In Latin America, since 1959, the United States has been unable to oust the Communist regime of **Fidel Castro** in Cuba.

- In the Middle East, U.S. recognition and support of Israel has antagonized many Arab nations and jeopardized the flow of oil.

- In 1990, when Iraq invaded Kuwait, President George H. W. Bush's administration sent Iraqi leader **Saddam Hussein** an ultimatum to withdraw his troops. Hussein ignored the warning, and in January 1991 operation **Desert Storm** was launched to liberate Kuwait. When the military action began, the United States had 500,000 troops in the **Persian Gulf** region. Kuwait was freed.

VIII. The Present
Key question: *What sorts of domestic issues has the United States faced in the last forty years?*

- Since World War II, the U.S. government has been confronted with a variety of problems and challenges. Slowly, the nation moved toward becoming an integrated society.

- President Truman desegregated the armed services by executive order.

- In 1954, the Supreme Court declared segregation (the tradition of separate but equal) unconstitutional in ***Brown v. the Board of Education of Topeka***. The principal attorney in the case was **Thurgood Marshall.** In 1967, President Johnson named Marshall the first African American Supreme Court Justice.

- In 1955 in Montgomery Alabama, a seamstress named **Rosa Parks** refused to give up her seat on the bus to a white passenger. The bus driver called police and she was arrested. News of her arrest spread rapidly and the National Association for the Advancement of Colored People (NAACP) quickly organized a boycott of the buses in Montgomery. They asked a young pastor named **Dr. Martin Luther King, Jr.,** to lead the boycott. For 381 days, African Americans refused to ride the buses. The boycott remained nonviolent. In late 1956 the Supreme Court ruled in response to a lawsuit brought by one of the boycotters that bus segregation was unconstitutional. The Montgomery Bus Boycott proved that ordinary people could unite and organize a successful protest movement.

- When the Soviet Union launched **Sputnik** in 1957, President Eisenhower played an active role in establishing the **National Aeronautics and Space Administration** (NASA) and passing the **National Defense Education Act** to train more scientists and engineers.

- During the 1960s, Dr. Martin Luther King, Jr., helped make Americans aware of continuing racial injustices.

- Some African Americans did not feel that the Congress had done enough to remedy the centuries of segregation and discrimination. Angry rioters often took to the streets. There was a growing movement that believed that African Americans should take complete control of their communities. One of the movement's leaders was **Malcolm X.** His followers did not take the nonviolent approach that Dr. King's followers had used.

- After Malcolm X was assassinated in 1965, racial tensions increased. In 1966, *Stokely Carmichael* issued a call for "**Black Power.**" Also in that year, *Huey Newton* and *Bobby Seale* founded a political party known as the **Black Panthers** to fight police brutality in predominately African American neighborhoods.

- In 1963, **President John F. Kennedy** sent a bill to Congress that would guarantee equal access to all public accommodations and gave the U.S. Attorney General, Robert Kennedy, the power to file school desegregation lawsuits. To help persuade Congress to pass the bill, more than 250,000 people, including 75,000 whites, came to Washington. There, Dr. King delivered his most famous oration, the "**I Have a Dream**" speech. At that time, the **March on Washington** was the largest demonstration ever held in the United States.

- In 1963, President Kennedy was assassinated in Dallas. Lyndon Johnson, the Vice President at the time, became President. President Johnson continued to pursue Kennedy's civil rights agenda.

- President Kennedy and his brother, the Attorney General of the United States, Robert Kennedy, were concerned with the needs of the poor. However, important domestic poverty legislation was only passed after President John Kennedy was assassinated.

- Under President Johnson, Congress enacted the **War on Poverty** to provide job training and rebuild inner cities. It also passed **Great Society** legislation such as **Medicare,** insuring the health of the elderly, to improve the quality of American life. Unfortunately, the cost of the war in Vietnam was responsible for cutting the budget money available for many of Johnson's social programs.

- Congress passed the **Civil Rights Act of 1964,** barring discrimination in housing and establishing the Equal Opportunity Commission.

- In 1968 the United States lost two great civil rights figures. Both Dr. Martin Luther King, Jr., and Robert Kennedy were assassinated.

- President Kennedy vowed to get a man on the moon by the end of the 1960s. In 1969, President Nixon congratulated **Neil Armstrong** when he became the first man to walk on the moon. With the explosion of the space shuttle **Challenger** on January 28, 1986, U.S. space programs underwent review.

- Abuse of power became a major problem during Richard Nixon's presidency. Nixon and his advisors withheld and covered up information concerning a burglary at Democratic National Headquarters in the **Watergate** building complex during the 1972 presidential campaign. The president and his aides had also used government agencies, such as the FBI and the IRS, for political purposes. When Congress took steps to impeach him, President Richard Nixon resigned from office.

- Through the efforts of **Rachel Carson** and others, America became aware of the need to clean up and preserve the environment. During the Nixon administration, Congress established the **Environmental Protection Agency** and passed legislation to provide clean air and water.

- The economy has been a constant source of worry to U.S. presidents. Under President Johnson, inflation increased at an alarming rate. Presidents Nixon, Ford, and Carter found it difficult to control inflation, especially because Arab oil policies raised the price of energy, thereby affecting the costs of manufacturing and transporting goods. Under President Reagan, inflation was finally halted, but the mounting **budget deficit** became a major problem. President Reagan, however, was able to virtually end the Cold War with the economic collapse of the Soviet Union and the removal of the Berlin Wall, joining East and West Germany.

- **George H. W. Bush** acted to stop the aggression of Iraq when it invaded Kuwait, sending troops (a good many of them were women in support and air positions) into **Desert Storm.**

- During his first term, **Clinton** was involved in a number of controversies ranging from alleged wrongdoing in an Arkansas land deal known as "White-water" to charges of sexual misconduct. The strong economy and the lack of a significant Republican challenger resulted in Clinton's reelection in 1996. Clinton became the first Democrat since FDR to be reelected President. In December 1998 Clinton became the second president in the history of the United States to be **impeached.** Like President Andrew Johnson, Clinton was tried and acquitted.

- In 2000, the Republican Party nominated for President Texas Governor George W. Bush, son of the former President George H. W. Bush. This resulted in one of the closest presidential elections in history. This presidential election was complicated by the news media incorrectly proclaiming Gore as the winner; the withdrawal of an initial concession by Gore; butterfly ballots, hanging chads, and a recount of votes in Florida; and several court challenges. Finally, Bush was declared the winner.

- There have been recent terrorist incidents in the United States. In 1993 a terrorist bomb exploded in the parking garage of the **World Trade Center,** killing and injuring over 1,000 in New York. Four Islamic militants were tried and convicted in this attack. In 1995, 168 people were killed and around 500 people injured when the Murray Federal Building in Oklahoma City was bombed. Timothy McVeigh was tried, convicted, and later executed for his role in the attack. His accomplice, Terry Nichols, was convicted of conspiracy and sentenced to life in prison.

- On **September 11, 2001,** symbols important to the U.S. economy and military—the twin towers of the **World Trade Center** in New York and the **Pentagon** in Washington, D.C.—were attacked by hijackers who flew commercial airplanes into the buildings. The twin towers collapsed and thousands died in what has been referred to as the worst act of terrorism in U.S. history. Advisors to President Bush have determined that **Osama Bin Laden** was the primary suspect in the attack, resulting in the invasion of Afghanistan to stop Al Qaeda terrorists and to remove an oppressive government, the Taliban, from power.

- In the spring of 2003, the United States accused Iraq of links with terrorists and harboring weapons of mass destruction. When Iraq's leader, Saddam Hussein, failed to reveal and destroy these weapons, the United States invaded Iraq. After a three-week blitz, combat operations were declared at an end. This war was characterized by technological weapons aimed specifically at the opposing army and its leaders rather than civilians.

Texas History

IX Earliest Inhabitants
Key question: *Who were the first Texans and in what activities did they engage?*

- Anthropologists believe that the first Texans, called **Paleo-Americans,** or Old Americans, crossed the land bridge connecting Asia and Alaska over 37,000 years ago.

- These Old Americans of the Ice Age were hunters.

- They roamed the High Plains of West Texas in search of ancient American elephants, mammoths, mastodons, ground sloths, and giant bison. These bison were twice the size and four times the weight of the modern buffalo.

- Eventually, the Ice Age ended and the lush land of Texas became hotter and drier. Soon the animals that the Old Americans had depended on for food became extinct.

- Before the land bridge disappeared, around 7,000 years ago, a new group of humans made their way across it and eventually to Texas. These were the people of the Archaic Period, called **Amerinds.**

- These new people, like the Old Americans, were nomadic hunters and gatherers. The Amerinds of North America displayed almost identical racial or physical characteristics, with only minor variations of height or color, but became differentiated culturally. They split into linguistic stocks, and then adopted mutually unintelligible languages within each linguistic group. They made their tools and artifacts in different ways. The early Amerinds left twenty-seven different kinds of dart points on the Edwards Plateau alone.

- Culturally varied, speaking different languages, nomadic and constantly impinging on each other, the hundreds of bands of Amerinds could only follow the oldest human logic: They made war. Each new folk wandering from the north invaded already appropriated hunting grounds, and the first wars stemmed from the most logical of reasons—the defense of territory. But a constantly roaming, constantly colliding people soon imbedded the idea and act of warfare deep in their cultural heart. Fighting became a central part of their lives. Therefore, the center of society and most important member was the warrior. Because the male warriors were too busy preparing for war and actually fighting to work, women performed most labor.

- The **Neo-American Age,** around 3,000 years ago, is marked by an "agricultural revolution." The people of this age began to domesticate crops including maize (corn), beans, squash, tomatoes, potatoes, and cotton. These people have been referred to as **Mound Builders** because of the burial and temple mounds they erected in the Piney Woods of East Texas.

- The largest group of these Mound Builders was the **Caddo Nation,** once the largest and most powerful Indian group in Texas. The Caddo settlements were relatively permanent. They hunted game as a supplement rather than a staple. They grew many varieties of several crops and lived in villages made up of large timbered houses, domed and thatched. Because they were agricultural and war was no longer a central part of their culture, the Caddoan tribes were remarkably amiable to white men in the first years of contact and with disastrous results to their tribe. The Europeans brought with them diseases that had devastating effects on the tribes that had little or no immunity to them.

- Racially, all Texas Indians were quite similar, except for minor differences of height and skin shade. In their tribal customs, habits, and economies, they were extremely different.

- South of the Caddo nation, along the Gulf Coast, lived a number of smaller tribes. One of the most powerful was the **Karankawa.** These Indians inhabited an area from Galveston to Corpus Christi.

- West of the Karankawa country, on a line ranging through San Antonio to Del Rio, was the territory of a number of small bands of **Coahuiltecans.** Their territory was one of the harshest in the state. Because of the heat and the dry conditions, there were not enough game animals to support a hunting society. Farming was also futile in this area. These people learned to use almost every native plant that grew in South Texas. They made flour from agave bulbs, concocted a "fire-water" from mescal and maguey leaves, and roasted mesquite beans. They consumed spiders, ants, lizards, and rattlesnakes.

- The **Tonkawas** lived above the country of the Coahuiltecans, over the Balcones Escarpment. They ranged across the Edwards Plateau to the Brazos valley. They lived by hunting, fishing, and gathering fruits, nuts, and berries. They lived on the edge of bison country in buffalo-hide tepees and used large domesticated dogs as beasts of burden. Horses and cattle, brought by the Spaniards in the 1500s, were still unknown to these early Indian tribes. The Tonkawas did not hunt or raid very far north on the Texas plains. They were relatively confined to the Edwards Plateau by another, fiercer tribe that commanded the largest buffalo territory: the Apache.

- The **Apaches** inhabited the High Plains of Central Texas. Here there were millions of bison, elk, deer, and antelope. Each spring and fall bison congregated on the southern plains and grazed in a northward direction throughout the summer months. Anthropologists believe that the typical buffalo-hunting cultures of the Plains evolved first in Texas, and then spread north; the Eastern Apaches were certainly the dominant stereotype.

- The **Plains Indians** centered their lives around the buffalo. The great hunts took place in the spring and fall, when small herds were surrounded by men on foot and shot with arrows until all the animals were killed. Immediately, the women set to work with their flint knives. Every part of the buffalo was used. Most of the meat was roasted and the intestines were cooked to provide a special treat. Some lean flesh was sun dried, or jerked, to be eaten over the winter. Some organs were cleaned and dried to be used as bags to store water. Bones were made into picks and other tools. Hides were dried for clothing, shelter, and blankets. Apaches made teepees of buffalo skins and light frames of sotol sticks. These were flapped with bearskins for doors, and open at the top for escaping smoke. Four to twelve people lived in one teepee. Fires were built in the centers and they were furnished with hide blankets. The bison hide was tanned so fine that rain could not penetrate or stiffen it.

- In the hot months Apaches wore very little. In winter they wore deerskin shirts and heavy buffalo robes. Apaches possessed little besides their clothing, tools, weapons, and teepees. During the hottest months of the summer the herds moved north to follow the grass and the rains and avoid the blazing sun. During this period, the Apaches, still hunting on foot, were limited in their pursuit of the herds. Therefore, they were forced to supplement their economy with other foods. They learned to domesticate crops, planting them in small patches along the infrequent rivers and streams. While these crops ripened, Apaches settled down for long periods beside the waters. The Spanish called these semipermanent camps *rancherias.*

- The **Comanches**, exceptional horsemen, dominated the Southern Plains. Originally, the Comanches migrated south because of the greater access to the mustangs that roamed wild after the Spanish brought them to America. The warm climate and abundance of buffalo were additional incentives. Like many of the Plains Indians, Comanches were nomadic. The buffalo was extremely important to their way of life, providing them food, clothing, and shelter. They supplemented their meat diet through trade with agricultural tribes such as the Wichita and Caddo. Because of their trading skills, Comanches controlled much of the commerce of the Plains. The Comanches came to the Plains later than other groups so they became accustomed to conflict. The Apaches and Comanches became mortal enemies. Forts were established throughout much of Texas as protection for white settlers. The most famous chief of the Comanche was Quanah Parker, whose mother, Cynthia Ann Parker, had been captured in a raid on Fort Parker.

X. Early European Exploration and Development

Key question: *What was the primary function of the Spanish missions?*

- In mid-1519, sailing from a base in Jamaica, **Alonso Alvarez de Piñeda,** a Spanish adventurer, was the first known European to explore and map the Texas coastline. This event marked the beginning of Spain's rule in Texas and the first of **six flags** that would wave over the state.

- In 1528, **Cabeza de Vaca** shipwrecked on what is believed today to be Galveston Island. His small band wandered the area for approximately six years, trading with the Indians of the region. He later explored the Texas interior on his way to Mexico City. Once there, he related the legend of the ***Seven Cities of Gold.***

- From 1540 to 1542, **Francisco Vasquez de Coronado** led an expedition of over 300 soldiers, Mexican Indian allies, women, and priests through present-day New Mexico, western and northern Texas, and as far north as Kansas, searching for those cities of gold. Though he found no gold, he did strengthen Spain's claim on Texas.

- One of many Spanish conquistadores, Coronado claimed for Spain all the territory he explored.

- Priests began to settle and build missions in the conquered territory so that they could "civilize" and convert to Catholicism the Indians of the area. The **first Spanish mission** was Corpus Christi de la **Isleta** established near **El Paso** in 1682.

- The **French** claim on Texas rests on the Robert Cavelier, Sieur de **LaSalle,** visit in 1685. He established **Fort St. Louis** in the Matagorda Bay area. Two years later, he was killed by his own men.

- In 1689, Spanish explorer **Alonso de Leon** set out from Mexico, reaching Fort St. Louis and finding it abandoned. It is believed that Indians and disease destroyed the remainder of the French force. In 1995, a team of archaeologists from the Texas Historical Commission discovered the *Belle,* one of La Salle's frigates in the waters of Matagorda Bay. In 1996, the exact location of Fort St. Louis was pinpointed near Victoria.

- Alarmed by the French presence in Texas and the French settlements in the Louisiana area, the Spaniards established **Mission San Fransisco de los Tejas** in 1690 as the first East Texas mission.

- Throughout the eighteenth century, Spain established Catholic missions throughout Texas. Missions were located near the major population centers of all the major Indian tribes of Texas, except for the Apaches of the higher plains. Most all of these missions failed and were abandoned.

- European diseases such as measles and smallpox spread rapidly among the Indians and decimated their populations. By the end of the eighteenth century, the Caddo Indians had almost disappeared. Ironically, the diseases brought by Spaniards and Catholic priests of these missions helped exterminate the very people they had come to save.

- In 1718, the same year the French founded New Orleans, the tiny Spanish mission of **San Antonio de Valero (the Alamo)** was established.

- Viceroy San Antonio de Valero, for whom the mission was named, began to build a complex around his mission. For protection from the Indians and French, he established Fort **San Antonio de Bejar** (or Bexar) named for a brother of the Marques de Valero.

- More and more people began to move to the San Antonio area. By 1726 there were 200 men, women, and children, not counting Native Americans, living in the town of San Antonio.

- Other Spanish towns founded in this same time period are Goliad and Nacogdoches.

- **Jane Long** became known as the **Mother of Texas** because of the birth of her child on Bolivar Peninsula in 1821. She referred to herself as the first English-speaking woman to bear a child in Texas. However, the census between 1807 and 1826 revealed that children were born to a number of Anglo-American women prior to 1821.

- By 1800, Mexican colonization of the Rio Grande area affected Texas more than all the missions. It did three things: Mexican cattle kingdoms entered North America; it established land titles and other related Spanish laws in the region; and finally, it brought a new kind of settler to the area—the tough Mexican frontiersman who came to stay, unlike the priests and soldiers who came before them.

- In 1821, the year Mexico gained independence from Spain, **Stephen F. Austin,** known as the **Father of Texas,** received permission from the Mexican government to settle a colony of 300 families, now known as the **"Old Three Hundred,"** in the Brazos River region in southeast Texas. Stephen F. Austin was continuing the work that his father, **Moses Austin,** had begun the year before. Unfortunately, Moses died before he could complete his plan.

- Although Anglo-Americans were already living in Texas at the time, Austin's settlement was the official beginning of Anglo-American colonization in Texas. This trickle became a flood as Americans heard about the fertile land in Texas. **GTT** (Gone to Texas) was a sign left on many doors as settlers moved from U.S. states and territories.

- Despite Mexican restrictions, by 1836 there were between 35,000 to 50,000 Anglo settlers in Texas. By 1830, Mexico had become so concerned about the rapidly increasing numbers of Anglo-American settlers that the Mexican government banned any further emigration into Texas by settlers from the United States. With the increasing Anglo population, a strain quickly developed in the relationship between the Texans and Mexico due to government, language, and religion.

XI. Revolution, Republic, and Statehood
Key question: *How did Texas ultimately break with Mexico and gain independence?*

- Early in 1835, Stephen F. Austin announced that he was convinced that war with Mexico was necessary to secure freedom.

- Growing tension in Texas was the result of cultural, political, and religious differences between the Anglo-Americans and the Mexican government. In response to the unrest, Antonio Lopez de **Santa Anna,** the president of Mexico, reinforced Mexican troops in Texas.

- Gonzales, a town in central Texas, owned a cannon to protect itself from Native American attack. Mexico did not want the town to retain this weapon. A battle was fought at Gonzales on October 2, 1835, in which the Mexican forces were thwarted in their efforts to retrieve it. This gave rise to the famous Texas flag bearing the words "Come and Take It." Though there were earlier minor skirmishes, **the Battle of Gonzales** is generally considered to be the first battle for the independence of Texas from Mexico.

- Santa Anna gathered a substantial army to sweep through Texas. **General Sam Houston,** commander of the Texan army, ordered **William B. Travis** to the **Alamo.** There, a small group of Texans and others made a stand hoping to give other Texans a chance to organize for a stronger defense.

- The **Texas Declaration of Independence,** March 2, 1836, was produced, literally, overnight. Its urgency was paramount, because while it was being prepared, the Alamo in San Antonio was under siege by Santa Anna's army of Mexico. The Texas Declaration of Independence is similar to that of the United

States Declaration of Independence. There is a statement on the nature of government, a list of grievances, and a final declaration of independence. Separation from Mexico was justified through a declaration that charged, among other things, that the government of Mexico had ceased to protect the lives, liberty, and property of the people.

- The **Battle of the Alamo,** lasting nearly two weeks, ended on March 6, 1836, with the deaths of all its defenders (numbering about 189). The mission was defended by Anglo-Texans, Hispanic-Texans and others from the United States who had heard about the fight for freedom. The Mexican army of Santa Anna numbered 4,000 to 5,000 during its final charge. Among those killed were **David Crockett, Jim Bowie,** and **William B. Travis.** A small number of women, children, and slaves were spared by Santa Anna. Principal among them was **Mrs. Susanna Dickinson,** whose husband had been killed in the fighting. These witnesses were told to spread the word of what had happened at the Alamo and to tell Sam Houston that resistance was hopeless.

- A subsequent execution of **James Fannin** and nearly 400 Texans who, after hearing about the slaughter at the Alamo surrendered at the mission of **Goliad** on March 27, 1836, led to the battle cry of Texas' independence, "Remember the Alamo! Remember Goliad!"

- As Texans heard about the Mexican advance, many abandoned their property and belongings and headed toward the safety of Louisiana, across the Sabine River border. This was called the **Runaway Scrape.** The flight was marked by panic and lack of preparation. The people, mostly women, children, and the elderly, used any kind of transportation they had, and many died on the run. Often they were buried where they fell. The flight continued until the war was over. Even then, people did not immediately believe they could return home because of false rumors.

- **The Battle of San Jacinto** was fought on April 21, 1836. In a surprise attack during the Mexican army's siesta near the present city of Houston. Santa Anna's entire force of 1,600 men was killed or captured in less than 20 minutes by **General Sam Houston**'s army of 800 Texans; only nine Texans died. This decisive battle resulted in Texas's independence from Mexico. Texas was now its own country and would fly its "Lone Star" flag for the next ten years.

- Envoys from Texas had been meeting with officials from the United States well before the end of the war. The Texans wanted to join the United States once they gained independence from Mexico. However, when the war ended in 1836, many in the United States opposed the annexation of Texas because it would have affected the balance of slave and free states. Representatives from the free states believed that Texas would certainly enter as a slave state and the Congressional power of those from free states would be diminished. After winning independence from Mexico, Texas spent ten years as a separate nation.

- In 1836, five sites served as temporary capitals of the country of Texas (Washington-on-the-Brazos, Harrisburg, Galveston, Velasco, and Columbia) before Sam Houston moved the capital to Houston in 1837.

- In 1839 the Texas Congress first met in the new town of **Austin,** the frontier site selected for the capital of the Republic.

- **Sam Houston** was the first president of the Republic of Texas. He was also governor of the state of Texas from 1859 to 1861. The second president, **Mirabeau B. Lamar** (1838–1841), is called the "Father of Education in Texas."

- Even after declaring independence from Mexico, there were clashes between the Texans and their southern neighbors. In 1843, an expedition of Texans was captured; while they were being marched to Mexico City, many of them escaped. Within a week, 176 of them were recaptured. It was decreed that all who participated in the escape would be executed. The order was later modified to kill every tenth man. The Mexican commander put 176 beans into a jar, 17 of them **black beans,** to determine those who would die. Observers of the drawing later described the dignity of the men who drew the beans.

- By 1846, increasing westward expansion and an overwhelming belief in manifest destiny gave President James Polk a mandate to admit Texas as the 28th state on December 29, 1845.

- The **Mexican-American War** in 1846 ignited as a result of disputes over claims to Texas boundaries. The outcome of the war fixed Texas's southern boundary at the Rio Grande River.

- In 1861, Texas seceded from the federal Union following a vote by the Secession Convention to become part of the **Confederacy.** Governor Sam Houston was one of a small minority who opposed to secession.

- The last land engagement of the Civil War was the Battle of **Palmito Ranch** in far south Texas in 1865.

- In 1866 the abundance of longhorn cattle in south Texas and the return of Confederate soldiers to a poor reconstruction economy marked the beginning of the era of Texas trail drives to northern markets.

- The United States Congress readmitted Texas into the Union in 1870.

- The present Texas State Constitution was ratified on February 15, 1876.

- Six flags have flown over Texas: the Spanish, the French, the Mexican, the Texan, the Confederate, and the United States flag.

- The symbols of Texas are well known. The state song is "**Texas, Our Texas.**" The state flower is the **bluebonnet.** The state tree is the **pecan,** and the state bird is the **mockingbird.** The state flag is red, white, and blue with a single large star, dubbing Texas the "**Lone Star State.**" The state name *Texas,* or *Tejas,* comes from the caddo word meaning "friend," giving the state is motto "**friendship.**" The state pledge is said daily in classrooms throughout Texas: "Honor the Texas flag; I pledge allegiance to thee, Texas one and indivisible."

Key question: *What technological discoveries have affected America's history?*

- There have been many inventions that have changed the lives of Americans. Beginning with Benjamin Franklin's experiment with a kite one stormy night in Philadelphia, **electricity** eventually became one of the most important inventions in history. In the mid-1800s, everyone's life changed with the invention of the electric light bulb. Early in the nineteenth century, the **automobile** changed people and society. Cars gave people the freedom to move farther from their workplace, which gave rise to suburbs. Demand for cars resulted in a search for faster and cheaper ways to build them. Henry Ford's **assembly line production** changed the way the manufacturing industry operated. Support industries developed in response to the mass production of cars. Glass for windshields and rubber for tires were just two of these. Cars also made the construction of roads, bridges, and tunnels necessary. Road construction also produced new goods and services industries. In 1920 KDKA in Pittsburgh was the first commercial **radio** station to go on the air. By the mid-1930s almost every U.S. household had a radio. The first successful **television** transmission was in New York in 1927, although television sets in homes were not commonplace until the 1950s. These two broadcast technologies soon gave rise to the **advertising** industry.

- Advertising encouraged people to buy things such as household appliances.

- **Household appliances** dramatically changed the twentieth-century lifestyle by eliminating much of the labor of everyday tasks. Engineering innovation produced a wide variety of devices, including electric ranges, vacuum cleaners, dishwashers, and dryers. These and other products gave us more free time, enabled more people to work outside the home, and contributed significantly to our economy.

- The **computer** is a defining symbol of twentieth-century technology. It is a tool that has transformed businesses and lives around the world, increased productivity, and opened access to vast amounts of knowledge. Computers relieved the drudgery of simple tasks and brought new capabilities to complex ones. Engineering ingenuity fueled this revolution and continues to make computers faster, more powerful, and more affordable. The **Internet** is changing business practices, educational pursuits, and personal communications. It provides global access to news, commerce, and vast amounts of information.

- Perhaps the most amazing engineering feat of the twentieth century is the human expansion into **space.** We have progressed from the early test rockets to sophisticated satellites. The development of spacecraft has expanded our knowledge base and improved our capabilities. Thousands of useful products and services have resulted from the space program, including medical devices, improved weather forecasting, and wireless communications.

- **Nuclear technologies,** although generally controversial, are among the most important achievements of the twentieth century. The harnessing of the atom has changed the nature of war forever. Nuclear technologies also gave us a new source of electric power and new capabilities in medical research.

Consider the following practice question:

Mr. McCarthy assigned his fourth-grade class a research project on the earliest immigrants of Texas. Which of the following groups were first?

A. Spanish.
B. English.
C. French.
D. Amerinds.

The Spanish did not come to Texas until the 1500s, more than 5,000 years later than the Amerinds. The answer is *D*, Amerinds. These were nomadic hunters and gatherers who came to Texas around 7,000 years ago.

STANDARDS V AND IX: GEOGRAPHY AND CULTURE

The social studies teacher applies knowledge of people, places, and environments to facilitate students' understanding of geographic relationships in Texas, the United States, and the world. The social studies teacher understands cultures and how they develop and adapt, and uses this knowledge to enable students to appreciate and respect cultural diversity in Texas, the United States, and the world.

Competency 018 (Geography and Culture): The teacher demonstrates knowledge of geographic relationships among people, places, and environments in Texas, the United States, and the world; understands the concept of culture and how cultures develop and adapt; and applies social science skills to geographic and cultural information, ideas, and issues.

The beginning teacher: applies knowledge of key concepts in geography (e.g., location, distance, region, grid systems) and knows the locations and characteristics of places and regions in Texas, the United States, and the world; understands geographic patterns and processes in major historical and contemporary societies and regions of Texas, the United States, and the world; demonstrates knowledge of physical processes (e.g., erosion, weather patterns, natural disasters) and their effects on patterns in the environment; knows how humans adapt to, use, and modify the physical environment and knows how the physical characteristics of places and human modifications to the environment affect human activities and settlement patterns; understands the concept of culture and the processes of cultural diffusion and exchange; understands the contributions of people of various racial, ethnic, and religious groups to Texas, the United States, and the world and demonstrates knowledge to the effects of race, gender, and socioeconomic class on ways of life in the United States and throughout the world; understands similarities and differences in how various peoples at different times in history have lived and met basic human needs, including the various roles of men, women, children, and families in past and present cultures; relates geographic and cultural information and ideas to information and ideas in other social sciences and in other disciplines; knows how to formulate geographic and cultural research questions and uses appropriate procedures to reach supportable judgments and conclusions; understands research relating to geography and culture and knows how social scientists in these fields locate, gather, organize, analyze, and report information using standard research methodologies; knows characteristics and uses of primary and secondary sources used for geographic and cultural research (e.g., databases, maps, photographs, media services, the Internet, interviews, questionnaires, artifacts); analyzes information from primary and secondary sources; and evaluates information in relation to bias, propaganda, point of view, and frame of reference; applies evaluative, problem-solving, and decision-making skills to geographic and cultural information, ideas, and issues; knows how to communicate and interpret geographic and cultural information and ideas in written and visual forms, including maps and other graphics; analyzes data related to geography and culture using appropriate analytical methods.

Consider the following practice question:

Ms. Arcain is teaching her first grade class about the environment. An important concept in this lesson is understanding resources. She wants to make sure that the students understand the difference between natural (renewable) and nonrenewable resources. For review, she asks students:

Which of the following is NOT a renewable resource?

A. Water.
B. Trees.
C. Copper.
D. Wind.

Copper is a metal ore that is a nonrenewable resource. In other words, when it is used up, it is gone forever. The correct answer is C.

Teaching Geography

Geography doesn't simply begin and end with maps showing the location of all the countries in the world (Davis, 1992). In fact, such maps don't necessarily tell much at all. Geography should raise important questions about who people are and how they developed in their own ways and then provide clues to the answers. It is impossible to understand history, international politics, the world economy, religions, philosophy, or patterns of culture without taking geography into account. Unfortunately, students identify geography as a least favorite subject, just as they do history. Teachers too often concentrate on recitation and memorization rather than allowing students to make meaningful connections between their lives and geography learning.

Traditionally, a central focus of geography has been on map reading and globe skills. Young children can begin to learn map skills, but globe mapping skills are not age-appropriate for preK or kindergartners. For grades 1 through 3 globes should be used to pique curiosity and help children understand the physical roundness of the Earth (Seefeldt, 1997) and that we have large land masses and great oceans. However, young children, ages 5 to 7, are able to begin learning about symbols: the idea that something represents another thing. This is a key concept in understanding maps and globes. Children can best begin to learn about symbols by first manipulating blocks to represent their classroom, as discussed earlier, or they might use milk cartons and boxes to make a model, showing desks and other features. Children might next work as a class to draw a representation of their classroom from a bird's view, developing symbols to represent desks, centers, sink, clock, and other features. They might compare this to a picture they draw or a digital photo they take from their own desk to understand how a two-dimensional drawing can represent real life. From this point, students move to map their school, playground, and neighborhood. By third or fourth grade, students are ready to deal with the landforms and other geographical features.

Relative location (where in relation to _____ is _____) is also an important concept for young children to learn. Teachers begin this concept through many questions and games ("I'm thinking of something very near my desk . . . who can guess what it is?"). Teachers also continuously ask young children questions such as, "Who is behind Anil? Who is nearest the sink, so he could bring a towel?" The concept of direction should follow the introduction of symbols. Prior to entering kindergarten, many children have only started to learn the basics of direction (left and right, up and down, in front of, beside, behind, etc.). Left and right may not come easily to children until age 9. Many of the games and songs popular with very young children—such as *Hokey Pokey, Simon Says,* and *Mother May I*—help them learn these concepts. Once students understand these simple directions, they will be better able to understand cardinal directions (north, south, east, and west). *Simon Says* and *Mother May I* can be modified for older students using cardinal directions ("Turn west and clap twice."). Then meaningful connections can be made ("It looks like we have a storm coming from the north. What do you think we should wear tomorrow?"). Once the concept of direction has been learned, students may be given opportunities to construct their own maps such as the neighborhood and popular sites. Treasure hunts constructed by the teacher and by students offer exciting activities in formulating and following directions.

Many trade books can reinforce the concepts of maps and map skills. There are also works of fiction that deal with travel and treasure hunting. Trade books can also be used to help students gain understanding of other people and places in the world. For help in choosing appropriate trade books for geography and other social studies subjects, the National Council for the Social Studies annually reviews new trade books for children. The results are published in a special pullout in the May/June issue of *Social Education.*

Materials for the Social Studies Classroom

There are a number of other materials that should be available for geography skills for lessons or to be placed in centers. A globe invites children to explore in primary grades. By the later elementary grades students should be able to answer questions placed in a globe center ("Twirl the globe and stop it with one finger. In which hemisphere did you stop? If it is a landmass, what country? What do you think the weather is like there and why?"). Classroom maps for older children and age-appropriate map puzzles help children spatially in locating shapes of regions, states, countries, and/or water boundaries.

Sand and water in a center is especially necessary for increasing physical knowledge of landforms. Adding safe props such as houses, buildings, cars, trains, and so forth encourage children to build neighborhoods, farms, and cities as well as mountains, valleys, rivers, and so forth. Children should be allowed time to play in this type of center as well as to be directed to specific tasks at times. Teachers should ensure that sand stays moist for easy construction by adding water when needed. Children can also use the water to discover properties of erosion on the land. Sand centers can be constructed of anything that will hold well (rubber or plastic swimming pools, or even a large roasting pan for older children). Blocks have been mentioned. Children should first be allowed to explore all of these materials and then gradually begin to construct increasingly complex known forms in their environment. For older elementary children, modeling clay should be used as a manipulative for landforms.

Props in a center provide for sociodramatic play depicting workers or community helpers (police hats, an astronaut helmet, doctor's bag, a chef's hat and kitchen items, etc.). These can be supplemented with other tools, play furniture, and clothes or uniforms of various jobs or of other eras. Other props for social studies skills might include play money and a cash drawer for econom-ics, store items, and doll families (of diverse ethnicities/skin colors, of various types of families, and of various ages, including grandparents). Seefeldt (1997) also suggests that books be put in a doll center for "reading babies to sleep."

The art center can also easily become integrated as a springboard to social studies by providing cultural items or artifacts. During the year, the teacher can insert a piece of Native American pottery or jewelry, a mask, an Oriental ink drawing, or a picture of a clearly different era for students to interpret and use for inspiration. The music center may work similarly—as the teacher can rotate recordings and instruments from various eras or cultures.

Picture files are one of the most effective tools for social studies. A teacher can gather many examples (and nonexamples) of one concept for children such as transportation (cars, planes, cycles, trains, hot air balloons, skis, dog sleds, snowmobiles, etc.). A mountain file, for example, might include volcanoes, forested mountains, snow-capped rocky peaks, island peaks, dry west Texas peaks, or villages in mountains in various countries.

Other resources may consist of speakers, field trips, having vehicles come to school, and many other diverse options.

Geography Content

In general, children are fascinated by our world. It is important that EC-4 teachers encourage this fascination among their students. Geography and culture offer many opportunities for children to explore their world and the many people who inhabit it. The content in the geography competency, like the history competency, is fairly large. To make the geography content more accessible, it will be broken down into the following subheadings:

- The study of geography
- Climates
- Natural resources and the environment
- Texas geography

Each subheading has a question to help you as you read each topic. These questions should be useful to organize your reading and to help in your review of the information covered in each section. A section on the culture portion of the competency follows the Geography section.

I. The Study of Geography
Key question: *What are two major areas of the study of geography?*

- Geography studies our planet and the people who live on it.
- There are two main branches of geography—physical geography and cultural geography. **Physical geography** focuses on the Earth and its physical environment. Changes in the Earth's crust have created the mountains, plateaus, and other landforms. Factors such as weather, earthquakes, and volcanic eruptions continue to alter these landforms. Also included in physical geography are soils, vegetation, climate, and resources, and anything that pertains to our land, water, or atmosphere.
- **Cultural geography** studies how human groups have lived and changed in relation to the physical environment. Cultural geographers have defined various useful concepts to aid them in this study. One such concept is population density, or the average number of people living within a given amount of space such as a square mile. Urban areas, or cities, are more densely populated than rural areas. Migration is another important concept, since it refers to the movement of groups of people out of (emigration) or into (immigration) different regions.

- Physical geography also involves describing position through **absolute location** (precise points on a map or grid) and **relative location** (expressing a location in relation to other sites: San Marcos is about 25 miles south of Austin) (Brophy & Alleman, 1996).

- For mapping purposes, Earth is divided into four hemispheres (Northern, Southern, Eastern, and Western). The United States lies in the Northern and Western Hemispheres.

- The Earth is further divided horizontally by **parallels** showing **latitude** and vertically by **meridians** showing **longitude.** All locations on the Earth can be located in **degrees** of latitude and longitude.

- **Relief maps** have raised features to show elevation. **Topographic** maps show detailed elevations with various colors (and other details) but are flat maps.

- The geography of the United States is a result of changes caused mainly by plate tectonics, volcanic activity, and glaciers over millions of years. When viewing a topographical map of the United States from the east coast to the west coast, the land that borders the Atlantic Ocean and south around the Gulf of Mexico coastline is coastal plains (primarily lower, flat land). The **Appalachian Mountains** appear next, stretching from the south in Alabama to the Canadian border in the north. The geography caused the New England area and the southeastern states to be settled first, until a way over the mountains was discovered by **Lewis and Clark** with the help of **Sacajawea.** These mountains open out further west to miles and miles of **Great Plains,** covering most of the middle of the United States stretching from Texas to the Canadian border. In early history, it was in this area that the great buffalo herds roamed (and supported many Native American tribes) because this rolling plain was once covered by lush grasslands. The **Mississippi,** North America's greatest river, runs through this plain from north to south, ending in a large delta area near New Orleans. These plains are finally broken by the Rocky Mountains running from Colorado north to Canada. On the west side of the **Rocky Mountains,** a strip of desert stretches from Arizona northward. The high desert area is caused by other ranges of mountains that line the Pacific coast in the west (the Sierra Nevadas and, father north, the Cascades). When Pacific moisture hits these mountains, it moves upward, cools, and drops most of its precipitation on the west side of these mountains.

- The Hawaiian Islands, our 50th state, are the tips of high ocean volcanoes.

- Huge glaciers cut deep lakes and valleys in the northeastern and northwestern parts of the country.

- High mountain ranges were the result of shelves of rock coming together and being forced upward (plate tectonics).

- Some educators suggest that the combined physical and cultural study of places be coupled with nine basic human activities:
  1. Protecting and conserving life and resources
  2. Producing, exchanging, and consuming goods and services

3. Transporting goods and people
4. Communicating facts, ideas, and feelings
5. Providing education
6. Providing recreation
7. Organizing and governing
8. Expressing aesthetic and spiritual impulses
9. Creating new tools, technology, and institutions (Hanna et al., as reported in Brophy & Alleman, 1996, p. 118)

■ Other areas of cultural geography include the development of political systems (e.g., how physical factors such as mountains and rivers help set the boundaries of nations), the development of economic systems (e.g., how the amount of rainfall in an area helps determine its economy), languages spoken, and the geography of natural resources (e.g., how the presence or absence of resources affects population distribution).

II. Climates: How and Why They Differ

Key question: *What are the types of temperate climates?*

■ Wherever people live, climate has an important effect on the way of life. It influences the clothing worn, food grown, housing constructed, and transportation used.

■ **Climate** refers to average weather conditions over a long period of time, taking into account temperatures, wind, and amounts of precipitation (rain, sleet, snow).

■ **Weather** is the atmospheric conditions during a short period; weather may change from day to day.

■ To a large extent, climate depends on the amount of the sun's heat that reaches a place. Because Earth is tilted as it **revolves**, or circles around the sun, the strength of the rays varies in different parts of the Earth.

■ When the Earth is tilted closer to the sun, the rays are stronger and that hemisphere experiences summer. In the winter the hemisphere is tilted away from the sun.

■ The rays are least strong on the **polar regions,** around the North and South poles. Polar climates are cold with light precipitation, usually in the form of snow. As only mosses and small plants can live on the frozen ground, the area is unsuitable for agriculture. Polar regions are sparsely populated.

■ The sun's rays are most strong and direct in the **tropics,** the area near the equator.

■ The **equator** is an imaginary circle on the surface of the earth, equal distance from each pole and dividing the earth into northern and southern hemispheres.

■ **Tropical climates** are almost unchanging, very hot, humid, and wet. Jungles and rain forests with their abundant plant life are difficult to clear for agriculture. The tropics are also not heavily populated.

- The middle regions between the poles and the equator are temperate zones. **Temperate climates** do not have extremes of heat or cold and are characterized by four distinct seasons. Crops can be grown for a good part of the year.

- The **Tropic of Cancer** is an imaginary line around the earth that marks the northern limit of the tropics. This line crosses Mexico, the Caribbean Sea, the Sahara Desert of Africa, central India, Southern China, and the Pacific Ocean just north of Hawaii.

- The **Tropic of Capricorn** is an imaginary line around the earth that marks the southern limit of the tropics. This line crosses south central South America, southern Africa, the island of Madagascar, the Indian Ocean, central Australia, and the Pacific Ocean just south of Tonga.

- Climatologists identify four kinds of **temperate climates**: marine, continental, desert, and mountain.

- The **marine climate**, which is found near seacoasts, is mild with moderate to heavy precipitation in all seasons.

- The **continental,** or Mediterranean, climate of inland regions is characterized by hot summers, mild to cold winters, and light precipitation.

- The **desert climate** is hot and dry with scarce precipitation.

- The **mountain** or highlands climate tends to be cool with moderate precipitation. Nearby places in a highlands region may have rather different climates if they have different elevations or different positions relative to winds.

- Most of the world's population is found in temperate zones, where the climate is favorable for mental and physical activity, and natural resources for agriculture and industry are accessible.

III. Natural Resources and the Environment
Key question: *What are the basic types of resources?*

- Any material supplied by the Earth that people can put to use is called a **natural resource.**

- **Renewable resources** are those that can be replaced in the foreseeable future. For example, forests can be replanted after trees are cut, and the water supply is replenished by rain.

- Examples of **nonrenewable resources** are minerals in the Earth's crust. Metal ores (iron, gold, silver) and fossil fuels (coal, oil, natural gas) are among the most important nonrenewable resources in today's world.

- Researchers are working to find substitutes for some metals that may be used up and to find new energy sources to lessen our dependence on fossil fuels.

- A region's economy develops in part according to its available resources. Arable land (land suitable for farming) and fertile soil are needed for an agricultural economy to succeed. The lumber industry is important in forest areas, as is mining in regions with mineral deposits.

- People usually settle in areas where water is available. Fresh water is needed for both home and industrial use. Water is used to turn wheels and generate electricity known as hydroelectric power. Waterways serve as important transportation routes for ships carrying raw materials and manufactured goods. **Port cities** develop where there are good harbors or waterways.

■ Wherever people live and work, they affect the air, water, soil, and mineral resources. Dirty, or **polluted,** air and water are often unsafe for all living things. Industries sometimes pollute rivers, lakes, and oceans by dumping toxic, or poisonous, wastes. Oil spills are another hazard for plants and animals.

■ Most air pollution is caused by exhausts from automobile and industrial emissions. In addition to polluting the air, some smoke can combine with moisture in the air to form acids. These acids return in rain to pollute the land as well as bodies of water. Air pollution is dangerous to health and may cause severe respiratory problems. Local health departments and a federal government agency, the **Environmental Protection Agency** (EPA), monitor air and water and track down polluters. The government also protects the environment by banning the use of cancer-causing chemical pesticides such as DDT and regulating vehicle exhausts.

■ Pollution remains one of the world's most serious problems. Our industrialized society must learn to take responsibility for the environment.

IV. Texas Geography
Key question: *What are the four geographic regions in Texas?*

■ Texas is the second largest state in population and in territory. The largest state in terms of population is California, and Alaska is the largest state in terms of territory.

■ With an area of 267,339 square miles, Texas is larger than most nations and contains every major landform: mountains, plains, plateaus, and hills.

■ There are four major land regions in Texas: the Gulf Coastal Plains, the North Central Plains, the Great Plains, and the Trans-Pecos Region.

■ The **Gulf Coastal Plains**, an immense lowland area in the south and east portion of Texas, covers about a third of the state. The Gulf of Mexico provides a long border to the south. Two large port cities are Houston and Corpus Christi. Houston began its growth as a port city. The Houston Ship Channel, a 52-mile inland waterway, connects Houston to the Gulf of Mexico. In 1998, the port of Houston ranked first in the United States in foreign tonnage and eighth worldwide in total tonnage.

■ The **Piney Woods** makes up the eastern section of the Gulf Coastal Plains. The area of vast pine forests and the lands immediately to the west are suitable for diversified farming and livestock.

■ The **Valley** located on the south/southwest border with Mexico and the Gulf of Mexico makes up the southern sections of the Gulf Coastal Plains. Cotton and citrus fruits, such as oranges and grapefruit, are among the notable crops grown in the area. Crops can grow all year here.

- At the west edge of the Gulf Coastal Plains stands a line of southward- and eastward-facing hills. These balcony-like hills, called the Balcones Escarpment, mark the boundary between lowland and upland Texas, the beginning of the **North Central Plains.** The land is generally treeless except for areas along streams. Most of the land in this area is used for raising cattle.

- Farming in the **Great Plains** region of the Texas Panhandle depends on irrigation from underground water supplies. Some of the areas of the Great Plains offer grasses, weeds, and trees suitable for cattle, sheep, and goats.

- An **aquifer** is a geological formation that is water bearing, or that stores and/or transmits water. The largest of these in the North Central Plains is the Edwards Aquifer. The **Edwards Aquifer** has been designated as the most productive aquifer in the United States. It is designated by the EPA as a "sole source" drinking water supply for the 1.5 million people of San Antonio and the Austin–San Antonio corridor. The aquifer is also vital to the agricultural and light industrial economy of the region. Springs flow from the Comal and San Marcos Springs areas, providing water for the tourist and recreation industry.

- The **Trans-Pecos** region is located in the southwest corner of the state. The region is rocky and very dry. With the recent discovery of groundwater reserves, there is some limited agriculture production of cotton and alfalfa. This region contains all the state's mountains and best scenery, making this a popular tourist area. Big Bend National Park is located in far-west Texas in this area.

- Texas has several of the largest urban areas in the United States: Houston, the Dallas/Fort Worth metroplex, and San Antonio.

Culture

The increasing cultural diversity of the United States challenges educators to understand differing values, customs, and traditions and to provide responsive multicultural experiences for all learners. Currently one in four Americans has African, Asian, Hispanic, or Native American ancestry. By the year 2050, that number will be one in three (Duvall, 1994, p. 2).

Teachers must work harder than ever before to educate the diverse children of today's classrooms. According to the Houston Independent School District (H.I.S.D.) website, 91 different languages are spoken by students in the city schools in Houston, Texas. Imagine being a teacher in one of these schools and trying to communicate with students. Unless you spoke all these languages you would have difficulty communicating the most basic information to some of the children. How would you teach them social studies? How to use the library? How to find the bathroom?

Traditionally, the United States tried to create unity through the public education system by assimilating students from diverse racial and ethnic groups into a single "American" culture. Of course, assimilation required self-alienation—denying who you are in order to become someone else. Once everyone was assimilated, all cultures would *melt* together into *American.* While the United States is one nation politically, sociologically we are far from it. The melting pot theory is no longer considered a viable model, much less a means of achieving a just, equal, and accepting society (Manning & Baruth, 2000, p. 30). Educators need to develop an understanding of cultural, ethnic, racial, socioeconomic, gender, and individual differences, especially in light of the wealth of cultural diversity of the nation that increases daily. This invokes the "salad bowl" theory, where though mixed together, the flavors of the various ingredients retain their individual flavor.

Today's teacher, as part of developing his or her vision for the future, must recognize the intelligence and potential in each child. Teachers are expected to set challenging expectations and provide a strong and supportive instructional environment for all students. Without this commitment—a conviction that all children are bright and will learn—it is "unlikely that teachers can overcome the old institutional habit of low expectations for some children and high expectations for others" (Parker & Jarolimek, 2000, p. 5).

These issues of multicultural education are different from those of global education. Multicultural education generally deals with the people who are called *Americans* and situations mainly found in the United States. Global education, on the other hand, looks at the connections between *Americans* and the other people in the world. These two entities are not mutually exclusive. They both stand for freedom and universal values, "essential concepts in today's ethnically polarized and troubled world" (Massialas & Allen, 1996, p. 191). Both multicultural education and global education are necessary components of a new multidimensional citizenship that is developing in the world today.

According to Chapin and Messick (1999), multidimensional citizenship requires more than just knowledge. Multidimensional citizenship "calls for viewing problems from a global perspective using critical thinking skills." It also involves a commitment to the following convictions:

1. We are all global citizens who share a responsibility for solving the world's problems and for creating the world we desire.
2. We are all members of the family of humankind. We are responsible for understanding and caring for people of cultures different from our own.
3. We are stewards of Earth, which is our home and life-support system. (Chapin & Messick, 1999, p. 212)

The bumper sticker *Think Globally, Act Locally* summarizes the goals of multidimensional citizenship. Instruction should incorporate a global perspective on, for example, ecology, resources, cultures, and human choices. Children should be shown that nations and people depend on each other for survival. A change in a Pacific current, such as El Niño, can have ramifications for the entire world. Limiting oil production in the Middle East can automatically cause concern for the rest of the world. The record-setting gas prices in the United States in the first few months of the new millennium is one consequence. These were nothing in comparison to the gas lines experienced in the 1970s in the United States, Europe, and many other parts of the world when the flow of oil was disrupted. The stock price drop of over 10 percent in the Hong Kong market in 1997 immediately affected all the stock markets of the world. It is difficult, if not impossible, to find any major event in any area of the world without implications for the rest of the world.

Teachers who make a difference in the lives of children recognize the potential for success for all children. Gay (1991) explains, "the primary message from previous research on cultural diversity and learning social studies is that cultural socialization affects how students learn" (p. 154). For the social studies classroom, this means that the most important responsibility that the teacher has is to create a classroom environment that respects and supports the unique backgrounds of all children. There are some things to consider that will help develop this type of classroom:

1. Cultural perspectives must be integrated into the total social studies curriculum. Do not rely on special days, weeks, or months (such as Black History Month) to incorporate multicultural perspectives.
2. Understand the existence of the "hidden curriculum" that generally centers events around Western European experiences. There are many groups who traditionally have been relegated to the margins of U.S. history. These people deserve to be recognized in the main "texts" of history.
3. The social studies curriculum should include the contributions of the many cultures to American life. Much of the strength of this nation derives from the diversity of its ethnic heritages and cultural origins.

While the main focus of the culture standard is on multicultural diversity and its implications for social studies education, gender equity must also be considered. While most of the blatant portrayals of women in merely subservient roles have been eliminated from the textbooks and other classroom materials, there is still a need to remain watchful. Stanford (1996) discovered that two major patterns emerged in student–teacher interactions and gender discrimination: (1) Teachers give boys more attention, both positive and negative; and (2) boys demand more teacher attention. Stanford (1996) recommends several things for teachers to do in the classroom, including becoming conscious of the attention they give each gender in classroom interactions; modeling gender equity by providing an equitable environment; and selecting nondiscriminatory curricular materials that contribute to a sense of gender equity in the classroom. The contributions of women to the life, culture, and development of this nation must not be overlooked, nor merely relegated to Women's History Month in March.

Consider the following practice question:

Mr. Chancellor's fourth-grade class was studying the geographic regions of Texas. Students first investigated the different regions then, in small groups, designed travel brochures for their region. For the group assigned the Valley region, what characteristic of the region should they emphasize?

    A. Orange and grapefruit production.
    B. Mountains.
    C. Pine forests.
    D. Cattle, sheep, and goat ranching.

Mountains are found in the Trans-Pecos region; pine forests are found in the Piney Woods region; and sheep, cattle, and goat ranching is predominant in the Great Plains. The answer is *A*, orange and grapefruit production.

STANDARDS VI, VII, AND VIII (ECONOMICS, GOVERNMENT, AND CITIZENSHIP)

The social studies teacher knows how people organize economic systems to produce, distribute, and consume goods and services, and uses this knowledge to enable students to understand economic systems and make informed economic decisions. The social studies teacher knows how governments and structures of power function, provide order, and allocate resources, and uses this knowledge to facilitate student understanding of how individuals and groups achieve their goals through political systems. The social studies teacher understands citizenship in the United States and other societies, and uses this knowledge to prepare students to participate in our society through an understanding of democratic principles and citizenship practices.

Competency 019 (Government, Citizenship, Economics): The teacher understands concepts and processes of government and responsibilities of citizenship; knows how people organize economic systems to produce, distribute, and consume goods and services; and applies social science skills to information, ideas, and issues related to government and economics.

The beginning teacher understands the purpose of rules and laws; the relationship between rules, rights, and responsibilities; and the fundamental rights of American citizens guaranteed in the Bill of Rights and other amendments to the U.S. Constitution; understands fundamental concepts related to life in a democratic society (e.g., importance of voluntary participation and the expression and tolerance of differing points of view, roles of public officials); knows the basic structure and functions of local, state, and national governments and their relationships to each other and knows how people organized governments during the early development of Texas; understands the key principles and ideas of the U.S. and Texas Declarations of Independence, Constitutions, and other significant political documents; understands basic economic concepts (e.g., economic system, goods and services, free enterprise, interdependence, needs and wants, scarcity, roles of producers and consumers), knows that basic human needs are met in many ways, and understands the value and importance of work; understands the characteristics, benefits, and development of the free-enterprise system in Texas and the United States and knows how businesses operate in the U.S. free-enterprise system; demonstrates knowledge of patterns of work and economic activities in Texas and the United States, past and present, and knows how a society's economic level is measured; understands the interdependence of the Texas economy with that of the United States and the world; relates information and ideas in government, citizenship, and economics to information and ideas in other social sciences and in other disciplines; knows how to formulate research questions related to government, citizenship, and economics and uses appropriate procedures to reach supportable judgments and conclusions; understands research in government, citizenship, and economics and knows how social scientists in these fields locate, gather, organize, analyze, and report information; knows characteristics and uses of primary and secondary sources used for research in government, citizenship, and economics (e.g., databases, maps, media services, the Internet, biographies, interviews, questionnaires); analyzes information from primary and secondary sources and evaluates information in relation to bias, propaganda, point of view, and frame of reference; applies problem-solving, decision-making, and evaluation skills to information, ideas, and issues related to government, citizenship, and economics; knows how to communicate and interpret information and ideas related to government, citizenship, and economics in written and graphic forms; analyzes data related to government, citizenship, and economics using appropriate analytical methods; knows how to apply skills to foster good citizenship (e.g., negotiation, conflict resolution, persuasion, compromise, debate).

Consider the following practice question:

Ms. Thompson wants her kindergarten class to understand the importance of rules. How can she best communicate this idea to her students?

   A. Require that students memorize her list of five posted classroom rules.
   B. Bring a newspaper to class and have students talk about what the president does.
   C. Ask students to help develop a set of classroom rules.
   D. Ask the principal to explain the school's rules to the children.

The best answer is C, ask students to help develop a set of classroom rules. Creating rules and practicing the use of authority help develop a child's understanding of justice and fairness. Once children have experience in rule making, they may then relate their experiences to understand how rule making and enforcement occur in the adult world (Chapin & Messick, 2002).

According to Martorella and Beal (2002), elementary schools are excellent educational environments for developing good citizens. This is because elementary schools are relatively small, and the people in them (administrators, staff, teachers, and students) often form a close community. All of these people become concerned citizens of the school. Students and teachers are concerned not only with the school's policies and programs, but also with the physical appearance of their individual classrooms and the common areas of the building and surroundings.

Teachers should use this sense of caring to foster students' active involvement in their school community. Democratic classrooms are essential to encourage and model activism. A simple definition of democracy is "rule by majority, or a government of the people." In a classroom setting, democratic ideals such as respect and cooperation are central. Students play an active role in establishing goals and rules. On the first day of school, EC-4 teachers should involve students in establishing classroom rules. This will give the students a sense of involvement in their new community.

Playing an active role in establishing classroom rules will also give students the opportunity to understand one of the fundamental principles of democracy: that rights come with responsibilities. Democracies are characterized by hard choices. Choices become difficult when they cause our values to conflict. For example, if we value freedom, we must also value justice. Values can sometimes be hard to reconcile; however, students must learn this most central feature of democracy. Personal choices are most often based on values. In a representative government like the United States, people elect representatives that share their values. Therefore, it is essential that children begin to identify and develop their own personal values. Economics concepts could also help children begin to identify personal values. A main concept in economics involves a "lesson" in hard choices: cost and benefit. Children should ultimately understand the importance of making decisions that provide the greatest satisfaction.

The remainder of this section contains content information for government, citizenship, and economics necessary for EC-4 teachers preparing to teach social studies.

Government Content

The subject of government studies and compares different types of political systems. Political scientists try to understand decision making in politics and how individuals and groups obtain and use political power.

Political systems and concepts broken down into the following subheadings:

- Foundations of government.
- Writing the Constitution.

- Development of federalism.
- Election process.
- Texas government.

I. Foundations of Government

Key question: *What fundamental ideals are expressed in the Declaration of Independence?*

- Any group of people living and working together needs certain laws and services. A **government** acts on behalf of the group, making and enforcing laws and providing for other needs.
- **Political science** studies how different types of governments function.
- Governments can be classified by how many people take part in the decision-making process.
- In a **monarchy,** one person (such as a queen or an emperor) usually inherits ruling power. An absolute monarch has complete authority to govern. A constitutional monarch has limited power and must work with other government officials.
- In a **dictatorship,** or totalitarian government, one person or a small group has total power and exerts extensive control over people's lives. Dictators often rise to power during times of national unrest.
- In an **oligarchy,** a small governing class rules.
- In a **democracy,** all of the people take part in governing the country.
- Ancient Greece was an example of a **direct democracy** because all the citizens met to make decisions.
- The United States is a **representative democracy** in which the people elect representatives, such as the members of Congress, to carry out the work of the government. The belief in a republican government (or government headed by an elected officials) is why the United States is referred to as a **republic.**
- When the thirteen colonies decided to free themselves from British rule, the writers of the Declaration of Independence expressed a political philosophy of **individualism** that is still basic to American government today. "Rugged individualism" emerged from those who moved into the West and carved out the land self-sufficiently.
- One of the tools that governments use is **propaganda.** Propaganda is a strategic technique used to persuade another person to believe or act upon an idea. By using certain symbols or words a good propagandist can make a person feel angry, sympathetic, apathetic, or any number of emotions. Other important concepts to understand are **point of view,** or the perspective from which something is told (ownership), and **frame of reference,** which is a structure of concepts, values, customs, and/or views by which an individual or group perceives or evaluates data, communicates ideas, and regulates behavior.
- The philosophy of the Bill of Rights emphasizes the equality of all people and the right to "life, liberty, and the pursuit of happiness."

■ The U.S. government exists to protect these rights, and the power of the government comes from the consent of the people. If the government ignores the people's will, the people have the right to elect new officials.

II. Writing the Constitution

Key question: *At the Constitutional Convention, what compromises were required?*

■ Five years after the U.S. Declaration of Independence was written, the first national constitution governing the United States was approved, or ratified, by all of the states. This document was known as the **Articles of Confederation.**

■ The Articles created a central government with very limited powers. It could not make laws without unanimous state agreement, nor could it settle conflicts between states. There was no president or national court system. It soon became clear that these weaknesses had to be corrected.

■ In 1787, 55 delegates from all the states, referred to as the **Founding Fathers,** met at the Constitutional Convention to develop a new system of government.

■ A debate about the nature of representation of individuals and of states was settled by the **Great Compromise.** Under the terms of this compromise, a two-part, or **bicameral,** congress consisting of a **House of Representatives** (representation determined by state population) and a **Senate** (two representatives for each state) was created.

■ The new U.S. Constitution also provided for shared power and responsibilities in three ways: (1) a **separation of powers** that defines three branches of government with distinct powers, (2) a system of **checks and balances** that allows each branch to oversee the other two, (3) a **federal system** that divides governing power between the national government and state governments.

■ The three branches of the federal government are the **executive branch,** whose main power resides in the presidency; the **legislative branch,** which includes the two houses of Congress; and the **judicial branch,** which includes the Supreme Court and lower federal courts.

III. The Development of Federalism

Key question: *How does the federal system provide for the sharing of power between the states and the federal government?*

■ After much debate between **Federalists** (those who favored the ratification of the Constitution) and **anti-Federalists** (those against ratification), the Constitution was finally approved by the required number of states in 1788.

■ Because the anti-Federalists were concerned that the Constitution did not provide strong enough guarantees of state power or of individual liberties, the Federalists promised to pass a Bill of Rights during the first Congress.

■ The first ten amendments to the Constitution are called the **Bill of Rights.** Nine of these placed limits on Congress by forbidding it to infringe on certain basic rights: freedom of religion, speech, and the press; immunity from arbitrary arrest; that no one may be derived of life, liberty, or property without due process of law; speedy public trial by jury; no excessive bail or cruel and unusual punishments; and others. The Tenth Amendment reserved to the states all powers except those specifically withheld from them or delegated to the federal government.

- Thus far, there have been a total of 26 amendments to the Constitution. The **Thirteenth Amendment** prohibited slavery in the United States. The **Fifteenth Amendment** guaranteed the right to vote to all men, no matter their race. The **Nineteenth Amendment** guaranteed the right to vote to everyone, including women. The **Twenty-fourth Amendment** declared poll taxes and similar measures designed to prohibit people from voting unconstitutional. The **Twenty-sixth Amendment**, the final amendment to the Constitution, was adopted in 1971. This gave 18-year-olds the right to vote.

- These amendments were passed following one of the two methods outlined in the Constitution. An amendment must be proposed by two-thirds of both houses of Congress or by two-thirds of the state legislatures. Approval by three-fourths of the state legislatures is needed for amendment ratification.

- The **federal system** was a logical compromise that allows the national government and the states to share power.

- Powers given specifically to the national government, such as establishing post offices and coining money, are **delegated powers.**

- Other powers—those not specifically granted to the national government and not denied to the states—are called **reserved powers** of the states. Examples would include the administration of education and the regulation of police forces.

- **Concurrent powers** such as tax collection are shared by both the national and state governments.

- Because powers are divided in various ways, no group or part of government can become too powerful. The principles of the Constitution encourage national, state, and local governments to work together to serve the American people.

IV. The Election Process

Key question: *How does the method for electing the president differ from the way in which members of Congress are elected?*

- Elections and voting are the foundations of U.S. democracy.

- On the federal level, voters elect the president and members of Congress.

- At the state and local levels, voters cast ballots for governors, mayors, state legislators, and city or town council representatives.

- Voters also have opportunities to express their opinions on laws and amendments. Any citizen 18 years of age or older may register to vote.

- Political parties are not provided for in the United States Constitution. However, political differences beginning early in our history brought about a two-party system: the Democrats and the Republicans. Despite the strength of the two parties, the history of the United States is filled with third parties that have achieved limited and temporary successes. The most successful third party candidate was **Theodore Roosevelt.** His Progressive or **Bull Moose Party** won 27.4 percent of the vote in the 1912 election.

- Today, **Democrats** usually favor a strong federal government involved in economic and social issues. **Republicans** usually want less federal involvement and greater state responsibility.

- The parties nominate candidates for various public offices.

- In most states, **primary** elections are held to choose **presidential candidates.** At these preliminary elections, voters from each major political party select delegates who will decide on the party's candidate for president. These delegates generally pledge to vote for a particular candidate at the party's national convention.

- Presidential elections are held every four years.

- Citizens do not directly elect the president or vice president. Rather, they choose electors to represent them in the **electoral college.** Each state has a number of electors equal to the total number of its senators and representatives. In most states, the electors are usually pledged to vote for the candidate who won the popular vote in their state. There are three instances where the person who won the popular vote did not win the presidency. In 1824, Andrew Jackson received more popular votes and more electoral votes than did John Quincy Adams; however, while he did receive a plurality of the votes, he did not receive a majority. This meant that the election had to be decided by the House of Representatives. The House voted for Adams. And in 1876 Samuel Tilden received more popular votes than his opponent, Rutherford B. Hayes; however, Hayes won the presidency by one electoral vote. In the 2000 election of George W. Bush, Albert Gore, Jr., received a majority of the popular vote.

- To be elected, a presidential candidate needs a majority of electoral votes. If no candidate receives a majority, the president is chosen by the House of Representatives (this happened in 1800 and 1824), and the vice president is chosen by the Senate.

- The **House of Representatives** has 435 members. This total is divided or apportioned among the states according to population. Representatives serve two-year terms.

- There are 100 **senators,** two from each state. Senators are elected for six years, with a third of the Senate being elected every two years.

- Both senators and representatives are elected by direct popular vote.

V. Texas Government

Key question: *How is the Texas government similar to the U.S. government?*

- After Texas became independent of Mexico, **Sam Houston** became the first president of the Republic of Texas. The second president, **Mirabeau B. Lamar** (1838–1841), is called the "Father of Education in Texas."

- The last president of the Republic of Texas was **Anson Jones** (1844–1846).

- When Texas became a state, ten years after independence, the first governor of the state was **James Pinckney Henderson** (1846–1847).

- In 1874, the election of **Richard Coke** began a Democratic Party dynasty in Texas that continued unbroken for over 100 years.

- In 1888, the dedication of the present state capitol in Austin ended seven years of planning and construction.

- **James Hogg** took office as the first native-born governor of Texas in 1891.

- **Miriam A. "Ma" Ferguson** was the second woman to serve as governor in the United States. Because of the date of elections in Texas, she was technically the first woman elected to that office. She served from 1925 to 1927 and again from 1933 to 1935.

- The present Texas State Constitution was ratified on February 15, 1876.

- Currently, the Texas Legislature convenes in Austin for a 140-day regular session every two years in odd-numbered years.

- The **governor** of Texas is elected to a four-year term in November of even-numbered, nonpresidential-election years. There is no limit on the number of terms a governor may serve.

- The governor may call additional 30-day special sessions in which the Legislature may consider only the subjects submitted to them by the Governor.

- The **Texas Senate** consists of 31 senators elected to four-year overlapping terms of office.

- A statewide elected official, the **lieutenant governor** is the presiding officer of the Senate and serves a four-year term. In Texas, the governor and lieutenant governor do not run on a combined ticket as those who seek the offices of president and vice president in the United States. Therefore, it is fairly common for the governor and lieutenant governor to be from different political parties.

- The **House of Representatives** consists of 150 representatives elected in even-numbered years to two-year terms of office. At the beginning of each regular session, the House elects a Speaker of the House from its members to serve as the presiding officer.

- The **Legislative Budget Board** (LBB) primarily develops recommendations for legislative appropriations and performance standards for all agencies of state government. The LBB also prepares fiscal notes and impact statements that provide the Legislature with information and analysis on bills being considered for enactment.

- The **Office of the State Auditor** (SAO) functions as the independent auditor for Texas state government. The SAO reviews state agencies, universities and programs for management and fiscal controls, effectiveness, efficiency, performance measures, statutory compliance and compliance with administrative rules and regulations.

Citizenship

Many of the important decisions affecting our lives are political decisions. However, "to most students and adults, the study of the institutions and processes involved in these matters is confusing and uninteresting" (Maxim, 1999, p. 302). Richard Brody (1989) is convinced that apathy toward civic life (the public life of a citizen) is the result of a "failure of civic education. Americans fail to see connections between politics and their lives because they have not been taught that the connections exist and are personally relevant" (p. 60). Maxim (1999) writes that democratic education traditionally has studied the structure and functions of governments without regard to how they affect one's life. Essentially, democratic education was equated with democratic knowledge.

Barber (1989) argues, however, that, "if democracy is to sustain itself, a richer conception of citizenship is required" (p. 355). Barber (1989) calls this richer concept *strong democracy* and describes it as follows:

> If the point were just to get students to mature into voters who watch television news diligently and pull a voting machine lever once every few years, traditional civics . . . would suffice. But if students are to become actively engaged in public forms of thinking and participate thoughtfully in the whole spectrum of civic activities, then civic education and social studies programs require a strong element of practical civic experience—real participation and empowerment. (p. 355)

Maxim (1999) explains that the role of citizens in a strong democracy "includes real, active participation in civic processes (such as helping with a local effort to provide shelter for the homeless) and institutions (such as volunteering to lead a group of Girl Scouts)" (Maxim, 1999, p. 302). Active participation of informed and responsible citizens is the ultimate goal of democratic education.

In order to effectively participate in a strong democracy, citizens must be able to think critically to make reasoned decisions and work out societal problems. Productive thinkers are those who possess knowledge on which to base thought, can represent information from several points of view and understand multiple perspectives of others, have the motivation to use the thinking skills acquired, and can combine thought processes into strategies to solve problems. In order for students to become productive thinkers, they must be challenged to make their own meanings, not merely to remember the meaning of others.

The words *discovery learning, inquiry, problem-solving, inductive thinking, thinking,* and *thinking skills* all refer to the processes that everyone uses to discover knowledge, make decisions, and solve problems. Rather than being given answers in social studies, it is a more active process to have students actively seek answers on their own. Our knowledge about subjects can change, fade, or become obsolete, whereas our ability to think remains constant. Productive thinking strategies allow us to acquire the necessary knowledge and apply it appropriately. One of the goals of social studies education is to foster effective higher-order thinking skills that are needed outside the classroom by all members of society.

Economics

Consider the following practice question:

Ms. Laine "created" two chocolate factories in her fourth-grade room. In one, she place four "employee volunteers": a mixer (a person whose job it was to take the chocolate out of the container), a pourer (to put the chocolate into the mold), a remover to "take the chocolate out," and a wrapper "to wrap the chocolate in a special foil." The other "factory" was a sole proprietorship, where a lone owner did all the jobs. Mrs. Laine provided mixing bowls, forms, and aluminum foil as wraps so students could pretend to be doing their jobs. When Ms. Laine called, "Go," each "factory" went to work to produce as many chocolates as it could in a designated length of time. The assembly line won. In the next round, however, she had the mixer in the assembly line "go home sick." The assembly line stalled because no one else knew this job and the sole proprietorship won. Mrs. Laine was teaching that:

A. Blue-collar workers are often in an assembly line position.
B. Specialization of an assembly line also requires cross-training.
C. The demand of a product increases the price.
D. It would be better to have a corporation.

Mrs. Laine wanted to show children that an assembly line works very well, but all can come to a halt if only one worker knows one job. The best idea is to have cross-training (*B*).

Economics focuses on the production, distribution, and consumption of a country's goods and services. Economic factors have an important influence on how people in a society live. The economics standard is broken down into more manageable segments:

- Types of economic systems.
- Consumer influence.
- Structure of business.
- Government revenues and expenditures.
- Business cycles and government regulation.
- International economics.
- Economics of Texas.

I. Types of Economic Systems

Key question: *What is the role of the government in the three different types of economic systems?*

- **Economics** is the study of the ways in which goods and services are created, distributed, and exchanged.

- The **standard of living** of a society is the material well-being of its members. The United States has one of the world's highest standards of living.

- Societies must make decisions about what and how much to create in the way of goods and services.

- Societies also must decide who gets the goods and services. The ways in which these decisions are made depend upon the type of economic system.

- There are three major types of economic systems: communism, socialism, and capitalism.

- **Communism** is an economic system in which the government owns all businesses and makes all production decisions. All citizens are supposed to share equally in the country's wealth. Communist economies are often planned economies with set national goals for different areas of the economy.

- **Socialism** is also based on the idea of a cooperative society in which wealth is equally distributed. The government controls some basic industries and public utilities, whereas other businesses are owned by individuals. Socialist governments provide many social welfare programs such as health care and aid to the poor.

- **Capitalism** is an economic system in which individuals control the means of production, distribution, and exchange. The government usually does not interfere in business. Capitalism is a free-enterprise system because, with the exception of some limitations imposed by the government, citizens may engage in whatever business they choose and may produce and charge what they want.

- Most modern countries have mixed economies that emphasize one system but use elements of others. For example, the United States has a capitalist system. However, because of the complex nature of our society, the government needs to exercise some control over business and industry. There are also government-owned and operated enterprises in the United States, including the Postal Service, the public schools, some railroad lines, and social welfare projects such as public housing developments.

II. Consumer Influence

Key question: *What is the relationship between the price of and the demand for a product?*

- An individual who buys or uses goods and services for personal wants is a **consumer.**

- Consumers buy more of some products than others. The ways in which consumers spend their money (demand) influence producers' decisions about which goods to make or which services to provide (supply).

- Businesses must always consider supply and demand.

- **Supply** is the amount of available goods and services. The **assembly line** has meant faster production of goods and also standardized products. An assembly line is an arrangement of machines, equipment, and workers for a continuous flow of pieces in mass production operations, where everyone one has a specialized job.

- **Demand** is how many people want to buy the product or service. Goods and services can be sold at different prices. Usually, prices affect demand. An increase in price results in a decrease in demand. A lower price means a greater demand. However, this relationship is not always true.

- The demand for some goods and services is not greatly affected by price. For example, the demand for milk or bread does not change much even if prices go higher. The demand for these products is said to be **inelastic.**

- In contrast, the demand for video recorders or computers is greatly increased when the price drops. The demand for these products is **elastic.**

- Businesses study the changes in supply and demand for their goods and services to determine an **equilibrium point**—the price at which consumers will buy exactly the amount supplied by the producer.

- When there is overproduction, a **surplus** is created, and prices fall. When there is underproduction, a **shortage** occurs, and prices rise.

- Because of the importance of consumers, businesses try to gain favor for their goods and services through advertising. **Consumer protection groups,** like Nader's Raiders founded by Ralph Nader, check the safety and reliability of products and services and the accuracy of the claims in advertisements.

III. Structures of Business

Key question: *What three elements are needed for the operation of any business?*

- To create goods or services, a business needs three things—natural resources, labor, and capital. These things are known as **factors of production.**

- **Natural resources** are materials that can be found in nature. Metal ores, water, wood, and land are examples of natural resources.

- **Labor** is the human activity that is required to produce goods or services. Labor can be classified into two types: blue-collar and white-collar. Blue-collar workers are manual laborers such as construction workers, electricians, or factory employees. White-collar workers are employed at "desk jobs" in offices. Examples include lawyers, bankers, and journalists.

- **Capital** is wealth used to produce more wealth. Machinery, tools, and equipment are examples of capital. Money also is capital if it is producing more wealth, as in interest-paying savings accounts. Money can be used to buy other capital or to buy natural resources or labor.

- **Business** is any activity in which goods and services are exchanged for profit.

- Businesses are organized in different ways: sole proprietorships, corporations, and conglomerates.

- A **sole proprietorship** is a business owned by one person. Today, sole proprietorships make up over 75 percent of U.S. businesses. About 8 percent of U.S. businesses are partnerships, in which two or more people are owners and operators.

- A **corporation** is a business that is licensed, or chartered, by state or local governments. Corporations are owned by people who buy shares, or stock, in the business. Stockholders receive dividends, or earnings from the business, based on the number of shares they own. Stockholders elect a board of directors to make decisions for the business. About 17 percent of U.S. businesses are corporations.

- A **conglomerate** is a corporation that owns or controls companies in many fields.

- **Scarcity** occurs when there is an insufficient supply or amount of something needed. The availability of a good will affect the price consumers have to pay.

- **Price** is the amount of money, or other goods, that you have to give up to buy a good or service.

- **Barter** is an exchange of goods for goods without using money.

- **Free enterprise** is a system in which sellers and buyers are free to own property and engage in commercial transactions.

- **Laissez faire,** which literally means "hands-off," is a doctrine of government noninterference in the economy except as necessary to maintain economic freedom.

- Goods and services are anything that anyone wants. **Goods** are all options or alternatives of things. **Service** is the performance of any duties or work for another.

- **Interdependence** is a term used to describe how one industry depends on the work of another. For example, the building of a house requires several goods and services. Lumber mills, window manufacturers, and so on supply the goods to construct a house. Architects and construction workers provide some of the services required to build a house.

- **Profit** is the excess of income over all costs, including the interest cost of the wealth invested. This means the money made after one has paid all the expenses in a business.

- **Need** is a specific quantity of a specific good for which an individual would pay any price. These are the goods and services a person must have.

IV. Government Revenues and Expenditures

Key question: *What are two main sources of government revenues?*

- The U.S. government raises and spends billions of dollars each year. To pay for its activities, the government accumulates revenue (income), mainly through a variety of taxes.

- The **personal income tax** brings in the most revenue.

- The second largest amount of revenue comes from **social insurance taxes** such as that for Social Security (a proportional tax taken out of payroll).

- Substantial amounts of revenue also come from corporate income taxes, excise taxes (taxes on nonessential items), customs duties and tariffs (charges levied on imported items), state income taxes, school and property taxes, highway tolls, fines, licensing fees, and sales taxes.

- In recent years, government expenditures have been greater than revenues; this results in a **budget deficit.**

- The accumulated total of these deficits is called the **federal debt.**

- To get the money it needs, the government borrows money through the sale of **bonds.**

- The largest government expenditures are for payments made directly to Americans in the form of Social Security and Medicare benefits, federal retirement pensions, unemployment compensation, and social welfare programs.

- **Defense** is the second largest spending category.

- Interest on the federal debt is the third largest cost and will continue to be a major expense for many years.

- Economists and government officials propose different ways to reduce the debt: reducing government spending, raising taxes, or a combination of both of these approaches.

- The government also spends money on public health programs, job training, research, veterans' benefits, and payments to state and local governments to operate publicly funded programs.

V. Business Cycles and Government Regulation

Key question: *What methods does the government use to fight inflation?*

- Most countries experience periodic changes in the economy.

- The movement from one level of economic activity to another and back again is known as the **business cycle.**

- When the economy moves down from prosperity to **recession,** production decreases and unemployment increases.

- A very bad recession, such as the one the United States experienced in the 1930s, is called a **depression.**

- Another condition that has an adverse effect on the economy is inflation. **Inflation** is a general rise in prices. People can buy less with the same amount of money. The real value of the dollar declines.

- During periods of recession or depression, the government tries to stimulate the economy with public works projects and low-cost business loans.

- The government can also influence business cycles through monetary policy. The **Federal Reserve System** (or the Fed), consisting of twelve regional Federal Reserve Banks, is a regulatory agency with the power to supervise the country's banks and adjust the money supply. The Fed can lower the amount of cash reserves banks must keep, making more money available for loans. Raising the reserve limit decreases the amount of available money.

- The Fed can also adjust interest rates. Higher rates mean fewer loans to people and businesses, which then have less to spend. In this way, the Fed can shrink the money supply to combat inflation.

- The government makes decisions affecting the economy by studying various statistics. The **Consumer Price Index** (CPI) is a way of measuring the dollar's value. The CPI is the average price of essential goods and services, such as food, housing, and transportation.

- Another important economic statistic is the **Gross National Product** (GNP). The GNP is the value of everything produced in one year. GNP is the total income that residents of the country earn within the year. Total income equals total spending when calculated for the country as a whole. Therefore, GNP is the sum of spending by consumers on food, clothing, rent, durable goods, personal services and other items, plus government expenditures on goods and services, plus business outlays on capital equipment and new factories and commercial buildings, plus the spending of foreigners when they buy exports of the United States.

VI. International Economics
Key question: *Why are protected markets created?*

- Most Americans wear clothes, drive automobiles, consume food, or use radios or TVs that were manufactured in other countries.

- As the leading trade nation, the United States imports and exports billions of dollars of goods annually. The combination of imports and exports makes up a country's **balance of trade.** A country has a favorable balance of trade when it exports more than it imports. If a country imports more than it exports, then it has an unfavorable balance of trade.

- Imports mean a greater variety of goods and allow consumers to purchase some products at lower prices. However, some U.S. industries complain that they cannot compete with foreign manufacturers that are able to produce goods more cheaply than U.S. companies.

- The United States exports many goods that other countries do not make or cannot produce as cheaply. Many of this country's industries—especially agriculture—depend on exports for a large share of their profits.

- Although exports increase sales and provide employment for U.S. workers, heavy exports of some goods can sometimes keep prices high at home.

- Countries trade with one another for their mutual economic benefit. However, most countries find it necessary to regulate foreign trade to protect their economies. If the United States imposed no limits on imports of certain products, many U.S. businesses would be forced to close. Special taxes, or **tariffs,** are therefore sometimes imposed on certain foreign goods to make them more expensive so people might buy U.S. products.

- When tariffs are used to make foreign goods more expensive than similar items made at home, then a **protected market** is created. If restrictions that trading partners impose on one another become too severe, however, both countries can suffer economically.

- Sometimes, countries prohibit their usual trade with each other because of a political conflict. A ban imposed on trade because of foreign policy is called an **embargo.**

VI. Economics of Texas
Key question: *What are the major economies of Texas?*

- Until recently, the Texas economy was land based and colonial in structure. Texas produced, processed, and shipped its agricultural and mineral products to outside markets. Texas was dependent on external demand and the prices paid for its cotton, cattle, or petroleum.

- The first real economy in Texas was created by southern planters and was based on large slave plantations. Cotton has helped shape Texas history as a major cash crop. As early as Stephen F. Austin's original colony, the leading export was cotton. **Cotton** was barged down Texas rivers to the Gulf of Mexico to be shipped to Europe or the United States. Cotton was the heart of the economy during the era of the Republic of Texas and early statehood. After the Civil War, the plantation system was replaced with sharecroppers. In the early 1900s, the **boll weevil,** a type of beetle, inflicted serious damage on Texas cotton crops. In 1904, an estimated 700,000 bales were lost at a cost of approximately $42 million. The boll weevil caused a steady drop in Texas cotton yields over a thirty-year period. The economy diversified, but cotton is still an important part of the Texas economy. Texas harvests still account for a third of the total cotton production in the United States.

- The **cattle kingdom,** inherited from the Mexicans, spread across the entire American West in the late nineteenth century. Initially, the cattle business involved rounding up stray cattle and driving them north to Kansas railheads. The demand for beef created a link between the western frontier and the industrial marketplace. Like King Cotton, the cattle kingdom drew people and money from outside the state and involved agricultural products shipped to distant markets.

- By 1866, cattle had replaced cotton as king in Texas. The abundance of longhorn cattle in south Texas and the return of Confederate soldiers to a poor reconstruction economy marked the beginning of the era of **Texas trail drives** to northern markets. Cattle that sold for $4 a head in Texas brought $30 to $40 in the North.

- For much of the twentieth century, **petroleum** was the basis for the Texas economy. From the first major oil discovery at **Spindletop,** near Beaumont, by mining engineer Captain A. E. Lucas in 1901, Texas and the production of crude oil have been synonymous. Between 1900 and 1901, Texas oil production increased fourfold. In 1902, Spindletop alone produced 17 million barrels, 93 percent of the state's production. The massive amounts of money involving oil production brought great prosperity to the entire state.

- After World War II, the United States market sought cheaper oil in the Middle East. However, the oil embargo by the Organization of Petroleum Exporting Countries (OPEC) in 1973, a year after Texas reached its peak in oil production, caused an economic boom during the 1970s as prices were driven upward.

- This boom, of course, was followed by the bust of the 1980s when, in 1986, the price for West Texas crude fell below $10 a barrel. In 1981, the petroleum industry contributed 27 percent of the state's gross state product (GSP). Ten years later, in 1991, the industry contributed only 12 percent to the GSP.

- In recent years, the Texas economy has diversified from oil production. **Computers** and **electronic products** are now Texas's largest export. The communications equipment industry is also very important to the Texas economy. This industry is composed primarily of establishments that manufacture telephone, radio, and television broadcasting and wireless communications equipment.

Consider the following practice question:

Ms. Henning's fourth-grade class is ending their unit on the different economies of Texas. To ensure their understanding, Ms. Henning asks them the following question:
Which of these is not one of the major economies of Texas?

A. Tourism.
B. Oil.
C. Cattle.
D. Cotton.

Oil, cattle, and cotton have been much more important economies for the state of Texas, though some areas of Texas do enjoy a great deal of tourism (San Antonio, South Padre Island, etc.). The best answer is A.

SUMMARY

As you have probably gathered, many of the competencies covered in the social studies component of the TExES overlap in their coverage. This makes the organizing principles established in the introduction of this chapter important considerations as you prepare to take the TExES. Both the TExES social studies competencies and the social studies TEKS are based upon three areas: skills, knowledge, and values. Understanding the interrelatedness of the TExES standards and the TEKS should facilitate your study and review of the social studies information that may appear on the TExES. Hopefully, too, this organizing technique will help you as you move from pre-service teacher into your role as a classroom teacher and begin to think about teaching social studies in your classroom.

Teachers today have the responsibility of shaping the future through their work with children. This is an awesome responsibility since many of these children will become tomorrow's leaders. Thinking of education merely in terms of the present is no longer sufficient. It is important for all teachers to have a vision of the future for the children they teach. This vision will reflect their passion and drive to work with children and will give purpose and direction to their decisions about instruction. We hope that you will carry this vision throughout your days as a social studies teacher.

REFERENCES

Barber, B. (1989). Public talk and civic action: Education for participation in a strong democracy. *Social Education, 53,* 355.

Berg, M. (1988). Integrating ideas for social studies. *Social Studies and the Young Learner, 1,* unnumbered pullout section.

Brody, R. (1989). Why study politics? In *Charting a course: Social studies for the 21st century.* Washington, DC: National Commission on Social Studies in the Schools.

Brophy, J., & Alleman, J. (1996). *Powerful social studies for elementary students.* New York: Harcourt Brace College Publishers.

Chapin, J., & Messick, R. (1999). *Elementary social studies: A practical guide* (4th ed.). Boston: Allyn and Bacon.

Chapin, J., & Messick, R. (2002). *Elementary social studies: A practical guide* (5th ed.). Boston: Allyn and Bacon.

Davis, K. (1992). *Don't know much about geography: Everything you need to know about the world but never learned.* New York: William Morrow.

Duval, L. (1994). *Respecting our differences: A guide to getting along in a changing world.* Minneapolis: Free Spirit Publishing.

Ellis, A. (2002). *Teaching and learning: Elementary social studies.* Boston: Allyn and Bacon.

Farris, P. (2001). *Elementary and middle school social studies: An interdisciplinary approach.* Boston: McGraw-Hill.

Fritzer, P. (1999). *Social studies content for elementary/middle school teachers.* Coral Springs, FL: Bassett Press.

Gay, G. (1991). Culturally diverse students and social studies. In J. Shaver (Ed.), *Handbook of research on social studies teaching and learning* (pp. 144–156). New York: Macmillan.

Grant, S., & Vansledright, B. (2001). *Constructing a powerful approach to teaching and learning in elementary social studies.* Boston: Houghton Mifflin Co.

Hernandez, H. (1989). *Multicultural education: A teacher's guide to content and process.* Columbus, OH: Merrill.

Johnson, A. (2000). *Up and out: Using creative and critical thinking skills to enhance learning.* Boston: Allyn and Bacon.

Levstik, L., & Barton, K. (2001). *Doing history: Investigating with children in elementary and middle schools.* Mahwah, NJ: Lawrence Erlbaum.

Loewen, J. (1995). *Lies my teacher told me: Everything your American history textbook got wrong.* New York: New Press.

Manning, M., & Baruth, L. (2000). *Multicultural education of children and adolescents.* Boston: Allyn and Bacon.

Martorella, P., & Beal, C. (2002). *Social studies for elementary school classrooms: Preparing children to be global citizens.* Upper Saddle River, NJ: Merrill Prentice-Hall.

Massialas, B., & Allen, R. (1996). *Crucial issues in teaching social studies K–12.* Belmont, CA: Wadsworth Publishing Company.

Maxim, G. (1999). *Social studies and the elementary school child.* Upper Saddle River, NJ: Prentice-Hall.

McGowan, T., & Guzzetti, B. (1991). Promoting social studies understanding through literature-based instruction. *The Social Studies, 82,* 16–21.

National Council for the Social Studies (1994). *Expectations for excellence.* Washington, DC: Author.

National Center for History in the Schools (1996). *National standards for history.* Los Angeles: Author.

Parker, W., & Jarolimek, J. (2000). *Social studies in elementary education.* Upper Saddle River, NJ: Prentice-Hall.

Savage, T., & Armstrong, D. (1996). *Effective teaching in elementary social studies.* Upper Saddle River, NJ: Prentice-Hall.

Seefeldt, C. (1997). *Social studies for the preschool-primary child* (5th ed.). Upper Saddle River, NJ: Merrill.

Social Studies Center (2000). *Texas social studies framework.* Available online: http://socialstudies.tea.state.tx.us/

Stanford, B. (1996). Gender equity in the classroom. In D.A. Byrnes & G. Kiger (Eds.), *Common bonds: Anti-bias in a diverse society* (pp. 79–94). Olney, MD: Association for Childhood Education International.

Swartz, R., & Perkins, D. (1990). *Teaching thinking: Issues and approaches.* Pacific Grove, CA: Midwest Publications.

Texas Education Agency. (1999). *Texas social studies framework kindergarten–grade 12: Research and resources for designing a social studies curriculum.* Austin: Author.

ABOUT THE AUTHOR

TRENIA L. WALKER, Ed.D., is an assistant professor at the University of Pittsburgh, Department of Instruction and Learning. Dr. Walker formerly taught social studies methods at the University of Houston for several years. Her current research explores transformative learning theories and the implications for technology, popular culture, and globalization in social studies teaching and learning.

Preparing to Teach Science

Mary E. Wingfield
University of Houston

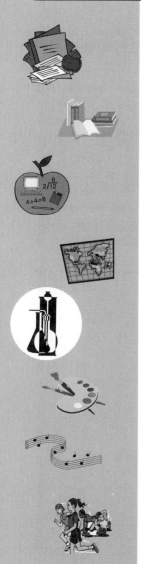

This chapter contains three sections of information about science in the elementary classroom. A brief introduction to science education provides the theoretical basis for the state's standards. Then, each of the science standards and relevant practice questions will be discussed. Finally, a model science lesson and evaluation by standards, a resource list, and references are presented.

According to the National Science Education Standards (National Research Council, 1996), "Lifelong scientific literacy begins with understandings, attitudes, and values established in the earliest years" (p. 114). Therefore, teachers of elementary-school-aged children must remember to foster a sense of wonder, design investigations, ask questions, and promote curiosity. Today's science teachers benefit from newly designed curriculum materials and kits that include developmentally appropriate manipulative materials. Textbooks are no longer viewed as a tool for memorizing definitions but as one of many resources available for information. Finally, appropriate instructional strategies should be employed that encourage inquiry, problem solving and higher-order thinking, cooperative learning, and concept attainment.

Science education reform efforts have relied on research studies from the National Science Teachers Association, the American Association for the Advancement of Science, and the National Science Foundation. The effort to improve science education has resulted in the establishment of new state guidelines and National Standards. Texas teachers see these reform efforts detailed in the Texas Essential Knowledge and Skills (TEKS) for science for each grade level (access at http://www.tea.state.tx.us/teks). The format of the TEKS reflects national reform efforts through its introduction at each grade level. One example notes that "In kindergarten, science introduces the use of simple classroom and field investigations to enable the development of students' skills of asking questions, gathering information, communicating findings, and making informed decisions. Using their own senses and common tools such as a hand lens, students make observations and collect information. Students also use computers and information technology to support their investigations" (TEA, Chapter 112.2 (a) 1). Texas children are evaluated on their knowledge of the elementary TEKS in the new TAKS test (Texas Assessment of Knowledge and Skills).

The TAKS tests focus on an understanding of scientific processes, the nature of science, and the content strands of life, earth, and physical science. Correlations with the National Standards, TEKS, and district guidelines ensure that students are benefiting from a concerted effort by numerous scientists and science educators to provide meaningful, inquiry-based, student-centered, "hands-on" science instruction. The next section of this chapter highlights each of the eleven Texas science standards for the Elementary Comprehensive EC-4 TExES (Competencies 20–23).

STANDARD I (SCIENCE INSTRUCTION)

Competency 020:   The science teacher manages classroom, field, and laboratory activities to ensure the safety of all students and the ethical care and treatment of organisms and specimens.

The beginning teacher considers safety considerations as essential in the hands-on science classroom of today. Curiosity and immaturity combine to present hazards with even the most common materials. *This standard requires that the teacher knows and understands safety regulations and guidelines, procedures for responding to an accident in the laboratory, including first aid, legal issues associated with accidents, potential safety hazards, and modification of equipment for students with special needs. In the classroom, the teacher employs safe practices by arranging the space for storage, traffic flow, and access to each student. The teacher is responsible for reading the Materials Safety Data Sheet (MSDS) and other chemical labels and for ensuring that safety equipment, including eye washer, a fire blanket, and a fire extinguisher, is available. The teacher needs to check all materials prior to use and must create an environment where rules and safety procedures are important. Potential hazards in the field, including insect bites, poisonous plants, and allergies, require planning and preparation. They should not, however, be used an excuse for avoiding field investigations listed in the TEKS grade level. Finally, classroom pets are a wonderful way to promote responsibility and encourage scientific observations. Considerations must be given to the possibilities of allergies, appropriate instruction in care and treatment, and extra supervision to ensure the careful handling of animals.*

Consider the following practice question:

Ms. Davis, a third-grade teacher, intends to continually reinforce the importance of safety in the science classroom and makes sure that:

A. Safety rules are posted in the room.
B. The class previews each activity together to identify potential hazards.
C. Signed safety contracts are required at the beginning of the year.
D. Safety is part of the students' grade.

The teacher realizes that even if grades are used (*D*), safety rules are posted (*A*), and safety contracts are signed at the beginning of the year (*C*), students will need constant reminders for each activity because it may include specific hazards. The correct answer is *B*.

Laboratory safety begins in the planning stages, where activities need to be evaluated and risks minimized. Plastic containers are substituted for glass; food allergies considered; and appropriate management, preparation, and proactive measures are employed. However, accidents can happen even in the most carefully planned instruction. Therefore, safety procedures must be practiced.

In 1965, the Texas Board of Health adopted standards for eye and face protection. Later, the U.S. Congress passed the Occupational Health and Safety Act (OSHA) and in 1986, Texas enacted the Texas Hazardous Communication Act (HazCom). These acts govern how employees (and students) must be informed of potential risks involved in handling scientific materials and how materials that may harm the environment are to be disposed of. This information is found on the Material Safety Data Sheet (MSDS) for every chemical substance with which employees (and students) come into contact, including cleaning agents, laboratory chemicals, and other products. Schools *must* keep an up-to-date record of all

MSDSs for every chemical on site. This record is displayed in a centralized location and available for inspection.

Safety equipment should be available in every room. Even with proper use of safety goggles and safety glasses, an emergency eye washer (either fixed or portable) is essential in case of eye contamination from chemicals or foreign material. Fire extinguishers, fire blankets, and practiced procedures of "stop-drop-and-roll" are necessary whenever flame or heat is used. The use of personal protective equipment (goggles), proper storage, use, and disposal of materials, and the need for a safety contract and clearly posted rules are all included in this competency.

Numerous sources are available for additional safety information. Each campus should have a copy of the "Texas Safety Standards" (www.tenet.edu/teks/science/stacks/safety/safetymain.html). At minimum, the major safety points to remember include:

- Obtain and review all state and district guidelines and policies.
- Provide appropriate safety instruction, including a safety quiz and safety contract for students and parents to sign.
- Instruct students on proper use of safety equipment—goggles, fire extinguishers, etc.
- Provide practice sessions for safety rules and procedures.
- Identify potential hazards and provide appropriate safety precautions before each activity.
- Instruct students to immediately report any personal injury, damaged equipment, and hazard potentials.
- Do not permit students to handle science supplies or equipment until they have been given specific instruction in their use.
- Prevent loose clothing and/or hair from coming into contact with science supplies, chemicals, or equipment.
- Instruct students in the proper care and handling of classroom pets and organisms.
- Expect the unexpected, never taking hazards for granted.

Try the following practice question:

After using cabbage juice, vinegar, lemon juice, egg white, and baking soda to identify acids and bases with litmus paper, the teacher should:

A. Dismiss students to their next class immediately.
B. Instruct students to return unused chemicals to their original containers.
C. Instruct students to clean work surfaces and wash their hands.
D. Have students move away from tables so that the teacher can clean the area properly.

The best answer is C. Returning unused chemicals to original containers (*B*) might lead to contamination. Other labeled containers should be used to store unused chemicals. Answers *A* and *D* fail to promote safety consciousness and appropriate practices, leaving little responsibility to students, although answers *C* and *D* list two appropriate procedures for chemical use with children.

STANDARD II (USING SCIENCE TOOLS, MATERIALS, EQUIPMENT, AND TECHNOLOGIES)

Competency 020:   The science teacher understands the correct use of tools, materials, equipment, and technologies.

The beginning teacher knows and understands concepts of precision and accuracy in the process of data collection. The teacher can use grade-appropriate equipment and technology for gathering, analyzing, and reporting data. This includes the use of the International System of Measurement (i.e., the metric system) and the ability to perform conversions within and across measurement systems. Scientific communications include the teachers' ability to organize, display, and communicate data in a variety of ways (e.g., charts, tables, graphs, diagrams, written reports, and oral presentations).

Consider the following practice question:

After providing laboratory equipment for her fourth-grade students, Ms. Estrada notices that the triple beam pan balance is not even. She should:

A. Instruct the students to add a few gram masses until the balance is even.
B. Use that balance for only weighing large objects because it is not accurate.
C. Level the balance by using the adjustment dial.
D. Use a different balance.

The triple beam balance has an adjustment dial that balances the pan with the beam masses. Adjustment is necessary after the balance has been relocated. Answers *A* and *B* might work as solutions, but they do not model the importance of accuracy in science. Option *D* is unnecessary. The correct answer is C.

In the collection of data through observations, scientists use many tools. Magnifying (hand) lenses, microscopes, telescopes, and measuring devices (e.g., Pyrex beakers, graduated cylinders, and balances) would be included in a science classroom. Equipment for the EC-4 classroom needs to be developmentally appropriate. For example, double-pan balances in early grades are used to indicate less-than and more-than relationships. Teachers also must be familiar with the correct terminology and use of the equipment so they can instruct their students.

For example, a liquid tends to adhere and curve upward on the sides of graduated cylinders. Measurements must be taken by reading the bottom of this curved liquid, called a meniscus, in order to obtain an accurate measurement.

Try the following practice question:

Mr. Landry starts a lesson on the proper use of a microscope and *first* has children:

A. Identify the parts of the microscope: the stage, eyepiece, and arm.
B. Make slides to view under high magnification.
C. Explain the difference between high- and low-power magnification.
D. Predict the total magnification power of the instrument.

The student needs to correctly identify and name the parts of the microscope. This procedure facilitates subsequent important instructions for microscope use. Although *B, C,* and *D* might be appropriate at some point in the lesson, the students would need the microscope terminology to use and follow directions. The correct answer is *A.*

Data collection and interpretation are included in this standard, and the teacher is expected to promote scientific communication through graphing. The third- and fourth-grade TEKS include the following student expectations related to scientific inquiry: "construct graphs, tables, maps, charts to organize, examine, evaluate information" and "analyze and interpret information to construct explanations from direct and indirect evidence" and "communicate valid conclusions."

Students will be able to interpret graphs if they have had experience in constructing them. Teachers should provide numerous opportunities for students to collect and organize data. Bar graphs are used for data of groups, sets, or categories. Early grades often collect categorical data and organize bar graphs, for example, for types of weather, car and bus riders, and birthday months. Line graphs are useful for comparing two sets of continuous numbers and finding the relationship between those data. Technology can also be used to collect data on simple spreadsheets, design graphs, and communicate results using presentation software.

Consider the following practice question:

Mr. Gray's paper recycling project allowed the third graders to collect data. Children presented the information each week as pie charts showing percentage of mass recycled per class. At the end of the year, the children wanted to know how the percentage for their grade had changed throughout the year. How should the data be represented?

A. Pie chart.
B. Line graph.

C. Bar graph.
D. Data table.

The pie chart (*A*) was used for weekly results, but this format would not show change over time. A bar graph (*C*) would best show categories on the x-axis (i.e., types of paper recycled such as newspaper, copy paper, etc.). A data table does organize data, but this format does not have visual impact to depict changes throughout the year. The correct answer is *B*, a line graph. The manipulated variable on the x-axis (horizontal) would be numerical and continuous (weeks per year), and the responding variable on the y-axis (vertical) would be third grade percentage each week. A line graph would depict clearly the relationship between these variables, and the trends of increasing or decreasing recycling would be evident and visual.

Let's look at the pie chart used by Mr. Gray's students to show the percentage of weight recycled each week by each class. Note that weekly data would best be represented as the *pie chart* in Figure 5.1.

In order to organize and analyze information, data are often recorded in tables. A *data table* is organized lists of information or observations that should be titled and labeled for clear understanding (an example is shown in Table 5.1).

This information can be visually represented on a line graph (as in Figure 5.2) because the data for both variables (time and population) are continuous and numerical.

During this week, the third graders
recycled 50% of the total weight.
The fourth graders recycled 25%.
The second graders had 15%,
and first graders had 10% of the total.

Pie charts visually present the fraction,
percent, and proportion of the whole.

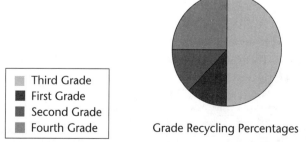

Third Grade
First Grade
Second Grade
Fourth Grade

Grade Recycling Percentages

FIGURE 5.1

**TABLE 5.1 Yearly Catfish
Population in Big Star Lake**

Year	Catfish Population
1999	550
2000	800
2001	1200
2002	700

The *manipulative variable* (MV) is always plotted on the x-axis (horizontal), and the *responding variable* (RV) is plotted on the y-axis (vertical). Line graphs allow us to determine increasing and decreasing trends (e.g., the catfish population increased from 1999 to 2001) and to determine data values that fall between collected data points on the graph line. For example, what was the population halfway in between 1999 and 2000? (The answer is 675.) Teachers should ask many questions, including which year had the highest catfish population, the lowest population, and so forth. They can also ask the students to (1) identify patterns and trends—which year looks different than the rest, (2) make inferences—explain what happened to the population between 2001 and 2002, and (3) make predictions—what do you think will happen to the population in 2003? Thus, the line graph is the best format to depict the annual data for fish in a nearby lake for Mr. Gray's class.

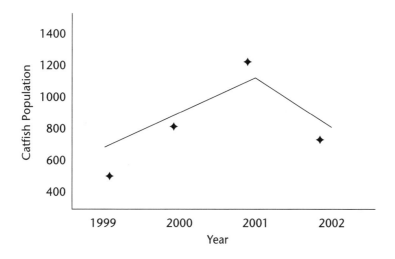

FIGURE 5.2

Try the following practice question:

During a kindergarten science lesson on animals, Ms. Lowe gave each student a box of animal cookies and asked them to sort the animals by shape. These animal data could be visually represented best as a:

A. Data table.   **C.** Pie chart.
B. Line graph.   **D.** Bar graph.

The categorical data (type of animal) would be the manipulative variable (MV) on the x-axis (horizontal), and the number of that type would be the responding variable on the y-axis (vertical). A data table (*A*) could list this same information, but it is not visual. A line graph (*B*) is used for continuous, numerical data. A pie chart (*C*) helps to show data collected as parts of a whole. The bar graph would clearly show which type of animal was most represented and which was least represented. The correct answer is *D*.

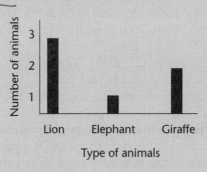

FIGURE 5.3

Finally, this standard on tools, equipment, and technologies includes emphasis on measurement and the metric system.

Consider the following practice question:

A first-grade teacher wants to introduce measurement to her students. She gives each group of students five objects to observe and asks them to compare the objects to a:

A. Metric ruler.
B. Standard ruler.
C. Student's shoe.
D. Yard stick.

First-grade students should use measurement aids without numbers to compare and develop *greater than* and *less than* concepts. Upper-grade students would use standard measurement tools—*A, B,* or *D*—where divisions and markings are clearly understood and are appropriate for the task. The correct answer is *C*.

Scientists use measurement to quantify their observations. For example, an observation of a "large" butterfly has no frame of reference, but a butterfly with a 4 centimeter wingspan is more specific. Scientists are careful that the measuring instrument is appropriate for the task. For example, a graduated cylinder with 1 milliliter markings is more accurate than a beaker with 50 milliliter lines. Graduated cylinders are designed and manufactured specifically for liquid measurement. Measurements are often repeated and averaged to increase their validity and reliability.

The *International System of Units* or the *metric system* was adopted internationally for use in 1960. All but two countries quickly made the conversion to the metric system, and this system is used internationally for commerce and scientific work. The metric system was designed to relate mass, distance, and volume for pure water. A cubic box that is one centimeter on each side has a volume of $1 \times 1 \times 1 = 1$ cubic centimeter (volume = length × width × height). The amount of water that would fill such a box is defined in the metric system as one milliliter, and it has a mass of one gram (at standard temperature and pressure).

The metric system makes use of base units—*gram* for mass, *meter* for length, and *liter* for volume. Prefixes (e.g., kilo-, deci-, milli-) modify the base units.

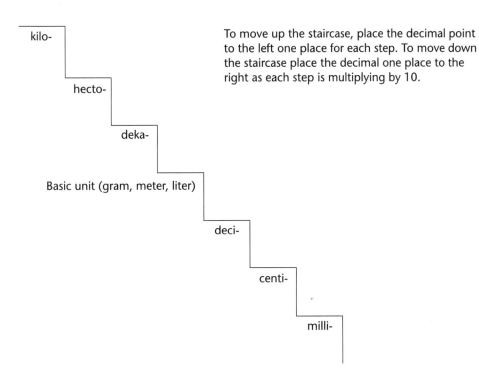

kilo-

hecto-

deka-

Basic unit (gram, meter, liter)

deci-

centi-

milli-

To move up the staircase, place the decimal point to the left one place for each step. To move down the staircase place the decimal one place to the right as each step is multiplying by 10.

FIGURE 5.4

Converting within the metric system is as easy as adding a zero or moving the decimal point, because each prefix represents a factor of ten. The staircase depicted is a visualization of how these prefixes are related. To help you remember this order, you might use a memory model for the first letter of each word (King Henry danced [a] dizzy, crazy minuet) or one of your own.

For example, since there are 10 millimeters in each centimeter, 10 centimeters in each decimeter, and 10 decimeters in a meter, there are 1000 (10 × 10 × 10) millimeters in a meter. A kilogram is a measure of mass that represents 10 hectograms, 100 dekagrams, and 1000 grams.

Try the following metric conversions.

__460__ centiliters = 4 liters (L)   27 meters = __27,000__ millimeters (mm)

__5__ dekagrams = 50 grams (g)   5 liters = __500__ centiliters (cl)

__14__ kilometers = 140 hectometers (hm)   .05 kilometers = __.05__ meters (m)

__75,000__ centigrams = 75 dekagrams (dcg)   65 kilograms = __6,500__ dekagrams (dcg)

Answers: 400 centiliters = 4 liters; 5 dekagrams = 50 grams; 14 kilometers = 140 hectometers; 75,000 centigrams = 75 dekagrams; 27 meters = 27,000 millimeters; 5 liters = 500 centiliters; .05 kilometers = 50 meters; 65 kilograms = 6,500 dekagrams. Also note the abbreviations used.

Several common but important measurements and their metric values are listed below:

- Boiling point of pure water at sea level: 100 degrees Celsius (212 degrees Fahrenheit)
- Freezing point of pure water at sea level: 0 degrees Celsius (32 degrees Fahrenheit)
- Normal human body temperature: 37 degrees Celsius (98.6 degrees Fahrenheit)
- Distance from the sun to the earth: 149,637,000 kilometers (93,000,000 miles)
  (Conversion factor, 1 mile = 1.609 km)
- Weight of 10 pound bag of potatoes: 4.54 kg
  (Conversion factor, 2.2 pounds = 1 kg)
- 15 gallon tank of gasoline: 56.775 liters
  (Conversion factor, 1 gallon = 3.785 liters)

Try the following practice question:

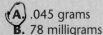

Mrs. Henry is teaching her third-grade students to measure mass in the metric system. Which of the following measurements represents the smallest mass?

A. .045 grams
B. 78 milligrams
C. .009 kilograms
D. 333 hectograms

The least amount of mass cannot be determined until all choices are converted to the same unit. For example, one yard is more than 27 inches, even though the number 27 is greater than the number 1. "Apples" must be compared to "apples" to make a comparison. Converting all the choices into grams would yield (*A*) .045 grams, (*B*) .078 grams, (*C*) 9 grams, and (*D*) 33.3 grams. Clearly, .045 grams is the least value. The correct answer is *A*.

STANDARD III (SCIENCE INQUIRY)

Competency 020:   The science teacher understands the process of scientific inquiry and its role in science instruction.

The beginning teacher understands that the type of scientific investigation used depends on the questions to be answered. The teacher understands the use of technology in scientific research and the principles and procedures used in conducting descriptive studies, controlled experiments, and comparative data analysis. The teacher links prior knowledge and experience to the investigations and focuses inquiry-based activities from questions and issues that are relevant to the students. The teacher models the processes of scientific inquiry by using combinations of the following:

- *Asking a scientific question, formulating a testable hypothesis.*
- *Selecting appropriate equipment and technology for gathering information.*
- *Making observations and collecting data.*
- *Organizing, analyzing, and evaluating data to find trends and patterns and making inferences.*
- *Communicating and defending a valid conclusion about the hypothesis under investigation.*

Consider the following practice question:

Mr. Lopez has completed a fourth-grade unit on the environment and intends to assess students' ability to use higher-order thinking skills to draw conclusions based on experimental data. Given a graph of alternative fuels and the resulting air pollution, the students would be able to:

A. Evaluate which alternative fuel would be best for the environment.
B. Describe the process of measuring resulting air pollution.

C. Predict what new alternative fuel will be invented in the future.
D. List three alternative fuels.

As this is an evaluation-level question, the student is required to use knowledge and synthesis to think at a higher level. Correctly reading the graph could include answer *D*, but the listing task requires only the lowest level of knowledge. Basing the conclusions from the graphed information in this case would not enable the student to describe the process (*B*) or to predict (*C*) future events. The correct answer is *A*.

Science teachers are able to promote the scientific attitudes related to inquiry and skepticism through careful investigations and analysis of results. Challenging students to (1) make predictions; (2) develop research questions; (3) form hypotheses; (4) conduct descriptive, experimental, and correlational investigations; and (5) correctly analyze the results enable them become problem solvers and critical thinkers. Questions from all levels of Bloom's taxonomy allow students to use the knowledge of facts and vocabulary to build comprehension through explanations in their own words and applications of the knowledge in other contexts. Higher levels of thinking include analysis—taking apart, comparing/contrasting; synthesis—putting together, designing/creating; and evaluation—recommending/judging based on selected criteria. Assisting students in developing higher-order thinking prepares them for the level of scientific literacy they would need, for example, to read a newspaper story about a new medical discovery (or diet drug) and be able to question the report's authors, their sources of information, the investigation's methods, and the interpretation of the data. In an effort to promote the science educational reforms that produce a scientifically literate society, students need authentic experiences with critical thinking and analysis in real-world contexts. Teachers should promote conversations between young scientists to encourage them to see each other as resources and demonstrate that more is learned when scientific information is shared.

Try the following practice question:

During a second-grade science lesson about states of matter and heat, Ms. Curtis allows children to observe the physical changes of an ice cube placed in a sunny spot on the playground. Which of the following questions regarding the melting of the ice cube would be most effective in encouraging students' use of higher-order thinking skills about the effect of heat on matter?

A. What is the amount of time it takes for the ice cube to melt?
B. What would happen if the ice cube were placed in the shade?
C. Why does the melted liquid look bigger than the original ice cube?
D. What is the temperature of the sunny spot?

Making predictions would require students to use their observations to hypothesize about the amount of heat and the effect of the heat on the ice cube in the shade. Although the time (*A*) and temperature (*D*) could be recorded, these answers do not require higher-order thinking. Option (*C*) would allow students to make predictions but does not directly involve the effect of heat on states of matter. Making use of students' questions is a good way for teachers to advance higher-level thinking and problem solving. Teachers should be flexible, continuing the investigations and promoting student inquiry. The correct answer is *B*.

Consider the following practice question:

Mrs. Glenn, a first-grade teacher, wants her students to understand the scientific process of classification. She provides a container of different rocks to each group of students. What question should she first use to direct the students?

   A. How many rocks does your group have?
   B. Can the rocks be sorted into two groups? Explain the grouping of each rock.
   C. Can you predict where each of these rocks came from?
   D. How can you find more about each rock?

Although answers *C* and *D* might be interesting and appropriate for instruction, the objective is to practice classification. Answer *A* requires a response based on low-level knowledge, one that does not require classifying. The correct answer is *B*.

Teachers realize that scientific inquiry is promoted through the practice and the use of science process skills. Each of the TEKS grade levels begins with an emphasis on science process skills that can be used in the classroom on a daily basis.

The **basic science process skills** include:

- **Observing:** Using the five senses to describe objects and events. Observations can be qualitative (e.g., color, shape) or quantitative (e.g., length, mass, volume).
- **Classifying:** Sorting objects or events into groups based on common characteristics or attributes.
- **Measuring:** Determining the length, volume, mass, temperature, or area to describe and quantify objects.
- **Communicating:** Sharing observations and explanations of objects or events with others.

The **integrated process skills** include:

- **Inferring and predicting:** Explaining or drawing conclusions about an object or future event based upon observations.

- **Using variables:** Studying effects of manipulating and controlling variables.
- **Representing data:** Organizing observations and measurements to make data useful.
- **Experimenting:** Using the process skills necessary to ask a question, plan an investigation, collect data, and form a conclusion.

All children can use their curiosity to observe the natural world around them. Children must be encouraged to use their senses to make observations and gather data. When children are able to use their own senses to gain information, they remember it much longer than when told or read. Science with the senses literally comes alive. Even preK and kindergartners routinely communicate selected weather conditions at calendar time, classifying their results and representing the data through pictures or graphs. Teachers can often integrate these skills throughout other content areas by infusing prediction into a reading assignment, measuring into a mathematics lesson, or observation into fine arts.

Consider the following practice question:

The second-grade TEKS (2.7A) expect children to "observe, measure, record, analyze, predict and illustrate changes in size, mass, temperature, color, position, quantity, sound, and movement." The teacher supplies thick and thin rubber bands stretched over cardboard box lids. The students design a controlled experiment with a testable hypothesis to find if sound produced by plucking the thick and thin rubber bands is different. Their design must include:

A. Manipulative variables—thick and thin rubber bands.
B. Responding variables—same or different sounds heard.
C. Controlled variables—same-size box lids, and same person plucking each rubber band with the same force.
D. All of the above.

The correct answer is *D*. Controlled experiments should also be repeated and the data averaged when necessary.

Scientists use a specific processes and criteria to investigate and interpret the natural world. This procedure is called the *scientific method,* and it involves seeking observable evidence in a systematic process. This process begins with *observations* that can be gained from the senses and/or enhanced through technology. For example, a thermometer provides a quantitative measurement rather than a vague sense of feeling hot or cold.

For scientists, observations lead to questions about "why?" or "what if?" These questions lead to the examination of existing knowledge on the subject in order to learn more about the phenomena they are questioning. This research step is important because the problem may have already been studied or an answer discovered, or new findings could lead the scientists toward a different possible *hypothesis* or "educated guess" about the solution. The *experiment* is a means of comparing an unknown set of circumstances to one that is known or controlled. A *variable* is a factor that affects the outcome of the experiment. Manipulative variables are able to be changed—such as changing the thick rubberband to the thin ones to see what new outcome in sound will occur in the preceding question. An ideal experiment tests only one variable at a time and compares the result to a control setting (where the variable is not present or consistent). This method helps to clarify or examine the outcome, identify possible cause-and-effect relationships, and make predictions for further study. After a hypothesis has withstood repeated testing and experimentation, the hypothesis can be called a *scientific theory*—a general explanation of a group of related phenomena.

Teachers should continuously use events and activities that stimulate students' questions and curiosity. Students should have opportunities to explore these events. Sometimes this exploration can be unstructured and more play like. Instructional structure is needed at other times. This format is conducive for the investigation procedures described above. This instructional approach is often called inquiry-based or discovery. Its goal is to foster engagement, scientific thinking processes, and student-generated generalizations.

Consider the following practice question:

Third-grade students notice that recently planted bushes near the edge of the playground are all brown. The teacher uses their observations to promote inquiry about plant growth and environmental conditions. What step should they take next to follow the scientific method?

A. Research the plant type to determine its ideal growing conditions.
B. Write a report for the school newspaper about their observations.
C. Formulate a testable hypothesis or an educated guess.
D. Plant some new bushes and add water daily.

The students' observations lead to questions, and now they must undertake research to narrow their possible explanations. Then they can (C) form a testable hypothesis and set up an experiment where water, soil conditions, sunlight, and/or temperature can be investigated. The cause of the plant's condition may not be a matter of water (D), and their scientific reporting (B) should be undertaken after they have tested their hypothesis. The correct answer is A, research what they can find out about the situation first.

STANDARD IV (TEACHING SCIENCE)

Competency 020: The science teacher has theoretical and practical knowledge about teaching science and about how students learn science.

The beginning teacher knows the developmental characteristics of students and how that influences science learning. The teacher understands the importance of play for the preK child at a water table and the need for manipulatives and concrete experiences for the young child. Teachers use developmentally appropriate methods to plan and implement inquiry-based science programs. They establish a collaborative scientific community that supports actively engaged learning and make accommodations for the needs of all students. Teachers must use strategies that assist students in the development of content-area vocabulary; word meaning in content-related texts; and comprehension before, during, and after reading content-related texts. Teachers must understand common student misconceptions in science and learn theories about how students develop scientific understanding. In the classroom, teachers will sequence learning activities in a way that allows students to build upon their prior knowledge and challenges them to expand their understanding of science. This can be done through lab and field investigations that promote curiosity, openness to new ideas, and skepticism. Teachers will use a variety of instructional strategies to ensure all students' reading comprehension of content-related texts. They will assist students in locating and retaining content-related information from a range of texts and technologies. Teachers will also help students to locate the meanings and pronunciations of unfamiliar content-related words through dictionaries. Teachers will respect student diversity and use questioning strategies to move students from concrete to more abstract understanding. As a facilitator, teachers will expect students to be active participants through individual, small group, and whole-class strategies. Working with others provides a model of the scientific community where researchers often communicate and share findings.

Consider the following practice question:

Ms. Peters has been teaching her second-grade science unit on dinosaurs by reading about dinosaurs and having students color pictures. After all, she says, there are really no hands-on approaches to studying dinosaurs because they aren't around anymore. Which activity would be *least* consistent with developments in science education about how students learn science?

A. Include hands-on experiments about fossils—pressing shells in play dough for example.
B. Include hands-on measurement activities to compare dinosaur size to animals of today—lifting strings with helium balloons to show and compare the heights of some dinosaurs, for example.
C. Include use of computer technology to visit an archeological site.
D. Show the video of *Jurassic Park*.

The hands-on activities (*A* and *B*) are developmentally appropriate and in keeping with research about how second graders—who are concrete learners—would best learn. *C* stresses technology, and a computer archeology site would provide a visual of authentic science—opportunities for career discussions and connections of relevance to the real world. Showing a video (*D*) is not the best choice as it is passive, and students may not be involved. The correct answer is *D*.

Understanding how students learn and making modifications in instructional strategies are hallmarks of an effective teacher. Learning theories from *Piaget, Bandura,* and *Vygotsky* provide the teacher with a theoretical framework and tools for success in the classroom. Most pre-service programs require an educational psychology course, and the early childhood focus usually outlines the stage theory of Piaget's cognitive development. From sensorimotor to preoperational stages, language development is rapid, because speech is used to express understanding of observations of their world. The concrete operation stage is characterized by *conservation*—the ability to hold or save a mental picture (a short wide jar holds the same amount as a tall thin one) and ability to reverse physical change. It is important to realize that children in the elementary grades need hands-on experiences and manipulative materials because they are concrete learners and often unable to visualize an abstract concept. Piaget's final period of formal operations from age 11 through adulthood is a period when students are able to solve problems in a logical and systematic way. Using the scientific method independently, they can then design experiments and refine the skills taught in earlier grades. According to Piaget, children acquire physical knowledge, logico-mathematical knowledge, and social knowledge through the interactions with their environment. Teachers of young children should provide stimulating, concrete experiences and promote problem- solving activities to enhance knowledge development.

Vygotsky, who theorized about the role of cognitive development in social interactions, developed the *Zone of Proximal Development* concept—an area of cognitive development that can be enhanced with instruction that presents ideas and materials that are just ahead of the child's current cognitive status. Both Piaget and Vygotsky stress the importance of the *construction of knowledge* by the learner. Unlike a blank slate to be filled by the teacher, the child comes with experiences and prior schema (sometimes misconceptions) that need to be challenged.

The instructional strategy of the *learning cycle* fits the view of constructivists' learning theory. Often described as "5Es," the steps include: *Engage, Explore, Explain, Elaborate,* and *Evaluate.* First, the teacher gains attention and uses a focus to introduce the lesson. Asking questions generates curiosity about the concept, *engages* the learner, and can be a means to assess prior knowledge. Using a *KWL chart* (what I know—what I want to know—what I learned), for example, the teacher can *identify concepts and misconceptions.* Next, students *explore* the materials—a natural response that encourages curiosity and stimulates more questions. As a facilitator, the teacher challenges students' observations and *prompts discussions.* In the third step of *explaining,* it is the teacher's role to define vocabulary, clarify results, and help draw conclusions. The *elaboration* step allows the student to use and transfer the concept knowledge in a new way. These are usually the extension activities or try-at-home examples that students design on their own. Finally, *evaluation* includes the numerous ideas and examples in Standard V that follows.

In the classroom, there are numerous programs and opportunities to include technology and enhance learning. The videodisc format of *Windows on Science,* information searches on the Internet, CD-ROM and simulation activities, data collection and participation in programs like the international GLOBE (http://www.globe.gov/ghome/educators.html) all help to compress or expand time and space while ensuring safety and availability of experiences. Teachers and students may also use simple database programs to organize information and word processing or visual presentation software programs to report and share results.

Consider the following practice question:

Ms. Helms recognizes that her students are struggling with a social studies chapter and the concept of community when one student declares, "Look, it's like the ants in our ant farm. Some work, some take care of the young—but together, everything can get done." Ms. Helm's best response is:

A. Good point. But ants are animals, and people are people.
B. Well, yes, how else can you compare these two systems?
C. Well, yes, but ants are just acting out of instinct.
D. Good point. But we're studying social studies now—not science.

Using an ant farm in the first place was a great science lesson for Ms. Helm's students. Integrating the concrete example as a model for the abstract concept of community is developmentally appropriate and cognitively beneficial for the students. Higher-order thinking through analogies establishes more cognitive connections for the students. Answer (*D*) does not promote interdisciplinary learning. Answers (A) and (C) do not enable students to make connections in learning. The correct answer is *B.*

STANDARD V (ASSESSMENT)

Competency 020: The science teacher knows the varied and appropriate assessments and assessment practices to monitor science learning.

The beginning teacher knows the relationship between curriculum, assessment, and instruction and understands the importance of monitoring and assessing students' science knowledge and skills on a regular, ongoing basis. In the area of assessment, the teacher knows the importance of validity, reliability, and absence of bias. Also, the teacher knows the purposes and uses of various types of assessments, including diagnostic (before), formative (during), and summative (after). Teachers know strategies for assessing students' prior knowledge and can use assessment to inform instructional practice. They share evaluation criteria with students and engage students in meaningful self-assessment. In the classroom, the teacher can use formal and informal assessments of science performance including rubrics, portfolios, student profiles, journals, and checklists and can base decisions regarding instructional content, methods, and practice on information about students' strengths and needs gathered through assessment.

Consider the following practice question:

Second graders are learning the scientific process in TEKS 2.10 where they are expected to describe and illustrate the water cycle. The teacher provides numerous hands-on activities for students to observe evaporation, condensation, and precipitation related to the water cycle. She asks questions during the activities and reteaches when necessary. How should the teacher grade the students on their understanding of the objective?

A. Give one final written test with matching items.
B. Have students write definitions of the vocabulary.
C. Use a rubric that contains knowledge and skills attained.
D. Have students do a self-assessment.

The teacher should grade students' understanding of the objective through multidimensional means rather than by a single attribute (*A*). Although definitions might be part of the instruction, they do not allow the student to "describe or illustrate" or show understanding of the water cycle (*B*). The rubric contains the knowledge and skills attained and can be used to grade students on their activities, questions and answers, cooperative group participation, and understanding. Self-assessment, though desired, does not allow for a grade. The correct answer is C.

Reform efforts in science education include mandates for instruction and for assessment. We cannot continue to evaluate students with one unidimensional measurement. Knowledge and understanding should be assessed through formal and informal means. Authentic assessment includes observations by the teacher with a shift from a behavioral to a cognitive view of learning. Teachers should use tasks that represent meaningful instructional activities that tap productive thinking and problem-solving skills. Children should be encouraged to collect their work over time and develop portfolios or presentations of their knowledge. With multiple learning styles comes assessment through audio, visual, tactile, and kinesthetic means. Student performance of the water cycle could include a skit of a water drop, the sun, a cloud of water vapor, a thundercloud full of water, rain, and all the processes of evaporation, condensation, and precipitation clearly represented through materials, songs, and hand motions.

STANDARD VI (HISTORY AND NATURE SCIENCE)

Competency 020:   The science teacher understands the history and nature of science.

The beginning teacher knows the limitations of the scope of science and the use and limitations of physical, mathematical, and conceptual models to describe and analyze scientific ideas about the natural world. He or she knows that science ideas and explanations must be consistent with observational and experimental evidence but realizes that science is a human endeavor influenced by societal, cultural, and personal views of the world. Teachers understand that scientific theories are constantly being modified to conform more closely to new observational and experimental evidence about the natural world. They understand how logical reasoning is used in the process of developing, evaluating, and validating scientific hypotheses and theories. They appreciate the principles of scientific ethics and the role of publishing and peer review in the development and validation of scientific knowledge. Teachers understand the historical developments of science and respect the contributions that diverse cultures and individuals of both genders have made to the body of scientific knowledge. In the classroom, teachers can analyze, review, and critique the strengths and weaknesses of scientific explanations, hypotheses, and theories using scientific evidence and explanation. Viewing science as a way of knowing, they can provide students with opportunities to examine types of questions that science can and cannot answer. They can use examples from the history of science to demonstrate the changing nature of scientific theories and knowledge. They can analyze ways in which personal or societal bias can affect the direction, support, and use of scientific research and design instruction that accounts for the contributions of individuals from a variety of cultures.

Science is often viewed as a body of knowledge that resulted from years of experiments. Formal science training often included the memorization of endless concepts, terms, and formulas. Today, science education is viewed as a verb—as a way of thinking and acting and as an expanding body of knowledge that cannot possibly be memorized. In fact, estimates of the knowledge explosion predict that scientific information doubles every two to five years. Teaching your students how scientists developed their experiments and analyzed their results will be more useful than simply memorizing a definition that they may not understand. Learning about the people involved in the production of scientific knowledge will give students a sense of career awareness. They need role models, guest speakers, and diverse cultural examples to make science come alive. Learning about the struggles of science will teach lessons of persistence, patience, and the excitement of discovery.

Numerous resources are available for the teacher to integrate the history and nature of science into the classroom. The National Public Radio presentations of Dr. John Lienhard's "Engines of Our Ingenuity" are broadcast twice daily and are available from the website at http://www.uh.edu/engines. A simple web search of "scientists" gives links to women in science at http://www.astr.ua.edu/4000WS/4000WS.html, to African Americans in the sciences at http://www.princeton.edu/'mcbrown/display/faces.html, and to numerous pages on Albert Einstein (theory of relativity), Thomas Edison (electricity), Sir Isaac Newton (laws of motion), Madame Curie (radioactivity), Antonio Novello (first Hispanic Surgeon General), Mae Jemison (first African American woman in space), Dr. Daniel Hale Williams (African American doctor who performed the first successful heart surgery), Louis Pasteur (pasturization), Barbara McClintock (only woman to win Nobel Prize in Physiology or Medicine for genetic research), and others.

Students should know that Lewis Latimer, the son of slaves who escaped to freedom in Boston, drew the patent for Alexander Graham Bell's original telephone and himself invented the carbon filament for the incandescent electric light. They should realize that Charles Drew, another African American, was a pioneer researcher in the area of blood plasma preservation, saving thousands of soldiers' lives in World War II through establishment of blood banks. Yet he died from loss of blood following a car accident near a hospital that admitted only whites. We can have a greater appreciation for the contributions to science made by people who overcame discrimination. Women like Rachel Carson, who wrote *Silent Spring* in 1962, testified before Congress and withstood the attacks of the chemical industry who denounced her as a hysterical woman for her attention to environmental issues. Women like Sally Ride, who became the first U.S. woman to go into space, serve as examples for females in the classrooms today.

STANDARD VII (PERSONAL AND SOCIAL DECISION MAKING)

Competency 020:   The science teacher understands how science affects the daily lives of students and how science interacts with and influences personal and societal decisions.

The beginning teacher knows the role that science can play in helping to resolve personal, societal, and global challenges. The teacher understands how human decisions about the use of science and technology are based on factors such as ethical standards, economics, and societal and personal needs. Teachers understand the properties of natural ecosystems and how natural and human processes can influence changes in the environment. They know about concepts related to changes in populations and to characteristics of human population growth that impact consumption on the renewal and depletion of resources. Finally, they understand that scientific concepts and principles relate to personal and societal health, including the physiological and psychological effects and risks associated with the use of substances and substance abuse. In the classroom, the teacher can use situations from students' everyday lives to develop materials that investigate how science can be used to make informed decisions. They can apply scientific principles to analyze factors that influence personal choices concerning fitness and health and factors that affect the probability and severity of disease. They can demonstrate how factors such as population growth, use of resources, overconsumption, technological capacity, poverty, and societal views can influence changes in the environment. They can demonstrate how science can be used to make informed decisions about societal and global issues through the analysis of advantages and disadvantages of a course of action.

Understanding the relationship between science-technology-society (STS) helps students to appreciate the need for science in their daily lives. If they can observe the pollution problems from automobiles (technology) and realize that government decisions about air quality and emissions testing are possible societal responses, they can use their science information to make informed decisions. Older elementary students should be encouraged to collect newspaper articles about current STS issues in their community and in the world. Cutting down the rainforest, using government lands for oil exploration, transporting oil in tankers that spill and pollute the oceans, overpopulation, and overconsumption are current events issues that demand decisions about the future. Students can access data collected from other students throughout the world—or establish their own research site. The international GLOBE program (http://www.globe.gov/ghome/educators.html) trains teachers to work with their students in authentic inquiry. Activities from tracking El Niño temperatures, tree budding times, acid rain values, and global warming conditions can be accomplished by classroom "scientists." Teachers can also choose numerous texts that emphasize STS issues, including *Investigating and Evaluating STS Issues and Solutions* (Hungerford et al., 1997) that enhance critical thinking and problem-solving strategies by providing sample vignettes to analyze and rubrics with identified skills. Hopefully, these same students will become knowledgeable citizens of the future who can make better choices about environmental policies, land use, and government regulations.

STANDARD VIII (PHYSICAL SCIENCE)

Competency 021: The science teacher knows and understands the science content appropriate to teach the statewide curriculum (Texas Essential Knowledge and Skills) in physical science.

The beginning teacher has a basic understanding of physical science concepts and processes. These include properties of objects and materials; concepts of force and motion; concepts of heat, light, electricity, and magnetism; as well as conservation of energy and energy transformations. In the classroom, the teacher conducts demonstrations and facilitates experiments and experiences that promote understanding of these ideas.

In order to teach effectively, the teacher needs an understanding of the science concepts and definitions presented to the student at each grade level. A review of the TEKS for science at http://www.tea.state.tx.us/teks, teachers' manuals, and curriculum guides will provide a start into this vast area. Other resources include textbooks, dictionaries, CD-ROM encyclopedias, and Internet searches for key terms. Although TEKS at all grade levels begin with a stated emphasis on classroom and field investigations, scientific inquiry, critical thinking and decision making, and tools and process skills of science, they also include examples of developmentally appropriate concepts and content. Stated concepts at lower grades may be studied again in upper grades at greater depth. For example, kindergarten TEKS state that the student is expected to "record observations about parts of plants including leaves, roots, stems, and flowers." The seventh-grade student also studies plants but is expected to "identify that radiant energy from the sun is transferred into chemical energy through the process of photosynthesis."

The following are examples of science concepts included in the TEKS for grades K–4:

- Kindergarten: Studies *changes* (weather, seasons, life cycles); explores the *natural world* (rocks, soil, water); and observes and describes living *organisms* (plants, animals).
- Grade 1: Studies *sources of water* (streams, lakes, oceans); compares *characteristics of living organisms;* identifies and tests ways that *heat* may cause change; manipulates objects to show relationship between *parts to the whole* (for example, a flashlight needs batteries to make it "whole").
- Grade 2: Collects information using *tools,* including meter sticks; describes and illustrates the *water cycle;* demonstrates change in *motion* by applying force (push or pull); studies functions of *plant and animal parts.*
- Grade 3: Studies the sun and planets in our *solar system;* investigates *magnetism* and *gravity;* observes *states of matter* (solids, liquids, and gases); compares *adaptations* and *needs* of organisms, including habitat.
- Grade 4: Constructs *complex systems* (an electric circuit); draws conclusions using *fossils;* identifies the sun as a major source of energy; studies *properties of matter* (density); observes *patterns in nature* (metamorphosis, weather).

The following provides key science ideas selected from concepts included in the elementary TEKS.

Physical Science: Key Ideas
- All *matter* is made of particles called atoms. Matter is anything that occupies space and has mass. *Mass* and weight are not the same. Mass is the amount of matter in an object. *Weight* refers to the gravitational force between objects. Thus, weight is the measure of the amount of force that the earth exerts on an object. Mass remains the same, but weight varies, depending on the size and distance of the objects (for example, an empty box and a full box of the same size have the same mass but different weights). *Density* is the ratio of mass/volume and helps explain how objects sink or float.
- *Matter* is found in three states—solid, liquid, and gas. Matter converts from one state to another by heating or cooling. When materials are heated, the

molecules (combinations of atoms) move faster and spread farther apart so that the material expands. The *Law of Conservation of Matter* states that in ordinary chemical reactions matter is neither created nor destroyed but only changed from one form to another. All the existing molecules recombine into new combinations.

- *Atoms* contain protons and neutrons in the nucleus and electrons outside the nucleus (the core of the atom). Elements are composed of the same kind of atoms. Each element has a different number of protons and electrons. Compounds have combinations of two or more kinds of atoms.
- *Mixtures* are not chemical combinations and can be physically separated. In a *solution,* the substance that dissolves is the *solute,* and the substance that does the dissolving is the *solvent.*
- *Energy* is defined as the ability to do work. Energy can be changed from one form to another. Stored energy is *potential energy.* When stored energy is released, it is changed to kinetic energy or motion energy. *Kinetic energy* depends on the mass and the speed of the object.
- The following forms of energy exist: light, heat, sound, chemical, nuclear or atomic, mechanical, and electric. Physical interactions typically convert one form of energy to others. For example, a flashlight converts electrical energy to light and heat energy. An automobile engine converts the chemical energy in fossil fuels to mechanical energy (chemical → mechanical).
- *Electricity* is a form of energy from electrons that provides light and heat. Two types of electricity are *static electricity* (when two materials rub together, and electrons are transferred) and *current electricity* (when electrical energy flows through a conductor in a circuit). *Conductors* are materials that allow the energy of electrons to move easily. *Insulators* are materials that resist the electrical flow of energy.
- *Heat* is a form of energy that transfers from one object to another by *conduction* (contact among moving molecules in solids), by *convection* (contact among moving currents of liquids and among gases), or by *radiation* (waves from the sun or other sources).
- *Magnets* exert a force (a push or a pull) within a region called a magnetic field. The *Law of Magnetic Attraction* states that two unlike poles attract each other, and two like poles repel each other. An *electromagnet* is a coil of conducting wire wrapped around a metal core. As electric current flows through the wire, the core becomes a temporary magnet.
- Newton's three *Laws of Motion,* established in the 1700s, state that an object at rest remains at rest unless a force acts on it to move it. That is, all objects have inertia—the tendency of an object to resist a change in the state of motion (First Law of Motion). This rule explains the importance of seat belts in auto accidents. Acceleration is any increase or decrease in the speed or direction of an object. It is related to mass and force in the following equation: F = ma (force = mass × acceleration). When forces are exerted on something, the greater force "wins." The Third Law of Motion states that

for every action there is an equal and opposite reaction. This rule explains the forces operating in rocket, auto, and boat engines. Newton's laws opened the door for scientists to determine other laws that control our world.

- *Velocity* relates the speed and direction of a moving object. *Speed* is the distance an object moves in a given period of time.
- *Gravity* is the force that pulls (attracts) all physical objects toward each other.
- *Work* is force multiplied by the distance an object moves. In the metric system, force is measured in newtons. Thus, work is measured in newton-meters, more commonly called joules.
- *Simple machines* change how work is done by increasing/decreasing the amount of force or speed of force applied, changing the direction of the force, or transferring the force from one place to another. Examples of simple machines include *levers*—three classes of which differ by position of the fulcrum; *pulleys*—fixed and movable; *wheel and axle; inclined plane; wedge;* and *screw. Compound machines* contain one or more simple machines.
- *Waves* are described by their wavelength (frequency), speed, and amplitude. The electromagnetic spectrum is an arrangement of light and other electromagnetic waves of different frequencies. The *visible spectrum* includes the seven colors of light. These are red, orange, yellow, green, blue, indigo, and violet. *Opaque* objects are the color of light reflected; a *transparent* object is the color of light transmitted. Smooth surfaces reflect light waves. Light waves often bend (are refracted) when passing through one material to another. Laser light is an intense, narrow beam of light of one wavelength.
- *Sound* is created by the vibrations of a material and is transmitted via a material medium that can be a solid, liquid, or gas. Sounds are described by their pitch and intensity.

Consider the following practice question:

Using a relevant application for science knowledge, Mr. Allen explains that the construction of homes built in the southern United States differs from those built in the northern United States in many ways. The placement of the heating/air-conditioning vents in Texas homes and buildings is usually in the ceiling because:

- **A.** Cold air is less dense than warm air and conduction can occur.
- **B.** Warm air needs to be forced to circulate to the ceiling.
- **C.** Warm air is less dense than cold air so it doesn't move.
- **D.** Cold air is denser than warm air and convection can occur.

Cold air is denser (thicker) than warm air and will sink to the floor as the warmer air rises producing a convection current that moves air within the room. If the cold air was released from floor vents, the air would not circulate because the warmer, lighter air would remain warmer near the ceiling. Using knowledge of density and convection in a real world context shows students that science is relevant to their lives. The correct answer is *D*.

STANDARD IX (LIFE SCIENCE)

Competency 022: The science teacher knows and understands the science content appropriate to teach the statewide curriculum (Texas Essential Knowledge and Skills) in life science.

The beginning teacher knows and understands the fundamental concepts and processes of living systems, including the ideas that different structures perform different functions, that organisms have basic needs, and that organisms respond to external and internal stimuli. Important life science concepts include an understanding of the life cycles of organisms, the relationship between organisms and the environment, and how species and populations evolve and adapt through time. The teacher provides activities and examples and describe stages in the life cycle of common plants and animals. Through observations, students identify adaptive characteristics and explain how adaptations influence the survival of populations or species. Students compare inherited traits and learned characteristics and explain how hereditary information is passed from one generation to the next. Students also analyze the characteristics of habitats within an ecosystem and identify organisms, populations, or species with similar needs and analyze how they compete with one another for resources. The following provides more explanation of these ideas.

Life Science: Key Ideas
- *Living things* are able to reproduce, grow, respond to change, excrete and secrete waste, and die. Living things *adapt* (change) to the unique conditions of their environment. They interact with and affect their environment, and the environment affects living things. Living things inherit and transmit the characteristics of their ancestors.
- Living things are classified in one of *five major kingdoms:* animals, plants, protista (including viruses and slime molds), monera (including blue-green algae and bacteria), and fungi (including various types of fungus). The kingdoms are further classified into increasing smaller groups, including phylum, class, order, family, genus, and species (then varieties and hybrids). For example, a dog's classification is:
Kingdom—Animalia
Phylum—Chordata (animal with backbone)
Class—Mammalia (animal with body hair)
Order—Carnivore (animal that eats meat)
Family—Canidae (animal with dog like features)
Genus—Canis
Species—familia
- All plants and animals are made of *cells.* Each cell is surrounded by a cell membrane that controls what enters and exits the cell. Plant cells have a cell wall (an outer, rigid covering). Cells are controlled by the nucleus that contains chromosomes made of the genetic codes called DNA (deoxyribo-

PREPARING TO TEACH SCIENCE

nucleic acid). Cells obtain energy to do processes through an energy reaction involving ATP (adenosine triphosphate). Cells undergo the processes of *mitosis* producing two new, identical cells. *Meiosis* in sex cells produces two new cells with half the original chromosomes. Groups of cells that work and function together are tissues. A group of tissues working together is called an organ. And a group of organs working together are called a system.

- Living things reproduce in two ways: *sexually* and *asexually.* Asexual reproduction occurs in simpler species (yeasts, bacteria, etc.) when one organism produces new offspring. Sexual reproduction occurs with male and female organisms and enhances variation in the genetic diversity, which enhances the long-term survival of the species.
- Plants undergo several life processes. *Photosynthesis* is very important because it is the sole chemical process that captures, converts, and stores solar energy. Further, it is the source of oxygen in the atmosphere. Photosynthesis involves the ability of green plants with chlorophyll to trap the sun's energy, take in carbon dioxide and water, and produce to make food (carbohydrates) and oxygen. Plants, just like animals, undergo respiration using oxygen and releasing energy and carbon dioxide as by-products. Plants also use the processes of *digestion* to break down and use nutrients, the process of *transpiration* (the evaporation of excess water through stomata in leaves), and *capillary action* (the transportation of materials within the plant parts).
- Plants have behavior and structural *adaptations* for survival in their environment and in various other functions. Major structures for growth include: roots (for anchoring the plant and for taking in nutrients from the ground), stems (for support and transportation of nutrients), and leaves (for the ability to make food and oxygen). Major structures for flowering plants' reproduction include the stamen, pistil, petals, and sepals on the flower. Fertilized egg cells from the ovary divide and multiply, eventually forming seeds. Each seed consists of stored food, a seed coat, and the tiny plant called an embryo. Seeds need favorable conditions to germinate and grow. Temperature, water, and air are all external variables that affect seed germination and plant growth. These factors and sunlight affect plant growth.
- Animals are commonly divided into two groups—animals with backbones, called *vertebrates,* and animals without backbones, called *invertebrates.* Only the chordate phyla have backbones and include classes of fish, mammals, reptiles, birds, and amphibians.
- The vast majority of animals are invertebrates and include the phyla of arthropods (insects, crayfish), mollusks (clam, oyster, snail), echinoderms (starfish, sea urchin), annelids (earthworms, leech), aschelminths (hookworms, pinworms), platyhelminths (tapeworm—a parasite living and feeding in its host), coelenterates (jellyfish, coral), and poriferans (sponges).
- *Insects* have three body parts—head (with pair of antennae), thorax (with three pair of legs and two sets of wings), and an abdomen. Some insects undergo complete *metamorphosis* with four stages for change—egg, larva,

pupa, and adult. Other insects undergo partial metamorphosis with three stages—egg, nymph, and adult. Some insects are social and live in colonies with genetically defined, specialized roles (bee societies include the queen, drones, and workers).

- *Spiders* (class arachnida) are not insects; they are arthropods with eight legs.
- *Fish* breathe through gills located on each side of the head that exchange the dissolved oxygen in the water and release carbon dioxide, a by-product of cell respiration. Fish are cold-blooded animals with fins; their body temperature is the same as that of surrounding water.
- *Amphibians* (including frogs, toads, and salamanders) live in water in young stages but live on land near water as adults.
- *Reptiles* (including turtles, snakes, and alligators) are cold-blooded, breathe through lungs, and have rough, thick, dry skin.
- *Birds* have porous or hollow bones that make them lighter and able to fly. They are warm-blooded, which means that their body temperature remains the same regardless of the temperature around them. Many birds migrate or move throughout the year because of unfavorable weather conditions. Egg incubation is the process of adults' sitting and warming the eggs until they hatch.
- *Mammals* have hair (even a whale has a few bristles), have lungs for breathing, are warm-blooded, and usually have live young that are fed milk through mammary glands. Mammals have many adaptations for living in different environments. Some of those adaptations are very similar from animal to animal and some are very different. Bats use a guided flying process, detecting objects through sound echolocation. Whales, dolphins, and porpoises have lungs but live only in oceans. Some mammals (e.g., woodchuck) hibernate all winter. Others (e.g., bears and skunks) have a long winter sleep where inactivity and slowed breathing allow survival using stored food during harsh weather.
- *Man,* a mammal, has used other animals to do work and to provide food and clothing. Man has also tried to protect animals that are *endangered* (few in number) and prevent *extinction* (no longer exist on this planet). Man's activities have resulted in many endangered and extinct plants and animals. Climatic changes have also resulted in extinction of many plants and animals.
- The human body is made of millions of tiny cells that undertake specialized work. Five main types of *tissues* include: muscle, nerve, epithelial, connective tissue, and blood. The main *body systems* include: skin, skeletal, muscular, digestive, circulatory, respiratory, excretory, nervous, reproductive, and endocrine.
- Three main areas of the body are the head, or *cranial cavity* that includes the brain; the chest, or *thoracic cavity* that includes the heart and lungs; and the *abdominal cavity* that contains the stomach, intestines, liver, pancreas, kidneys, bladder, and reproductive organs.

- The *human heart* is strong muscle tissue that acts like as a pump by contracting and relaxing. It has two sides separated by a wall called the septum. It has four chambers—two atria and two ventricles. The right atrium receives blood from the veins and pumps it into the right ventricle where it is then pumped into the lungs to exchange carbon dioxide (a by-product of cell respiration) for oxygen (necessary for respiration). The blood returns to the left atrium and is pumped to the left ventricle and into parts of the body through a large artery. The heart, arteries, and veins along with small, branching capillaries make a closed circulatory system.
- The *respiratory system* includes the nose, nasal passages, throat (pharynx), windpipe (trachea), voice box (larynx), bronchi, bronchial tubes, alveoli (clusters of little air sacs), and the lungs.
- Knowledge of genetics, antibodies, vaccines, and immunity continues to give us new procedures to protect us from bacteria and viruses. The history of medicine provides examples of how scientists obtain, modify, and advance their knowledge.

Try the following practice question:

Ms. Garcia's third graders are studying animal habitats and food chains. She wants her children to know that the herbivores in an ecosystem depend upon which of the following organisms for their survival?

  A. Carnivores.
  B. Omnivores.
  C. Producers.
  D. Decomposers.

In a food chain, producers (plants) make their own food for energy. Consumers either eat the producers and/or other consumers to obtain energy. They are classified as *herbivores* (plant-eaters), *carnivores* (meat-eaters), or *omnivores* (eating both animals and plants). For example, the hamburger and bun that you eat (consumer-omnivore) came from a cow (consumer-herbivore) that ate grass (producer). The grass trapped the energy of the sun in order to grow and this energy is passed throughout the food chain. The correct answer is C.

STANDARD X (EARTH AND SPACE SCIENCE)

Competency 023: The science teacher knows and understands the science content appropriate to teach the statewide curriculum (Texas Essential Knowledge and Skills) in Earth and space science.

The beginning teacher knows and understands the properties of Earth materials as well as changes in the Earth system. Students should participate in investigations of properties and uses of rocks, soils, and water. They could describe characteristics of weather and collect data with simple weather instruments. The teacher assists students with models that demonstrate changes in the earth's surface due to earthquakes, weathering, glaciers, etc. Finally, the teacher can describe the basic characteristics of the sun, moon, and stars—especially the position of the planets in relation to the sun and the consequences of the moon's orbit around the earth (phases of the moon each month), the Earth's orientation (23 degree tilt) and movement around the sun, and the Earth's rotation (spin) on its axis (day, night, seasons). The Earth's tilt increases the amount of sunlight striking the sections of the Earth that tilt toward the sun and decreases the amount of sunlight in those sections tilted away from the sun. As the Earth moves (revolves) around the sun every 365 days, the sections receiving more-direct and less-direct sunlight change and reverse. The combination of tilt, revolution, and energy transfer act together to cause weather changes and seasons. The Earth's rotation on its axis moves a given position on the Earth's surface into the path of sunlight and then away from that path. Sunrise, day time, sunset, and night are the result.

Earth Science: Key Ideas

- The solid section of the earth contains four major layers. The *inner core,* the *outer core,* and the *mantle,* consisting mainly of rock, and the *crust* that is the thin (3 to 30 miles) outer layer on which life exists.
- There are three basic types of rocks found on earth—*igneous, sedimentary,* and *metamorphic*—all formed of one or more minerals. The rock cycle is a description of the mixing and changing of rock material found in the Earth. These changes results from heat, melting, cooling, chemical reactions, and pressure. Rocks are classified by physical characteristics and rated by hardness (on the Mohs scale), luster, and specific gravity.
- *Continental drift* refers to the theory that all land masses were once joined together as a single unit called Pangaea and have since moved as separate continents. The evidence includes the apparent "puzzle-fit" of the current continents, the similarity in fossil record among continents, climate, and mountain range locations.
- Studies of the age and appearance of the ocean floor helped scientists form the theory of *plate tectonics,* explaining that the upper layer of the Earth's surface is made of approximately twenty huge plates that move in different directions causing spreading, colliding, and fracture/fault boundaries.
- *Earthquakes* and *volcanoes* occur most often at plate boundaries as the plates push against each other. Volcanoes can arise from these pushing forces, forming shield, cone, and composite cones and releasing hot, molten rock materials as well as sulfurous gases as soot and dust particles. Earthquakes also can result from plate pressure. Their intensity is measured by a seismograph and compared on the Richter scale.
- Other Earth processes that cause change include the formation and movement of glaciers and weathering by wind erosion, water erosion, and freezing and thawing. Ancient glaciers are responsible for cutting deep

gashes in the earth's surface, sometimes hundreds of miles long, that sometimes fill with water (such as the fjords in Norway and Alaska or lakes and valleys in other areas).

■ Earth's *atmosphere* is divided into several layers. The troposphere (where we live) consists of 78 percent nitrogen, 21 percent oxygen, and 1 percent other gases, including helium, and carbon dioxide. The next layer is the stratosphere with its ozone layer that absorbs the sun's ultraviolet radiation, a health risk to many living things. The next layer is the mesosphere, followed by the ionosphere, and finally the thermosphere.

■ The *water cycle* consists of the movement of water between the Earth's surface and the atmosphere. The water cycle includes precipitation (rain, snow, sleet, hail, etc.), the collecting and falling of rain and snow from clouds to the Earth as a liquid; the movement and accumulation of surface and ground water in streams, lakes, underground tables, rivers, and oceans; evaporation from the water's surface due to heat or wind; and condensation of water vapor in the air to water droplets due to cooling. The Earth's surface, land forms, air temperature, and wind (caused by uneven heating of land and water surfaces) all contribute to our climate and weather conditions.

■ Our planet is just one of nine in our *solar system* that also includes moons, asteroids, comets, and meteors. In orbit around the sun are Mercury, Venus, Earth, Mars, Jupiter, Saturn, Uranus, Neptune, and Pluto. The sun is a star, radiating energy (heat and light). Our solar system is part of a huge galaxy of many stars and their solar systems. The Milky Way is one of the most famous star clusters (with intersteller gases) in our galaxy. Our *moon* is a satellite of our planet that revolves around the Earth and reflects the sun's light. The moon has phases during each month (full, quarter, etc.): depending upon its position, we are able to see a certain amount of its shaded side and of its "light" side.

STANDARD XI

Competency 020: The science teacher knows unifying concepts and processes that are common to all sciences.

The beginning teacher knows that scientific literacy relates not only to facts and information but also to understanding the connections that make this information useful and relevant. The teacher knows how the concepts and processes listed below provide a unifying framework across science disciplines:

- *Systems, order, and organization*
- *Evidence, models, and explanations*
- *Change, constancy, and measurements*
- *Evolution and equilibrium*
- *Form and function*

    Teachers realize that systems and subsystems can be used as a conceptual framework to organize and unify the common themes of science and technology. They know that patterns in observations and data help to explain natural phenomena and allow predictions to be made.

In the classroom, the teacher can apply the systems model to identify and analyze common themes that occur in physical, life, and Earth and space sciences. They can analyze a system (the ocean, a cell, a flashlight) and general features of a system (input, process, output, feedback). They can analyze the interactions that occur between the components of a given system or subsystem and can use the system to model and analyze the concepts of constancy and change.

Consider the following practice question:

The new fourth-grade teacher is overwhelmed with the curriculum guides, time demands, and preparation for all the content areas of a self-contained classroom. The teacher proposes the following solution at a team meeting.

- **A.** Have the principal hire a science specialist.
- **B.** Have all the fourth-grade teachers share ideas and develop integrated units.
- **C.** Have all the fourth-grade teachers concentrate only on TAAS content areas.
- **D.** Have guest speakers come in more often.

The fourth-grade TEKS require the student to "identify patterns of change such as in weather, metamorphosis, and objects in the sky." An integrated unit about weather could include science process skills of observation and data collection, organizing, and reporting. It could also engage students in writing, reading, and research (language art requirements). Fiction and nonfiction trade books can also be added for the students' enrichment. The data collection and graphing provide authentic opportunities in mathematics and the social studies for investigations of science careers, severe weather's impact on society, and climates and conditions around the world. Science is a part of our daily lives and its integration with other content areas can only help students to learn more. Although (*D*) speakers and (*A*) specialists could often be used for additional instruction, the self-contained classroom teacher best knows how to maximize effective content connections. The correct answer is *B*.

In the classroom, interdisciplinary emphasis (between content areas—e.g., science and math are discussed in the AIMS program at http://www.aimsedu.org) enables the teacher to reinforce learning and fit curricular pieces together. Science should also have an intradisciplinary focus (not just separate life, earth, and physical) that is relevant and meaningful.

A TEXES SCIENCE LESSON

In the classroom, a teacher facilitates the following long-term investigation of mealworms. Your task is to analyze and evaluate this student-centered science activity for its compliance with the standards. The results will yield examples of the unifying concepts of systems, change, properties, patterns, models, and survival, all embedded within the format of this investigation.

Focus: Children will be given a "critter" population (5 to 10 mealworms). Their task is to diligently observe and record what they see and learn. This population will change over the next few weeks.

Directions to the students: You will need a wide-mouth, transparent container with a small amount of dry oatmeal. The critter population should be maintained at room temperature and sustained with a small slice of apple or potato. The slice should be changed regularly. Because the population cannot escape, a lid is not needed. The population might, however, be transferred temporarily to a flat surface (like a shoebox lid or wax paper) for easier study. The critters are not harmful; they do not transmit disease. They are, however, fragile and must be handled with care. The log/diary will be submitted for grading after at least six weeks of observation.

The log should:

a) Contain a minimum of two to three observation entries per week, noting changes and/or behaviors of the critters. The observations should be dated and organized into a systematic format of your choice.

b) Reflect an "inquiring mind." Communicate questions, feelings, speculations, predictions, and intuitive leaps that you experience as you are, indeed, thinking about what you see.

c) Communicate evidence of informal "sciencing." Devise and try simple experiments. Report what you tried, what happened, and what you learned. You should also communicate ideas you would like to try but could not, given consideration of the animal, safety, time, and/or equipment.

d) Contain a number of simple, labeled drawings that visually communicate observations.

e) Contain one- to two-page summary of what was observed and what was learned about these critters. A small group will meet and report/share findings in order to coordinate a master report to be presented to the class.

Lesson Evaluation Using the Standards

The critter assignment is inquiry based and student centered—encouraging higher-order thinking as well as promoting curiosity and independent student "sciencing." Obviously, the basic science concept of metamorphosis is investigated as well as basic needs requirements and care for living things. Use of laboratory and instructional materials is encouraged and metric rulers, scales, and magnifying lenses are all available. The assignment addresses safety with regard to the harmless nature of the critters and the materials used for observation. The science process skills are emphasized as observations are used to make and test hypotheses. Students must take measurements to collect and organize data and, finally, to present findings through scientific communication.

The assignment is authentic and parallels how scientists would approach the process of learning about the natural world. The observations lead to experimental designs with testable hypotheses that can be repeated. Students can find out if the critters prefer light or dark, respond to sound, and eat more oatmeal or cornflakes. Students can also answer other original questions. The assignment stresses interdisciplinary learning as it integrates language arts through journal writing and reporting, math through measurement and graphing, and fine arts through drawings with details.

Recent developments and research in science education have reinforced the use of discovery, inquiry, cooperative group reports, science process skills, and the use of technology for research. Mealworm information can be found online at: http://www.minnetonkak12.mn.us/support/science/lessons23/mealworm. html or http://www.ndsu.nodak.edu/instruct/devold/twrid/html/cmeal.htm).

REFERENCES

Hungerford, H. R., Volk, T. L., & Ramsey, J. M. (1997). *Science-technology-society. Investigating and evaluating STS issues and solutions.* Stipes Publishing.

National Research Council. (1996*). National science education standards.* Washington, DC: National Academy Press.

Texas Essential Knowledge and Skills (TEKS) access at http://www.tea.state.tx.us/teks

INFORMATION RESOURCES

Information for science teachers working with students with disabilities includes:

- Visit your regional service centers for viewing assistive technology.
- Review Ed Keller's Internet page: Strategies for teaching science to students with disabilities: http://www.as.wvu.edu/~scidis
- Write for information from:
  SAVI/SELPH Center for Multisensory
     Learning
  Lawrence Hall of Science
  University of California
  Berkeley, CA 94720

Additional safety information can be obtained from: www.tenet.edu/teks/science/stacks/safety/safetymain.html

American Chemical Society
1155 16th Street NW
Washington, DC 20036

Texas Department of Health
Occupational Health Program
1100 West 49th Street
Austin, TX 78756

Flinn Scientific Inc.
P.O. Box 219
Batavia, IL 60510

ABOUT THE AUTHOR

MARY E. WINGFIELD, Ed.D., is a science methods professor for preservice elementary teachers in the field-based teacher preparation program at the University of Houston. She has served on State Board of Educator Certification Oversight Teams to assist in reviews of certification performance at entities throughout the state. As a former science teacher, she is interested in helping to enhance the efficacy of new science teachers and in promoting scientific literacy in Texas elementary school children.

Preparing to
Teach Art

6

Sara Wilson McKay
University of Houston

As long as art is the beauty parlor of civilization,
neither art nor civilization is secure.
John Dewey, 1934, p. 344

This chapter addresses the art standards of the EC-4 comprehensive exam. The standards range broadly to include art objects and their relationships to their makers and their cultures. As Dewey points out in the quote given above, the role of art should not be limited to what is beautiful. Rather, art plays a large role in how civilizations perpetuate themselves. Accordingly, this exam explores more than just what young students can construct in the classroom. Even at the early childhood level (EC-4), students are expected to engage with ideas about how art is created; art histories of diverse cultures; and analysis, interpretation, and evaluation of works of art.

Art in the early childhood classroom plays an important role in the learning and development of young children. Gardner (1983) maintains that art allows perception, awareness, judgment, and the expression of ideas to occur in ways that are not purely linguistic or mathematical, such as in reading, writing, science, and technology. These alternative ways of knowing may be most visible in young children who are not always able to clearly express themselves verbally (Wright, 1997). Early childhood specialist Malaguzzi (1993) identifies a stumbling block in early education, citing that spoken language is increasingly imposed on children through imitative mechanisms that are typically devoid of meaning. In contrast, Malaguzzi advocates that children learn best through strong imaginative processes linked to experience and to the problems of experience. Art, especially when it is integrated into a learning program rich with problem-solving projects, involves precisely the kind of imaginative processes advocated for the early childhood classroom. Wright (1997) agrees by suggesting that art provides "a powerful means with which to promote future-oriented learning, particularly for young children, because [it] involves nonverbal, symbolic ways of knowing, thinking and communicating" (p. 365). Through art, young children play active roles in the processes of discovery, self-awareness, personal communication, social interaction, perception, skill use, analysis, and critique. These goals for young children in art are consistent with the standards for the visual arts addressed in the EC-4 comprehensive TExES exam. The understanding of artistic development as a domain of human growth, like development in the intellectual or social domain, points to the important role of early childhood professionals (Kindler, 1996). This crucial role is underscored by the clear standards EC-4 teachers are expected to meet.

Consistent with the design of the previous chapters, this chapter is structured with an overview of the various art standards that are, in turn, correlated to the Texas Essential Knowledge and Skills for Fine Arts. Additionally, for each standard, there is a sample item with responses and rationales for why test takers selected their answers. This sample section will be followed by a discussion of the correct and consequently incorrect responses. For each standard, a brief related body of knowledge is included, and a final assessment item follows that also discusses the possible responses in order to check your understanding.

TEKS-RELATED CORRELATIONS

There are five art standards for the EC-4 comprehensive exam and, in the past, the art section has comprised roughly 11 percent of the test. Statistically, this is an area that has been an obstacle for many test takers due, perhaps, to the incredible breadth of what is encapsulated by the term *art* and a general lack of emphasis on these areas throughout the present educational system. This may be the case because of the limits placed on art just like the ones John Dewey warned to avoid. Generally, people approach art without keeping in mind all that it can do. Rather, they assign art a role, such as decoration, and forget to ask for what else it might be important, especially at the youngest levels of education. Thus, in addressing these standards, you will find that they go beyond a single limited view of art; therefore, a broad perspective about art will help in thinking about these proficiencies. Additionally, these standards are in line with the Texas Essential Knowledge and Skills (TEKS) for Fine Arts for students and are therefore reasonable for an early childhood teacher to understand.

The TEKS for Fine Arts are designated in four basic strands:

- *Perception:* The student develops and organizes ideas from the environment.
- *Creative Expression:* The student expresses ideas through original artworks, using a variety of media with appropriate skill.
- *Historical/cultural heritage:* The student demonstrates an understanding of art history and cultures as records of human achievement.
- *Critical Evaluation:* The student makes informed judgments about personal artworks and the artworks of others.

The TEKS chapter 117 for Fine Arts goes on to say:

> *Four basic strands—perception, creative expression/performance, historical and cultural heritage, and critical evaluation—provide broad, unifying structures for organizing the knowledge and skills students are expected to acquire. Students rely on their perceptions of the environment, developed through increasing visual awareness and sensitivity to surroundings, memory, imagination, and life experiences, as a source for creating artworks. They express their thoughts and ideas creatively, while challenging their imagination, fostering reflective thinking, and developing disciplined effort and problem-solving skills. By analyzing artistic styles and historical periods, students develop respect for the traditions and contributions of diverse cultures. Students respond to and analyze artworks, thus contributing to the development of lifelong skills of making informed judgments and evaluations.*

In the discussion of the various standards outlined below, watch for correlations among these TEKS strands and what the test covers. You will definitely see significant overlaps, which require a broad understanding of what art is.

STANDARD I (PERCEPTION IN ART)

(Note: Competency 024 applies to all art standards.)

The EC-4 teacher understands how ideas for creating art are developed and organized from the perception of self, others, and natural and human-made environments.

The EC-4 teacher assists students in their ability to perceive and reflect on the environment. The teacher uses correct terminology for the art elements (i.e., color, texture, shape, form, line, space, value) and the art principles (i.e., emphasis, contrast, pattern, rhythm, balance, proportion, unity) in order to help students analyze art and their environment. The teacher constructs art lessons that foster creative thinking and problem-solving skills. The EC-4 teacher also plans lessons that encourage observation and reflection on life experiences, and s/he identifies visual symbols that can be analyzed and compared in both natural and human-made subjects.

This standard relates directly to the first of the TEKS, requiring teachers to emphasize student perception of their environment for both art making and evaluation of art. It requires that teachers understand the value of multisensory experiences for EC-4 students and necessitates that teachers know that life experiences and imagination are sources for artistic creation. Along with Gardner's theory of multiple intelligences, perception may govern young children's views of reality, and it is often the basis for their developing logic (Wright, 1997). The early childhood teacher knowledgeable of this standard understands the important role of perception in education and knows that the basic elements of art and principles of design help students gather and assess what is perceived. Because this standard requires knowledge of the elements and principles of art, teachers need to know how to recognize the relationships among these elements and principles in works of art.

Consider the following example:

The following reproduction of Marcel Duchamp's *Nude Descending a Staircase* (1912) best shows:

   A. Texture.
   B. Movement.
   C. Balance.
   D. Line.

Test taker 1 answered *C*, claiming the reproduction has equal amounts of visual weight on each side. Test taker 2 answered *B*, because her eye went from the top left corner to the bottom right and that showed her movement. Test taker 3 answered *D*, because she saw a lot of lines. Test taker 4 answered *B*, because of the title of the work "*Nude Descending . . .*" Test taker 5 answered *A* because he knows paintings sometimes have texture.

To answer this question well, a limited knowledge of the elements of art and the principles of design would be helpful. However, the logic of test takers 2 and 4 proved successful because they had evidence of their answers in the artwork. Choice *A* is not correct because the reproduction shows no *tactile* evidence that one area is rough and another area is smooth. Although the test taker was right to think about some paintings and sculptures having *texture*, he should have looked closer to support his decision with visual evidence. Choice *B*, *movement*, is supported with visual evidence and the test taker stated it well by identifying how her eye reacts when looking at the reproduction. Noticing that her eye moved with the reproduction from one side to the other gives the test taker visual evidence for her answer (not to mention the title of the artwork!). Choice C is a valid choice, but is it the *best* choice? This is an asymmetrically *balanced* artwork, but when looking at this work of art, do you feel an overwhelming sense of balance? When a question asks you for what it shows *best*, it is looking for what is overwhelmingly exemplified. Keep this in mind. Choice D actually falls to much of the same logic as Choice C. A reproduction that best shows the *use of line* would most likely consist primarily of clear, overt lines, not ambiguous lines that are hard to follow. If they are hard to follow or hard to identify, they might be suggesting something else is important (such as in this case with the emphasis on movement). The correct answer is B.

1950-134-59
Duchamp, Marcel, "Nude Descending a Staircase, No. 2"
Philadelphia Museum of Art: The Louise and Walter Arensberg Collection. Used with permission.

In order to be able to address this standard about perception, we need to pay special attention to what art encompasses. In one respect, art uses a common language called the *elements of art* and the *principles of design*. Below you will find definitions of the major building blocks of art and descriptions of how they can be arranged in a composition. There is also a chart that may be helpful in trying to understand how an artist uses various elements of art in order to achieve certain principles of design. For example, using conflicting shades of color might suggest contrast in a design, whereas using similar shades of color might suggest unity in a design. This is just an example of the kinds of things to look for when you analyze a work of art structurally.

The Elements of Art

Line: The path of a moving point, a mark made by a tool or instrument as it is drawn across a surface.

Shape: A two-dimensional area that is defined in some way, perhaps with an outline or solid area of color. Shapes may also be *implied*.

Form: Objects that have three dimensions (length, width, and depth) therefore have mass and volume.

Space: Shapes and forms exist in space. On a flat surface, artists can employ various means to imply the illusion of three-dimensional space such as modeling to show volume, objects diminishing in size as they move to the background, overlapping, and showing more detail and brighter colors in the foreground with duller colors and less detail in the distance.

Texture: The way a surface feels or appears to feel if you could touch it.

Color: The aspect of objects caused by the varying quality of reflected light. Color is possibly the most expressive element of art but the most difficult to describe. Colors appeal directly to our emotions and can stand for ideas and feelings.

Value: The relative lightness or darkness, whether in color or in black and white.

The Principles of Design

Rhythm and Movement: The repetition of visual elements, such as shapes, lines, or spaces. Visual rhythm creates the sensation of movement as the viewer's eyes follow the "beats" through a work of art.

Balance: The arrangement of elements in works of art. This may be symmetrical, asymmetrical, or radial.

Proportion: The relative size of one part to another.

Contrast: The degree of difference between colors, shapes, tones, or other elements in a work of art.

Variety: Combination of elements using diversity and change. Too much sameness might be dull; thus, artists add variety to their work to make it more interesting.

Unity: Allows the viewer to see a complex combination as a complete whole. If all the parts are joined together in such a way that they appear to belong to a whole, the work of art will be unified.

Emphasis: Center of interest in a picture; the focal point. Artists generally designate the most dominant part of the work by using some of the elements above to emphasize the most important point.

The chart in Figure 6.1 (adapted from Mittler, 1994) is helpful when looking at an artwork in order to determine how a composition is arranged. Use this chart to organize your thoughts about the artist's techniques.

		Principles of Art (how the artist organizes the work)			
		Unity	Variety	Balance	Emphasis
Elements of Art (building blocks)	Color				
	Line				
	Shape				
	Texture				
	Value				

FIGURE 6.1

And now, a final assessment item:

In a kindergarten class, how can a teacher best relate art to daily life?

A. Have an art center where students draw whatever they feel in their journal.
B. Ask students where they see art in the world.
C. Give students 15 minutes of free art time at the end of the school day.
D. Ask students to describe aspects of their environment in terms of colors, shapes, and light.

Choice *A* is not appropriate because there is no specific assignment that asks students to look at their surrounding culture in the form of daily life. Similarly, Choice *C* gives children no direction in using that free time. Consequently, there would be very little learning about the relationship of art to daily life. Choice *B* is a good question; however, for kindergartners it is too broad and vague. This idea allows students to use their homes, the outside world, school, etc., to identify art. The problem, however, lies in the fact that these choices might overwhelm a kindergartner, who would not know where to focus first. With the prompting of various settings and good questions, teachers might be able to salvage this choice and get to larger connections of art and daily life, but this is not the best answer. The most specific way to address the connection between art and life with kindergartners is to use the informal way of describing art suggested in Choice *D*. This choice is the most concrete answer. Kindergartners need concrete assignments to let their imagination expand. Plus, the variety of answers inherent in the question means that discussion of possible student responses will yield a rich understanding of the multiple ways art is reflected in daily life. The best answer is *D*.

STANDARD II (CREATIVE EXPRESSION IN ART)

The EC-4 teacher understands the skills and techniques needed for personal and creative expression through the creation of original works of art in a wide variety of media and helps students develop those skills and techniques.

The EC-4 teacher demonstrates a basic understanding of techniques used to create various forms of art, including drawing, painting, printmaking, construction, ceramics, fiberart, and electronic media. The teacher is also able to help students use the art elements and principles in making art in various media and understands age-appropriate activities. The EC-4 teacher helps students see their artworks as personal expression and based on relevant ideas in students' lives (i.e., ideas, experiences, knowledge, and feeling). Also, the EC-4 teacher helps students differentiate between copy art and original works of art, focusing on the use of critical and creative thinking while making art. The teacher also demonstrates safe and appropriate use of materials and equipment.

This standard basically corresponds to the second point of the fine arts TEKS pertaining to creative expression. This requires that teachers know how to differentiate between two-dimensional and three-dimensional forms of art and are familiar with the qualities and uses of various media used to produce artworks (i.e., paint, crayon, chalk, clay, etc.). The EC-4 teacher knows how the art elements and principles are used to create art in a variety of media. The teacher also understands the ways personal, social, and political ideas are expressed through works of art and encourages the use of experience, memory and imagination as sources for making original art.

Consider the following example:

Third-grade students are exploring pattern and repetition in art. How might a teacher best extend this knowledge from two-dimensional media to three-dimensional media?

A. Let students make prints from Styrofoam plates.
B. Have students experiment with weaving by making bracelets.
C. Ask students to create shoebox houses and decorate the outside with patterns they draw.
D. Have students make a whistle out of clay.

Test-taker 1 selected D because clay whistles are definitely three-dimensional. Test-taker 2 selected A because printmaking lets students repeat their images. Test-taker 3 selected B because weaving requires that students repeat motions and choices to create patterns in their bracelets. Test-taker 4 selected C because shoebox houses are definitely three-dimensional and the teacher had the students put patterns on them.

Choice A is incorrect because printmaking is a two-dimensional medium. Choice C is a poor choice since students merely apply flat (2-D) designs on top of a 3-D model, therefore they don't use pattern and repetition in the construction of the three-dimensional part of the artwork. Choice D, while definitely a three-dimensional product, makes no mention of how pattern or repetition might be used in constructing the artwork. Had there been mention of using Pre-Columbian patterns on the whistles, it may have been a stronger answer, but as it stands, weaving is the most direct translation of repetition and pattern from two dimensions to three dimensions. The best answer is B because the motions of weaving will reinforce the idea of repetition in making various patterns in the bracelets, which are three-dimensional.

In addition to needing to know the basic vocabulary of art, the teacher should also be familiar with ways of art-making for the classroom. Visual creations are also forms of communication. In general, you should be mindful of what is required of the student and whether the emphasis is on process or product. An art project that results in 24 identical bird feeders, although popular *not* for its educational reasons, is also not an appropriate art-making activity if there is no individual input from the student. Recipe-oriented art activities that require children simply to do what the teacher does (or wants) do not allow children to develop artistically (Szyba, 1999). Additionally, some students may not be able to relate to the relevance of a product (such as a bird feeder, for example), due to their own living conditions. In trying to conceptualize appropriate art-making activities, think through the following techniques that, when paired with solid content and student input, will be strong activities where the students' process is augmented and the students' communication is enhanced. In working with young children, teachers should welcome conversation among the children as they are working and praise original ideas, encouraging each child to find his or her own way of working with the art material and the problem posed (Szyba, 1999).

> *Drawings:* Making marks on a flat surface of material, usually paper. Contour drawings trace the outside edge of an object, and gesture drawings are quick drawings to get the idea of an object. Use charcoal (black chalk-like substance), colored chalk for paper (not chalkboards), conte crayons (available in black, brown, and sienna), pen and ink, pencils or wax crayons and pastels (similar to chalk but finer and available in a wider range of colors).

> *Paintings:* Usually more color-dependent than drawings. Use acrylics (quick-drying, water-soluble), tempera (used in schools, dries quickly, opaque, inexpensive, water-soluble), and watercolor (transparent, used with soft brushes).

> *Printmaking:* An original artwork made in multiples. Images are raised or scratched into a surface (like scratch-foam, linoleum, wood blocks, potatoes, erasers) and ink is rolled onto the surface. Either the raised part or the nonscratched part is then pressed or stamped onto paper or fabric. This can be repeated. Fingerprints are a basic form of this artform.

> *Collages:* Paper, fabric, and various found materials combined to adhere to a surface. Making collages is *not* just cutting things out of a magazine and pasting on what you like. They involve placement and thought about the other elements of art and principles of design and usually revolve around a central idea.

> *Sculpture:* Free-standing, three-dimensional, and viewed from all sides. These include carving (stone or wood cut or chipped to create a form), modeling (clay shaped into a form—ceramics), casting (a form is created, a mold is made, and then filled with melted metal or plaster), and assembled (different materials are collected and joined together to create a form).

> *Fiberarts:* Use of textiles, fabrics, yarns, threads, etc., to produce weavings, quilting, needlework, basketry, and fiber sculpture. Fiberarts also can include spinning of yarn and thread from raw materials.

> *Electronic media:* Technology-assisted image making. This may include draw-and-paint software programs as well as more sophisticated software such as Adobe Photoshop. Issues such as copyright and originality are explicit when working with this kind of media and should be taught to children.

General age-appropriate art-making activities include:

Kindergarten:
- Spontaneous drawing and painting
- Scribbling and naming scribbles
- Combinations of ordinary things to design imaginative places (Szekely, 1999)
- Use and identification of primary colors
- Choices of color based on emotional appeal, not realism
- Identification and use of patterns and textures

First and second grades:
- Use of different kinds of lines, spacing, shapes
- Building forms with clay or wood to develop concepts
- Using more realistic color
- Mixing of colors in painting
- Repeating shapes in a rhythmic flow
- Creating patterns
- Making rubbings of various textures

Third and fourth grades:
- Making lines with a variety of tools
- Contour drawing and gesture drawing
- Understanding of shading concept
- Realization of various points of view
- Recognizing emerging themes like permanent vs. temporary or natural vs. man-made (Miller, 1999)
- Mixing colors and shades
- Using a compass for radial balance
- Organizing compositions using the principles of design (Linderman, 1997)

These guidelines do not suggest that there are no exceptions to these activities; they are provided for general age-appropriateness. However, the most important component in designing art-making activities for students should emphasize strong content, individuality, thoughtful process, and open criteria. This allows children to be successful in their attempts at visual communication.

Now, try your hand at this assessment item:

Which of the following techniques would be best for showing pattern and creating texture in a first grader's artistic composition?

I. Crayon rubbing of the bottom of student's shoe.
II. Printmaking using small found objects.

III. Perspective drawing showing depth.
IV. Sculpting a figure out of wire.

A. I & II only
B. I & IV only
C. II & III only
D. III & IV only

Rubbings show patterns and textures, and printmaking lends itself to making patterns because you can use the prints again and again. Perspective drawings are too advanced for first graders and wire sculptures show neither texture nor pattern. Therefore, the best answer is *A*. Based on what we learned about pattern and texture from the elements of art and the principles of design, crayon rubbings and printmaking with small objects are the most age-appropriate activities because both choice I and II incorporate pattern and texture into the activity.

STANDARD III (APPRECIATION OF ART HISTORIES AND DIVERSE CULTURES)

The EC-4 teacher understands and promotes students' appreciation of art histories and diverse cultures.

The EC-4 teacher describes, compares, and contrasts art of different periods and cultures and explores reasons why different cultures create and use art. The teacher can describe the role of art in everyday life and is able to describe the main idea in works of art from various periods and cultures. The EC-4 teacher is aware of the role of art in storytelling and documenting history and can describe the role of art in different careers. The capable teacher is able to demonstrate how ideas have been expressed using different media in different cultures and at different times.

The capable teacher meeting this standard understands the characteristics of a variety of art forms of *multiple* cultures from both the Western and non-Western traditions. This standard requires that teachers know characteristics of art from various historical periods, including various reasons cultures created and used art and continue to do so. Teachers are knowledgeable about careers in the arts and they understand the various roles of art (e.g., storytelling, documentation, personal expression, decoration, utilitarianism, inspiration, and social change) in different cultures.

This standard clearly relates directly to the historical/cultural heritage strand of the arts TEKS. The teacher's understanding of the roles of history and culture and their relationships with art is intrinsic to being able to help students experience and explore diverse cultures through the arts. Meeting this standard entails inquiring into art and its origins and seeking connections across cultures. Early childhood educators advocate that developing art appreciation in young children deepens their understanding of the world and enriches their daily lives

(Epstein, 2001). Even simple discussions with children about the choices involved in designing a storybook or the design of tiles on the floor develop young children's ability to discuss art in the context of their cultures (Johnson, 1997). These kinds of discussions reinforce the value of talking with even the youngest of learners about art in their daily lives as well as art they see from various cultures.

Consider the following example:

Use the reproduction of *Green Coca Cola Bottles* (1962) by Andy Warhol to answer the next question. A third-grade teacher wants to show that art can reflect a society's beliefs. In the context of this painting, the teacher could best do this by asking the students to suggest why:

I.   The Coke® bottles are all full?
II. The same bottle is repeated over and over?
III. The artist chose Coke® bottles as his subject?
IV. The artist didn't use Pepsi® cans?

A. I & II only
B. I & IV only
C. II & II only
D. IV only

First, let's look at the questions the teacher might ask.
Option I asks the students to focus on a detail of the artwork that is more of a descriptive fact than something to be interpreted about society. If, however, one of the bottles was deliberately empty or half-full, then this might be an interesting question to ask, but as it stands, it gains the student no insight about social beliefs. Option II asks students to consider what repetition might represent. This question allows students to interpret multiple possible meanings from this overwhelming element in the artwork. The entire artwork consists of repetition and is therefore important to interpret for social beliefs that may be expressed through repetition. Option III similarly asks students to interpret the other main feature of this work of art, the subject matter. This entire work of art uses Coca-Cola® as its subject matter. It is appropriate, then, to ask questions about the significance of this choice. One test taker understood the importance of subject matter choice for artists such as Andy Warhol and extrapolated the correct answer from this knowledge. Option IV asks students to exchange essentially apples for oranges, Coca-Cola® for Pepsi®. Although this may be an interesting question, the shift to consider Pepsi® in place of Coke® does not significantly shift the social beliefs being communicated in this work. Therefore, answer C is the best answer.

Teachers should recognize art, regardless of whether it is labeled "fine" or not, as a product of its culture. Independent of exclusive criteria, art reflects its producing culture in the questions it asks, in what it holds up as art, and in what content it chooses to represent. An understanding of the relationship between art and culture is probably one of the most important things the EC-4 teacher can pass on to young students, as it is an understanding that results in the creation of a window into the world. In order to have some sense of the historical events that are contemporaneous with the developments and movements in art, Table 6.1 presents a very brief overview of a primarily Western history of art (but with many non-Western references), which is organized to show how art reflects principal social and cultural ideas of its time. This overview is in no way meant to represent all that is "important" about art and history. Rather, it is intended

TABLE 6.1 Western History of Art—Overview

Period/Style	Social Issues and Historical Events
Paleolithic (25,000 B.C.E.): First examples of pigment being placed on a surface (cave drawings). Abstract sculptural figures in stone.	"Magical" explanations for natural phenomena, including procreation. Shelter limited to cave dwellings or other preexisting natural forms of protection.
Egyptian (3000 B.C.E.): Proportion in figurative art—rigidity reflecting strength of Pharoah.	Development of pyramids. Pharaohs are the sons of god, and the focus is on life after death.
Greek Art (500–325 B.C.E.): Art and architecture reflect concerns with order and rationality. Unparalleled naturalistic style in sculpture.	Beginning of Western culture as we know it. Human body elevated to highest ideal. Gods given human form and human weaknesses. Advent of philosophy, democracy, medicine, geometry, algebra, and astronomy.
Roman Art (500 B.C.E.): Contributed realism in figurative sculpture and painting.	Took over Greek and Etruscan culture and adopted it. The idea of republic develops.
Asian Developments (1200–300 B.C.E.): Animal style prevalent in early bronzes. *Pi* disc reveals Chinese desire for unity. In India, dome-shaped shrines house relics of Buddha.	Development of Confucian principles for living. Advent of Taoism, Chinese philosophy. Birth of Buddha in 537 B.C.E. Rise of Buddhism, with its belief in reincarnation and Nirvana.
Byzantine Art (to 1000 C.E.): Domed churches; mosaic becomes highly developed art form. Naturalism and realism totally lost.	Beginning of Byzantine culture, Eastern Orthodox religion. Gradual decline of western (Roman) empire. Muslim empire gains strength.

(continued)

TABLE 6.1   Continued

Period/Style	Social Issues and Historical Events
Gothic Art (c. 1300): Pointed arch introduced, along with buttress system, lending extraordinary height to the interior. Images mostly religious; reflects religious stories and stories of major events.	Abbot Suger of St. Denis equates light in architecture with ethereal presence.
Developments in Islam and Asia (600–1100): Principal form of Islamic architecture is the mosque, featuring a tower (minaret) used in calling to prayer.	Islamic empire expands from 662. Crusades begin.
Renaissance (1350–1650): Ever-increasing naturalism; linear perspective invented; exactness and order is reborn from the classical Greek and Roman times. The importance of the individual is emphasized. Exploration takes these new ideas to Germany and the Netherlands.	Humanism: A philosophy that emphasizes the value of each person; no limits to arriving at the level of genius. The popes commission artworks that reflect balance, serenity, perfection, and beauty. Trade and the printing press encourage intellectual freedom and exploration.
Art in China: Landscape painting is held as pursuit of the founding principle of the universe and is therefore the highest artform. Exiled artists make political art showing bamboo that will bend but not break under Mongol rule and orchids that flourish without soil around their roots.	Marco Polo visits China in 1275. Mongol ruler Kublai Khan rules as a tyrant and forces artists into exile. In 1368, Mongols are overthrown.
Pre-Columbian Art: Olmec (1500 B.C.E.–300 C.E.) focused on pyramids and large stone statues. In Mayan (300–900 C.E.) culture, narrative relief sculpture dominates. Aztecs (1300–1500) celebrate calendars with connections to nature and body systems.	Because of European exploration during the Renaissance, Hernán Cortes conquered the Aztecs in 1519. This art is termed "pre-columbian" because it predates the "discovery" of it by explorers in the age of Columbus.
Baroque (1600–1700): Most notable for its theatricality and drama in art that is achieved by use of light and monumentalizing.	To combat rising Protestantism, the Vatican intended to turn Rome into the most magnificent city in the world. Art became a commodity to the large group of middle-class bourgeoisie.
Rococo (early 1700s): Curvilinear style of the Baroque is modified and refined to be more delicate. Painting and sculpture begin to reflect sensuality.	Decadence of France under Louis XVI and Marie Antoinette who lead needlessly extravagant lives. Aristocratic values at their crest.

Peirod/Style	Social Issues and Historical Events
Romanticism (1750–1850): Color and expression of subject matter reign supreme. Painting shows passion of subject. In landscape painting, human's insignificance in the face of the infinite is called the sublime.	Individuality and the power of the individual mind become prevalent social themes. Writings by Thoreau and Emerson contribute to renewed interest in nature.
Realism (1850–1900): Romantic idealism fades in favor of depiction of reality—the "here and now"—especially in the face of the reality of war.	The advent of photography brings about new vision of society. Social inequities examined in art and literature. Marx writes the *Communist Manifesto*.
Impressionism (late 1800s): Focuses on the pleasures of life, backing off from Realism and Social Realism. Leisure is the main subject. Optical mixing is interesting and the fleetingness of time becomes key to represent.	Progress of industrialization creates a "leisure class." Artists have the sole occupation to observe the habits of a city and comment on their observations with flair.
Post-Impressionism (late 1880s): No dominant visual style, but there is an increase in the expressive possibilities of color. They critique modern life and the elitist qualities of the Impressionists. There is a new emphasis on space and form.	Travel to the outskirts of cities and even islands is possible. The world's fairs in Paris create impetus for social critique of the elite.
Cubism (early 1900s): Trying to see the three-dimensional world in two-dimensional terms. Emphasis is on trying to see the world in terms of the cylinder, the cone, the sphere, and the cube.	Much industrial progress is seen in the first airplane flight, first radio transmission, and the opening of the Henry Ford plant. Also Einstein's theory of relativity in 1905 brought up a new notion of time and space.
Futurism (1910s): Champions speed, motion, energy, and the machine. Painting and sculpture show movement.	WWI begins and there is a celebration of the new science of the twentieth century.
Dada (1920s): Art reflects a nihilistic point of view. Nonsensical juxtapositions of ideas attack tradition and challenge the status of art's sacred or precious images.	WWI ended with nearly everyone feeling the effects of great loss. Women's suffrage gains strength in the United States.
Surrealism (1930–40s): More positive than Dada, exploration of dream images and incorporation of chance events into compositions.	Theories of Freud and the significance of the subconscious is explored by the Surrealists. The Great Depression takes place and Hitler begins to rise to power.

(continued)

TABLE 6.1 Continued

Period/Style	Social Issues and Historical Events
Abstract Expressionism (1950s): Energetic use of line and color along with the ability to document the actions of the artist.	In response to WWII with the Holocaust and the atomic bomb, artists turn inward to abstract representations of feelings. The center of the art world moves from Paris to New York.
Pop Art (1960s): Art reflects more humorous, less serious approach. Common images from popular culture, advertising, television, magazines abound. The transformation of the commonplace into the monumental is a dominant theme.	Postwar United States is very commercialized and consumer oriented. Fast food is inaugurated with McDonald's and the TV dinner.
Minimalism (1970s): Artists seek to simplify in the face of the excess of 1950s culture. The notion of space and the material presence of shape and form are key.	With the beginning of the space race at the Soviet launch of Sputnik, schools and art take a back seat to the basics approach to life.
Postmodernism (1960–present): Pluralistic art incorporates diverse ideas and cultural values. Art reflects new and old technologies intermixed. Reevaluation of traditional canons of art history, particularly roles of women artists. The question of identity is key along with other social and political issues.	The Civil Rights movement, the military involvement in Vietnam, the assassination of Martin Luther King, the feminist movement, the AIDS epidemic, the collapsing of the Berlin Wall all signify the pluralistic state of current society.

Source: Adapted from Sayre (1997).

to provide a way of recognizing the manifestation of social and historical issues in art of a particular culture.

The most important element in thinking about art and culture is to be cognizant of the ever-reflective relationship of art and the society that produces it. In relating art and its culture to young students, be sure that children can relate aspects of their own culture (their own world around them) to the cultural aspects of the artwork in question. Also ask students to look at their own surrounding culture to identify possible sources of art. Be sure that this is specific and appropriate for each grade level, too. Young students have varying understandings of what culture is as they go through various grade levels depending on their focus. For example, in general, second graders are going to be less aware of fashion trends than sixth graders simply because of how these two groups think about their surrounding society. Kindergartners will more likely focus on their immediate family as culture, whereas fourth graders can begin to generalize to the state and national levels. This varying understanding of culture is important to remember in making age-appropriate cultural connections to artworks.

Consider the following example:

A fourth-grade class is studying masks from a West African tribe. The teacher explains that the symbols and colors of the masks have different meanings depending on the ceremony for which it was created. Masks celebrating a good hunt have different symbols and colors than a mask celebrating a birth in the tribe. Which of the following activities would be the most appropriate and effective art activity for supporting students' understanding of this subject?

- **A.** Students design their own symbols based on those found on African masks.
- **B.** Students make a mask in the African style based on their own important ceremony.
- **C.** Students make a detailed copy of an African mask and then paint it.
- **D.** Students make Mardi Gras masks, using symbols from African masks.

Test taker 1 selected Choice *D* because the students love to make masks for Mardi Gras. Test taker 2 selected Choice *A* because the students get to study actual symbols and also create at the same time. Test taker 3 selected Choice *B* because this activity would build a student's self-esteem by allowing him or her to highlight some important ceremony. Test taker 4 selected Choice *C* because it provides a model for the student.

Choice *A* is incorrect because it does not make the connection of important cultural symbols to ceremony. Rather, it devalues the African symbols by encouraging students to fabricate their own. Likewise, Choice *D* devalues the symbols by transferring them to a nonrelated event, Mardi Gras. Choice *C* does not challenge the students to make any connection through the replication of these masks. It is simple copying, which rarely serves any educational purpose. Choice *B* is the best choice, although not for the reason the test-taker proposed. Other good rationales for Choice *B* are that it incorporates students' experiences as well as some African history; it encourages students to personalize this knowledge; and most of all, it creates understanding about why African masks are important to tribes. Additionally, this choice stresses the importance of ceremony and ensures that students understand West African culture before making their own masks. The best answer is *B*.

STANDARD IV (ANALYSIS, INTERPRETATION, AND EVALUATION OF ART)

The EC-4 teacher understands and conveys the skills necessary for analyzing, interpreting, and evaluating works of art and is able to help students make informed judgments about personal artworks and those of others.

The EC-4 teacher assists students in developing skills necessary to analyze, interpret, and evaluate works of art as well as the visual world around them (visual literacy). The teacher also helps students to substantiate their understanding and interpretations by determining and describing their own personal criteria for interpreting and evaluating the main idea in artworks.

This standard relates directly to the fourth strand of the art TEKS—focusing on critical evaluation. Today's highly visual world requires that even young students are able to process and make meaning from the barrage of images that make up our image-laden culture. Because of this, visual literacy—or the ability to make meaning from what is seen—requires that young children be given the tools needed to create meaning from the bombardment of imagery, be it television or the Internet, in order to become critical citizens. The tools required to accomplish such a task relate directly to the development of higher-order thinking skills in the visual realm. The conscientious early childhood teacher uses all of this knowledge to encourage critical thought.

In the early childhood classroom, critical evaluation requires that teachers develop meaningful art experiences for young children. They should avoid potentially harmful activities that require children to work with preformed objects (like templates or coloring book pages) that subliminally tell children there is only one best way to create or interpret (De la Roche, 1996). But, additionally, teachers must engage children with genuine interest in their responses. Respectful responses to young children's observations about artworks of adults and the artworks of their peers teach children to value the aesthetic concerns of others. These aesthetic observations can stem from easy conversations about common objects such as cups or chairs (for example, "Why is one more comfortable to hold or to sit on? Which one is nicer to look at?") Obviously, there are no "right" or "wrong" answers to either of these questions, but these types of questions give students the tools to justify their own critical responses in positive ways. Additionally, discussions about which of the child's artwork should be kept or discarded help young children articulate their own value systems and their own criteria for evaluating art—again, a transferable skill to our own consumer culture, which often preys on children's inability to discern what they like and why (Johnson, 1997).

Consider the following example:

A third-grade teacher wants to encourage students to apply skills of interpretation and aesthetic awareness in a visual context. Which of the following activities would be most effective and appropriate for achieving this goal?

- **A.** Asking each student to write a short poem and then to create a small drawing that expresses the feeling of the poem.
- **B.** Showing an artwork to the class and then having each student write a story that he or she thinks the artwork is telling.
- **C.** Having students look at two portraits in two widely differing styles and then discuss what mood is expressed in each portrait and how the mood was created.
- **D.** All of the above.

Test-taker 1 selected *B* as the answer because it most directly corresponds with a skill that is tested on the annual standardized test. Test-taker 2 selected *A* as the answer because it fits best with his language arts specialty and brings art into language arts. Test-taker 3 selected *D* because all three ideas are interactive and imaginative, and they give students a chance to express themselves and see art with their own ideas.

Choice *A* requires students to interpret their poems by translating the ideas in their poem into a visual form. It follows that students would then need to aesthetically evaluate their artwork to see if it adequately expresses the intended emotion. This activity achieves the teacher's goal. Choice *B* clearly allows students to construct their own meaning or interpretation of the artwork by evaluating the work aesthetically. Choice *C* asks students to evaluate moods and compare and contrast. It takes these skills into the visual realm by asking students to tell how, in each painting, that mood was created. This also clearly achieves the teacher's objectives. Therefore, agreeing with test-taker 3, *D* is clearly the best answer because all three of these options allow room for students to interpret, or draw their own meaning from, the visual art in some way. Choice *D* is the correct answer.

Any standard addressing higher-order thinking skills requires a quick review of Bloom's taxonomy in terms of art that outlines levels of critical-thinking skills:

- *Knowledge,* in which students recall art terminology, titles, dates, and such; recognize, name, identify, label, define, examine, show, and collect information.
- *Comprehension,* in which students explain, describe, translate, interpret, and summarize collected information.
- *Application,* in which students go beyond the concept or principle they have learned and use that principle in a new, imaginative, or hypothetical situation. Here they can think creatively, make preferences, and project ideas. They can experiment, predict, imagine, and hypothesize as they attempt to solve problems.
- *Analysis,* in which students make connections and establish relationships, categorize, compare and infer, classify and arrange, and organize and group information.
- *Synthesis,* in which students critically design, plan, combine, construct, and produce.
- *Evaluation,* in which students critically examine their own work and the work of others as they learn to criticize, judge, appraise, and make decisions.

Art in the early childhood classroom is a wonderful way to build skills in each of these critical thinking categories. Critical evaluation for students (as the TEKS advocate) requires that teachers be confident interpreters of works of art, taking into account important contextual information about the art in question. Teachers who critically challenge their students must also approach art critically. They must take on the responsibility to elevate art instruction beyond the level typical of holiday art or take home projects that all resemble the teacher's model.

In fact, there is an art criticism model in use in many early childhood classrooms that help teachers do just that. The Feldman Model of Art Criticism suggests four steps to engage with works of art meaningfully: *Describe*—observers take visual inventory of a work of art, *Analyze*—observers think of how the parts relate to the whole, *Interpret*—observers create possible stories and meanings from visual evidence, and *Evaluate*—observers think through the "whys" of the artwork, ultimately developing their own criteria for judgment about the work of art (Feldman, 1992). There are obvious correlations among Bloom's higher level thinking and Feldman's steps for art criticism. Look for such correlations in Table 6.2.

In thinking through some of these questions, the key to determining whether higher-order thinking skills are employed is to look for the kind of student action required. Those that require children to go beyond mere counting, graphing, and organizing to a level of application, synthesis, and evaluation are going to be more effective in addressing higher-order thinking skills.

Now let's try a final assessment item to see whether the relationship of art to higher-order thinking skills has been clarified.

A fourth-grade teacher shows a painting of a serene landscape and then a wild abstract gestural painting. Which of the following questions about these two pieces would best promote the students' use of higher-order thinking skills?

A. Have you ever seen these paintings before, and where did you see them?
B. Are the colors used in the second painting also used in the first painting?
C. How does each artwork make you feel, and why does the painting make you feel that way?
D. What would you name each of the paintings?

Answer *A* is merely a recalling exercise. Choice *B* is a comparison question. Choice *C* asks students to account for their feelings, thereby requiring the most student action. Choice *D* might require some degree of creativity in coming up with the titles, but there is no place for the student to explain the name that was created. Thus, Choice *C* is the best answer because of the kind of effort required by the student.

STANDARD V (COGNITIVE AND ARTISTIC DEVELOPMENT)

The EC-4 teacher understands how children develop cognitively and artistically and knows how to implement effective, age-appropriate art instruction and assessment.

The EC-4 teacher is able to evaluate and assess curricula and instruction in art as well as the skills and abilities of individual students. The teacher is able to address the strengths and needs of each child and monitor and encourage growth of students'

TABLE 6.2 Sample Questions to Stimulate Higher Order Thinking

Recalling (Knowledge and Comprehension)—generally straightforward questions (NOT usually higher-order thinking skills)

Naming:	What is the title of this painting?
Listing:	What do you see at the top, bottom, and sides of the painting?
Describing:	What are the figures in the boat doing?
Matching:	Which picture goes with the word *sad*?
Defining:	What is meant by *cool* colors?
Observing:	What is the woman wearing on her head?
Identifying:	Which building is the lightest value of blue?
Counting:	How many apples are in the still life?
Completing:	This type of artwork is called (sculpture, landscape painting, portrait painting, and so on).

Processing (Application and Analysis)—open-ended questions (some are more geared to higher-order thinking than others)

Comparing:	How is this mask like (unlike) that mask?
Explaining:	Why did the artist place the horizon so high (so low)?
Inferring:	From looking at these paintings, what can we infer about space and diminishing sizes?
Sequencing:	Arrange the paintings in order, from those with the brightest and most intense colors to those with the dullest colors.
Classifying:	Which sculptures of figures are most realistic? abstract? expressive?
Explaining cause and effect:	How did the artist use repetition and pattern to emphasize the face?
Contrasting:	How does the texture on the helmet differ from the fur collar?
Making analogies:	Can you think of another artist (or culture) who produced art similar to this one?

Application (Synthesis and Evaluation)—hypothetical questions and personal interpretations (higher-order thinking skills)

Forecasting:	If this artist had lived fifty years longer, how do you think his or her style might have changed?
Predicting:	Which artist, in this group of six, do you think will be best remembered for his or her technique in a hundred years?
Judging:	Which painting do you think shows the most artistic merit?
Imagining:	How do you imagine this artist would have painted a horse? Would he or she have used the same style and technique as in painting this landscape?
Applying:	How would *you* paint a cubist picture of a penguin?
Hypothesizing:	How do you think this sculpture would have looked if the artist had painted it with bright colors?

Source: Adapted from Herberholz & Herberholz (1998).

thinking in art. Teachers recognize and utilize the valuable interdisciplinary structure of the early childhood classroom, keeping in mind stages of mental, social, and physical development. Teachers also engage in professional development in art, including most recent research and contemporary practices about art teaching at the early childhood level. This also requires that teachers are able to communicate effectively about the value of quality art programs in the EC-4 curricula.

This standard is basically the rationale for why the TEKS in the fine arts were deemed necessary to develop and worthwhile to teach. Teachers who meet this standard know about children's stages of development (intellectual, social, emotional, and physical) and how these apply to art. They also know how to determine appropriateness of curricula and art activities while showing relevance of these skills in other subjects (e.g., reading). Successful EC-4 teachers are aware of Discipline-Based Art Education (DBAE) and its goal of applying learning from the arts across the curricula. Effective assessment and management of all students in the art curriculum is also a necessity. Knowledge of professional development sources for art education is also important. The Texas Art Education Association (TAEA) (http://www.coe.uh.edu/taea/) and the Center for Educator Development in the Fine Arts (CEDFA at http://www/finearts.esc20.net/) are both extremely useful resources for the EC-4 teacher.

A teacher's ability to teach the TEKS to students in the best manner possible requires that he or she knows the most current developments in the field. The specific recent development in art education called disciplined-based art education (DBAE, discussed at length later in this section) is a good example of how the four strands of the TEKS are met through its shared emphasis on art making, art history, art criticism, and the philosophy of art. Clearly, this recent development in art education incorporates all four strands of the TEKS.

Again, Gardner's theory of multiple intelligences confirms the early childhood teacher's knowledge of sound art instruction for the young child. There are multiple forms of cognition—visual and spatial being one of them. Art instruction that is mindful of this strengthens cognitive growth across the board (Wright, 1997). Logically, what follows is an *interdisciplinary* approach to learning through the arts. This means applying these very same standards in the realm of art with an eye for making many possible connections between art and other subject areas. Connections to the arts should figure prominently in any cross-curricular endeavor because thematic links transport the arts into everyday experiences (Pitri, 2001). In terms of the TEKS, cross-curricular connections ask that children put their knowledge of the arts to work reinforcing their learning. Perception skills are aligned with skills in science, for example. Creative expression becomes art-making with a purpose. Historical and cultural heritage take on a broader significance by virtue of their connections with other subject areas. Drawing significance from links among other subjects requires critical evaluation.

Consider the following example:

Which statement reflects current thinking about art education in the elementary school?

A. Developing students' technical skills by having them select and then work with a single art medium for an extended period of time.

B. Developing students' drawing skills by having them view and attempt to copy reproductions of drawings by famous artists.

C. Developing students' knowledge of art history by having them focus on important periods of artistic achievement before moving on to other areas (e.g., perceptual awareness).

D. Developing students' critical skills by encouraging them to assess their own artwork in the act of creation using what they have done so far to guide what they do next.

Test taker 1 guessed at Choice C because once when babysitting she saw that kids had to learn history in art. Test taker 2 selected *A* because this is what he remembers doing in school. Test taker 3 selected *D* because the "big thing" in schools right now is critical thinking. Test taker 4 selected *B* because once a student learns how to draw a little bit, then he or she can learn everything else.

Choice *A* does exemplify past modes of art education where the emphasis was on technical products, so the test taker was right in remembering this aspect. However, current thinking of art education in the elementary school values *process* over product. The emphasis in Choice *B* on drawing by copying does not allow students to develop cognitive skills at the same time. Current thinking in art education emphasizes purposeful art-making. Choice *C* is a partial component in current thinking in art education because there is an emphasis on art history in addition to art criticism, aesthetics, and art-making. This choice strays from current thinking in the field by separating out history from perceptual awareness, etc. This choice does not support integrated art education that is emphasized in the field. Choice *D* encourages critical thinking by having students engage in reflective art-making where they are able to compare what they did with what they are doing now. This kind of art education is congruent with teaching students art in ways that make them critical and reflective about their own activities (which current thinking supports). The best answer is *D*.

Discipline-Based Art Education (DBAE)

Current thinking in art education is characterized by what is known as discipline-based art education (DBAE) in which art education incorporates four strands of art: art history, art-making, art criticism, and aesthetics (or the philosophy of art). Consider the diagram in Figure 6.2 on page 280 (adapted from Wilson, 1997).

Discipline-based art education (DBAE) is:

- Different from past approaches to art education that generally focused on students' free expression and art-making.
- Not a set curriculum but rather a set of principles based on the domains or disciplines that contribute to creating and understanding art: art criticism, art history, art-making, and aesthetics (the philosophy of art).

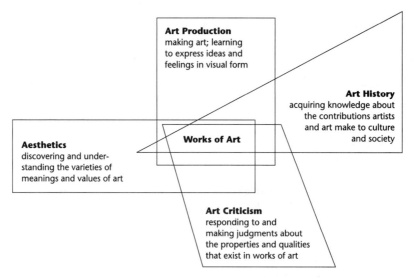

FIGURE 6.2   Discipline-Based Art Education Model

- A holistic, comprehensive, multifaceted approach to art education focusing on artworks at the center of thematic inquiry and instruction.

Through DBAE, students:

- Make art.
- View and study art (original and reproductions).
- Respond to and discuss art.
- Speculate about meaning and value in art.
- Read and write about objects that have cultural significance.
- Develop multiple skills and capacities for making art and responding to, interpreting, and evaluating their own art and the art of others.
- View and study works of art from many cultures and times, including fine arts, folk arts, and applied arts.
- Learn how art relates to the rest of the school curriculum, how art influences culture, and how culture influences art.

From the preceding lists it is easy to see how easily DBAE mirrors and incorporates the arts TEKS. Curricula should enable children to develop their creative abilities for making art (also called studio art); to understand art's cultural and historical context and the contributions that artists make to society (art history); to respond to and evaluate the qualities of visual imagery (art criticism); and to raise questions about the nature of art (aesthetics). DBAE uses adult role models from each of the art disciplines as sources for ideas and methods. This enables the teacher in a DBAE classroom to provide students opportunities for a much wider encounter with art than has traditionally been the case in art programs that only emphasize production activities. Through cumulative learning, students in grades K–12 are able to experience art at many different levels with increasing competence and sophistication.

It is key to recognize the important role *works of art* play in DBAE; they are at the center of this approach to art education and are the link between the four art disciplines. Works of art are selected for study because they have relevance to both the actual communities and the communities of interest in which students live. Students are encouraged to create works of art in which the themes and topics, subjects and ideas found in the works of artists are adapted to their own interests and the interests of contemporary society. Through this process, DBAE has acquired a depth that is lacking in much of contemporary education. DBAE encourages inquiry, knowledge, competence, caring, freedom, well-being, and social justice, which some educational reformists cite as the "moral purpose" necessary for reform (Fullan, 1993).

Appropriate student activities in a DBAE format include the following questions, some of which obviously should be reworded for the actual grade-level use.

Art-Making
- What might have been the sources of the artist's visual idea, and how are these eventually manifest in a given art object?
- What are the steps involved in working in a given medium to make it ready for the artist to use?
- What are the impacts of work habits on the production of art objects?
- Is the artistic impetus or idea a new one, is it a variation on an old or established idea, or does it build through elaboration or revision of other works or traditions?
- What processes does the artist appear to utilize in order to work out a visual solution?
- How might the creative work of artists depend upon the character of their lived experiences?

Art Criticism
- What is the subject or theme of the work, and what does the work say about the intentions, interests, or social or political concerns of the artist?
- What are the significance and meaning of the objects, nonobjects, or visual effects in the work, and how do the visual and tactile elements contribute to an effective and meaningful statement?
- What do critics say the work means, and how is the work regarded overall in the development of the artist and of other artists?
- How do different audiences relate to or interpret this work and how does its context influence its meanings?
- Does this work sustain attention and involve active discovery of new things?

Art History

- Where, when, why, and by whom was the work made?
- What are the traditional meanings of the objects and symbols in the work?
- What are the distinguishing characteristics or qualities that identify the work and relate it to other works of art?
- Who and what in the artist's life affected him or her most?

Aesthetics

- How can we assign value to what various perceivers say about works of art?
- Should artworks that are deemed sacred, privileged, or private by groups within one culture be publicly displayed by another culture for all to see?
- To what extent should a viewer substitute his or her own personal perceptions, ideas, and judgments for expert and academic testimony?
- Is the alteration of a work of art the destruction of an existing work of art or the creation of a new one?
- Should we honor the deathbed request of an artist who wants his or her unsold works destroyed?
- Do citizens have the right to remove public artwork, paid for through taxes, if some members of the public find it offensive? Who decides? What arguments would make the case one way or the other? (Dobbs, 1998)

These questions should help in understanding the goals of DBAE. In general, we can characterize current thinking in art education as a shift from product to *process,* an emphasis on *connected, integrated learning* in and through art and a *multifaceted approach* to art education.

Interdisciplinary connections are key to making art education in the early childhood classroom meaningful. As Howard Gardner suggests in his *Frames of Mind* (1983), students who engage with the arts have the opportunity to be smart in different ways because of the different perspectives that art encourages. Consider the following:

> *The arts contribute to an overall culture of excellence in a school. They are an effective means of connecting children to each other and helping them gain an understanding of the creators who preceded them. They provide schools with a ready way to formulate relationships across and among traditional disciplines and to connect ideas and notice patterns. Works of art provide effective means for linking information in history and social studies, mathematics, science and geography . . . opening lines of inquiry, revealing that art, like life, is lived in a complex world not easily defined in discrete subjects. (The Power of the Arts to Transform Education, 1993)*

Because our lives do not naturally fall into 50-minute segments during which we focus on one subject at a time, it is important that teachers integrate multiple disciplines in their instruction, with an eye on making learning more meaningful for students (Cornett, 1999).

It is imperative, moreover, that teachers focus on the word *meaningful* used in Cornett's sentence directly above. Teachers should be cautioned that artworks should not be used merely to illustrate topics and concepts (Wilson, 1997). Critical-thinking skills in the arts are transferred to other subjects (Boyer, 1995) and should be recognized and used as such. Projects or assignments that are purported to be interdisciplinary but only address the educational objectives of one subject matter are not using the arts meaningfully. In successful interdisciplinary connections, students are *challenged* in a subject area and in art. Look for this dual feature in the following interdisciplinary examples. In evaluating the artistic component, bear in mind the other standards already addressed as guidelines. The greatest issue with regard to interdisciplinary art is that there should be some openness to allow for more than one way to produce an assignment, even though criteria are set and will be used for assessment.

Relating Language and Art
- Write poems and stories and create artworks to complement them or vice versa.
- Make paintings, drawings, and murals that reflect books that you have read.
- Play a game that practices different types of language usage such as using gestures, action words, or facial expressions instead of words to suggest a mood or feeling. Practice drawing these gestures, actions, and expressions.
- Create puppets that offer opportunities for interpretations and expressions of ideas, thoughts, and feelings.
- Draw, rather than write, a book report.
- Dramatize a book in dance, costumes, music, and art.
- Make art using news articles as the impetus.

Relating Science and Art
- Study and draw the anatomy, structure, and workings of natural forms such as the human figure (or part of the body such as a hand, foot, ear, etc.).
- Make sculptures using the principles of balance, gravity, and kinesthetics.
- Design touch pictures and feeling boxes (pictures and boxes made from various textures and materials).
- Design and build bridges and buildings.
- Study how scientists use various chemicals to clean and restore paintings and sculptures (such as the Sistine Chapel).

Relating Mathematics and Art
- Draw pictures that show mathematical problems and solutions that involve weight, balance, measurement, and geometry.
- Introduce games that offer visual and spatial planning such as chess and checkers. Relate spatial planning to drawings.
- Create optical art by dividing spaces on paper.

- Use mathematical tools such as rulers and compasses to create drawings and designs.
- Engage in art activities that require measurement and planning such as weaving and architectural models.

Relating Social Studies and Art

- History becomes alive through art. Visually interpret—that is, draw, sculpt, or paint—historical events or developments.
- Study the history of a country (or a state) through artists' paintings.
- Draw and compare similar artifacts of various cultures.
- Create maps of a city as seen through the eyes of an architect and a city planner. (Linderman, 1997)

Many teachers, in examining TEKS, wonder how to include art when they must teach so many other TAKS requirements. As the demands on educators' time and other expanding responsibilities encroach, teachers must see interdisciplinary learning as a solution to cutting out one area in preference for another (Dobbs, 1998). The end result is stronger learning in both the arts and the subject area because learning will have to be cognitively transferred from one domain to another within the same lesson, thus requiring the student to be more fully engaged in the learning process.

One last assessment item:

A teacher wants to link his or her second-grade science curriculum with art. The best example of a lesson that would accomplish this goal would be:

- **A.** Children make a papier mache mobile of the solar system.
- **B.** Children draw, color, and label the stages of metamorphosis of a caterpillar into a butterfly.
- **C.** Children enlarge and paint encyclopedia drawings of flowers and diagram their parts.
- **D.** Children imagine an animal to which they assign certain characteristics and create a three-dimensional habitat for it.

While students may enjoy doing both Choices A and B, these are not the best answer. Choice C clearly promotes little learning in either science or art. Little is gained in the process of copying. Both A and B result in students' most likely creating relatively similar products. This aspect is completely avoided in Choice D, wherein students creatively design animals with characteristics that require them to practice their knowledge of adaptation and animal habitats in their creating process. Certainly, it is great to give students hands-on activities to reinforce learning such as in Choices A and B, but be careful to differentiate between a hands-on activity and an interdisciplinary lesson. Because Choice D involves critical application of both scientific and artistic knowledge, this choice is the best interdisciplinary lesson.

SUMMARY

This chapter has explored the foundations of art education within the context of the EC-4 TExES exam. The hope, however, is that the components delineated here in helping you understand the five standards for the Visual Arts section will be put to good use when you enter the early childhood classroom. This chapter should serve as a review for the comprehensive exam but, more importantly, should be useful in the classroom setting. The standards addressed here are not meant to stand outside of classroom practice. Rather, these strategies are solid ways to ensure that art plays an important role in your curriculum.

Early childhood educators have identified ten distinct barriers to establishing a strong base for later learning in the arts in young children. They are: (1) succumbing to stereotypes, (2) assessing children's work in terms of personal ability, (3) reducing art to following instructions, (4) concentrating on precociousness, (5) searching for exotic materials, (6) forgetting who creative teaching is for, (7) avoiding the fine arts, (8) believing that creativity and chaos are synonymous, (9) failing to teach techniques, and (10) neglecting professional development in the arts (Jalongo, 1999). Given the discussion of this chapter, do not let these factors be barriers to your students' future learning in the arts. Use your knowledge to break down these barriers and open up the role that art can play in your early childhood classroom.

Art should play a crucial role in your curriculum development for many reasons, including those rationales given within the discussion of the various standards. However, let's return to Dewey's words, from the beginning of this chapter, about art ensuring civilization. In particular, contemplate the following association of art and democracy:

> If democracy is a fundamental value of this country, art must play a central role in education. It is art that encourages critical thought and respect for diverse points of view. It is art that practices novel solutions to age-old problems and encourages freedom of expression. It is art that allows us a window of understanding into those around us. The practice and study of art enacts democracy where diversity is valued and respect is instilled even in the earliest learning years.

Seriously consider the role art can and should play in your early childhood classroom. Democratic civilization is not secure without it.

 REFERENCES

Boyer, E. L. (1995). *The basic school: A community for learning.* Princeton, NJ: The Carnegie Foundation for the Advancement of Teaching.

Cornett, C. E. (1999). *The arts as meaning makers: Integrating literature and the arts throughout the curriculum.* Upper Saddle River, NJ: Prentice-Hall.

De la Roche, E. (1996). Snowflakes: Developing meaningful art experiences for young children. *Young Children, 51,* 82–83.

Dewey, J. (1934). *Art as experience.* New York: Perigee Books.

Dobbs, S. M. (1998). *Learning in and through art: A guide to discipline-based art education.* Los Angeles: The Getty Education Institute for the Arts.

Epstein, A. S. (2001). Thinking about art: Encouraging art appreciation in early childhood settings. *Young Children, 56,* 38–43.

Feldman, E. B. (1992). *Varieties of visual experience.* New York: H. N. Abrams.

Fullan, M. (1993). *Changing forces: Probing the depths of educational reform.* London: Falmer.

Gardner, H. (1983). *Frames of mind: The theory of multiple intelligences.* New York: Basic Books.

Herberholz, D., & Herberholz, B. (1998). *Artworks for elementary teachers: Developing artistic and perceptual awareness.* Boston: McGraw Hill.

Jalongo, M. R. (1999). How we respond to the artistry of children: Ten barriers to overcome. *Early Childhood Education Journal, 26,* 205–208.

Johnson, M. (1997). Teaching children to value art and artists. *Phi Delta Kappan, 78,* 454–6.

Kindler, A. M. (1996). Myths, habits, research, and policy: The four pillars of early childhood art education. *Arts Education Policy Review, 97,* 24–30.

Linderman, M. G. (1997). *Art in the elementary school.* Madison, WI: Brown & Benchmark.

Malaguzzi, L. (1993). History, ideas, and basic philosophy. In C. Edwards, L. Gandini, & G. Forman (Eds.), *The hundred languages of children* (pp. 41–90). Norwood, NJ: Ablex.

Miller, S. A. (1999). Shape it! Sculpt it! *Scholastic Early Childhood Today, 13,* 46.

Mittler, G. A. (1994). *Art in focus.* New York: Glencoe.

Pitri, E. (2001). The role of artistic play in problem solving. *Art Education, 54,* 46–51.

The power of the arts to transform education. (1993). Los Angeles: J. Paul Getty Trust.

Sayre, H. M. (1997). *A world of art.* Upper Saddle River, NJ: Prentice-Hall.

Szekely, G. (1999). Designing BRAVE new worlds. *Arts & Activities, 126,* 46–47.

Szyba, C. M. (1999). Why do some teachers resist offering appropriate, open-ended art activities for young children? *Young Children, 54,* 16–20.

Wilson, B. (1997). *The quiet evolution.* Los Angeles: The Getty Education Institute for the Arts.

Wright, S. (1997). Learning how to learn: The arts as core in an emergent curriculum. *Childhood Education, 73,* 361–365.

ABOUT THE AUTHOR

SARA WILSON MCKAY, Ph.D., is Assistant Professor and Program Area Coordinator of Art Education at the University of Houston. Her research interests include theories of vision and perception, cultural reproduction, and art and democracy. She advocates critical thinking in education through art experiences that emphasize the value of diverse points of view and multiple interpretations. She is currently developing the Houston Area Visual Resource Center and has published about contemporary issues in elementary art education.

Preparing to Teach Music

Janice L. Nath
University of Houston-Downtown

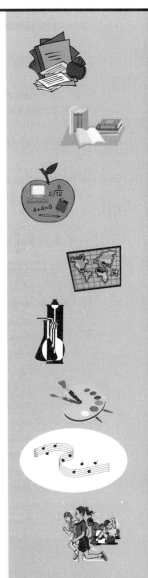

Teachers who will take the Generalist test should be familiar with many aspects of music, as the state of Texas has established music standards for all of those who will teach in grades preK through 4. Under each music standard Texas has provided information that includes *Teacher Knowledge* (what teachers should know about music) and *Application* (what teachers should be able to do when teaching EC-4 music). These standards are given in this chapter, but they can also be downloaded in chart form from http://www.sbec.state.tx.us/SBECOnline/standtest/standards/ec4music.pdf.

Many of you are probably wondering why the state of Texas requires elementary teachers to know about teaching music, as you may have grown up in (or are teaching in) a school where there is a special teacher for all music classes. You may not realize that there are *no* specialized music teachers in many Texas schools, particularly in grades preK through 4. Therefore, if any music is to be taught in those schools, it is you—the regular classroom teacher—who will be responsible. It would be a terrible thing, I hope you will agree, for children to grow up without learning about music—both in the sense of appreciating the wide range of music the world has produced and in learning the songs and music that bind our culture. You may be the one person who opens the door for a child's love for music, special musical talents, or even a career in music. Therefore, our state wants to offer students the opportunity to have a teacher who can bring music into each Texas classroom, even if a district is not able to provide a music specialist for each school.

This chapter is not only written to help those teachers-to-be who have had little, if any, music training but also to provide a good review for those who may have had some experience with music. Let us take a closer look at the standards that will be tested here.

STANDARD I (VISUAL AND AURAL KNOWLEDGE)

(Note: All music standards are covered under Competency 025.)

The music teacher has a comprehensive visual and aural knowledge of musical perception and performance.

> *The early-childhood-through-fourth-grade teacher, in addition to other subject areas, should know and understand the standard terminology used to describe and analyze musical sound. Thus, he or she should be able to identify and interpret music symbols and terms, use standard music terminology, and identify different rhythms and meters. In addition, she or he should be able to identify vocal and instrumental sounds and distinguish among timbres; recognize and describe the melody, harmony, tempo, pitch, meter, and texture of a musical work; and identify musical forms. Teacher knowledge should also include how to demonstrate musical artistry both through vocal or instrumental performance and by conducting vocal or instrumental performances. The teacher should be able to perceive performance problems and detect errors accurately.*

There are many concepts in music that you should know as a beginning teacher of young children because you may be required to teach music as one of your subject areas. The main concepts taught through fourth grade include duration, rhythm, pitch and melody, form, dynamics, tempo, instrument families, and timbre and tone color.

Duration

One of the first concepts about which young children learn in music is **duration** of sound—that is, there are *long sounds* in the world all around us (sirens, mooing cows, etc.), and there are also *short sounds* (jackhammer, clicking sounds of a computer keyboard, etc.). These variations of length of sound (or duration) are also found in music and can be represented by symbols or *musical notes*. Each symbol, or written musical note, represents a certain length (or count) that the sound should last. The longer the count or length held, the "less darkened, encumbered, or decorated" that note is when written. For example, the symbol for the longest tone in music is called a **whole note** and looks like a hollow circle—almost the same as the letter "O." If we were to sing one tone or note ("la-a-a-a," for example), while we slowly counted to four in our heads, that would be about the length of a whole note's duration. To begin to teach very young children this concept, you may want to begin with long animal sounds and have them "sing" whole notes.

O   O   O   O

Moooooo!   Moooooo!   Moooooo!   Moooooo!

There is an easy connection in determining duration of musical notes to mathematics (fractions, to be exact). If the whole note gets four equal counts in a certain piece of music, then we would read the next shorter tone as getting two counts. The symbol for this tone is called a **half note.** If you divided the whole note that you sang before into two half notes, they would sound like "La-a" "La-a" (if we counted 1-2 in our heads for the first "La-a" and 3-4 for the second "La-a"). Half notes are described as hollow circles with a stem. The half note tones can then be divided into shorter **quarter notes,** which would be sung or played as "La," "La," "La," "La," as each receives one short count (1, 2, 3, 4). The quarter note looks like a half note with a stem, but the circle is filled. To continue to teach young children about the length of sound here, you may want to have them continue with less sustained animal sounds.

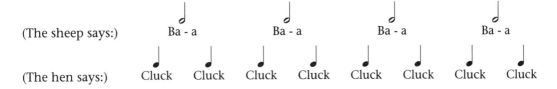

(The sheep says:)   Ba - a   Ba - a   Ba - a   Ba - a

(The hen says:)   Cluck   Cluck   Cluck   Cluck   Cluck   Cluck   Cluck   Cluck

We can continue to divide these length or duration symbols into eighth notes, sixteenth notes, and so on, each getting half as much time as the note before. The shorter the note, the more that it is darkened in and the more "flags" it has attached. Let us see how this might look in music. As you sing "La" to yourself, hold each note as long as the count below it shows.

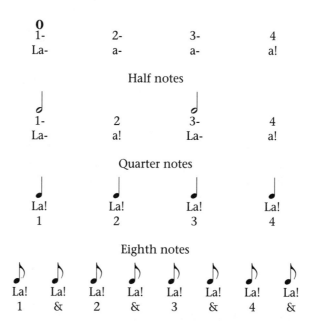

A whole note

0			
1-	2-	3-	4
La-	a-	a-	a!

Half notes

1-	2	3-	4
La-	a!	La-	a!

Quarter notes

La!	La!	La!	La!
1	2	3	4

Eighth notes

La!	La!	La!	La!	La!	La!	La!	La!
1	&	2	&	3	&	4	&

To continue to explain this concept to children, you could compare a whole note to a telephone ring or siren. The half notes are similar to the length of a grandfather clock's "bonging." The quarter notes are like a clock ticking or a car blinker, and the eighth notes are like someone typing fast on the computer. You can see how these symbols work in the song "Old MacDonald" below. Try singing the song by counting the numbers below rather than the words and you will have an idea of how the shape and design of the note tells you how long to hold it.

Old	Mac-	Don-	ald	had	a	farm	E	I	E	I	Oh—!	**0**
1	2	3	4	1	2	3-4	1	2	3	4	1-2-3-4	

On	his	farm	he	had	some	chicks,	E	I	E	I	Oh—!	**0**
1	2	3	4	1	2	3-4	1	2	3	4	1-2-3-4	

There is also a symbol for when *no* music should be played or sung—the **rest.** When you see a rest symbol, it means to "rest" your voice or instrument by *not* singing or playing for a certain time period. Rest symbols (or notations of silence) are also designed, as we have seen with the values of musical notes, in (1) whole rests, (2) half rests, (3) quarter rests, (4) eighth rests, (5) sixteenth rests, and so forth. Again, these symbols indicate a period of time when there is no sound for an established duration. Each rest appears very different from the others, unlike the notes we saw above to which flags and darkening are added as the note gets shorter in value. Rests with their counts are shown below. Remember that there will be a length of silence for each rest, according to its value.

One important thing to remember in teaching the duration of notes and rests is that the sound (or, in the case of rests, *no* sound) occupies the entire space in time until the next note or rest value is written. If one is singing or playing a whole note with the value of four counts, for example, each count must be equal—including the last count. One cannot count, "One—two—three—fo-One—two—three—fo—One. . . ." It must be, "One—two—three—four—One—two—three—four. . . ."

whole rest	half rest	quarter rest	eighth rest
1-2-3-4	1-2 3-4	1 2 3 4	1&2&3&4&

Rhythm

The concept of **rhythm,** or sound organized in time, is an important one in music and strongly relates to the discussion above. If you have ever marched, played a "pat-slap" game, chanted while jumping rope, or participated in a rap, you have experienced the beat, or pulse, of music. This pulse of the music can normally be felt easily through toe-tapping or dancing and is, perhaps, the most fundamental, though not the whole concept of rhythm. For example, sing the words to "Baa Baa, Black Sheep" and tap your foot at the same time. You will experience a very *steady beat* in sets of 2s (count "1, 2" over and over as you hum the tune). Notice that each set is divided by a bar. The distance between bars, in music, is called a *measure* and separates sets of beats into groups—in this case, sets of 2 beats per measure.

	MEASURE		MEASURE		MEASURE		MEASURE	
2/4	1	1	1	2	1	2	1	2
	Baa,	baa,	black	sheep	Have you any		wool?—	

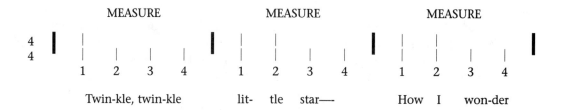

In "Twinkle, Twinkle Little Star," there is a steady beat, or foot tap, in sets of four. In most Native American music, there is a very steady pulse of four beats. In stereotypical Native American music, such as we hear in Wild West cartoons, a very *strong beat* comes on the first of the four beats (ONE-two-three-four, ONE-two-three-four). Think of the drum beat associated with stereotypical Native American music and see if you can tap it out below. In authentic Native American music this loud-soft-soft-soft rhythm is not so distinct.

The beat changes, however, in "On Top of Old Smoky" and "Happy Birthday." When you toe-tap to either song, you should feel beats in sets of three with a very *strong beat* on the first beat (ONE-two-three, ONE-two-three). This is a rhythm also seen in many waltzes.

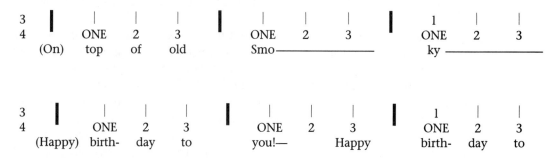

Try tapping or patting each of these songs to see if you feel the beat. Another type of music that has a strong beat is a march. This type of music is easy for many people to follow, as in a marching band or military group, because it helps people to walk in time together: "left, right, left, right; 1, 2, 1, 2." "Yankee Doodle" is a march that demonstrates this beat. Try to move your feet to feel this rhythm as you count to the melody.

	One	Two		One	Two		One	Two		One	Two
	Left	Right		Left	Right		Left	Right		Left	Right
	Yankee	Doodle		went	to town,		riding	on a		po-	ny

One way to see if you are keeping the beat regularly is to set a **metronome.** This is an instrument that sounds like a loud clock and "ticks" to the beat that a composer has written or a musician has selected for each piece of music. It takes the place of a director when playing or singing alone, so that one does not speed up or slow down the music inadvertently. Thus, a singer or instrumentalist can be sure to practice the correct beat in a very *steady* manner throughout a piece of music.

Now that you have a "feel" for what beats are all about, how do composers tell players or singers to play what they intended? At the beginning of each piece of music, as shown below, you will see the **meter** sign that indicates how many beats per measure the composer desires. This is indicated by two numbers that are one on top of the other called the **time signature.** The number on top of the time signature indicates how many beats there are per measure, or, for our purpose, divided "tap or pat sets." The bottom number tells what kind of note gets one beat. For example, a "2" on the bottom means that a half note gets one beat, but a "4" on the bottom would mean that a quarter note gets one beat. There can be many combinations, but here we will deal with only the most common time signatures. Let us look at the following signatures written below.

4 There are four equal quarter notes to a set (1-2-3-4; 1-2-3-4)
4 The 4 on the bottom indicates that a quarter note gets one beat (or think math again . . . a 1/4 of a whole note gets a beat = a quarter note).

2 There are two even quarter notes to a set (1-2; 1-2) as in a march.
4 A quarter note gets one beat.

3 Three even quarter notes to a set (1-2-3; 1-2-3) as in a waltz.
4 A quarter note gets one beat.

If we now combine the two concepts discussed above, we can see that the notes have a *value length* (duration) and the composer can arrange a *set of notes* together. When we tapped the beat of "Baa, Baa, Black Sheep," we were in 2/4 time, "Twinkle, Twinkle Little Star" was in 4/4 time, and "On Top of Old Smoky" and "Happy Birthday" were both in 3/4 time. A question in the exam may ask you to determine this time for a familiar piece of music.

Sometimes music changes time signatures in the middle of a song. If you see measures that look like the ones below, you can see that the beat pattern changes. Using time signature changes is the way in which composers tell us that the beat of the song should change, for example, from a waltz beat to a march beat. This does not happen very often in popular vocal music, but we see, hear, and feel the change in instrumental music frequently.

We have spent some time talking about the beat or pulse and the duration of notes and silence, but another element that contributes to rhythm is the patterns of accented and unaccented sound that occur in music. We can also find these in poetry. For example, in "Jack and Jill went up the hill," there is a heavy accent on the words Jack/Jill/up/hill with other less accented words between, although there is still a steady 1-2/1-2 beat that we can tap. The same occurs in music. This concept might be compared to our heart providing a steady, consistent beat, while we go about running, jumping, stopping, stepping, and so forth. In music, all of this organization of sound is rhythm.

Children seem to develop musical abilities as they mature. By about age 7 to 9 rhythmic coordination improves dramatically, and by the fourth grade most children should be able to discriminate among elements of duration (length of sound) and meter. The ability to *perceive,* recall, and reproduce musical elements precedes the ability to read, or decode, and make sense of rhythmic phrases and other musical features. To help children learn about rhythm, first promote the natural tendencies of children in rhythmic play when they are moving to the music, then use direct music instruction to teach the elements of rhythm. Thus children should first internalize "how the music feels" before they are introduced to the process of decoding music symbols. Clapping to music or having students listen to a beat that you play will help them "feel" the rhythms. Relating words to rhythm is also helpful, as you have seen above. All words have a rhythm, so select words to match rhythms you wish to teach. For example, say the following words in a rhythmic pattern —"Hou-ston, Dal-las, Wich-i-ta Falls!" This activity also helps young readers with determining syllable division. Can you perceive the rhythm of each word and of the phrase as a whole? Model such patterns often, then ask students to echo or clap what they hear. This is an excellent way to introduce the idea of rhythm, and young children love pat-clap or echo games and will follow along easily. As with the psychomotor domain, it is best to break instruction and performance into small tasks. As children grow in their abilities with rhythms, ask students to differentiate between rhythm patterns and explain their thinking or sort out several patterns. At first, discriminate rhythm examples within songs children know rather than using abstract or unknown music.

National and state standards tell us that children should be able to create, notate, and perform simple rhythmic patterns. Another good way to help children understand and perform the concept of rhythm is to have rhythm instruments available. Instruments can be genuine or can be created from anything that students can beat, rattle, or shake to the beat. Some typical instruments for beginning rhythm activities might be rhythm sticks, hand drums, bongos, maracas, guiros (ridged gourd instruments), jingle bells, tambourines, claves (hardwood sticks), sand blocks, wood blocks (hardwood blocks with a hardwood striker), slit drums, cowbells, hanging cymbals, finger cymbals, triangles, resonator bells, and glockenspiels or xylophones. As an aside, some of these instruments can be rather expensive, but this is an excellent time to begin to teach children the value of taking care of instruments and treating them with respect. Computers and other technologically based devices, including keyboards, sequencers, synthesizers, and drum machines, can also be used. Having a variety of instruments gives students choices in improving and/or creating their own sound composition.

Pitch and Melody

The next concept or idea you will need to know (and teach) is, "How do you know what tone to sing or play?" This question is related to another beginning musical concept for younger children: *Some sounds are high, and some are low.* Again, this is a concept that you would first want to compare with sounds that are familiar to children. For example, a mouse usually has a high "squeak" while a cow has a low "moo-o." High and low sounds go together to form a **melody.** When you hum a tune, you have hummed the melody, or the tones or pitches that are put together to create a unique piece of music that is recognizable as a particular song. Thus, if asked to sing or hum "Mary Had a Little Lamb," you are humming or singing the melody of that song. The melody may have other parts of music that are added, but if these *other* parts were played or sung alone, we would not be able to recognize it as a particular song. Think of the melody as the "main plot" of a song. As in a story, there can be many details that you could add in the telling; but if you were to tell these details alone, no one would be able to follow the storyline. Also, as in literature, there may be a **musical theme.** A melody may, thus, have a pattern that occurs several times throughout a piece of music. This is usually recognized at once and serves to bring the piece of music together as a whole. If you know the popular instrumental song "The Entertainer," you will quickly catch the idea of theme and of how the same patterns are repeated to create a theme. We will investigate *form* later in this chapter as an element that helps provide musical unity.

A good way to beginning to teach children about melody is to have children move their hands up and down as they sing a melody, or they may draw a graphic representation. For example, a part of the melody of "Jingle Bells!" (Jingle bells! Jingle bells! Jingle all the way!) might be drawn like this:

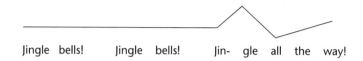

Jingle bells!   Jingle bells!   Jin- gle all the way!

Each musical **note,** or symbol of sound, not only shows us length (as discussed above in duration) but is also given a name from the musical alphabet based on its tone—or how high or low the sound should be. The musical alphabet only uses seven letters *A* though *G*, then repeats itself in tone higher or lower. An *octave* is a set of tones from a named tone (such a C note) to the same tone (C), only higher or lower. For example, sing the first two notes of "Somewhere over the Rainbow," and you have an octave. If you can, go back now and hum all the notes in between step by step. You will find that, altogether, you have hummed eight notes. An octave can be from any note, but must end on the same one higher or lower (for example, C—D, E, F, G, A, B—to a higher C; C/C is an octave). A piano and a harp are two instruments with a great number of octaves.

But how do you know what key or string to play? The answer is where a note is located on a musical staff.

The name of a note is related to the place where it is found on a **musical staff** (the five lines and five spaces on which all music is written). There are a treble staff and a bass staff in music. The staff for high notes/sounds is called the **treble** and is marked by a **treble clef** symbol while the staff for low notes/sounds is marked by the **bass clef.** Normally (but not always), the melody is written on the treble clef. If you are singing a part for a **soprano** (high voice) or **alto** (mid-high voice), usually for a female or young boy's voice, or if you were playing an instrument with a high sound (such as a flute, a violin, clarinet, etc.), music is read from the treble clef. If you have a male mid (**tenor**), mid-low (**baritone**), or very low (**bass**) voice or are playing an instrument with a lower sound (such as a tuba, trombone, string bass, etc.), music is read from the bass clef. In simple music, we may only see the staff with the melody on it. When other notes are added in a more complicated piece for harmony, there is a staff of music for treble and one for bass—each marked with its clef sign. Naturally, since these staffs are written one on top of the other, the treble (for high sound) clef is on top, and the bass clef (for lower sounds) is on the bottom. Note the symbols for each clef below:

Treble

Bass

Again, part of understanding how music is made involves understanding the relationship of size, length, and tension to sound. The higher the sound, the smaller and shorter the vocal chords or instrument and vice versa. Children's voices are high because their vocal chords are still very small. If you are playing an instrument that has both high and low notes, such as the piano, two clefs are presented—the treble on top and the bass clef on the bottom. If you open up the top of a piano, you can see that the high notes are played by a hammer striking shorter, thinner strings. If you also look at the strings of a guitar, you will see that the higher notes (treble) are played by the fingers strumming the thin strings, while the lower notes (bass) are played on thicker strings. The same is true with a harp. The lower the note, the longer and thicker the string. Tension is also considered in pitch. When a trumpet or trombone player wishes to play a higher pitch, he or she blows air through tautly stretched lips but produces lower tones by blowing through relaxed the lips. A singer also uses tension. For example, note the tension of your vocal chords increasing as you singer higher and higher. **Pitch** is caused by vibrations of the materials of the instruments or by the vocal chords. The higher the pitch, the faster the vibrations. The lower the tone, the more slowly the vibrations move.

Music is designed to be able to easily "read" pitch as well. Each musical note written on a staff has a *pitch,* or tone of sound that is high or low and that is associated with its name. For our purposes, we will only learn the name of the notes where the melody is often found—the treble clef. Beginning music students have always remembered the names of the notes written on the treble clef by two easy methods. The notes arranged in between the lines of the treble clef spell "FACE" (from the bottom up). The notes arranged on the lines of the treble clef are EGBDF ("Every Good Boy Does Fine" or "Every Good Boy Deserves Fudge") from the bottom up. By remembering these placements on a staff, you can easily read the name of the note. Vocalists can read, then remember, and sing the correct pitch while instrumentalists play the note by reading it from the staff. Remember that these five lines and four spaces are known as a musical staff. There are also notes above and below the staff, continuing in the order of the musical alphabet. Look at each staff below.

Notes in Spaces	Notes on Lines	Together
E C A F	F D B G E	E C A F / F D B G E

You may have heard the song "Do, Re, Mi" from the *Sound of Music* or heard someone sing a scale (or the eight notes of a musical octave) "do, re, mi, fa, sol, la, ti, do," where each note gets progressively higher. You can also sing or play back down each scale. Many music texts teach students to sing using the concept of these tone names first rather than notes.

Steps, leaps, and repeated tones are important concepts in music. When you hear a **scale** (do, re, mi, fa, sol, la, ti, do) or part of a scale (do, re, mi), you are hearing an example of notes or tones arranged in **steps**—that is, the sound moves from one note to another without skipping a tone. However, if a tone *does not* change its pitch, it is called a **repeated tone,** such as you hear in the first few notes of "Jingle Bells" ("Jingle Bells, Jingle Bells . . ."). Sing this first line of the song. Note that your voice does not change its tone at all—that is, your voice does not go up or down. This is a repeated tone.

There is another way that tones are arranged—in **leaps.** When tones leap, the pitch moves up or down, but it skips tones in between as it moves. As you continue to sing "Jingle Bells" from above, the next few words go "Jingle all . . ." This line of music has a high leap, then a low leap ("Jingle all"), then ends in steps ("the way"). Think about how this whole first line of music puts together *repeated tones, leaps,* and *steps* to form a *melody.* The following may help you to see that visually.

repeated tone	repeated tone	repeated tone	repeated tone	repeated tone	repeated tone	repeated tone	leap	leap	step	step

[staff notation with circled notes]
(A) (A) (A) (A) (A) (A) (A) (C) (F) (G) (A)

| Jin- | gle | bells! | Jin- | gle | bells! | Jin- | gle | all | the | way! |

Music also can be arranged in half steps or tones. When you see a piece of music that has a symbol known as a **flat** (♭) or a **sharp** (♯), the composer means that your voice or instrument should only move up a half step or tone for *sharps* or move down a half step or tone for *flats.* When a composer wants to indicate a *flat* or *sharp* in the middle of a piece of music, it is called an *accidental.* Note how the following accidentals (in this case, *sharps*) are written in this example:

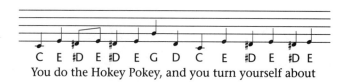

C E ♯D E ♯D E G D C E ♯D E ♯D E
You do the Hokey Pokey, and you turn yourself about

A composer can also indicate a sharp or flat *every* time a particular note is played or sung in his or her piece of music by placing a flat or sharp symbol at the beginning of a piece of music on the line or space of the note desired, where the note(s) is normally written. In the first example below, we see that the composer wants us to play or sing a B *flat* every time we come to a note on the B line. In the second example, we can see that the composer asks us always to play a *sharp* when we come to F notes, as a sharp symbol has been placed on the space where F is normally found (FACE). If we skip down to the next line of music, we can see that the composer chose to put three *flats* into this composition. By looking at the lines and spaces, we can see that we have a flat on the line where B is located ("Every Good Boy...") and the spaces where A and E are (FACE) located. Therefore, when we are reading this music, when we come to B, A, and E, we would automatically play or sing half steps or tones instead of whole steps. Note the following examples:

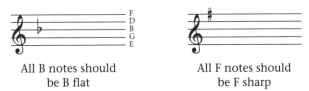

All B notes should   All F notes should
be B flat   be F sharp

In the next example, a composer begins with three flats. He or she can change this in the middle of a piece of music as well. In other words, the composer may say, "I want this music to start out with all B flats, but in the middle, I want to change to all B flats plus all E flats. This would be call a **key change,** and it makes a difference in the sound of the music. The music can change from no flats at all to one to seven flats or no sharps at all to one to seven sharps (one half tone up or down for each note in the musical scale—A, B, C, D, E, F, G). A key change usual creates an emotional surge in music. The staff below shows a key change from three flats to one flat.

Key and *key changes* are important concepts for other reasons. Have you ever started to sing a song and found that the tone on which you started made it impossible to hit the high notes (or maybe the low notes) as you continued singing along? This is a fairly common occurrence in singing "The Star-Spangled Banner." What did you do? Usually, if you were singing alone, you probably began again—either on a higher note or lower note, which would have helped you hit those notes that you could not sing the first time. This whole concept is related to the *key* in which a song is played or sung. You may have seen a movie where a singer is trying out for a part, and she or he ask the piano player to accompany him or her in a certain key ("Can you play it in C?"). Almost all simple children's songs are written either in the key of C, F, or G. These keys are the most popular because they offer easy accompaniment on many instruments.

All of the arrangement of the tones that we have discussed creates a melody. Again, melody is a sound pattern that often allows us to easily sing or hum along with a piece of music or to recognize a particular composition when we hear it played.

Form

Music is written with an overall plan, structure, or **form.** The elements that help shape music into forms are repetition, contrast, and variation. For example, a **melody pattern** is one that can be heard to be repeated several times throughout the music. We use the letters of the alphabet or even shapes to help us identify form, where contrasting parts of music are heard. For example, a song might have an ABA pattern or an ABAB pattern:

One can see this very easily in simple popular songs that have verses but come back to one chorus or *refrain* (part of the song that repeats). Looking again at "Jingle Bells, we know that the song begins with one melody pattern (A) and ends with a different melody pattern in the refrain or chorus (B), thus the form is AB:

A   Dashing through the snow, in a one horse open sleigh
O'er the field we go, Laughing all the way
Bells on bobtail ring, Making spirits bright;
Oh, what fun to ride and sing a sleighing song tonight!

B   Oh, Jingle Bells! Jingle Bells! Jingle all the way!
Oh, what fun it is to ride in a one horse open sleigh!

"Oh, Susannah!" is another good example of a song with a different form. It is written in *AAB* form, where there the pattern is three sections, the first and second verses repeat the same melody, while the ending verse (refrain or chorus) is different.

A   Oh, I come from Alabama with my banjo on my knee
And I'm going to Louisiana, my own true love for to see.

A   Oh, it rained all day the night I left, the weather was bone dry
The sun so hot, I froze to death, Susannah don't you cry.

B   Oh, Susannah! Don't you cry for me,
For I come from Alabama with my banjo on my knee.

"The Bear Went over the Mountain" is a simple example of ABA:

A   The bear went over the mountain,
    The bear went over the mountain,
    The bear went over the mountain,
    To see what he could see.

B   To see what he could see,
    To see what he could see

A   The bear went over the mountain,
    The bear went over the mountain,
    The bear went over the mountain,
    To see what he could see.

Music can be written in any of these combinations (even adding other forms such as C, D, etc.). A **rondo** refers to a musical form that has different sections. The A pattern is repeated after each different section.

When singing or playing songs with repeated *forms,* we often see repeat signs. A **repeat sign** (:‖) is a handy symbol that tells the musician when to go back and play or sing a passage again. The musician either goes back to the beginning of the music and repeats all of it *or* finds this sign (‖:) and begins from that point again.

Why would form be important to know as a musician? First of all, it is very useful for singers. If a singer masters the melody of one of one section, such as the melody of *form A* in "Oh, Susannah!" above, and knows that the next verse is exactly the same form, then he or she can repeat the melody easily. It is also easier to "sight read," or sing without the help of a musical instrument, when that form appears. For instrumentalists it is the same. However, knowing form really helps musicians memorize their music. In instrumental music, form can be of great importance in arranging more sophisticated orchestra pieces.

Teaching children about melody is much like teaching rhythm. By about age 8 children should be able to have a fairly stable tonal recall ability. To help children learn about melody, first promote the natural tendencies of children in known and invented melodies, then use direct music instruction. Model melody patterns often, then ask students to copy what they hear—as in echo melody games. As with rhythm, break instruction and performance down into small tasks. Ask students to differentiate between melody patterns and explain their thinking, and help them sort out several patterns. Again, when giving direct instruction on melody, isolate examples of melody within songs children know rather than offering examples with which they are unfamiliar. Have them recognize the same melody pattern played on different instruments. Encouraging students to invent short melodies and write them down where someone else could read them helps children understand the decoding process. Learning to match the exact pitch of a song is usually the last element of acquiring a song (as you may well know from trying to sing along with your favorite vocalists on the radio). Begin with concentration on words, then melody contours, and finally work on matching exact pitches.

Dynamics

We are not yet through with the way we decode written music. There are some other very important ways that a composer shows us to how read music. For instance, another question (when we want to play or sing) is, "How loud or soft should the whole piece or a particular part of the music be?" Composers indicate volume by writing terms or abbreviations of those terms into a piece of music. They are usually seen in italics and in Italian, so if you speak that language, you are already ahead in knowing about **dynamics** (how loud or soft the music should be). The most common words relating to dynamics, or volume, are *forte, mezzo forte, mezzo piano,* and *piano.* The symbols for those are *f (forte), mf (mezzo forte),* and in contrast, *mp (mezzo piano),* and *p (piano),* and they are simply written right under or, in some cases, above the notes of the music. *Forte* means forceful, loud, or with strength (as in "that is really my forte" or my strength). *Mezzo* is "medium" or "between" two sounds (as in a mezzanine, or the floor in a building "between" two floors), so *mezzo forte* is medium loud or medium forceful. *Piano,* on the other hand, indicates softness, so *mezzo piano* means to play or sing in a medium soft manner. What would you think *ff* or *pp* would be? Exactly! Doubly loud or *very* soft!! If you will think of most music that you know, you will also realize that a song does not stay at one level of sound, but changes *dynamics* within the song just as a "dynamic" speaker would vary his or her voice rather than remain monotoned. There is a way to indicate this in music as well. The composer simply uses **crescendo** (gradually become louder) or *decrescendo* or *diminuendo* (gradually become softer) or the symbols for these words. A teacher may say that children should think of the small end as the smaller sound and the large end as the larger sound. These symbols below also mean the same things that they do in mathematics, if you will look at the notation mark in the following example:

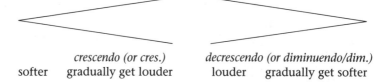

crescendo (or cres.)   *decrescendo (or diminuendo/dim.)*
softer   gradually get louder   louder   gradually get softer

The sound on this end should be **less than** the other end.	The sound on this end should be **greater than** the other end.

Another way to indicate a change in volume is with an *accent mark*. When an accent mark is used below a note, that note should be stronger or louder or more forceful than the sounds around it.

Tempo

Another Italian lesson comes with determining the **tempo** or speed of the beat—that is, how fast or slow the music should be played. Some terms that you might encounter are *largo* (very slow, as most *large* things move slowly), *adagio* (slow), *andante* (walking speed, not fast, or "my aunt walks not *too* fast") or *moderato* (moderate). In contrast, *allegro* (quick or merry), *allegretto* (very lively), and *presto* (very fast, as when you are pressed to hurry) are all terms that show when the beat should be played quite rapidly. Sometimes music speeds up during the song. Thus, it might be marked *accelerando* (get faster gradually, as in accelerating) or vice versa with *ritardando* (or slow down gradually, or retard your speed).

Yet another type of contrast in music is indicated by more Italian terms. For example, you may want to sing or play *smoothly* (*legato*) with a blended connection between notes, or a musical piece may require distinct precision in a way that each note is *detached* or *separated* (**staccato**). For example, in "Row, Row, Row Your Boat," the first part of the song is often sung or played smoothly with connection between notes (*legato*). Contrast that sound with the "Alphabet Song" (A, B, C, D, E, F, G . . .) where the voice or instrument clearly separates notes (*staccato*), much like a prancing horse.

Let's look at how many elements are combined now to allow us to read music:

Instrument Families

Elementary students usually begin to identify musical *instruments* of bands, orchestras, and even of other lands both visually and aurally, or by their unique sound. One way of identification involves classifying or grouping musical instruments into families. The *percussion* family instruments, for example, are those that are played by beating, shaking, scraping, or striking. Drums, tambourines, rattles, rasps, triangles, and xylophones are some examples. The piano, too, is often classified as a percussion instrument because the players' fingers strike the keys and, in turn, small hammers inside the piano strike the strings to make sound. Many of the percussion instruments are used to keep a strong beat in music such as the strong beat you hear when drums are played in rock and roll bands, the strong beat of Native American music, or the big bass drum being struck as a marching band goes by. These are instruments that are very old in the history of civilization, probably because many are very easily constructed. They are often the first instrument that children learn to play, for most have just one tone (unpitched instruments), though instruments such as timpani drums and xylophones do have many tones and are known as pitched instruments. Using unpitched percussion instruments, children are able to easily learn to read the rhythm and length of notes first—before they must worry with reading the names of notes for a melody.

Another group of instruments is known as the **woodwind** family. At one time all of these instruments were made of wood, though now you find these made of plastic and metal. Woodwind instruments are played by blowing air into a tube such as in the clarinet, oboe, saxophone, bassoon, pan pipes, English horn, flute, piccolo, and so forth. Many (but not all) of these instruments have a mouthpiece where a sliced piece of reed is fastened. This reed vibrates as the wind passes down through the tube to create a unique sound.

The **brass** family, obviously, has instruments that are made of tubes of brass. These long metal tubes are curled around and around, usually ending in a "bell" shape that "flowers" to the outside. The brass player make sounds by "buzzing" their lips inside the small, bell-shaped mouthpiece and moving a slide or pushing on valves to create different pitches. The trumpet, trombone, French horn, and tuba are all examples of brass instruments.

The last family is called the **strings.** String instruments include the violin, viola, cello, string bass, and so forth. Of course, all of these have strings and many are played with a bow that is drawn across them to vibrate the strings, thus creating the sound.

Another important concept to review when thinking about instruments is how the pitch is created for each instrument. The guideline is that the *smaller the instrument, the higher the sound.* Therefore, the small flute makes a much higher sound than the much larger tuba. To hear many instruments, go to http://www.dsokids.com/2001/instrument.char.htm.

Timbre and Tone Color

Each instrument has its very own characteristic sound, "voice," or **timbre.** A bell, for example, has a ringing sound all its own that it does not share with other instruments. Another name for this individual sound is **tone color.** Individual singers also have their own tone color, as most have a unique sound that is theirs alone, although we have all perhaps tried to imitate the tone color of our favorite popular singers—usually in the privacy of our showers. Combinations of instruments often create a unique sound as well. The choice of how a composer puts sounds together is as important as the artist's selection of colors. In Native American music one often hears a combination of drums, rasps, rattles, and flute that, when heard together, almost always creates a mental picture of this culture. The same is true of country and western music with guitar and fiddles, or Spanish music with castanets and guitars, and so forth. Also, there are many special instruments that have very unique sounds that are often associated with one particular area of the world. The samisen from Japan is one such instrument; the bagpipes from Scotland are another; and the digerido from the Aboriginal people of Australia is yet another example. There are many such unique instruments from Africa and other areas of the world.

All of the elements that we have spoken about up to this point—*tempo* (speed), *dynamics* (loudness), *meter* (beat), *key,* and *choice of instruments* affect the overall **mood** of music or the feeling that a piece of music creates for listener. A lullaby, for example, makes us feel quiet and gentle, while a march or rap song makes us feel excited and ready to move our feet. Each person may have a different reaction to the same composition, just as we may react differently to books, movies, and other art forms. However, it is not difficult to explain certain feelings when hearing certain types of music. The brooding mood of bagpipes accompanying "Amazing Grace" contrasts with the toe-tapping happiness of the fiddle in "Turkey in the Straw." Great compositions or even popular songs often have contrasting moods within the same piece as the elements discussed above work together. Emotion is the true power of music.

Another way that mood is created in music is through use of what we term *key.* There are two major divisions in Western music—major and minor keys. Most Western songs are written in major keys. The main difference when you hear a song written in a **minor key** is that it often sounds "bluesy" or sad. Two famous examples that you may know that are written in minor keys are "When Johnny Comes Marching Home Again" and "Summertime." **Ballads,** or songs that tell stories, are often (though not always) set in minor keys, especially when they tell sad stories.

When one instrument plays or one voice sings a main melody, it is called a **solo** performance, even though an instrument or instruments may *accompany* it in the background. Elvis Presley was, perhaps, the most famous *solo* male vocalist of the 1950s, though he was always accompanied by a guitar or group of musicians. The only time a solo singer or **chorus** (a large group of singers) has no instrumental accompaniment is when an arranger indicates that the voices should be **a cappella,** or for voices *alone* with no instruments. When there are two or more musical instruments playing different pitches together, one instrument playing different pitches at the same time (such as the piano, autoharp, guitar, etc.), or voices singing different parts, harmony is created. **Harmony** really means that two or more different tones are being played or sung together. When instruments of a band or orchestra are playing together or a choir of *many* people are singing different parts together, the harmony is usually very rich because there are many tones being played at once. A barbershop quartet usually has a four-part harmony. When three or more pitches are played together, we call this a *chord*. When a singer is accompanied by a guitar, autoharp, or piano, you are most likely hearing chords of a harmony being played.

There are other ways to create harmony. An *ostinato* is created by singing or playing a rhythm pattern over and over again throughout a song, normally as a part of the background. For example, in "Frere Jacques" ("Are You Sleeping?"), one voice or part can sing the lyrics of the whole song, while a second, ostinato voice sings the following words and melody over and over again, "Are you sleeping? Are you sleeping?" throughout the song—even though the other voice continues with the rest of the song. *Partner songs* also add harmony. This occurs when two different songs are sung or played together. A famous example of this is "Scarborough Fair" by Simon and Garfunkel. Two different songs are actually being sung at the same time, yet they blend together well. Singing or playing *rounds* is a very easy way to create harmony as well. This occurs when one group of musicians begins a song, and others wait to start until the group before it has finished the first musical phrase. There can be three to four groups waiting to sing at different starting points in a round. Most of us have sung "Row, Row, Row Your Boat" in a round. In a *counter melody,* a song is sung or played, but a different melody is also being played or sung at the same time. If you know the famous "The Stars and Stripes Forever" march, you may recall the end of the piece where the very high piccolos trill a counter melody against main melody as it continues.

The terms above also affect the **texture** of music—that is, how one voice (or instrument) alone sounds versus how different voices (or instruments) are put together. The quality produced by the number and kinds of instruments put together (or instruments and voices) also refers to texture. You can think of musical texture just as you might think of the weave of a cloth. Some weaves are thick and sturdy, while others are thin and delicate—and everywhere in between. The same is true of the texture of music.

Another term that you may need to know relates to music belonging to certain cultures—**musical conversation.** In African American spirituals, one may often hear a solo voice ask a question or make a statement while the refrain/chorus comes behind to answer or reinforce it. In "Deep River," for example, the musical question asked is, "Oh, don't you want to go to the Gospel feast, that Promised Land, where all is peace?" The answering phrase comes next, "Deep River, my home is over Jordan . . . . I want to cross over. . . ." A well-known musical conversation asks, "I looked over the Jordan, and what did I see?" "Comin' for to carry me home," is a reinforcer. The answer is, "A band of angels comin' after me. . . ."

All of the terms we have discussed in this section help us to begin reading music. There are many, many more terms in music, but these should be the basics to help you begin with EC-4. It is easy to access a number of other musical terms by typing in "music+theory" in many of the search engines on the Internet. For example, at www.essentialsofmusic.com and select the glossary to find definitions and play-back examples. In the next section, we will look at some elements that will help teach children music and help us to be better teachers of music.

First, test your knowledge on some sample questions from this section.

Mrs. Cottle had her first-grade students first clap their hands to a song, then stand up and walk in time to the music. She was trying to teach them about:

A. Timbre.
B. Dynamics.
C. Rhythm.
D. Instrument families.

Answer *A* cannot be the answer because timbre distinguishes the way one instrument or voice sounds different than another. A tuba has a different timbre (a very different sound to our ears) than a violin. Answer *B*, dynamics, refers to how loud or soft music is played or sung, so this cannot be the answer. Answer *D* cannot also not be the answer because there was no mention of the different instruments being played here. Answer *C*, however, is the correct answer. Having children clap or walk to music is a very good way to have them feel the rhythm of a piece of music. They would hopefully begin to feel the beat, an element of rhythm.

Ms. Botetourt wanted to teach her children about music with a strong beat. She selected a march to demonstrate two strong beats per measure, a Native American piece to demonstrate four strong beats per measure, and a waltz. How many steady beats per measure does a waltz have?

A. 5   **B.** 1   **C.** 8   **D.** 3

A march demonstrates *two* strong beats per measure, as it helps people (particularly in the military) keep together in marching. Since we only have two feet, a march has a beat for each . . . left, right, left, right; 1, 2, 1, 2. Native American music is often presented with a very strong ONE-two-three-*four* (4) beat, while a waltz has *three* strong beats per measure or set, often with a very strong first beat (ONE-two-three, ONE-two-three). The correct answer is *D* (3 beats).

Students in Mr. Spellman's class were given a writing assignment to describe a churning seacoast. He had waited for a rainy day for this assignment to set the mood. In addition, he put on a piece of music to heighten the effect. Before having students write, he asked, "Listen to how the composer used the string family and the percussion family to create a swirling, crashing mood. What instruments do you think you hear in the percussion family here?"

For what type of instruments were students suppose to listen?

A. Instruments such as the tuba and the trumpet.

B. Instruments with strings like the violin and the cello that are often (though not always) played by drawing a bow across the strings.

C. Voices accompanied by woodwind instruments.

D. Instruments that are struck, beaten, shaken, crashed, or scraped, such as the timpani drum, cymbals, bass drum, triangle, and so forth.

Answer *A* is not correct because the tuba and trumpet are members of the musical instrument family that are all made of *brass*. Answer *B* is not correct because, though he was probably going to ask them next about the string family instruments, he asked *first* about the percussion family instruments. Answer *C* is wrong because, although it mentions a family of instruments, it does not discuss the type of instruments in that family, *and* Mr. Spellman does not talk about voices. Answer *D* is the correct answer because instruments in the percussion family are those that are played by striking, beating, shaking, or scraping. Many orchestras use percussion instruments such as the timpani drums and cymbals to indicate dark, brooding power such as in a storm. Cymbals often imitate the sound of crashing lightning, while the triangle can be struck lightly to sound like raindrops.

STANDARD II (SINGING AND PLAYING)

The music teacher sings and plays a musical instrument.

The early childhood teacher must know methods and techniques for singing or for playing a musical instrument and must be able to sing or play an instrument while demonstrating accurate intonation and rhythm.

This standard also overlaps with Standards I and III, as the teacher must understand all of the information contained within those first so that the information and knowledge contained there can be applied to either playing an instrument or singing. Note the important message of this standard, however: The EC-4 teacher is expected to sing *or* play with his or her children often and in a way that maintains an accurate pitch and correct beat of the music. You may not have had the opportunity to have music lessons or to have been a part of a band or choir, but that does not mean that it is too late for you to learn to read music in order to sing or play an instrument. In days long past, there was often a piano in many elementary classrooms, and the teacher played while children gathered around to sing. Excellent recordings (often, *karaoke*-style) and "easy" instruments have often replaced this concept. Again, Texas expects you to be able to sing *or* play in order to teach children about music! One suggestion, if you do not already play an instrument that is conducive to accompaniment, is to invest in an autoharp or guitar. An autoharp is a stringed instrument that is an very easy to play, as you simply push down buttons that, in turn, create chords for harmony. Then, simply strum for accompaniment. A guitar is a bit harder, as you must learn which strings to press to create chords for accompaniment, but both are excellent instruments for the EC-4 classroom. It does take practice to feel comfortable, but the rewards of singing with your children and adding the harmony of an instrument are great. Both instruments offer the opportunity for children to gather in front of you or in a circle where you can easily see them. With knowledge of only a few chords, you can sing and play a large variety of easily learned children's songs. You should pay close attention to the information in the other standards for information for singing and/or playing an instrument.

STANDARD III (MUSIC NOTATION)

The music teacher has a comprehensive knowledge of music notation.

> *The early childhood through fourth grade teacher must know how to read, recognize aurally, interpret, and write standard music notation. This includes use of clefs, keys, and meters.*

You have been introduced to these concepts in Standard I in reading, interpreting, and writing music notation. Please review each, as this overlap indicates that they are of particular importance. The other emphasis in this standard, however, is recognizing musical concepts when you hear them—that is, aurally. Of course, that would be difficult to determine in a paper-and-pencil test, but as a teacher of musical concepts, you should be able to point out the concepts given in Standard I such as texture, mood, beat, and so forth, as you listen to music with children or as they sing or perform for you. For example, as they sing, you should be able to say, "Children, if you will *crescendo* (get louder gradually) right at this point in the music, it will give more power to the song," or as you listen to the song "Memories" from the musical *CATS!* together, you should be able to say, "Boys and girls, doesn't that *key change* in the middle just work to give you goose bumps! What a wonderful technique by the composer!" Begin to listen to music with a musician's ear and notice each of the concepts discussed in Standard I so that you can bring them to the attention of children. Music book series often group several examples of these concepts on tapes or CDs. This makes it easy for you to hear and teach examples to your children.

Ms. Glymph examined the sheet music that she wanted to teach her class for the PTO program next month.

This is   my country! Land of my   birth!

1. How does the dynamics symbol of this first line tell her it should be sung?
   A. Slowly.
   B. Rapidly.
   C. Loudly.
   D. Softly.

2. How many beats per measure does this song have and what note receives one beat?
   A. Two per measure and a whole note receives one beat.
   B. Four per measure and a quarter note receives one beat.
   C. Four per measure and an eighth note receives one beat.
   D. Two per measure and a whole note receives one beat.

3. For how many beats would the word *birth* be held in this line?
   A. One.
   B. Two.
   C. Three.
   D. Four.

In question 1, she would look for the dynamics symbol written in line with the notes that are affected. This is an *f*, or *forte*, so the song would begin loudly (*C*). In question 2, she would look at the time signature. In this music, it is 4/4. The top number tells her that there are four beats per measure and the bottom of the time signature tells her that a quarter note gets one beat (*B*). In Question 3, the measure with *birth* is represented by a whole note. In this song, a quarter note gets one beat, so a half note receives two beats, and a whole note receives four beats (*D*). Children would hold *birth* for four full beats.

Generalists are not responsible for Standard IV.

STANDARD V (TEXAS AND AMERICAN MUSIC HISTORY)

The music teacher has a comprehensive knowledge of music history and the relationship of music to history, society, and culture.

The teacher of early childhood through fourth grade should know how music can reflect elements of a specific society or culture and be able to analyze various purposes and roles of music in society and culture. Being able to recognize and describe the music that reflects the heritage of the United States and Texas is an important element in this area. Teachers should also know various music vocations and avocations.

Why should every child know about music? It is a universal human experience, although individuals and cultures certainly react to music in their own unique ways. Consider that humans may be somehow "wired" for music, since music has been a part of man's life since the beginnings of history. Music was often a means to preserve history and stories orally as well as to entertain. It was (and still is) used to honor people, places, events, and ideas. Music motivates people to do things such as support a cause, fall in love, worship, or even march into war. Music is used as comfort or to express joy, laughter, nonsense, yearning, anger, sorrow, protest, and celebration. In fact, music can be associated with and can express every human emotion. Just think about how bland your favorite movies would seem without the sound track enhancing the emotions that are being acted out. Imagine the emptiness of a wedding, graduation, or other ceremony that did not have traditional music as an accompaniment. We find that the rhythm of many kinds of labor has also been expressed through music—as well as the joys of play and diversion after work was done. People have used music to express traveling to new places and experiencing new things but also to remind them of their homelands and their lives before. Many different cultures of people share and express their music in distinctive ways and celebrate their traditions and holidays in song and dance. Music helps to unify people as a culture. To understand this musical part of a people is to understand them better as a whole.

The same can be said in reference to historical times. By analyzing instruments and the expressions of music from different periods of history, we can understand more easily the people who lived in those times. For example, is the music heavy and angry, or is it delicate and light? Does the music tell us that people danced and sang—or marched to war? Are the words set to music carefree, romantic, sad, fearful, or purposeful in some other way? Is the majority of the music of a population or period of time patriotic in nature? Elements such as these can tell us much about a society or culture and its times. But music can also transcend cultures, times, and ages. Good music may be enjoyed for centuries and by many different cultures throughout the world, thus becoming an instrumental or vocal *classic*. Thus music could almost be considered a universal human endeavor, as so many people of the world have created and enjoyed some type of music and musical traditions.

Texas Music

One requirement noted by this state standard asks you to teach children about our state and national music. As you drive through Texas today, scan radio stations and listen to the many kinds of music that the people of Texas love. Texas music is truly a reflection of the many cultures that exist here today and the rich history of Texas.

The first people of America and Texas were Native American tribes. We know little about some of these tribes, but others still exist today and have recordings and videos of song and dance. Although each Native American nation has developed its own unique music, musical instruments of Native Americans often include various drums, handmade flutes, and rattles. Voices often accompany songs and dances in sing-song chanting in their tribal language. Generally, there is a strong beat. Native American songs exist for almost every aspect of men's and women's tribal life—work, planting, hunting, social dances, celebrations, and other rituals of a people. Honor songs are sung to pay special homage to those who are deserving. Much Native American music deals with the forces of nature, myths, legends, and the spiritual aspect of life. Though there has been some melding of Native American music with more modern music, by and large this music has remained unaffected by other cultures.

Following along through the history of Texas, we note the exploration and settling of Texas by those from Spain, and later Mexico. During these early days when the flag of Spain, then Mexico, flew over Texas, religious festivals were held throughout the year honoring the saints and events found in the Roman Catholic religion—the religion of those of European descent living in Texas at that time. Many of these continue throughout Texas today, particularly in communities with Hispanic traditions and ties. *Las Posadas,* for example, commemorating Mary and Joseph's search for shelter in Bethlehem, is a popular combination of religious and mariachi-style music that remains as a part of San Antonio's December celebrations. Barges carrying performers of the pageant and of many other groups cruise the river singing Christmas songs. Mariachi music, typically joyful and exuberant, is very typical of Mexico and is heard often in Texas communities throughout the state. Musicians in traditional black and silver Mexican cowboy (charro) costumes stroll and sing in Spanish to the accompaniment of guitars, violins, guitarrons (bass guitars), and trumpets. They often sing *corridos* (Mexican folk ballads), *rancheras* (ranch songs), and *boleros* (romantic songs), often with much harmony. Many schools and several universities in southern Texas offer study in mariachi music. *Conjunto* music is also a sound heard often in Texas. Created by the working class along the border in the early 1900s, it is a bright and happy sound of Mexican-style music that has borrowed both its main instrument (the accordion) and some of its style (polka) from the Texans of German descent. With *conjunto* as its roots, the more modern *tejano* music today is music defined as current popular Hispanic-style music (rather than a very specific type of sound). Made famous by the tragic death of its star, Selena, it has gained considerable following in the past few years. One can hear all of these types of Hispanic-based music often in Texas, but the focus of the Hispanic community in Texas often centers on El Cinco de Mayo, a holiday celebrating a battle won in Mexico's fight for independence. During this holiday, there is a great deal of music, folk dancing, and even grand balls celebrated in some parts of Texas.

Music was an important part of the lives of the early settlers and colonists from the United States and the Texas Revolution as well. It is said that Texans went into the Battle of San Jacinto (the battle that won Texas independence) singing "Will You Come to the Bower?"

Early settlers who came from the United States to Texas brought ballroom dancing that was mixed with folk dances from the many European countries of their ancestries. During the early 1800s, upper-class circles of early Texas colonists and officials in the Mexican government attended sophisticated balls, while *fandangos* were street entertainment with music, dancing, and other activities. At *shindigs*, settlers with little or no formal music or dance instruction could attempt polkas and schottisches danced in an even more informal and frolicking way. In the formal dances of higher circles, groups danced to figures or quadrilles in the European style, and reminders about what to do next were often called out to the dancers. Over time, the person responsible for this became "the caller," and dancing depended less and less on the formal steps—thus merging into the style that we know as the *square dance*. One folk dance that was popular during this part of Texas history was the *play-party game*. Dancing to instruments was not considered proper among some religious leaders and groups, so the accompaniment to dances was sung or called, and the dance itself was called a "game." This "game" also had to serve when no music or not much music was available. Quite often in the early years of Texas there might only a fiddler at a function. The World Champion Fiddlers' Contest in Crockett, Texas, shows how important this type of musician was to the roots of Texas music.

Although Texas now boasts of several of the nation's largest urban areas, much of Texas still has deep roots in its cowboy heritage and music. This was music first sung and played by cowboys on the many cattle drives that originated on the ranges of Texas and moved north to Kansas railroads and markets in the mid-1800s. After the Civil War, many settlers had moved west from southern states, bringing traditional music of the South with them (ballads, hymns, and minstrel songs). Adaptations of these old songs of the range formed the basis of western swing in the 1930s, creating the roots of our modern country-and-western music. To go with this music, folk dancing in Texas developed its own style. The Cotton-Eyed Joe, for example, is a popular dance step that many Texans still learn. As radios became available, the traditional dances began to fade, replaced by the more popular American dances and music of the times during War War II. Later rock-and-roll moved to the popular front. However, country-and-western music and dance has always been a part of many Texas communities and has made a resurgence since the 1970s with popular country singing stars topping the charts. Several popular movies featuring country-style line dances and songs that have a more rock-and-roll rhythm help to keep this music in the minds of many Texans.

In the later part of the 1800s, many Germans began to leave Europe, fearing the rising militarism of Prussia and desiring to own land of their own. With them they brought their own unique music. Today, the *ohm-pa-pa* of German music is heard throughout many parts of central Texas, the area most settled by these groups. During the mid-1800s festivals centered around the homes and communities of German immigrants. In New Braunfels today, *Wurstfest* is always held in October and features German music, dancing, and food. The polka-style music, played most often by small brass bands in German communities, is also still heard in many Texas Czech communities.

Texans also hear and enjoy music that has its roots in African American cultures. You may have heard the expression "King Cotton" in reference to Texas prior to the Civil War. Many parts of eastern and central Texas were optimum for growing cotton, and because Texas was a Southern slave state, many African Americans were brought here as workers. With them, they brought their music. After *Juneteenth,* when Union forces brought the news to Texas that the slaves had been freed, many of these emancipated slaves began to look for work. This was a hard life, and most went into either sharecropping or became migratory workers. All hoped to find a place where discrimination and racism were not part of their day-to-day existence. The *blues,* the sound that emerged from these times, was a way for these people to express extreme feelings of sorrow, dejection, suffering, and, yet, even hope and humor. During the early 1900s African American composers contributed greatly to other genres of music. Scott Joplin from Texarkana, known as the "King of Ragtime" for his "Maple Leaf Rag," pioneered the energizing, lively sounds of ragtime. Jazz followed and formed a backdrop for rhythm-and-blues and rock-and-roll. This led the way for performers such as Texas-born Janis Joplin in the 1960s.

Attending festivals throughout the state give Texans an opportunity to hear music and see dancing from many of our Texas immigrants' historical backgrounds. The Lebanese-Syrian festivals in Austin, the National Polka Festival in Ennis, and the Greek Festival in Houston are only a few examples where the sounds of other cultures that make up Texas can be heard. In addition, certain cities and towns highlight other music. The Texas Folklife Festival is, perhaps, the most inclusive of all the festivals and is held annually at the Institute of Texas Cultures in San Antonio. Round Top is home to a renowned Classical Festival each year, Palo Duro Canyon hosts the outdoor musical "Texas" each summer, and the musical extravaganza "Fandangle" is performed at Fort Griffin in Albany, Texas. Several cities host excellent jazz festivals, including San Antonio, Corpus Christi, and Houston. Houston also has an excellent opera season, and famous musicals can be seen in most larger cities and/or on many university campuses throughout Texas.

Below are listed some of the many other famous singers and composers from Texas that have contributed in some way to Texas and American music.

Tex Ritter	Roger Miller	Trini Lopez	Buddy Holly
Gene Autry	Kris Kristofferson	Roy Orbison	
Dale Evans	Freddie Fender	Lyle Lovett	
Willie Nelson	Waylon Jennings	Selena Quintania	

Our state song, "**Texas, Our Texas,**" can often be heard and/or sung during morning announcement times, at assemblies, at some football games, and other opening ceremonies at many Texas schools and community events. Texas teachers should learn it in order to teach it to children and to help them understand the respect that Texans hold for our state's symbols.

American Music

National and state standards ask that students relate music to history, society, and culture. Because we can say that music is often a reflection of the times in which it is produced, it is helpful for you to know not only about the genres of American music but also about the period in history from which they come and what was happening in America during those times. Little is learned when a teacher just says, "Here is a song from ___ (colonial America or from another culture or another country)." The investigation of what makes that particular piece so unique is what will bring children to better understand an historical period or cultures—ours and that of others.

American music has a long history that parallels much of European musical history as well as the course of events that shaped our country. The first Pilgrim colonists were a very religious people who thought of music mainly for the part it could play in religion. They used only a few traditional English hymn tunes to sing a number of psalms. However, as the colonies quickly became settled, America took three turns in its music—one direction for the more cultured and wealthy; another direction for those many pioneers who lived more isolated, rural lives; and yet another for the slaves who were brought here early in our nation's history.

Where cities prospered, Americans integrated popular European music and dances into their colonial life. Many of the wealthier class listened to and danced European-style minuets and gavottes, mainly to the tunes played on harpsichords. The English and American aristocracy wished to replicate life from English courts on their plantations and by holding balls in flourishing urban areas. This type of music was from the Baroque era and would last almost until the Revolutionary War. In Europe during this time, Bach wrote many of his fugues (mainly for organ). Handel wrote his oratorio, *The Messiah*. An *oratorio* is opera without costumes, scenery, or action and is normally religious in nature. Vivaldi also wrote the set of four works known as *The Four Seasons*. You may have seen Baroque architecture that exuberantly "fills every space" with movement. Baroque music is very much the same in nature—highly ornate. This music was usually characterized by a single mood. If the work began with a mood such as sorrow or joy, that single feeling was maintained throughout most of the work.

Settlers soon began to move out from the East Coast into small and isolated rural homes (where not even a tavern supported music). In their own homes they sang folk ballads from their original homelands—mostly without accompaniment. If there was a musical instrument, it was probably a fiddle, a mouth harp, or a homemade lute.

Slaves were brought to America very early in its history and from many different African areas and countries. Slaves were forced to adapt to an unfamiliar world that led to a difficult new way of life, a new language, and a new religion.

Music became a way of life as slaves united the many cultures and sounds they brought from various parts of Africa and used music to pace their work, communicate, express feelings, and sing songs of worship and of hope. Often, one singer would start a song and others would answer (*field hollers* or *cries*) or join in on the refrain after a verse was sung. This music was mainly unaccompanied—sung with voice only (*a cappella*). *Spirituals,* religious songs that were really folk music in nature, developed as work songs combined with impression of hymns. Spirituals often retold Bible stories in a dialect more common to slaves and ex-slaves. *Spirituals* were eventually accepted into the general population and sung by Americans of many cultures, becoming widespread with the popularity of religious camp meetings in the later 1800s.

Let us return to the early days of America again to look at a different type of music. In the early days of America, England sent troops to its colonies. For the military, music was mostly from fife and drum during this time, but with the coming War for Independence against England, popular American songs such as "The Liberty Tree" (America's first patriotic song) and "Yankee Doodle" came to the forefront. "Yankee Doodle," a mockery used by the British to make fun of the "backwoods" colonists before and during the war, became so much of a symbol of defiance and pride that it was practically the national anthem for years following the Declaration of Independence. As the United States became more settled and people began to travel along established trails, rivers, canals, and seaport, many public houses, inns, or taverns began to appear. These provided a place besides church to go where people could hear and share music together. People also gathered together to celebrate festive occasions, and dance was often a part of those occasions. Folk dances of America developed during this time were the *play-party game* and *square dance* (discussed earlier in Texas music). *Long-ways* and *circular formation* dances (such as the Virginia Reel) developed, along with other round dances in which the general movement of all partners goes around the room (such as in the polka or schottische). **Square dancing** is seen very much as a true U.S. folk dance.

For those who remained in touch with the culture of Europe, the Baroque era in Western music was followed by the Classic Period (1750–1820), whose main composers were Mozart, Haydn, and Beethoven. As the Baroque period, most of these works were commissioned by the wealthy in Europe. The main composers were influenced by popular tunes of the times. A characteristic of this music is a range of emotions and themes displayed in each piece rather than maintenance of one mood throughout. The **symphony,** emerging from this period, was an orchestral work of four movements typically lasting from 25 to 45 minutes, with a fast section, slow section, dancelike section (like a minuet), and an emotional, fast end. *Chamber music,* using only a small number of instruments, also emerged from the aristocrats' or merchant classes' musical evening's entertainment. The signers of our Declaration of Independence probably attended dances where the popular dance sounds of Mozart were played.

As time marched on in Europe, the age of Romanticism in music (1820–1900), was full of uplifting aspirations and beautiful ideals. Music was no longer written just for commission but to fulfill an inner need of self-expression—particularly of yearning love. Also, composers began to look at national feelings—both their own and that of other countries—and drew on the folk songs, dances, legends, and history. Indeed, there was a great individuality of style based upon the concept of nationalism in many works of famous composers of that time such as Tchaikovsky and Chopin. *Program music,* based on a story, legend, or scene, was a popular style, as we see in Tchaikovsky's *Romeo and Juliet.* Interest in formal music boomed in the United States, as concert halls (such as Carnegie Hall) were built in many larger cities in the later part of the century.

A more informal type of musical entertainment began during the early 1800s in the United States, termed the *minstrel show,* and it became an important type of entertainment for a number of years. During these shows, comedy, dances, and songs were performed first by white entertainers with black face makeup but later on by African Americans. Dances were normally jigs and clog dances that later developed into **tap dancing**—a truly American form of dance. Accompaniment was often played by the fiddle, tambourine, and banjo, whose rapid, upbeat sounds subsequently influenced ragtime. As these programs became more elaborate with many performers, this type of entertainment eventually changed to *vaudeville.*

During the mid-1800s, a famous composer was working on a style of music that belonged to the United States alone. Stephen Foster wrote folk songs that articulated the U.S. character and spirit of work and the home. Much of his work vocalized plantation life and the life of African Americans during these times. Unfortunately, the United States became embroiled in the staggering Civil War just following this time period. From the Civil War, we remember marching songs such as "The Battle Hymn of the Republic" (from the North) and "Dixie" (from the South). Beginning in the very late 1800s reasonably priced, wholesome popular music and stage dance was presented in vaudeville shows such as the Ziegfeld Follies. Songs that were carefree and innocent, such as "A Bicycle Built for Two," were written and performed during this period when the United States was mostly at peace. Victor Herbert, sometimes called the father of popular music, wrote light operettas such as "Babes in Toyland" up through 1920. The marches of John Philip Sousa from this period, including "The Stars and Stripes Forever," also became world famous.

The years of the 1900s to the present have seen many styles of music. This was the age when the United States, like other nations, was changing from a rural, agricultural country to urban, industrial centers. The symbolism and expressivism created in modern art during this period was often mirrored by concert composers, as they experimented with unconventional, dissonant sounds and rhythms. George Gershwin and Aaron Copland, who composed during this time, are two of the most famous U.S. composers. Gershwin, with his

"Rhapsody in Blue," bridged popular music (jazz) with music for the concert hall. Copland, with his nationalistic agenda, wrote expansive music representing areas of the United States and American life that is still popular with adults and children today ("Billy the Kid," "Appalachian Spring," "The Red Pony," etc.). Spirituals were also changing to become *gospel songs*. These newly composed religious songs were more upbeat, with lively voices full of movement, accompanied now with instruments and (often) hand-claps.

Jazz, an American sound created from predominately African American roots, probably began early in the 1900s. The contributing elements were slavery and the hard life after Reconstruction. The heart of jazz lies in improvisation (creating music on the spot), syncopation (an "unexpected accent"), and call and response (where a voice or instrument is answered by other voices or instruments). The main styles of jazz included *ragtime* (player piano sound), the *blues, Dixieland,* and *boogie-woogie* (with its "walking bass" sound). In the 1920s many young people danced the Charleston to some of these sounds. In the 1930s radio brought music into U.S. homes throughout the country and allowed more people to hear more popular music. *Swing* (big band sound) of the World War II years, *bebop* or *bop,* and *"cool" jazz* of the early 1950s continued the jazz heritage. The years during World War II were filled with popular songs remembering those who waited and worked on the home front but portraying a clear determination to win the war. Glitzy musical movies with song and dance boomed during this era, too, as a way to escape from the hardships the war and the Depression that had preceded it. U.S. musical theater boomed through the new genre of *musical plays* of Rodgers and Hammerstein II *(Oklahoma, South Pacific, The King and I, Carousel, The Sound of Music,* and others). In the 1950s Leonard Bernstein became king of this genre by writing *West Side Story.* The late 1940s also saw *rhythm and blues* emerge from the African American communities, with artists such as Little Richard and T-Bone Walker. Later, *country and western* from rural communities appeared, along with *rock-and-roll.* In the mid-1950s songs like "Rock around the Clock" and stars such as Buddy Holly (from Lubbock, Texas) and Elvis Presley rocketed rock-and-roll to the top of popular music. *Rhythm and blues* (R & B), however, remained the main source of movements in pop music throughout the century. These genres influenced the evolution of *rock.* The event that ensured that rock would remain as an influential popular style was the first U.S. tour of the Beatles in the mid-1960s. Television also brought not only music but the faces of popular singers to the U.S. public, eventually leading to the development of popular videos of singers often shown now on MTV. Along with the more electric sounds of *rock (classical rock, psychedelic rock, acid rock)* came the folk influence of many of the protest songs of the "atomic age" and the Vietnam war. Softer folk songs of the times were reflected by such artists as John Denver who often sang about our states in such songs as "Country Roads." The reverberations of R & B and gospel united somewhat to produce the popular music called *soul* from the African American community. The 1970s saw a returned interest in partner dancing with the *disco beat,* and *country rock* became popular in some areas of the United States. *New wave, reggae,* and *heavy metal* sounds continued into the 1990s, and *rap* emerged as a hard, angry, chanting sound from urban African Americans. As music of this century moved from *jazz* to *rock* and *rock* to *rap,* melody became ever less important than the beat. Each popular music genre has not lasted a very long time in the United States during the past century, so it will be interesting to see what the "new modern style" will be.

Other more regional styles of music are a part of our national music history as well. Until recent times the isolation of the Appalachians and other eastern mountain regions kept the *folk music* there pure and uncorrupted by other types of music. The stringed dulcimer accompanies most of these songs, which have an Old English or Scottish sound, while the *bluegrass* sound of this region has a faster, upbeat mood with banjos, guitars, and other instruments. Cowboy and Native American music were discussed in the section on Texas music above. *Cajun music* from Louisiana is another unique type of U.S. music. Cajun's sad ballads are grounded in the forced migration of the Acadian French from Canada by the British, while the more exuberant sounds of their dance songs came from the mix of those who settled there long ago (from France, Africa, and the Native Americans of the area). The accordion, fiddle, and lyrical mix of French and the local dialect has a sound that is unique. *Hawaiian music* is another type of indigenous music that belongs to the native islanders of our fiftieth state. In old Hawaiian music, chants with heavy rhythms were accompanied by percussion instruments such as a hollow gourd (ipu) or bamboo sticks (pu'ili), though the more modern sound comes from a coupling of the Portuguese guitar (now the ukulele), steel guitar, and missionary hymns. Current trends combine traditional folk songs of the islands, modern instruments, and themes of life surrounded by water and the beauty of nature all around. The native dance, the hula, can be slow and graceful, fast and furious, or light and comical. Native Hawaiians love their children to be included in music, and there are many charming hulas for children.

Each of the genres and composers discussed above—and many that have not been—is described at length in music books and on the Web. In fact, much of the information for this standard comes from an excellent source, *The Handbook of Texas Online* (www.tsha.utexas.edu/handbook/online/index. html). It is important, however, for you to *hear* these different sounds. As a teacher of music and as an American, you should try to learn and understand our country's musical styles and history for all the richness music offers. Music in the United States will continue to change, but we should try to understand this part of our history and culture well.

As a note, when tragedy struck as a result of terrorists' actions in New York and Washington on September, 11, 2001, it was our patriotic songs such as "God Bless America," "America the Beautiful," "The Star-Spangled Banner," and others that helped to unite us as a nation. Every child in Texas deserves to feel that bond of belonging through knowing and being able to sing these American songs.

As a teacher, one should note that some religious affiliations maintain their Constitutional right for their children not to stand for the *Pledge of Allegiance,* considering it nationalism (in which they do not believe). This extends to teachers not requiring their children to stand for our national anthem, "The Star-Spangled Banner," or to sing other patriotic songs. Parents who belong to these affiliations will let you know. Other children should be reminded of the respect that stopping activity, standing, etc., shows for our national anthem in particular.

Musical Careers

Yet another element of this standard, and another rationale for teaching music, is teaching the many areas of employment that involve music directly and indirectly. Certainly, children should understand that people can grow up to become music educators/teachers of general music, play a particular instrument, or be a member of a band or choir, but they may not realize that there are many other occupations in which music is the focus. Some of the following could be leisure or volunteer activities listed below, but many are also employment opportunities for the future:

> Member or director of a: symphony, stage band, chamber orchestra, band pit orchestra, popular music band, and so forth.
>
> Member or director of vocal work or dance in a(n): chorus, choir, musical, opera, ballet, folk dancing group, or other performance shows, or as a choreographer. (Musicians above might work or enjoy performing in city or national organizations, religious institutions, theme parks, cruise ships, restaurants and private parties, weddings, radio, television, or movies.)
>
> Employment in the recording industry such as: composing, publishing, as a member of a road crew, in law or in studio technology, as an arranger, as a coach, as an equipment engineer, or as a composer for background music in television, radio, or movies, etc.
>
> Employment in technology: software designer, electronic instrument designer, sound manager, and so forth.
>
> Other areas might also include: composer, music historian, professional music critic, disc jockey, instrument maker or repairer, music therapist, music store owner, college professor, advertising (jingles), tuner, etc.

There are many areas that could involve music both recreationally and as a way to make a living.

STANDARD VI (EVALUATING MUSICAL PERFORMANCES)

The music teacher applies a comprehensive knowledge of music to evaluate musical compositions, performances, and experiences.

In this competency, it is important for teachers to know and understand the criteria used to evaluate and critique musical performances and experiences. Therefore, they must be able to recognize accurate pitch, intonation, rhythm, and characteristic tone quality. Teachers should also be able to diagnose performance problems and detect errors accurately. Finally, they should be able to integrate music with other subject areas.

Teaching Children to Sing

As the music teacher of younger children, a goodly number of your activities will involve children in singing. Here are some tips that you may want to use in teaching children to sing—and, we hope, to sing well. The first goal in music is to have children participate. Shyness or other reluctance is often overcome by providing inviting activities in a pleasing environment with musical games and lightness, rather than forcing children to "perform." Select songs in which children can find an interest and easily handle within their small voice range (i.e., songs where the pitches are not so far apart; that is, notes are not very high to very low). If a song can be integrated with other topics, that often creates interest as well, but one of the most compelling ways to involve young children is to use songs where their names are inserted in some way. Children (and the teacher) are usually more confident in a circle, where closeness gives the confidence to sing out. Treat the introduction of a song as you would a motivating introduction to a new book by setting the stage or a mood of inquiry. Memorize the song so you will be able to maintain eye contact. Then, introduce the whole song as it is supposed to be, so children catch the exact spirit of the music. Don't forget that songs often introduce new vocabulary or words that, when sung, may not sound like spoken words. Explain new vocabulary, and talk to children about the importance of pronouncing consonants clearly (e.g, the third line of "Silent Night" is *not* "all is Sprite" but "all is bright").

When seriously teaching a song, use your voice *without* accompaniment first. If you find it difficult to sing melodies, use a tape or a CD often as you sing along, too. It is important that students have a good models to imitate (sometimes adult and sometimes children's voices). Imitation is the main way children learn to sing. Give the correct beginning pitch (using a key on an instrument, if needed, a pitch pipe, or your voice) and begin the song. Then repeat the song several times during the introduction phase, so that children are not only introduced to the song but so they also "get well acquainted." Even though you may feel it is monotonous, don't hesitate to keep songs going for young children through many repetitions—sometimes singing, sometimes humming and doing motions if applicable. Repetition, however, does not always work without other motivation to keep children involved. The teacher who creates a reason for listening to the music (by asking questions about the music to heighten perception, playing a game, using dramatization, etc.) will find that students remain interested. The younger the child, the better to teach by rote (imitation) *only* and use short repetitive songs, chants, echo songs, or poems where only one or two things change in each verse and children's names are inserted often. Again, much repetition will help children learn to sing a song and enjoy many types of music. Young children do not value the unfamiliar in music—singing and/or instrumental. Yet, if they don't hear certain types of music or sing certain songs often, they will not be familiar with (or value) those forms.

Songs that combine movement and motions are developmentally good for children (see section on Teaching Children to Move). Again, they can be used to enhance concepts, teach directions, and so forth. Do not be concerned with singing or listening to *many* songs during music time. Most children will be more satisfied with one or two songs or musical activities that they find gratifying rather than glossing over many "half-tasted" experiences or practicing for very long periods of time. Let the mood of children be your guide when possible, as they will gain more from the experience. If they are getting too active, use a "quiet song" to bring down the level of activity—or invigorate a waning time with an exciting, active song. Also, do not be worried that very young children do not sing along all the time. A music listening center may encourage young children to listen or sing on their own quietly. We may not be sure how very young children are truly reacting in many ways to music. They may want to get up and leave a singing circle or move in different ways. Do not be too concerned, as they may just be discovering and reacting in a different way than we might expect. They may also be singing alone or at home.

There are some other factors that can encourage children to sing better as they grow. One common quality error in singing well occurs because the vocalist cannot sing whole phrases without breaking for a breath. During the learning process, have students read or speak sentences, noting where they should finish and take a breath, then do the same by singing. Finally, move to having children sing whole phrases. Because it is also very important that a singing voice project out to the audience, have older children repeat this process to someone across the room to encourage projecting one's voice as it remains controlled. However, forced projection can result in an unpleasant tone quality with younger children, so it would be better to emphasize breath support and use of breath. This will eventually lead to projection more naturally. During any musical performances where projection is needed, use a larger group of children or have a microphone available rather than force projection. It is also very important for students who are performing to stand or sit straight with both feet on the floor in order to get a full breath of air. If standing, children should also be straight, perhaps with one foot slightly in front of the other and resting on the ball of the foot with chins tilted at a lower angle. This will help them to learn to control their breath from the diaphragm rather than the chest, so they can hold notes out for extended periods or sing whole musical phrases or sentences rather than gulp for air in the middle. Some voice trainers suggest that singers draw in air for singing as if sipping through a straw, filling their rib cages well with air, then exhaling as if they were blowing to cool some hot food. Children should not tense up when singing but keep their shoulders relaxed. Doing some stretching exercises helps the whole body become ready to contribute. Singing with a tight jaw is also not desirable, so exercises are beneficial that have students begin a yawn or slow repetition of vowels and try to sing in a relaxed way.

Very young children should not always be expected to sing a tune on correct pitch, but by about the age of 7, they should begin to grow into this ability. If they are not able to do so, there are several things that might help. Young children tend to sing loudly, sing as they speak (using a speaking voice), or even shout rather than use the light voice that a child should have while singing. Singing on key can be improved by practicing with the Kodaly system of Curwen hand signals indicating on which tone the singer should be. In this system each note has a hand signal that represents its tone and name. A teacher can have students match their voices to the tone indicated by the hand signal (you may have seen this in the old movie *Third Encounters,* as scientists matched hand signals to the famous five tones played as communication by the spacecraft). Having children listen to recordings of children's voices singing (rather than adults all the time) and having children sing more softly should also help. Echoing pitch games with speaking and singing will also help, as will playing tapes of familiar voices in the school (for example, other teachers they know, the principal, friends, etc.) speaking and singing. Playing a pitch on an instrument, having the student "think the correct pitch," then having the child sing, can be helpful. Having those who use their speaking voice (rather than a singing voice) imitate other sounds such as animals, sirens, trains, and so forth, along with a range of human sounds (whispers, hisses, hums, shouts, etc.) develops a more flexible singing voice and increased range.

As mentioned, diction is also an important part of singing. If you hear children singing in a shrill or throaty manner, it may be because of faulty diction. Have students work on uniform production of vowel and consonant sounds. Articulation helps the listener understand. Sometimes teachers will present a song at such a fast-paced tempo that it is difficult for students to understand the words or carry the melody well. Also, have children practice singing words or phrases with pure vowels so that they can feel how their tongue operates if they are to sing clearly. Just as practicing an instrument is important in mastery, so is practicing singing correctly. Again, by selecting songs that have a small range of tones, rather than very high to very low, children can often grasp those sounds. Sometimes we laugh about family or peers who are "tone deaf," but some of our young singers will be, too. They may just need attention to tone and practice. Discuss with them the importance of being a good listener so that they can be a good "repeater" of things they hear. Train students to watch the teacher for hand directions, especially if you should be working on a program presentation. Tape and play many sounds for children to listen to and identify. Echo games are a must for practicing various pitches. If a child has continued problems with tone, it is also worth checking medical records to see if there is any reason this should be occurring. Telling a child he or she cannot sing or should not try to sing (unless, of course, there is a temporary or permanent medical condition) can create a stigma carried through life, dimishing the joy that singing can bring.

Teaching Children to Move

Development in the *physical domain* is another rationale for having a music program. Children, through musical response, learn how to control their bodies and refine large and small movements with the body and the voice. By using movement, many areas are heightened: dramatic response, imagination, and spatial perception. When songs are selected with simultaneous movements in a group, for example, students become more aware of the space around them, of their balance, and so forth. A teacher should realize, however, that developing physical skills takes time and much repetition for young children, especially to fine tune various movements. Finger plays and playing correct rhythms with percussion instruments require a great deal of repetition to coordinate eye/hand or finger control. These are an important part of development, without doubt, for young children, and music can make it an enjoyable process. Remember that young children are individual in their stages of development in the physical domain and that very young children may have some difficulty with movements such as skipping to music. Although most mid-elementary children can skip and hop, they may still have difficulty with control in dance steps until the later elementary years. Offer opportunities for both structured music and for free creative movement. Be certain that plenty of safe space is provided for freedom of movement. Also, without setting limits on most movements, set limits on behavior before movement activities that would make movement lessons disintegrate. Demonstrate many movements to children to give them guidance and choices—swaying, creeping, galloping, rocking, whirling, and so forth—without and with various types of music. When asking children to move, they should *hear* the music before they can respond. This allows them to imagine and make judgments on what their movements could be before they actually try it. Brainstorming ideas about "what the music is asking us to do" also aids in creativity. There should be opportunities for many types of movement: finger plays, singing games, and creative and free responses. At times, children should be encouraged to "do what they feel like" to the music. Those who do *feel* the music will, and other children may look to see what the teacher is modeling. Therefore, the teacher should be a participant, too. Other times, you as the teacher may make suggestions, such as, "Can you feel the heavy sounds? Can you move slowly like an elephant?" Provide opportunities to move in games or with groups as well as individual opportunities.

STANDARD VII (PLANNING AND IMPLEMENTING EFFECTIVE MUSIC LESSONS)

The music teacher understands how to plan and implement effective music instruction and provides students with learning experiences that enhance their musical knowledge, skills, and appreciation.

EC-4 teachers should know and understand the content and performance standards for music that comprise the Texas Essential Knowledge and Skills (TEKS) and the significance of the TEKS in developing a music curriculum. They should be able to use the TEKS to develop appropriate instructional goals and objectives for student learning and performance and provide students with multiple opportunities to develop music skills specified in the TEKS. By knowing the appropriate sequencing of music instruction and how to deliver developmentally appropriate music instruction, teachers should be able to provide students with an experience that is delivered in developmentally appropriate ways that encourage active engagement in learning and make instructional content meaningful. Teachers should know a variety of methods for developing an appropriate and effective curriculum and lesson plans for the music class and be able to adapt their instructional methods to provide appropriate learning experiences for students with varied needs, learning modalities, and levels of development and musical experience. Also, teachers should know learning theory as it applies to music education and be able to provide instruction that promotes students' understanding and application of the fundamental principles of music. They should understand the importance of helping students develop music skills that are relevant to their own lives and provide each student with opportunities to contribute to the music class by drawing from their personal experiences. Teachers should provide each student with varied opportunities to make music using instruments and voice, to respond to a wide range of musical styles and genres, and to evaluate music of various types. Early-childhood-through-fourth-grade teachers should provide each student with a level of musical self-sufficiency to encourage lifelong enjoyment of music and be able to use varied materials, resources, and technology to promote students' creativity, learning, and performance. Teachers know strategies and benefits of promoting students' critical-thinking and problem-solving skills in relation to music and can provide students with frequent opportunities to use these skills in analyzing, creating, and responding to music. While the teacher knows procedures and criteria for selecting an appropriate repertoire for the music class, she or he should teach students to apply skills for forming and communicating critical judgments about music and musical performance using appropriate terminology. Using technology and various other materials and resources available for use in music education is an important part of a teacher's knowledge base. Teachers should help students develop an understanding and appreciation of various cultures through instruction related to music history, and discussion of current events related to music that ties music to the past and present. They should also incorporate a diverse musical repertoire into instruction, including music from both Western and non-Western traditions. While knowing appropriate literature to enhance technical skills, teachers should also know the value of and techniques for integrating music instruction with other subject areas. Promoting music can be an integral element in students' lives, whether as a vocation or as an avocation, and encouraging students to pursue musical knowledge independently should be a part of a teacher's mission in music. Finally, teachers should be aware of and teach students proper health techniques for use during rehearsals and performances.

National standards for music suggest that there are four basic strands in which children should be involved in music: perceptions, creative expression, historical and cultural heritage and critical evaluation. However, *involvement* is the key for children in each case at this age, as they learn by *doing*.

Music in the Domains

Although good music instruction works to supports all major domains (the physical, the emotional, the social, and the cognitive), the domain most touched, perhaps, in music is the *affective*—that of feeling, emotions, and appreciation. The five stages of the *affective domain* are *receiving* (actively attending), *responding, valuing* (demonstrated by individual choices made), *organization* (ranking in importance), and *characterization by value* (acting consistently with one's values). You may easily see how this might work in the music classroom. Initially, in order for children to learn to love, appreciate, and critique music, they must first be given numerous opportunities to listen or actively attend, then respond. Because children will develop feelings about the many types and facets of music (through either good or bad examples), the teacher should be sure that encounters with music are positive in all ways possible. Teachers should also provide students with effective tools for judging the value of music. If they cannot actively talk about and use the elements, structure, and effect of a variety of musical examples (presented in Standard I), it will be difficult for them to evaluate and value choices.

Other domains are also part of music. The *cognitive domain* in music involves the acquisition of musical theory, history, and so forth, while the *physical domain* centers on both body movement and motor skill development (both large and fine). Music enhances athletic skills of growing children through movement. Musical finger plays and movement games should be a part of the physical and spatial development of every early childhood classroom, as children progress from common movements such as patting or clapping to the imitation of other animals or inanimate things to role-play and, finally, to organized musical games. Music provides a backdrop for kinesthetic learners by coupling learning to their developmental processes. Older elementary children should not be denied the kinesthetic modality either. The following example is a "silly song" that represents both the use of music as a memory model for remembering land forms concepts and a song that has students access kinesthetic movement to help in the learning process. It is written to "If You're Happy and You Know It."

I'm a mountain and I know it, climb my rocks! (Children first make a "peak" with their hands, then do a "climbing motion" with their hands.)

I'm a mountain and I know it, climb my rocks! (Repeat motions.)

I'm a mountain and I know it, and I've got steep sides to show it. (Children form a peak with their hands, then with their right hand point to the left "steep side.")

I'm a mountain and I know it, climb my rocks! (Repeat first motions.)

I'm a plateau and I know it, flat on top!! (Children form a "table top" plateau with their hands and arms.)

I'm a plateau and I know it, flat on top!! (Children form a "table top" plateau with their hands and arms.)

I'm a plateau and I know it, and I'm flat on top to show it. (Children form a "table top" plateau with their hands and arms and "smooth" the flat top.)

I'm a plateau and I know it, flat on top!! (Children form a "table top" with their hands and arms.)

Other verses and motions might include:

I'm a peninsula and I know it, I stick out! (Children form a "peninsula" by sticking the elbow out to the side.)

I'm a hill and I know it, round on top (Children form "hill" above head with hands.)

I'm a valley and I know it, a deep "V" (Children form a "V" by crossing their forearms almost at the elbow in front of them.)

Social skills develop when children are engaged in the many musical activities involving group or partner activities. The teacher should be a sharer and co-experiencer of each activity, but the learner him- or herself must listen, react, create, and perform to gain. All children have the potential to develop their skills and their appreciation for music, given opportunities by a Texas teacher.

Remember Your Pedagogy

For successful experiences, all music should be age-appropriate in terms of ability and subject matter *and* in terms of intellectual development, social development, and physical development. As a reminder, an important part of learning theory tells us that stages of each domain are not always tied to an exact age, so students may move through stages of these domains at different rates. In addition, the zone of proximal development theory (where children can function with help from an adult or capable peer) should be a part of music planning as well; we want to challenge young children with music rather than overwhelm them with concepts and skills that they cannot yet handle. Many concrete and manipulative experiences combined with visuals should be an important part of music instruction. Remember also that some movements that older children can accomplish to music are not appropriate for the coordination of the young child. On a serious note, teachers must consider that much of our popular music today no longer contains lyrics or messages appropriate for children. Listen to *all* songs that you will play in class carefully. You do not want children to hear some songs or repeat lyrics that would lead an angry parent and/or administrator to your doorstep. Children should be allowed to bring their own music to share, but do establish parental knowledge and rules for appropriateness. Select a variety of music throughout the day, though children will or may already have begun to develop preferences. Though certain types of music are not appealing to young children, your opinion matters, so if you also indicate distaste in certain music, young students may imitate your modeling.

When teaching music, foremost, do not forget other pedagogy from your *PPR (Professional Roles and Responsibilities) TExES*. Provide a classroom that is warm and open and that invites discovery, creativity, and improvisation. Establish rules and routines that help students become accepting of each other during performances and directions that show care with instruments and each other in movement. Positively encourage children always, especially in performance and creative areas. Provide for continuity and relevance for very young children by scaffolding with music that they may know or share from their home/community/culture. Follow lesson plans (both long-range and daily), as you would with other subject areas, that help students understand the objectives and the rationales for a musical experience. Download and use the music TEKS as a guideline for preparing goals and objectives for which you are responsible at the grade level in which you teach. Texas expects that you will do this for *every* subject, including music. Allow for both whole-class and individual experiences and for integrating other arts and subject areas whenever possible. Give children opportunities to to explore sounds. Provide them with thinking at all levels—particularly at higher levels. Such activities at the synthesis level might include creating musical introductions and accompaniments to stories or poems, improvising or writing short songs or simple operettas, designing new musical accompaniments to songs children already know, designing a new movement to a certain song, creating their own instruments, and so forth. Make judgments in terms of your objectives on how well children are progressing and use those assessments to reflect upon how it will impact what you do the next time in class.

There are other important reasons for teachers to understand the basics of music for the elementary classroom. The greatest potential for developing and encouraging musical interests and skills lies in the years of early childhood and elementary school. Also, multiple intelligence research identifies *musical* intelligence as one of several intelligences. As such, those children who have talent and intelligence in music should be provided a way "to shine," as they develop their talents more fully in the classroom. For other students, we know that to offer experiences in an intelligence area such as music, according to recent brain research, is to develop new physiological pathways. Children who learn best in kinesthetic or tactile ways also often "shine" during music classes, though, again, all children's skills in these areas can be enhanced. Music is one subject that can be developed both for playing, movement, and singing skill, as well as for appreciation. In the early childhood years a tremendous amount of musical growth can occur, *if* that growth is nurtured by a caring teacher.

Music is emotional in nature, and teachers can take advantage of that aspect. As with the background music to movies, classroom music can heighten students' experiences with certain subject areas such as writing and reading literature, or it can encourage a student to "be a part" of another land or era. For example, playing Native American music in the background as students enter their social studies classroom can set a mood for the day's lesson on the various tribes of Texas and can continue to involve students as they work on an independent project later in the hour with Native American music as a backdrop. Playing a focus song to lead into an activity can create considerable interest or close a lesson in a way that helps the lesson linger in the minds of students. For instance, a teacher who was planning a "science-heavy" unit on the Titanic might open or close with the popular theme song from that recent movie to connect science to the reality of human tragedy. And what student could not write a more vivid descriptive piece or poem on spring, for example, with Vivaldi playing softly in the background? Many songs can be found to introduce specific topics or concepts. Because music touches the emotions so easily, it can be used by a creative teacher to enhance the mood of the classroom and as an aid to increase creativity and learning across the curriculum. Often, music text series seek to combine works of art and poetry with works of music. This helps to further develop the affective domain, as students can relate to how a painter suggests feelings and emotions with color, lines, and shapes . . . to how a poet does the same with words . . . to how a musician does so with many variations of sounds.

Music Connections

Music has also been tied to learning in different subjects areas in other ways. You may have grown up with songs, for example, that helped you remember the alphabet, seasons, holidays, sequencing of letters and numbers, and so forth. This will be investigated in detail in a moment. You have already seen reasons why *mathematics* has a direct tie with music, particularly when looking at fractions. The study of the production of sound can easily be tied to *science* lessons, and, in *social studies*, there are many small and well-written operettas published for children in various historical periods. These provide students with motivating preludes to find out more about the times and persons upon which their roles in a performance may touch.

Multicultural studies and music go hand-in-hand when boys and girls begin to learn about people around the world. Simple songs written in other languages, may, for example, be a child's first experience with foreign language; they also help a child understand that many peoples throughout the world are the same in that they express similar feelings (and often do so through music). Music tells us much about the peoples of the world as well as the different regions of the United States. Music provides exciting differences for a child to see from place to place and from era to era, depending on who writes it, who performs it, for what occasions music is made and performed, and the different instruments and ways of singing that exist. The state music standards in almost every grade level require students to investigate diverse cultures by playing or singing songs or participating in musical games of other cultures. For young children, this aspect of introducing other cultures is extremely inviting. For example, a unit on Japan can include a "tea party" with traditional music of the country playing in the background as students sip their tea and learn about the new country. Other multicultural experiences and events should often include music.

Very compelling is the fact that music provides a very safe way of *reading* for students—as children follow along with choral lyrics. In this "low-risk" read-along situation, music can add to student confidence, and literacy is promoted through voice/print pairing.

Music, when played as a backdrop for reading or drama as a mood setter can enhance student creativity in dramatic roles. A play can be enhanced when students, using simple instruments, create a musical motif for each character. The matching musical motif is played each time the character enters or speaks. As the story becomes more involved and exciting, so does the instrumentation.

Art and music often fit together naturally, as the teacher selects background music that relates in some way to an art project while students work, or the teacher may ask students to "let the music tell them" what to paint or draw. Art is often combined as a part of music texts as a way for students to understand comparisons between art and musical elements such as texture, shape, and line.

Music also helps us to learn facts and acts as an aid to memory. Governmental processes, grammar, and math concepts have been set to music as an entertaining way for countless students to remember specified material (for example, how a bill goes through Congress). Many of you may still be able to name all the states by singing a song such as "Fifty . . . nifty . . .". Such productions as Schoolhouse Rock, for example, provide facts for social studies, grammar, money, multiplication, and science (to order, go to http://disneyvideos.disney. go.com and search for schoolhouse rock, or see lyrics at http://www.apocalypse. org/pub/u/gilly/schoolhouse_Rock/HTML/schoolhouse.html). Music can also be used as a memory model for students, as the teacher finds or composes words to popular melodies (or helps students create their own) that relate to a subject at hand. Many of you already know how a certain song or piece of music triggers a memory of a place, a date or time period, or a particular person. As a memory model for students, the teacher finds or makes up words to songs (as noted earlier in the song, "I'm a Mountain and I Know It . . ."), particularly popular melodies, that relate to a subject at hand. These lyrics can be quite serious or very silly. For example, recently, a fourth-grade classroom was being observed taking a test. Earlier, the student teacher had taught her students a song that she had made up to help them remember simple machines and their functions. Students did very well on their test, but interestingly enough, there was quite a bit of humming of the "machine song" going on in the classroom that day, as students "accessed" their lyrics and, thus, their definitions. Older elementary students also love to create these types of lyrics related to the various curriculum areas and put them to popular melodies, rap rhythms, and so forth, while younger children love to sing these types of songs because the melody is often already familiar. Do remember, however, that students coming from *outside* the United States may not readily know these tunes. You may need to teach the originals first.

Having students create their own music as an activity, of course, involves having them work at the *synthesis* level—a higher-level thinking activity. For example, in composing, students can create various rhythms or construct sound stories around a theme (holidays, a person, a trip, feelings, or another concept), where sounds that these represent to the child are collected on tape. A "sound tape" of human vocalizations (hums, whispers, hisses, sighs, shouts, etc.) that students write and record makes an interesting composition. They may create a poem or story backdrop (for example, a sound tape for each animal in a rain forest book), create lyrics and/or melodies, short operettas, chants, raps, and hand, body, or dance movements of their own.

A methodology, Suggestopedia, created by Bulgarian Georgi Lozanov, has been used since the 1970s in teaching foreign language in an accelerated manner. In this technique, Baroque music is used to relax the mind, as his research shows that a tense mind closes in learning languages. However, with music, learning in a new language can be easily accepted—for mental barriers are less taunt. Using the Suggestopedia techniques, the teacher often uses music in tandem with guided visualization or imaging. A scene is read containing a considerable amount of contextual clues along with known vocabulary. From this, students are able to gain understanding in the new vocabulary in a relaxed manner. Carrying this idea a step further into our elementary classrooms, new vocabulary in many different subjects may be "Greek" to our students, so the same method can be applied in various areas of study. For example, in a modified version of Suggestopedia, a teacher may play one of the many "nature" CD selections that are available of rain forest sounds combined with relaxing music. She or he asks students to relax, close their eyes, and "take a journey" into the rain forest. As the music plays, the teacher softly delivers a script that is full of contextual clues with new vocabulary words embedded within. New vocabulary and concepts are shown in boldface:

> *Close your eyes and relax and come with me now to the rain forest of Central America. The first thing that overwhelms our eyes here is the green vegetation—the incredible*

number of growing plants!! Everywhere you look the **vegetation** *is so green, and many of these plants have beautiful flowers. This green* **vegetation** *grows all year long— because the location is so warm and* **humid**—*that is, sticky and damp. About nine feet of rain falls here every year! How* **humid** *it is here! I am already sweating and my clothes are sticking to me. Most places in Texas receive only about one to two feet. There is so much rain in the rain forest that it cannot evaporate away, so the* **humidity** *(or moisture in the air) remains high all the time. Think about how it feels in Texas in the summer on a day when the* **humidity** *is high—you feel sticky, sweaty, and damp then. In the rain forest, there is even more* **humidity**! *That's one reason green for so much green* **vegetation**. *The* **vegetation** *gets so much moisture. Also, the* **vegetation** *never freezes here like it does in many parts of Texas. It is so warm here, so the* **vegetation** *grows and grows and grows! That is why, when we look down upon the rain forest from above, we view a "sea of green." So much* **vegetation**! *If we look closely, as we enter the rain forest now, we can see that we are standing in the* **understory** *of the* **vegetation**. *It is not like a jungle as I thought it would be from some movies. It is not a jungle, but a forest. A jungle is difficult to walk through because it is choked and tangled with undergrowth. In fact, here in the* **understory** *of the rain forest, there is almost no* **vegetation**—*most of the plants grow thickly above us. I can see why! It's so dark here on the* **understory** *floor—a little like a basement under the other stories of a house—the* **understory**. *There is very little light here because the* **vegetation** *growing above us almost covers the sun!! Look down and we can also see why there is little vegetation on the forest floor or the* **understory**. *The soil is clay—it is not a rich soil at all like a jungle would have! Reach down and take some soil from the* **understory** *in your hand. You could almost make a little clay bowl out of it, just like we mold clay in our art class. All around us in the* **understory** *there are just roots. . . . (the teacher would continue to introduce the* **canopy** *layer and the* **emergent** *tree layer).*

Speech and music also go hand-in-hand, as the spoken word has rhythms of which the child is not often aware. Singing, chanting, and rhyming words in the context of music help the child develop better speaking skills and understanding of pronunciation. Encouragement of experimentation of all types of verbal sounds helps the child to become more sensitive to his or her own speaking voice and develop that voice in a more dynamic manner.

Music can also be a mood adjuster for behavior. Teachers who have students enter a classroom where calming music is playing can often feel a difference in the way the class begins to focus. Conversely, music can invigorate a class after a long academic period of work or can help relieve some of the stress accompanying long test periods. Cute musical transitions have always been used by kindergarten teachers to move students from one activity to another, but clever teachers in all grades may find that age-appropriate music creates the perfect routine for changing activities or moving to new work areas in a more conducive manner. Very young children will need the consistency that certain songs can give, so teachers establish songs that build familiar routines for them during the day. Use familiar music before going on, so that they feel safe in branching out to explore the new.

Thinking about music can give children enjoyable ways to develop and reinforce thinking skills. Music can be a higher-level thinking activity in and of itself, as students compose or create their own compositions or think about sound in creating their own instruments. Boys and girls can analyze and evaluate music to determine their reasons for liking or disliking a song or composition and can interpret what a composer is trying to say through music. After comparing and contrasting, they can choose meaningful alternatives. Older elementary students can investigate music in relationships with other human endeavors. Thus, music becomes an integral part of students lives in many areas—rather than, "It's time for music class now!"

Try these practice questions:

For one musical activity, Miss Larson wanted a permanent music center in her early childhood class. She and a friend built a huge three-sided box that was comfortable enough for one or two students. The open side pushed up against the wall, so that when Miss Larson wanted to change the center, she could just pull it out from the wall. Light inside was provided by several holes in the top. Inside she placed only one or two instruments at a time (some with simple multiple tones capability, some that were monotoned). For example, one week she placed two drums, each with a different tone, while the next week she set up resonator bells (bells with three pitches and of three different sizes) and a mallet inside. Sometimes instruments were homemade (a durable box with seeds that could be shaken) and sometimes they were ordinary items (pot lids). She gave directions, mostly focusing on the care of the instruments. This center was:

A. Inappropriate because children do not know what to expect or do with the instrument(s) because no proper instruction has been given.

B. Inappropriate because young children cannot be expected to take care of the instruments when they are not in sight of the teacher, and they already have a chance to play with ordinary things at home.

C. Appropriate because it provides time and space for young children to spontaneously explore and create music.

D. Appropriate because young children need to have private time and the center is constructed so as to combine music time away from others.

Answer *A* is not correct for young children because, at times, they should be able to experiment independently in music. We would not select *B* either, because we expect that children will take care of the instruments, and, as music teachers, we continously instruct and enforce this concept. An important part of experimenting with sound is discovering what the environment has to offer (*C*). We cannot be sure that students have the opportunity at home to experiment. *D* is incorrect because the center is constructed to ensure that students are insulated when they are noisy (which we would expect here) rather than creating private time. Let's return to *C*. *C* is correct, as this type of center provides an inquiry-based time and space for young children to perceive information about the instrument (that is to experiment for data), analyze, and to come to some conclusions on their own. As new instruments are switched, they apply learned information to the new experience. Too many instruments at once would be overwhelming to the young child and would not give the child an opportunity to focus. An activity that should follow would be to have children make their own instruments, some of which may find their way to this center.

Mrs. Bradford's social studies class has been working on a unit on Africa for almost two weeks. Students have read about the continent of Africa, researched it on the Internet, seen videos, worked on art projects, and focused on African music as well. Tomorrow Mrs. Bradford plans on a test over this unit.

On this day, she first had children put away their things and relax. She put on a CD softly in the background entitled "African Safari" and proceeded to involve the class in a Concept Development model. She first asked students to brainstorm all the words that they could think of when they heard the word "Africa" and felt the music playing. As students thought of words, she wrote them on the board. Among the many examples that students contributed were:

drums	plains	tigers	singing	flutes
lions	safari	chants	many tribes	cheetahs
hunting	elephants	waterfalls	flamingos	Nile
ivory	gold	Lost Cities	desert	jungle
homemade instruments	big cities	colonies	many countries	
"The Lion King"				
dancing in the villages				
big mountains				

As the music was replayed, she asked her cooperative tables of students to classify the terms on the board into groups that belong together for whatever reason they think. Then, they were to label these groups with a name. They could also add any terms that they had left out that might belong in their categories. One cooperative group came up with the one of the following classifications and labels:

African Music	**They added to this category:**
handmade instruments	hunting dances
drums	story dances
flutes	masks
dancing in the villages	chants
singing	

Other categories emerged into land forms, African animals, and so forth. As each group read their categories, the class was asked to add anything else that came to mind about Africa.

Mrs. Bradford then asked each cooperative table to select one category and create one to three sentences using all of the words they listed. The cooperative group that selected African Music wrote, "In lots of villages in Africa, instruments like drums and flutes are handmade. The village uses these when they sing and dance. Lots of African music is just voices chanting without any music. The people there sometimes wear masks to act out stories—like a hunt." The music added an important element to this lesson because it:

A. Triggered memories of what students had seen about Africa in movies, videos, photos, etc., so it acted as a part of scaffolding and tapping past experiences.
B. Added another modality to the lesson.
C. Added interest to the lesson, so it helped with motivation.
D. All of the above.

The Concept Development model is an excellent way for teachers to determine what students know about a concept as a class. It is also helpful to begin teaching a lesson on a new concept. It helps a teacher determine prior knowledge so that students are not bored by the reteaching of information they know. As in this case, it is also extremely useful as a review for a unit test, etc., for students to self-monitor what they have gained prior to testing—and for the teacher to see what she or he might need to reteach. The music gives this lesson an added dimension in all of the areas mentioned, so the answer is *D*. In addition, if the teacher puts the same music on during the test, Suggestopedia experts believe that students will be able to access much more information.

Technology and Music

Technology has opened the doors wide to engage students in music. Not only does advanced technology in listening allow us to hear music more clearly than ever before, but also, as mentioned earlier, it allows students to hear their own music immediately, make judgments, and make alternative decisions to refine their performances. Electric instruments and sound equipment allow for amplification and purer sound. Music created totally through the use of synthesizers (electronic devices that create sounds) or music/sounds that are altered in some way by electronic devices is termed *electronic music*—rather than music played on electronic instruments such as the electric guitar or other amplified instruments. Music synthesizers that allowed sounds to be produced in almost any way a composer desired became available in the 1950s. Through the next decades computers made the process of composing easier and easier. Software programs work with computers to create sounds similar to almost any musical instrument, to save a composer's music and recall it for editing later on, and so forth. These are all excellent technology packages for budding musicians. Still other software packages teach students how to read music easily. Though working with MIDI (Music Instrument Digital Interface) is sometimes complicated, it can open a whole new world of possibilities with synthesizing. To hear what MIDI can do, go to the following site and select from the types of music that you would like to hear: http://midiworld.com/midifile.htm. Do not forget the Internet as a source for many types of music, biographies of composers, music history, and other pertinent information.

Resources

One question that you must be asking if you do not have a considerable background in music is, "How will I know what to teach and where will I get ideas?" Many schools have music books series such as Silver Burdett, McGraw-Hill, etc., although you may have to share one set per grade level. These series may come with student texts at all levels of elementary music instruction. Some investigation as to where these series might be found in your building or district may be in order, but it will be worth it for your students. Teachers' editions offer clear examples of appropriate scope and sequence along with many valuable activities. Most importantly, if these series are provided by your school, they often come with excellent, high-quality recordings (with both children's and adults' voices), written music for accompaniments or classroom instruments, charts and other visuals, cross-indexes for convenience, and so forth.

The TEKS (Texas Essential Knowledge and Skills) for music students are also a guide for teaching scope and sequence of skills and are a *requirement* for teachers to follow in Texas. There are TEKS expectations and elements for teachers in music (under Fine Arts) for young and elementary school children by grade level and can be accessed online. Again, TEKS for music are available for downloading at http://www.tea.state.tx.us/teks/117toc.htm. National Music Standards for young children are also available at http://www.menc.org/publication/books/prek12st.html.

Libraries can also be important places for you to find resources in music. You may find song and musical activity books, books about young musicians, biographies of famous composers, and recordings to check out for many age levels. Most university libraries have sets of teachers' editions and/or examples of student texts of music series from major textbook publishers to investigate.

Human resources can add to your musical program. The school district in which you work may have a musical specialist who oversees many schools. Other teachers in your school may also be a source of ideas and materials. Be sure to ask your principal about other teachers in your building who could become musical resources to you. It is most important for you to maintain a schoolwide network for the music program as well. Other teachers may want to share in various aspects of a program or performance, so be sure to communicate what is happening musically in your school. Other district schools (especially "feeder" schools) can be a resource of continuing interest in music for students, as you invite musical groups from intermediate, middle, and high schools to perform in your elementary school or class. Sparks of interest can be ignited in your children, as they see teachers in upper grades conducting exciting performances from older children. Inform your children and their parents about musical performances in your district or community that provide a source of interest and entertainment. Most school bands and choirs perform concerts and musicals during various times of the year, so making sure that you are a part of the information network (and can pass this information on) should be part of your commitment to music and your community. A quick guide to musical events around the state along with other information can be found at www.texasmusicguide.com. Also, parents can be excellent resources for musical experiences—as well as people from the community who take an interest in children and music. Be sure to ask parents through notes to the home or calls, or be resourceful in your community in searching for professional or amateur musicians who might add to the musical experiences of your children by volunteering in some way.

For teachers, the Internet offers a wide variety of resources—from finding suitable materials for any type of music desired, to finding organizations for music teachers, to quick examples of instrumental sounds. The Texas Music Educators site at www.tmea.org and the Texas Music Teachers site at www.tmta.org are two such sites that provide information and links to many other sites. The Internet has a great variety of "click on" songs and musical pieces from all eras. Musical histories and biographical information on great composers can be found at a moment's notice, and online music stores offer all types of musical recordings as well as books and sheet music. There are also a number of tapes and CDs suitable for these grade levels available from retail stores, school supply catalogs, or teachers' stores.

There are several journals that may act as resources of interest to teachers of music: *American Suzuki Journal, British Journal of Music Education, General Music Today, Canadian Educators Journal, Kodaly Envoy, Music Educators Journal,* and the *Orff Echo.* As with all subject areas, music has organizations to which teachers belong—both national and state—many of which publish good resource journals or offer beneficial conferences. The Texas Music Teachers Association (www.tmta.org), the Texas Music Educators (www.tmea.org), and the Music Teachers National Association all have websites for membership and information and act as good resources. Http://www.nats.org is a site for the National Association for Teachers of Singing. Http://www.isd77.k12.mn.us/resources/staffpages/shirk/k12.music.html is an excellent site with many other links to organizations that may be of help. Be creative and persistent in your Internet searches, and you will find what you need. Sites do change, so if any sites listed in this chapter are no longer found, try looking through a modified search by name or subject.

The Home, Community, and Music

One accepted element of pedagogy asks that the teacher seek to link the culture of parents and the community with instruction. This is also true with the music curriculum. This would be a scaffolding issue—that is, children will first relate to the type of music with which they are familiar. In planning, therefore, look carefully at the culture of the community and its unique engagement with music. In Texas, for example, we mentioned that there are rural communities that are of German and Czech descent whose children grow up learning to polka, while in other communities, children can two-step with country and western music almost before they begin school. Young African American children in many communities may have considerable experience with gospel music, while young Hispanic students may know the sounds of *tejano* very well. Of course, there are communities and individuals everywhere in between who relate to *many* types of music. One mission of schools is often seen as "supporter of a culture." Therefore, the mission of music in schools is not only to expose boys and girls to a wide variety of music, but to help students develop musical skills and songs that they can enjoy in their own world—that of their community's culture along with that of family and friends. Again, it is important for teachers to know what musical events are offered in the community around the school and capitalize on the connections. Parents are more likely to support programs with which they are comfortable musically, though most want their children to have a well-rounded education in music as well. Most young children love to perform, so school programs offer an excellent bridge to draw parents to the school. You may even have parents who are knowledgeable and willing to help with your programs—a great resource!!

Health and Safety in Music

There are some issues to which teachers must attend in music regarding the health and well-being of their students. Most importantly, if a teacher is lucky enough to have a classroom or school set of recorders (beginning instruments that look much like a clarinet), much care must be taken to ensure that these instruments are thoroughly cleaned in order to avoid having bacteria build up inside after use from warm breaths and to stop the sharing any type of illness or disease if children must share. Make sure to use a sanitizer that does not react with plastic. We know that germs can be easily spread through hand contact, so when children will be holding hands during musical activities or trading rhythm instruments, cleaning hands prior to and after the activity may save children passing colds, and other germs during epidemic times of the year. The loud volume of music can also be of concern. The hearing of children should be considered, especially those who are forced to sit continuously next to speakers or loud instruments.

Another safety issue concerns instruments that are played with mallets or strikers. Provide strict rules about the appropriate use of these on the instruments for which they were designed only. During musical movement exercises, song games, or dances, the teacher is responsible for making sure that space is cleared so that students do not trip over desks or other items as they become involved.

Special concern for children with exceptionalities, particularly those with physical challenges, should be made here. If students are going to be on stage or use risers for special programs, establishing rules and practicing moving on and off is a must for safety.

Special Needs Children at Music Time

Classrooms may have children who are differently abled that are a part of the classroom all day or may be mainstreamed for some subjects by reason of Public Law 94-192. If a child has been placed in a regular classroom for music as a part of the "least restrictive environment," teachers should make sure that they include those children and modify their objectives, if applicable, on their IEP (Individual Education Plan) as required by law so that these students can participate to the fullest of their abilities. Learn as much as you can about the child and his or her abilities and needs ahead of time and do not be afraid to call on the help of specialized teachers and parents as resources. If a child is coming to a self-contained classroom only for music, be sure to have music times set out clearly to work in coordination with the schedule of the special needs teacher. Your manner of acceptance and welcome will be the model for your students to follow.

Many children with mental differences or learning disabilities may need special attention in the music class regarding introductions to the instruments, as the sounds may startle, sensory "overload," or confuse them. Because music is emotional, these students may sometimes overreact during listening times to certain pieces or instrument sounds. Note short attention spans and be ready to change approaches if a child becomes too excitable or too bored. Clear structure and repetition (if children are unable to read long passages) is also a necessary part of instruction for some special needs children, even in music class. Try to begin and end the class in a routine way (perhaps with one particular welcome or greeting song and particular farewell song). Work on small portions of music at a time with immediate feedback to help eliminate failure. Establish clear signals to end music, as some students may become so involved that they do not stop. Children should be expected and encouraged to participate to the fullest of their abilities and praised well and often for their efforts.

For students with hearing difficulties, the teacher of music must go to further lengths to help in relating the lesson visually, through vibration in a tactile manner (by having students touch) and kinesthetically (through motions). Seating is especially important for these children, so that they may see visuals, feel vibrations, and catch the rhythms of movements. Many may not be totally impaired, so seating close to the music source or having a nonpitched instrument close to an ear may be vital—though it may depend on whether their hearing loss involves clarity or loudness (frequency) difficulties. Individual modification may need to be made for distortion in hearing devises for music and group singing. Be certain that students can see your face and speech movements during all instruction and singing, and use clear, distinct articulation. If a child has near or total impairment and signs, signing lyrics is also encouraged. Often these children face speech difficulties, too, so help in language development (diction, rhythm, etc.) is important in music class.

Students who are visually impaired may be able to participate fully in most lessons, though lessons that focus on listening and rote learning of songs *along with* tactile aids for some activities will increase learning. Children with visual difficulties may need physical guidance in any movements to music. If not fully impaired, large visuals in black and white or large-print song books may be provided. If students are learning Braille, see if there is a way to obtain Braille song books so they can follow along with words. When entering the classroom for music, always warn these students of new placements of sound equipment or instruments or of the fact that you have moved chairs in anticipation of an activity.

Children who are orthopedically challenged may need help with alternative movements, if applicable to the lesson, but they can often participate in most other ways. Sometimes the class can be very creative in helping in with design that helps these students move about and participate more easily. Watch phrasing of words used in movement activities so that all children can participate, depending on the particular circumstances, by providing alternatives for movements such as "Stand up and walk around in a circle" in classrooms with children in wheelchairs, for example. In playing rhythm instruments, special accommodations may be needed to help children hold a mallet or stick in some way.

Musically gifted students also require special attention as well. Some larger school district have magnet schools for musically talented children, although most are left to the school or classroom teacher. Be sure that you are providing opportunities for these children to work at their level through enrichment experiences.

There are other special needs and combinations of needs not covered here. Students who have learning disabilities that affect other subject areas will have the same difficulties in music classes (reading, sequencing, etc.). One important thing that teachers need to remember is that by law (PL 94-192) documentation needs to be provided for evaluation purposes on objectives set by the ARD (Admission, Review, and Dismissal) team. Continue to seek out resources to help with each type of need, and remember that each child is truly an individual and will have needs specifically for the extent to which he or she can participate. Music may offer special needs children an avenue of communication not open to them in many subject areas. It is often a nurturing force in their lives as well as an expressive one.

Consider the following practice question:

Ms. Mitchell told students that tomorrow would be a special writing day. They were going to experience "a concert" in class, then become *music critics* by writing about what they judged to be good or poor quality for two of the four pieces they would hear. They would choose two and evaluate what they heard, what they liked, what they didn't like—and why.

"To go to a concert," she told them, "tickets must be purchased. During certain times of the day today, you can to go back to the 'ticket booth' desk in the back of the room and select your seating for tomorrow's concert from the seating chart map. You will each get an envelope with 'money' for a seat." All envelopes would contain different amounts of money, so students would have to make a decision on where they could buy their seat based on the money in their envelope. As students purchased tickets, Ms. Mitchell put their names on those tickets in order to hand out tickets quickly the next day.

Ms. Mitchell went over the expectations for concert behavior: Wait for the usher to seat you, no changing seats, no talking once the concert has started, no getting out of one's seat during the music (and if you are not seated by the time the concert begins, you may not go in until there is a break), and show one's appreciation by clapping (and calling out "bravo" if the performance was very, very good). She also told them about the sequence of events for the orchestra: warm-up of the musical instruments at the beginning, applause at the entry of the concertmaster (first seat violinist), tuning of the instruments, entry of the conductor (applause), possible entrance of soloists; applause of the end of each piece, and applause at the end of the concert with standing ovations reserved for outstanding performances. She also reminded them of some longer pieces that they had already listened to in class that had different movements with silence in between. She laughed in telling them that sometimes audience members who don't know the music well start clapping between the movements— and the music is not really over yet! A good guideline, she noted, is to wait to see if lots of others begin applause, if unsure, or wait until the conductor actually steps down. She also told them that they should look particularly nice tomorrow. Though everyone who attends concerts does not dress up, it does show respect for the performers to look nice. Refreshments would to be served during intermission (with conversation), so all those who followed the rules would have something at that point. Finally, she quickly went over a bit of information on the composers that they would hear.

The following day, Ms. Mitchell had students line up at the door and gave out their tickets with "programs." She had two students role-play ushers, who seated students in their correct seats for the concert. She then introduced the music and had several students role-play the entrance of some of the orchestra members, and, finally, she had students listen to two exciting pieces of music. Punch and cookies were served at intermission, followed by "flashing of the lights," reseating, and two other pieces of music. At the end of the concert, Ms. Mitchell asked students to quietly return to their own seat to review the elements needed for critiquing, and begin the writing process, as she replayed the selections. This music class contributed the *most* to:

A. Introducing students to some of the great composers.
B. Having students understand concert etiquette.
C. Having students use thinking skills of comparing and contrasting.
D. B & C.

Standard 7.10s asks Texas teachers to teach concert etiquette. Role-play is the perfect introduction to a real concert. It is hoped that one field trip might include a musical performance of some type. Ms. Mitchell has also integrated this into her writing class, as she is asking students to compare and contrast the different pieces of music. The music that she selected for listening could be from the great composers but could also be chosen more for the enjoyment of this grade level. The emphasis here, however, was on the concert etiquette and the writing/thinking skills. Role-play might include any one of the many types of concerts that children might attend: symphony orchestra, chamber orchestra, recitals, choral and/or church music, operas, or ballet. The correct answer is *D.*

Generalists are not responsible for Standard VIII.

STANDARD IX (ASSESSMENT)

The music teacher understands student assessment and uses assessment results to design instruction and promote student progress.

> *The teacher knows the skills needed to form critical judgments about music. He or she knows techniques and criteria for assessing students' musical knowledge and skills and can use multiple forms of assessment and knowledge of the music TEKS to help determine students' progress in developing those music skills and understanding. Continuing, the teacher uses an understanding of ongoing results of assessment to continuously develop instructional plans. The EC-4 teacher can use standard terminology in communicating about students' musical skills and performance and can give constructive criticism when evaluating skills or performances. Meaningful prescriptions to correct problems or errors in musical performances can be easily offered.*

Texas provides several ways of knowing what is expected of children in EC-4 classrooms. Teachers can use these guidelines to assess if their children are receiving the information and experiences needed to meet these expectations and how well children are achieving in this area. For example, the online *Texas Music Curriculum Guidelines* for 3- and 4-year-old children shows that: Children should express themselves through singing and movement and by playing simple instruments. Children should learn to experiment with music concepts, volume, tempo, and sound. They should also begin to appreciate different types of music.

The child:

- Participates in classroom music activities
- Begins to sing a variety of simple songs
- Begins to play classroom instruments

- Begins to respond to music of various tempos through movement
- Begins to distinguish among the sounds of several common instruments

As another example, the TEKS for fine arts can be downloaded at www.tea. state.tx.us/rules/tac/chapter117/index.html). The following example shows some of the expectations for kindergarten (other grade levels can be found there as well):

> *Knowledge and skills:*
> 1. *Perception. The student describes and analyzes musical sound and demonstrates musical artistry. The student is expected to:*
>   A. *identify the difference between the singing and speaking voice, and*
>   B. *identify the timbre of adult voices and instruments*
> 2. *Creative expression/performance. The student performs a varied repertoire of music. The student is expected to:*
>   A. *sing or play classroom instruments independently or in a group, and*
>   B. *sing songs from diverse cultures and styles or play such songs on musical instruments*

EC-4 teachers should be sure that they are using these Texas expectations for their grade levels to prepare their plans and experiences to design short- and long-range plans to include all of the TEKS at their grade level, as teachers are accountable in this area. Using these as a base, teachers can also assess if children are receiving opportunities in all areas and to measure the quality and quantity of the experience. Criteria for judging individual achievement should be built into plans, as with other subjects that you teach. As children receive experiences, plans should either reflect progression or reteaching of information and/or skills in music.

Assessment and Evaluation

What areas should be included in music assessment and evaluation? Information on *all* the domains on which music touches may be included: (1) development of physical skills based on the ability to sing, play, and move at expected levels along with observed growth in perception through sensory responses or the ability to respond to musical differences; (2) growth in conceptual/cognitive development or thinking skills related to the elements of music, history of music, and so forth; (3) growth in the affective domain in terms of musical participation (both planned and free) in terms of musical preferences, creativity, and expressiveness; and (4) growth in the social domain, the interpersonal skills, and communication gained through musical participation.

Some responses to music are overt (or observable) but, more often than not, covert—that is, they take place inside the individual through the affective domain. For that reason, assessment and evaluation present some difficulty to teachers in music. However, teachers need to be able to communicate to children and their parents about student growth in music—as would be the case with other subject areas. With preK and kindergarten children this can be challenging because of widespread developmental differences. Young children do not respond well to paper-and-pencil testing, and children often know and can do much more than they can verbalize. However, parents appreciate and expect teachers to inform them about strengths in musical areas (for example, can a child coordinate a marching beat, does the child have good short-term memory in repeating rhythms, does the child have an excellent sense of imagination in creating new sounds, does he or she have a clear, pleasant singing voice, and so forth). These and other factors that the teacher can glean from music class are also hints that may help you understand how the student is developing in other subject areas. Supporting budding talent may also be a joint venture at home, if parents know their child is interested and/or talented.

As with other subject areas, we may evaluate the child in music *diagnostically* (to examine specific problems), *formatively* (over a period of time), and *summatively* (at the end of a specified period of time). Anecdotal records or observation sheets are favored by many teachers in music (especially for special needs children), while others use checklists or rating scales that can help more with issues of quality. Singing and using both directed and improvisional movement-to-music activities provides a way for the teacher to see what children are hearing and then translating into observable movements. A portfolio of audio- or videotapings may also be used to show development. Oral questioning provides a great deal of information. Paper-and-pencil-type sheets on the elements of music might be used for older students as they are asked to begin learning to read and write music. Excellent performance in music does involve a degree of talent, and some children may have the talent to become world-class performers, while others simply do not. However, because instruction and training can make a difference in how children appreciate music all their lives, teachers must be careful to use assessment in music in ways that are helpful and not hurtful. For that reason, we must use music terminology mentioned in the standards above with constructive criticism such as, "Listen carefully to the pitch that you hear now and try to match your voice carefully to it. Now try to make your voice go up just this much more (show hand signal)" or "Your audience will really appreciate hearing rising dynamics during this part because it makes the piece more powerful," rather than general comments such as, "You are hurting my ears today!" or "Can't you sing louder there?" Teachers alone may be responsible for children's loving or hating music. Teachers can affect children's desire for participation in music for the rest of their lives through our use of critique and assessment.

Assessing learning in music can be both written and performance based, but having children become good judges of music, including their own, is the best way for them to gain a lifelong appreciation of music. In addition to a teacher's assessments, children should critique their own performances by listening to their own tapes and by listening to many sources. Let them tell you, the teacher, how to make their performance(s) better. Here are some questions that may help young critics begin to think critically (depending on the instance):

> Was your musical performance played/sung on key?
>
> Was your instrument(s) in tune?
>
> Did your choice of instruments fit the music well?
>
> Did your piece or performance fit together with its forms?
>
> Did your piece/performance project a mood (how did you feel when you performed it)? If so, did it succeed? How well?
>
> How resourceful were you in creating a unique piece?
>
> Was the tempo/speed of the music correct to easily sing or play along?
>
> Was the tempo consistent or regular if so written?
>
> Was your choice of dynamics correct to express what the composer wanted?
>
> Was your sound too loud or too soft to be effective?
>
> Were the lyrics expressive?
>
> Was there enough variety in the music to make it interesting?
>
> What are some ways that you could have sung/played this song differently?
>
> What else could you or the composer/performer of a piece have chosen or done to make the music better?

The same questions could be asked of many other selected examples of music that a teacher introduces, including questions such as why a particular piece of music was interesting to them—with the criteria centering on the *musical elements* and what these elements do for music (intensifying and declining dynamics, feelings of tension and release, introduction and climax and closure, elegance and appeal of the notes of the melody, and so forth). Focusing on these elements will help students become excellent critics. It is difficult for children to understand how to describe their feelings without excellent modeling, however. The teacher should remember to carefully model often what she or he hears in music in order for children to be comfortable in their own assessments.

STANDARD X (PROFESSIONAL RESPONSIBLITIES)

The music teacher understands professional responsibilities and interactions relevant to music instruction and the school music program.

Teachers must know the legal and ethical issues related to the use or performance of music in an educational setting and be able to comply with copyright laws to make appropriate and ethical decisions. They must be able to comply with federal, state, and local regulations concerning the use or performance of music. In another area of professional responsibility, teachers must know strategies for maintaining effective communication with other music educators, the value of continuing professional development in music education, and the types of professional development opportunities that are available to music educators. Knowing strategies for and maintaining communication with students, parents/caretakers, and others in the schools and community about the music program and its benefits are also be a part of being an early-childhood-through-fourth-grade teacher (previously discussed in Standard VII).

Copyright Laws and Music

All teachers are tempted at times to take care of their needs for copies of sheet music or recordings easily and quickly. However, copyright laws help composers, musical artists, recording studios, and music publishers make their living. Without royalties, no money is received from their work. Some music is not copyrighted, but if a work is, the teacher must follow guidelines stated in laws. Most modern works are copyrighted, *even if* not specifically marked.

The following guidelines may help you understand copying music. Teachers are allowed to copy a single copy of a book chapter, article, short story, essay or poem, chart, graph, diagram, cartoon, or picture, but making multiple copies is a bit more complicated. Teachers can make multiple copies on a one-time basis but not more than one copy per student, and the copyright must be included. This must also meet a brevity test. Copying music, too, falls into this category. A music teacher can copy a part of a musical work (one per student) but not the whole work (no more than 10%). The teacher must also not take more than one short poem, article, story per author (or two excerpts) or take more than three items from a collected work. Copying should not be for more than one course per term, or there should be no more than nine instances of multiple copying per class term. When in doubt, buy multiple copies, or request permission, as the composer, publisher, or recording company can seek monetary damages. If you have just made the decision to use an item based on its value to the lesson and could not expect to get permission quickly, then you may follow the guidelines above. You may also make "emergency" copies to replace purchased copies that are not available for an impending performance. A music teacher may make some alterations to music and copy them, but not so much that the fundamental nature of the music or lyrics is changed. When using copyrighted music, teachers may record student musical performances and retain them for evaluation and rehearsal purposes *only*. One sound copy *only* of a copyrighted piece of music may be made and retained for rehearsal, exercise, or examination purposes, if already owned by the teacher or the school. A music teacher may not make copies that would, in essence, create his or her "own music series or book" or replace collective works. The copyright must always appear on the copy. Students or teachers may not include copyrighted songs or music on a website without permission. When adding any music to technology-based projects, permission must be obtained, if copyrighted. These serve as only very brief guidelines, and, as we know from the legal battles in which Napster (a company who allowed music to be downloaded from the Internet) engaged, legal issues change. Most of those involved in music are very glad for teachers to use materials, but they must be given the chance to agree. Several websites such as www.law.cornell.edu/cgi-bin/empower (then search for music) and http://library.austin.cc.tx.us/gen-info/copymusic.html or www.music.indiana. edu/music_resources/copy.html give more complete details of copyright laws and information on how to obtain permission to copy. When in doubt, be sure to check the details.

In addition to these laws, there may be other local policies and regulations that might affect performances in music. If you plan on children's performing in another area outside of school, you need to check carefully to make sure you have followed local guidelines. Communicating with parents and your school district about what music will be performed and in what context is also an important part of musical performance, as parents and the district have the right to exclude their children from certain types of musical performance. If you are planning a large performance, it is better to know sooner rather than later that a number of children may not show up at the performance or that your selections must be changed at the last moment.

 ## SUMMARY

With the information offered here, you should be able to have a good grasp of what you might need to pass most TExES questions about teaching music in EC-4. Learning musical terms will also get you started in teaching music, should you not have a specialized music teacher in your building. Even if you have never played an instrument (or have had others request of you, "*Please* don't sing!"), you should be encouraged to bring music to the classroom. Children honestly do not care about the quality of your voice (though they will also need to hear good models during your time with them), but they *will* learn to be embarrassed with their voices if you show

embarrassment over yours. However, they react to an enthusiastic singer, even if the voice is less than professional and will join in at a moment's notice. In the push for good TAAS scores many schools without music teachers may encourage teachers to drop everything but "the basics." As a creative teacher, however, you should be encouraged to use music in every way to support and enhance basic subjects rather than treat them as separate areas—for the many reasons stated in this chapter. Music is a lifelong joy for most human beings and can be more appreciated and enjoyed if there is some sort of background for understanding.

There is *much* more to be learned about music and many more musical terms. This introduction, however, can help you through the basics. It is difficult to only *talk* or *read* about these terms and genres. Listen when your radio is on at home or in the car for the musical terms and types of music that you have read about here and try to seek out as many examples as you can. If you are the only music teacher your children have, we hope this chapter will encourage you to teach music in the best ways possible—for your children! Enjoy musical times with your children—it will make your day much richer, too!

ABOUT THE AUTHOR

JANICE L. NATH, Ed.D., is currently a professor in the Department of Urban Education at the University of Houston-Downtown. She is the co-editor of Becoming a Teacher in Texas: A Course of Study for the Professional Development ExCET, Becoming an EC-4 Teacher in Texas: A Course of Study for the Pedagogy and Professional Responsibilities (PPR) TExES, and Forging Alliances in Community and Thought: Research in Professional Development Schools. She has taught K–8 music and has made music a part of her fourth-grade classrooms in schools where there has been no music teacher. Currently, teacher education is her main area of interest and research. She has been involved with field-based teacher education for many years, serving as the Coordinator of Elementary Education in a large field-based program. She has also served as president of the AERA (American Educational Research Association) Professional Development School Research Special Interest Group (PDRS SIG) and of the Texas Coordinators for Teacher Certification Testing (TCTCT). She is currently a member and officer of the CSOTTE Board (Consortium for Texas Teacher Educators).

Preparing to Teach Health and Physical Education

Mel E. Finkenberg
Stephen F. Austin
State University

Janice L. Nath
University of Houston-
Downtown

John Ramsey
University of Houston

D omain V of the Generalist EC-4 Test Framework addresses "Fine Arts, Health, and Physical Education."
This chapter focuses upon two of these areas:
health and physical education. Because many colleges and
universities do not require course work in these areas, this
portion of the test has been an obstacle for many test takers. However, as a result of the passage of Texas Senate Bill
19, it is anticipated that needed attention will be placed on
these two areas for teachers of young children. Senate Bill
19, authored by Senator Jane Nelson, requires school districts to provide daily physical activity as part of their
physical education curriculum for children in grade 6 and
below. Such activity must involve physical exertion of an
intensity and for a duration sufficient to provide positive
health benefits to students.

Studies consistently conclude that U.S. children are at risk due to the lack of health and fitness education opportunities provided in schools. The "fattening" of America can be directly linked to the diminished emphasis on physical education, particularly in the elementary schools where values are established. The document entitled *Healthy People 2000: National Health Promotion and Disease Objectives* was released as a governmental strategy to improve the health of *all* Americans, although a majority of the 300 target goals are specifically directed toward improving the health status of U.S. children and youth.

The recent release of the *Surgeon General's Report of Physical Activity and Health* (1996) documented many health benefits achieved through moderate and regular activity. The report showed that people of all ages benefit from regular physical activity. Never before, however, has a body of research been compiled to show such a strong need for activity and fitness in the lives of our youth. Activity programs are an absolute requisite for healthy youngsters. Yet helping children to become more active adults is not the only area educators view as important. Educators also believe that emotional development, safety, violence prevention, and other health-related issues can make a difference in a healthy life for children.

Consistent with the design of the previous chapters, this chapter is structured with an overview of the various standards and competencies within the health and physical education components of Domain V. These have, in turn, been correlated to the Texas Essential Knowledge and Skills (TEKS) for health and physical education. Additionally, sample items with discussion about the various alternatives are offered.

Standards are broad statements presenting the main idea of the knowledge and skills expected of a beginning educator. Each standard contains a list of specific knowledge and skill statements (the competencies) that further explain the main idea and requirements of each standard. The standards and their knowledge and skills statements are fundamentally based on the TEKS, the statewide curriculum for Texas public schools. In the discussion of the standards and competencies outlined below, correlations between these standards and the content of the Generalist examination will become apparent.

Many of the attitudes of lifelong mental and physical health for children are related to Bloom's Affective Domain. The **affective domain** influences lifelong learning and consists of the following levels:

1. **Receiving or attending.** The learner must first be ready, able, and motivated to receive and attend to information (i.e., listen, be aware of, observe, recognize, realize, be tolerant of).
2. **Responding.** The learner has to become engaged with the information in some manner (i.e., respond, cooperate, appreciate, comply, discuss).
3. **Valuing.** The learner selects the information and expresses a value about it (i.e., appraise, assess, evaluate, critique).

4. **Organization.** The learner places the value of the information in an order of importance (i.e., demonstrate, perform, uphold, engage in).
5. **Characterization.** The learner chooses to take the information and make it part of his or her life or a part of his or her character. (Bloom et al., 1956, in Cruickshank, Jenkins, & Metcalf, 2002)

A teacher must be certain that he or she plans health and physical education lessons with consideration of this domain in mind. For example, if a teacher wanted children to appreciate eating in a healthy way, children must first *receive* or *attend* to a rationale for the concept (self-esteem is connected to weight, mobility, health deterioration, dental decay, and so forth) and receive information on how this can be accomplished. Teachers might have children respond to the information, for example, through a tasting fair of healthy snacks, by designing a survey that shows which healthy foods are best liked, and by working comparison problems of the calories and food value of healthy snacks with nonhealthy snacks so that children become engaged with the concept. Learners may next be asked by a visiting nutritionist to prepare a healthy meal or snack tray by gluing cutout pictures of healthy foods from a variety of food items onto a paper plate and explaining why they selected each. Just as a teacher is requested to extend the knowledge and comprehension levels of thinking to higher levels in the cognitive domain, the teacher should go beyond just having children simply attend in this domain. Children should have opportunities to role-play, choose, discuss, and be actively involved and thoroughly engaged with these concepts. It is only after children *receive/attend* and *respond* that learners begin to value a concept. EC-4 teachers should always remember that children learn these types of health lessons and gain positive attitudes *throughout* the year. If only a few days are spent on a unit in any health area (nutrition, safety, stress, or so forth), the information and ideas will seem disjointed and unimportant. Teachable moments that reinforce health issues occur daily. A teacher should take full advantage of those moments (in addition to integrating health lessons with other subject areas) to bring the health issues discussed in this chapter to the forefront. Children revisit important topics in a spiraling curriculum throughout the early childhood and elementary years, establishing positive ways of growing into healthy lifestyles.

STANDARDS I AND II (HEALTH)

Competency 026: The health teacher applies knowledge of both the relationship between health and behavior and the factors influencing health and health behavior. The health teacher plans and implements effective school health instruction and integrates health instruction with other content areas.

A beginning teacher understands health-related behaviors, ways in which personal health decisions and behaviors affect body systems and health, and selects strategies for reducing health risks and enhancing wellness throughout the life span. The teacher also demonstrates knowledge of major areas in health instruction, including body systems (e.g., structures and functions of various body systems), illness and disease (e.g., types of disease, transmission mechanisms, defense systems, disease prevention), nutrition (e.g., types of foods and nutrients, maintenance of a balanced diet), stress (e.g., effects of stress, stress-reduction techniques), and fitness (e.g., components of fitness, methods for improving fitness). Understanding and teaching about substance use and abuse (including types and characteristics of tobacco, alcohol, and other drugs and of herbal supplements) are also expected of the beginning teacher, as is understanding the influence of various environmental factors (e.g., media, technology, peer and other relationships, environmental hazards) on individual, family, and community health. He or she should also understand types of violence and abuse (including causes and effects of violence and abuse and prevention). The Texas teacher is expected to select and use instructional strategies, materials, and activities to teach principles and procedures related to safety, accident prevention, and response to emergencies. EC-4 teachers should apply critical-thinking, goal-setting, and decision-making skills in health-related contexts and understand the use of refusal skills and conflict resolution to avoid unsafe situations. They should select and use instructional strategies, materials, and activities to help children build healthy interpersonal relationships (e.g., communication skills), demonstrate consideration and respect for self, family, friends, and others (e.g., practicing self-control) and understand the roles of healthcare professionals, the benefits of health maintenace activities, and the skills for becoming healthwise consumers. The teacher also applies knowledge of health content and curriculum, including the Texas Essential Knowledge and Skills (TEKS), and plans and implements effective, developmentally appropriate health instruction, including relating the health-education curriculum to other content areas.

Choosing a Healthy Life

Consider the following question:

Ms. Vasquez teaches elementary health and physical education. Her programs include a variety of personal health and safety skills. She has planned a unit in nutrition, focusing on healthy snacks. Which of the following activities would be most appropriate for this course?

A. Have students read from short "canned" skits to other students about healthy snacks.

B. Have students write paragraphs about what constitutes healthy snacks.

C. Hold a directed discussion in which children are led to discover the nutritional contents of a variety of their favorite snacks.

D. Divide the class into collaborative groups and have each group choose a different snack to present a nutritional report about what they have learned.

Test taker #1 selected *A* because it allows learners to discuss personal health. Test taker #2 selected *B* because writing paragraphs requires that learners study the topic in depth. Since writing is an essential skill, she thought that this option might provide the opportunity to use this subject matter in an interdisciplinary manner. Test taker #3 selected *D* because presenting findings through collaborative groups involves each learner in the determination of what constitutes healthy snacks. Test taker #4 selected *C* since the interactive discovery method is an effective means of imparting factual information and constructed ideas.

The correct answer is *D*. This option allows students to be active participants in the determination of nutrition concepts. Although each of the remaining options may meet the instructor's objective, this is the superior choice due to the active participation and knowledge construction of the learners.

This practice question relates to the health education component of the TEKS, whereby learners acquire the health information and skills necessary to become healthy adults and learn about behavior in which they should and should not participate. To achieve that goal, learners need the following understanding: (a) Learners should first seek guidance in the area of health from their parents; (b) personal behavior can increase or reduce health risks throughout the lifespan; (c) health is influenced by a variety of factors; (d) learners can recognize and utilize health information and products; and (e) personal/interpersonal skills are needed to promote individual, family, and community health.

Let's try another practice question:

Mr. Harris teaches elementary health and physical education. He wishes to teach health and safety skills that relate to the well-being of students, friends, and family. Which of the following instructional units would promote self-responsibility as it relates to family and friends?

A. Personal hygiene.
B. Exercise and fitness.
C. First aid.
D. Nutritional needs.

Test taker #1 answered *D*, maintaining that meeting nutritional needs relates to the well-being of students. Test taker #2 selected *A* because she believes that instructional units in personal hygiene would promote self-responsibility. Test taker #3 chose *B* because exercise and fitness relate to each of the remaining options; that is, if learners take responsibility for their health and fitness, perhaps they will take responsibility for personal hygiene, first aid, and nutritional needs as well. Test taker #4 also selected *B* because of the emphasis placed by the media on health and fitness. Test taker #5 also selected C since first aid relates to family and friends as well as to oneself.

The correct answer is C—first aid. The key phrase in this assessment item is health and safety skills "that relate to the well-being of students, friends, and family." Although choices A, B, and D relate to personal health and safety, they do not specifically correlate with others involved in the application of health and safety principles. The use of basic emergency aid procedures as identified in option C could directly affect the well-being of others, including friends and family. Further, these skills imply and develop decision-making and problem-solving skills that foster healthy interactions and promote learners' interpersonal skills.

Although many learning experiences related to caring for personal health take place in the home, sometimes children do not learn good personal health and safety patterns from parents and families. Teachers can therefore ensure that children are taught, encouraged, and reinforced with activities that maintain a lifestyle of appropriate personal health and safety.

Some believe that basic health is too personal to include in an educational curriculum. However, health education may never reach young students at the time it may be needed. Elementary and middle school children have many questions and concerns about such personal health matters as skin care, hair care, dental hygiene, and many other personal health matters. Apart from the formal learning and experiences that take place in a health instructional program, older elementary children often turn to less reliable sources of information such as popular magazines, product advertisements, radio and/or television, and peers. These sources may be biased or inaccurate.

Texas Senate Bill 19 also encourages districts to utilize the Coordinated Approach to Child Health program (CATCH), which is designed to prevent obesity, cardiovascular disease, and Type II diabetes in elementary children. CATCH offers a successful blend of physical education, classroom curriculum, nutrition awareness, student-directed activities, and physical education equipment designed to promote and maintain cardiovascular health in children grades K through 5. CATCH began as a research study founded by the National Heart, Lung, and Blood Institute. Its purpose was to establish the direct link between school health and physical education in developing healthier behavior among children in grades 3 through 5. Now expanded to cover grades K through 5, CATCH remains the largest and most rigorous school-based health promotion study to date. With more than 600 school programs, CATCH continues to impact students long after they complete the coursework. Published in the *Journal of the American Medical Association* (JAMA), results indicate that student intake of total fat and saturated fat was reduced while the intensity of physical activity performed both inside and outside school increased (Luepker, Perry, McKinlay, et al., 1996).

CATCH encourages kids to:

- Move, run, jump, and dance as they participate in moderate to vigorous physical activities using a variety of equipment.
- Develop good nutrition habits as they learn to recognize and monitor their fat and salt intake.
- Declare themselves "smoke-free!"

The four components of CATCH are the classroom curriculum, physical education, the school food service, and the family partnership. Teachers and staff are trained to implement and coordinate these components. These intervention strategies were shown to significantly increase the intensity and duration of physical activity and decrease the energy intake from fat and saturated fat in intervention school lunches.

School Health Facilities

Maintaining a healthy life also includes having regular medical and dental preventive care. Some children may have their first experience with healthcare in school. Children need to know enough about their bodies to tell the nurse, for example, exactly "where it hurts" and/or what symptoms may be present. A teacher should schedule a tour of the clinic facility or nurse's office early in the year, especially for younger children, as it could be a scary experience if the first visit is when the child is sent there ill. Teachers should ask the nurse to visit the class so young children know him or her better and understand the role the nurse plays in their healthcare. (Other healthcare workers can also be asked to visit.) Many teachers place appropriate real or play medical equipment in a "doctor's center" so that children can become familiar with these. In addition, teachers can provide stories that describe examination procedures, use puppets to role-play medical or dental procedures, or stage phone practice for help in an emergency. All young children can learn about emergencies and how to call for help at school or away from school. The school nurse also serves as a resource and teacher for many health issues.

As an aside, the EC-4 teacher is often the first to see underlying illness or health issues, as she or he is most often with children during many waking hours. The EC-4 teacher must be vigilant as an advocate for any health issues that are noticed, including abuse.

Nutrition

Consider the following practice question:

Mrs. Cleary, an elementary school teacher, is concerned about the eating habits of her students. Which of the following dietary guidelines should be stressed to elementary school students?

I. Eat a variety of foods from the basic food groups.
II. Eat primarily proteins and avoid carbohydrates.
III. Eat foods containing adequate starch and fiber.
IV. Eat only foods low in fat.

A. I and IV only.
B. II and III only.
C. II and IV only.
D. I and III only.

The correct choice is *D*—options I (eat a variety of foods from the basic food groups) and III (eat foods containing adequate starch and fiber). These two responses support a balanced diet. It is important to promote positive nutritional habits at the elementary grades because it is difficult to change eating patterns once they have been established.

Poor nutritional status may result in several problems. Although *undernutrition* can be a problem, in the United States the more common malnutrition problem is **overnutrition,** with about 15 percent of adolescents being overweight. Obese children are likely to suffer chronic disease risks later in life and are likely to suffer emotional stress as well. Healthy eating habits are best begun at an early age. In other words, the best way to maintain ideal weight and eat well throughout life is to learn how to eat and exercise early in life. Teachers should help parents teach their children proper eating habits and exercise. Of all the habits of living, the most important to good health is eating properly.

Teaching young children about food choices can begin with experimentation. The EC-4 teacher may offer a variety of healthy snacks, even using the opportunity to integrate social studies by a cultural or "theme" tasting ("Today, boys and girls, we are going to visit Hawaii. Let's look on the map to see where Hawaii is and why these wonderful fruits grow there . . ." as the teacher offers fresh pineapple chunks, mango, banana, passion fruit juice, and so forth). Cultural lessons can accompany these lessons with information on why, when, and with what foods are eaten in different cultures and why the food is a good choice. Because very young children cannot yet classify a number of ideas, it is suggested that children be asked to classify food into categories that are easier to sort, such as milk products, eggs, vegetables, breads, meat, fruit, nuts, and so forth. Later they can be introduced to the food pyramid with the number of recommended servings (bread, cereal, rice, and pasta at the bottom with the most servings allowed; fruit; vegetable; dairy; meat, poultry, fish, dry beans; and, with minimum servings, fats, oils, and sweets). This pyramid plays a major role in helping students understand how they can chose a healthy meal by selecting different proportions from different parts of the pyramid.

Parents can be used as a resource to reinforce trying foods at home and promoting healthy eating. Teachers should also remember to send a list of foods home that will be offered in class due to the possibilities of food allergies or cultural or religious desires for children not to eat certain items. At school, children should never be forced to eat what is offered in class. However, presenting foods in enticing ways should encourage children to try them. Teachers who reward young children with praise may also encourage others. Rothlein (cited in Brewer, 2001) suggests that only small amounts should be offered and the color, texture, and shape should be discussed. The teacher should also be a role model, and he or she should keep trying, despite children's reluctance. If reluctance is encountered, the teacher should try to determine if another way of serving a food would be acceptable (raw carrots versus cooked carrots). When children are involved in the preparation of foods, they are often more eager to try something new.

Healthy Relationships

This standard is addressed in a variety of components of the TEKS. Learners are expected to know healthy ways to communicate consideration and respect for self, family, friends, and others. Learners are expected to demonstrate skills in respectful communicating; describe and practice techniques of self-control such as thinking before acting; and to express needs, wants, and emotions in appropriate ways. Emphasis is placed on teaching children the skills necessary for building and maintaining healthy relationships. Children are expected to learn to identify characteristics needed to be a responsible family member or friend, to list and demonstrate good listening skills, and to demonstrate critical-thinking, decision-making, goal-setting, and problem-solving skills for making health-promoting decisions. Elementary school children should also be equipped with conflict resolution skills.

Despite a teacher's best efforts, conflict is often present in the schools. Conflict resolution represents a range of important skills for children to learn. Students should be made to understand the sources of conflict and instructed on how to manage the conflict. Three primary main conflict management techniques include:

- Avoid the conflict. This means walking away from a fight or not acting in a way that will provoke another person.
- Defuse the conflict. Adding humor to the situation or using delaying strategies can help defuse the conflict.
- Negotiation. This management technique means trying to find a way to compromise about the conflict.

Family members and teachers are especially important role models. Yet the media also offers many roles to children. Many American children spend more time watching television than they do working on schoolwork. Television has the potential to be a powerful educational medium. It is also apparent that violence on television can provide a violent or aggressive model for children. Teachers should provide as many other positive role models as possible to counter this effect (good literature, resources in the community, and others).

The issues of peer pressure, popularity, and high-risk behaviors impact even young children as they watch how to dress, what to say, and how to act. Children need to know that rejection is an unfortunate but inevitable part of life. It can be disappointing but should not be devastating. Part of good mental health is resiliency. Children must acquire knowledge and the ability to set limits, communicate effectively, and employ refusal skills. These basic skills are necessary to help students deal with daily pressures. Remember that peer pressure is not always a negative influence. Pressure to behave in a health-enhancing fashion can go a long way in helping a child. It is also essential that children understand that parents and other family members are not always opposing forces. Peers also do not always lead children astray. However, teaching children about what qualities make a good friend who would make a positive impact on their lives should also be a part of the EC-4 health curriculum.

Teaching about Illness and Disease

By understanding the difference between sickness and health in persons of all ages, learners will be able to explain ways in which germs are transmitted, methods of preventing the spread of germs, and the importance of immunization. In this way they will be able to identify causes of disease other than germs (such as allergies and heart disease) and explain how the body provides protection from disease. They should then be able to apply practices to control the spread of germs in daily life such as hand washing and skin care, noting that the skin is our body's major protector from germs. Teachers should schedule the *time* for healthy routines (such as always washing hands before eating and after visits to the restroom). The teacher can also be a role model whenever he or she has an opportunity with Think-Alouds ("I have a bit of a cold today, boys and girls. I am not going to come so close to you today to try to keep you from getting it," or "Excuse me a moment . . . I am starting to cough, so I am just going to get a tissue"). Teachers themselves should be very cautious with germs. If a teacher must aid a child in blowing a nose, for example, she or he should always wash his or her hands immediately afterwards. Gloves should be available and worn for cleaning up any bodily fluids as per universal precautions. Tables where young children work should be washed often.

Teaching children about the symptoms of common childhood afflictions can also be a good idea. Head lice, ringworm, pink eye, and other maladies may become less shared and less of a stigma if children understand how they occur and how they are cured (if handled in a matter-of-fact way). A teacher may also need to discuss HIV and AIDS. Depending on the age level, children may want to talk about it to help alleviate fears that people can contract AIDS from being around or touching someone with the disease. Certainly, children's fears need to be answered by teaching them that one cannot contract HIV/AIDS other than from infected blood, from intravenous needles often associated with drug use, from a mother with HIV to a baby in the womb or through nursing, and from unprotected sex. The EC-4 teacher must be appropriate in what she or he tells children with regard to age but should answer children's questions, for they see and hear much about disease and may understand very little.

Consider the following practice question:

Ms. Jackson has noticed that a number of her third-grade students have been coming to school with colds and flu-like symptoms. Which of the following strategies would be most useful for helping students understand self-responsibilities as they relate to friends and family?

A. Students will keep a log of their personal health attributes on a daily basis and discuss the logs each Friday.

B. Students will work in groups to discuss communicative and noncommunicative diseases and how they are transmitted.

C. Students will interview parents and friends in order to determine their health status.

D. Physicians and other healthcare practitioners will be invited to discuss with the students the health hazards they present when they come to school ill.

While maintaining health logs and discussing them with the class is a useful tool for assessing health status (*A*), it does not lend itself to assisting learners in developing self-responsibility. Choice *B* will give students the requisite information needed for preparing them to understand concepts and issues of health and self-responsibility; this is the correct choice. Choice *C* also does not provide the learner the opportunity to promote interpersonal well-being. Choice *D*, although having the potential for providing learners with a cognitive basis regarding health and safety issues, is not structured to provide the learner the opportunity to promote interpersonal well-being.

Substance Abuse

It is important to remember that individuals make choices about their health behavior. This requires teaching about decision making. Teachers must also enhance learner skills such that they can carry out their health-producing behaviors. For example, a fourth grader who is deliberating about trying tobacco or another harmful drug substance must be shown choices in order to make a decision and provided with occasions to practice the skills to avoid drug abuse. Bandura's (cited in Eggen & Kauchak, 2001) social learning theory is conducive to building these skills. For example, Bandura would suggest that the fourth grader who is contemplating drug use must: (1) understand what methods must be done to avoid it, (2) believe that he or she will be able to use the methods, (3) believe that the method(s) will actually work, and (4) anticipate a benefit after achieving the behavior. Social learning theory posits that children can learn these concepts, in part from watching others and with practice can develop the necessary skills required for any particular behavior.

The key focus for teachers is to select learning strategies that have proven effective, provide background information, assist in decision-making skills, support personal and social skill-building, and allow opportunities for practice. One activity is unlikely to fulfill all of these qualifications, so careful planning is required to accomplish this task.

HEALTHY RELATIONSHIPS. Students develop many different relationships throughout their elementary school years. For instance, relationships with family members, same-age friends, relatives, and teachers begin to change as children progress through school.

Although speech develops in most children in predictable developmental sequences, communication as a skill does not come naturally to all children. Effective communication includes a range of skills that must be learned. A person's ability to communicate can have a direct effect on self-esteem and the quality of relationships with others. Besides helping a child's self-esteem, good communication skills are important to help a child succeed in the classroom. Success in school depends on listening and speaking skills as much as on intellectual ability.

One important area in communications is the ability to recognize facial expressions and emotions. EC-4 teachers may use a number of activities such as identifying emotions when given pictures of faces, creating collages to represent a particular emotion, drawing, storytelling, questioning, and presenting good literature models. A record of what emotions each child is able to easily identify should be maintained. Teachers also should record whether children can identify the possible causes of emotions. Lack of emotional intelligence (Goleman, 1995) has been linked to adult failure in many ways. To help this area teachers should provide opportunities for students to work together in pairs, small groups, and teams. Providing roles in cooperative education situations and focusing on a social skill of the day can help children become aware of verbal and nonverbal behavior (Kagan, 1992).

Consider the following practice question:

All of the following are characteristics of good communicators, *except:*

A. People are sensitive to the needs of those with whom they communicate.
B. People are assertive without being aggressive.

C. People withhold their own opinions from the conversation.
D. People use "I" statements.

Three of these choices are appropriate communication skills. However, children should be taught that their opinions are important contributors to communication (C). When children first enter school, they are very self-centered and more concerned about their own needs. They rarely identify with the needs and characteristics of others. As they continue in school, they begin to develop an increasing awareness of others. As they age, children begin to redirect their personal concerns to intellectual concerns and group activities. They begin to expend more energy on friendships and the community around them. Children become less dependent on their parents, although parents are still important to them. The correct choice is C.

REFUSAL SKILLS. Refusal skills are part of good decision making. Children need good refusal skills when it is necessary to say "No" to an action or to leave a potentially harmful situation. Any situation that threatens personal safety or health, tempts children to break laws or norms, detracts from personal character, asks students to disobey parental rules, or results in loss of self-respect calls for strong refusal skills.

Catchy slogans and signing pacts have been criticized because they do not strengthen self-concept, social skills, and prosocial behaviors. EC-4 teachers should concentrate on these areas with particular attention to those children exhibiting difficulty in the areas mentioned above and offer opportunities for children to role play various situations to practice these skills.

Try this practice question:

Mrs. Smith's health class is discussing a model for using communication skills. In practicing refusal skills Jake responds to pressure to use the drugs by stating, "No, thank you." Which of the following is the *best* assessment of this refusal strategy?

A. Saying "No, thank you" is inappropriate because there is no need to thank people for an invitation to misbehave.
B. It's a good response because you are being polite.
C. It doesn't match his nonverbal communication.
D. It's a good response because it's short.

Students should be taught that in order to develop good refusal skills, they should:

- Employ assertive behavior. This allows others to know that you are in control of your behavior and the situation.
- Use body language that matches your assertive verbal behavior. Body language indicates that you are sincere. Students should make it clear that they do not desire to engage in unsafe situations.

- Avoid potentially harmful/dangerous situations.
- Be a positive role model. Children should act and talk in a manner that commands respect.

You don't have to say "No, thank you." There is no need to be polite when placed in a situation that may be unsafe. The correct answer is A.

Teaching about Violence

Violence as the answer to conflict has become all too common. Nowhere is the magnitude of the concern about the growing rate of violence reflected more urgently than in Goal 7 of the *Goals 2000: Educate America Act* (1994). Students in schools where violence occurs will likely not focus on meeting rigorous standards, not perform at high academic levels, or complete schooling. Students and teachers concerned more about their personal safety than about education cannot concentrate on teaching and learning. Violence and abuse in schools is not unique to public schools or urban centers. No geographic region is excluded. The public's concern about discipline and violence in schools is well warranted.

It is the responsibility of educators to help prevent violence. Violence prevention means two things: reducing our children's risk of facing violence in the future and preventing the immediate threat of violence to our children. As a teacher, you should recognize that there are behaviors and strategies that can help you safeguard yourself and the students in your classroom. Characteristics of teachers whose classrooms have been identified as relatively violence free include:

- Developing of positive relationships with students in the classroom and in the community.
- Taking preventive action by creating classroom environments where the teacher is clearly in control.
- Knowing how to diffuse a confrontation.
- Insisting on backup support when necessary.

Various programs exist that endeavor to teach children how to manage anger and conflict. These programs typically share the ideas that:

- Conflict is a normal part of human interaction.
- When individual prejudices are explored, students can learn how to appreciate people whose backgrounds are different.
- Disputes need not have winners and losers.
- Children who learn how to assert themselves nonviolently can avoid becoming bullies or victims.

- Children's self-esteem is enhanced when they learn how to build nonviolent, nonhostile relationships with their peers.

Incorporating the above principles in the health education curriculum is essential. Research has shown that comprehensive school health education is effective in influencing youth's behaviors and establishing a pattern of healthy behavior in the future.

Stress

Let's begin with a practice question:

Joey, a fourth grader, is having trouble coping with stressful situations in school and at home. This unresolved stress has caused him to become angry with his friends for little reason. What would be the *best* thing the teacher could do to help him?

- **A.** Have him begin an exercise program immediately.
- **B.** Discover his sleeping habits and see if he needs more sleep.
- **C.** Analyze his diet and make recommendations for a diet that will help reduce stress.
- **D.** Seek help from the counselor in the school.

Let's examine the alternative responses. Although it is true that exercise can reduce stress levels (*A*), it is apparent that there are a number of factors contributing to the child's demeanor. Exercise, while a valuable tool, will not necessary provide the results anticipated. Thus, response *A* is not correct. Although sleeping habits can impact behavior, there is nothing to indicate that the child's stress is a manifestation of lack of sleep. Answer *B* does not provide a comprehensive solution or one that the teacher could control. The same can be said for answer *C*. Typically, stress and the hostile behavior exhibited by students are a manifestation of several factors. The correct answer is *D*—seek help from a counselor. Though a teacher can try other stress-reducing strategies, the role of the counselor in schools is to professionally help individual students in cases such as this. The role of the counselor also may include advice for the teacher, working with parents, and working individually with the child for an extended time to try ideas, or perhaps explore testing or provide mini-lessons on various emotional-based topics.

Consider another question:

Members of a fourth-grade physical education class were running relay races. One boy exclaimed, "I was so afraid that I would drop the baton that I started sweating a lot, and my stomach felt funny. I was afraid that I'd let the team down." This statement best reflects the knowledge of what principles and practices needed by teachers?

- **A.** Teachers need to be aware that a learner's motivation is best gauged by stress symptoms and measures the learner's level of motivation.

B. Teachers need to recognize signs of stress demonstrated by learners, and they should use opportunities like this to teach coping skills that can be used by students.
C. Physical education instruction should include skills that are stressful during the early learning phases of motor activity.
D. Physical education instruction should include stressful situations to match those encountered in the learner's nonschool environments.

One of the unique advantages of physical education is that it provides the opportunity to view students in a variety of stressful situations. Teaching students that stress is a natural outcome of being placed in the competitive situation described is an excellent introduction to teaching students how to cope with stress. As a result, answer B is correct. Motivation and stress are not necessarily related to successful achievement of motor skill development, so A is incorrect. Providing stress during the early stages of skill development, as in item C, will result in frustration on the part of students. Teaching motor skills should result in a balance between mild stress and success. Item D is not correct, since the goal is to use these situations to teach students coping skills, not to purposefully create stressful environments.

It is possible to teach children skills in *coping* (the ability to deal with problems successfully) and *decision making* (a process in which a person selects from two or more possible choices) through instruction in physical activity. Specific strategies for teaching children coping skills include:

1. Admit that the problem exists and face it.
2. Define the problem and decide who owns it. (Is the problem theirs, or does it belong to others?)
3. List alternative solutions to the problem.
4. Predict consequences for oneself and others.
5. Identify and consult sources of help.
6. Experiment with a solution and evaluate the results.

Young children can formulate these into the following steps:

RED LIGHT: Stop! Calm down . . . and think before you act.

YELLOW LIGHT: Say the problem and how you feel. Set a positive goal. Think of lots of solutions. Think ahead of the consequences.

GREEN LIGHT: Go ahead and try the best plan (Goleman, 1995).

When making decisions, students should definitely consider each of the following steps:

1. Gather information.
2. Consider the available choices.
3. Analyze the consequences of choices.

4. Make a decision and implement it.
5. Evaluate the decision and begin at step one with a new plan if the decision did not have positive results.

The use of "challenge" activities such as climbing walls, rope courses, and other physically demanding activities have recently gained impetus because of their value in teaching both coping and decision-making skills. Teachers must remember that young children are still egocentric in development and children in poverty may not have the ability to navigate through decisions involving long-term goals. EC-4 teachers should help young children begin making decisions that deal with short-term goals first. Children who never are allowed or offered choices in a classroom never have the opportunity to practice making decisions.

Technology and Health

The technology revolution has had a dramatic impact on our ability to teach youngsters concepts related to health and fitness. An example is the use of heart rate monitors that permit children to gain a greater understanding of the cardiorespiratory system and the establishment of cardiorespiratory fitness. Another example is the use of video cameras to allow a child's performance to be filmed for immediate self-assessment. Audiovisual aids add another dimension to teaching concepts and are excellent for reinforcing learning. The Internet allows children access to a great deal of health-related fitness information and to set up interdisciplinary studies across distances to gather health-related data, share active games, and so forth. The Internet also provides teachers with the opportunity to communicate with others and to share their ideas and questions.

Technology also brings numerous products to consumers' attention. Teaching children about being a smart consumer of health products helps them understand that they must read labels, gather more information at times, and be constantly alert for false advertising. For example, having learners create their own "cure all" or "miracle weight loss" products along with a label and advertisements (which can be filmed) helps children understand this phenomenon.

Safety

The need for safety and efforts to provide it has been part of people's lives since the beginning of human existence. Although the hazards have changed over time, the fundamental problem is the same. Ever since humans sought shelter and developed weapons to protect themselves, the anticipation of danger and the ability to overcome it have been major keys to safety and survival. Instruction in safety and injury prevention is an important component of an elementary school curriculum. The leading cause of death among children ages 1 to 14 is unintentional injuries. Each year over 3,000 children between the ages of 5 and 14 die from unintentional injuries. Over half of these fatalities result from motor vehicle accidents (in which many children were not wearing seatbelts). For this reason, safety instruction cannot be ignored.

Attitude formation begins early in a child's life and has a major impact on safety behavioral patterns. Though innumerable factors influence attitude formation, the actions of parents and respected adults, including teachers, is a major force, particularly among children in the primary grades.

For health education to be effective in the elementary school, it is important that the school program be coordinated with health-promotion activities throughout the schools and community. Messages delivered in a consistent fashion and from several sources (teachers, parents, school staff, community leaders, and peers) are more effective in changing behaviors.

The elementary school teacher's responsibility is to instill in pupils attitudes that encourage them to act to protect their own safety, that of their families, and that of society. Safety education is not only training in conservation of life and the prevention of accidents but also instruction in how to be a good citizen. Other responsibilities of the teacher are to guide learners in molding sound values, direct their thinking and decision making, and help them regulate their behavior. According to the TEKS in health education, teachers should direct children's understanding of the health information necessary to become healthy adults and learn about behaviors in which they should and should not participate. To achieve that goal, students should understand the following: (a) Students should first seek guidance in the area of safety from their parents; (b) their own behaviors throughout their lifetime can increase or reduce safety risks; (c) a variety of factors affect and influence safety; (d) students can recognize and use safety information and products; and (e) personal/interpersonal skills are needed to promote individual, family, and community safety.

What safety issues are important for an EC-4 teacher to include in his or her class? Fire, traffic, sun, water, gun, poison (including another person's medications), and human predator safety are all issues of which children should be aware. Several of these can scare and worry children, so a teacher must be careful to balance information in a way that is completely age-appropriate. Drills (fire, violence or lock-downs, and bad weather) should be practiced until they become matter-of-fact. Instead of lining up in the routine way during the year, teachers can occasionally say, "Today, when we line up to go the library, we are going to do our fire drill line-up, so listen for my 'three bells'," or "When we come in from recess today, I want you to practice the lock-down routine," or "When we line up outside our classroom, let me see everybody practice the bad weather position." Outside resources such as fire departments and police departments can provide instruction in many of these areas. If outside resources are not available, EC-teachers must still provide instruction. "Stop, drop, and roll," exiting before calling 911, designating a gathering spot, and, of course, not playing with fire should be a part of all children's knowledge for school and home. Traffic safety instruction can include areas on the playground and in centers where children pretend to be vehicles or "drive" small toy vehicles according to traffic rules. In Texas, for example, young children need to learn about the out-of-doors safety with our direct sun and how to take measures that prevent skin cancer. Texas teachers should also be cognizant of sunburn and heat stroke when children are engaged in outdoor activities. Children should be taught about strangers through role-play, games, or puppet play. Many videos and police departments deal well with "good touching" versus "bad touching." Guidelines to help latchkey children be more safe (such as Internet and phone rules of never giving out one's name, parent's name, or address) (Brewer, 2001) should be communicated to children and parents. Teachers and parents should be careful about labeling children's clothing and materials on the outside to prevent a predator from easily identifying a name and calling out to a child.

Consider the following practice question:

An elementary teacher, Mrs. Santos, wishes to promote an understanding of community safety among her children. As the lesson is introduced, several children tell her that some children display unsafe behaviors while riding their bicycles to and from school. For example, they do not wear protective gear and weave in and out of traffic. Mrs. Santos would like her students to understand their roles and responsibilities in helping to ensure community safety while children are riding their bicycles.

Which of the following activities would be most appropriate for this purpose?

A. Making a list of inappropriate behaviors and the safety problems these behaviors cause.
B. Write a letter to school and city officials as well as the local police informing them of the bicycle safety problem and ask for assistance in eliminating the problem.
C. Suggesting to the well-behaved students that they avoid streets in which students practicing unsafe bicycle riding behavior is displayed.
D. Start a telephone campaign to report unsafe bicycle riders to the appropriate officials.

Let's examine the alternatives. Response A is not the correct answer, since it does not address the standard targeted in this question; that is, it does not address promoting an understanding of community safety among the students. Response B is the correct choice. By writing a letter to important community members, the learners are demonstrating an understanding of the concepts and issues of community health and safety and applying this understanding to the well-being of people collectively. By selecting this response choice, the elementary teacher demonstrates that she understands community health and safety issues and fosters learner understanding of the related responsibilities. Responses C and D are not correct, since the choices result in a failure to apply the concepts related to community health. Read the question very carefully to be sure you note nuances such as community versus personal safety.

Try another practice item:

During a discussion about community health in Ms. Arevalo's third-grade class, several children said that they often see others playing in an abandoned building known as a hangout for drug users. Ms. Arevalo would like her students to have an understanding of their own roles and responsibilities in helping to ensure community safety. Which of the following activities, suggested by the students in response to the situation, would be most appropriate for this purpose?

A. Suggesting to the students that they find a new place to play.
B. Making a list of the negative outcomes that could happen as a result of playing in an abandoned building.
C. Have students picket the abandoned facility in order to bring attention to it.
D. Make public officials aware of the dangers and possible hazards resulting from the abandoned building and asking them for their assistance.

Suggesting to children that they find a new place to play (*A*) helps to promote issues of health and safety but does not promote the well-being of people collectively. The same is true for options *B* and *C*. The correct choice, therefore, is *D*. By making public officials aware of the potential dangers and hazards, learners are better able to understand their roles in community safety. This promotes the idea of a responsible community; that is, if a situation is harmful and we do nothing and someone is hurt, we, too, are responsible to some degree.

The common thread interwoven throughout lifestyles and habits is that good health is often a choice, not chance. Children make daily choices about their health and in doing so establish early patterns of behavior. The learner who doesn't wear a seatbelt is at greater risk of injury. The learner who elects not to wear protective equipment while riding a bicycle also increases risk. The learner who refuses to wear eyeglasses exacerbates his or her vision problem. Choice of lifestyle impacts those around us. The injured child incurs medical costs for his or her parent(s) or may even become dependent upon the state healthcare system.

In contrast, learners who learn to brush and floss their teeth early are less likely to develop dental problems. Children who eat healthy snacks and remain within defined weight limits are less likely to suffer the many health problems associated with obesity. This reduces healthcare costs for all and places the family in a preventive mode rather than a treatment mode. Children must understand that in these and many other ways they are responsible for their health status. It is essential that they also know this responsibility is easily carried out if they make healthful decisions—decisions that are often simply a matter of applying common sense and information that they learn.

STANDARDS I–VI (PHYSICAL EDUCATION)

Competency 027:   The physical education teacher understands principles and benefits of a healthy, active lifestyle and motivates students to participate in activities that promote this lifestyle. He or she demonstrates competency in a variety of movement skills and helps students develop these skills. The teacher uses knowledge of individual and group motivation and behavior to create and manage a safe, productive learning environment and promotes students' self-management, self-motivation, and social skills through participation in physical activities. The EC-4 physical teacher uses knowledge of how students learn and develop to provide opportunities that support students' physical, cognitive, social, and emotional development and provides equitable and appropriate instruction for all students in a diverse society. Using effective, developmentally appropriate instructional strategies and communication techniques to prepare physically educated individuals is also a requirement.

The beginning teacher applies key principles and concepts in physical education (e.g., cardiovascular endurance, muscular endurance, flexibility, weight control, conditioning, safety, stress management, nutrition) and their significance for physical activity, health, and fitness. The teacher must also apply knowledge of physical education content and curriculum, including the Texas Essential Knowledge and Skills (TEKS), and of children in early childhood through grade 4 to plan and implement effective, developmentally-appropriate physical education activities. The EC-4 teacher also knows and helps children understand the benefits of an active lifestyle, and he or she modifies instruction based on individual differences in growth and development. The Texas teacher applies knowledge of movement principles and concepts to develop children's motor skills and selects and uses developmentally appropriate learning experiences that enhance children's locomotor, nonlocomotor, body-control, manipulative, and rhythmic skills. The teacher is able to select and use instructional strategies to promote children's knowledge and application of rules, procedures, etiquette, and fair play in developmentally appropriate games and activities. The teacher designs, manages, and adapts physical education activities to promote positive interactions and active engagement by children. Finally, the teacher evaluates movement patterns to help children improve performance of motor skills and to integrate and refine motor and rhythmic skills.

These standards are related to the component of the physical educational TEKS that states that learners acquire the knowledge and skills for movement that provide the foundation for enjoyment, continued social development through physical activity, and access to a physically active lifestyle. The goal is for the learner to exhibit a physically active lifestyle and understand the relationship between physical activity and health throughout his or her life. In elementary school, children learn fundamental movement skills and begin to understand how the muscles, bones, heart, and lungs function in relation to physical activity. Identifying personal fitness goals and beginning to understand how exercise affects different parts of the body are an important part of the instructional process.

Children should learn how to identify components of health-related fitness, including identifying sources of health fitness information and about appropriate clothing (including safety devises and equipment) and safety precautions in exercise settings.

Try this practice question:

The fourth graders at Moses Elementary School are learning about the risk indicators related to a healthy lifestyle. Which of the following factors would these students learn about that contribute most to an unhealthy lifestyle?

A. High blood pressure, smoking.
B. Watching television and playing videogames.
C. Diets high in unsaturated fats, lack of exercise.
D. A and C.

Test taker #1 selected A because it is apparent that smoking and high blood pressure are related and both are risk indicators that contribute to an unhealthy lifestyle. Test taker #2 selected C for the same reason; diets high in unsaturated fats and lack of exercise are risk indicators as well. Test taker #3 chose D since high blood pressure, smoking, diets high in unsaturated fats, and stress all contribute to unhealthy lifestyles. Watching too much television and playing videogames (B) concerns health educators, but this item does not talk about the time spent at these activities. Careful scrutiny of this question should make option D the apparent choice. Each factor cited is a risk indicator that contributes to an unhealthy lifestyle.

Recently, many elementary school physical education programs have incorporated more health-related aspects of human wellness into their curricula. The excessive number of overweight or undernourished children has created a need for programs that help children assess their eating habits and plan effective weight-control programs. Problems related to stress management and alcohol and drug consumption have prompted the physical education profession to redefine and emphasize new aspects of physical fitness. This new direction and emphasis toward a positive state of well-being has created a need for programs that help children understand how their bodies work, how they can monitor body changes, and how they can design personal fitness programs for improving and maintaining optimal levels of health.

Health-related physical fitness includes aspects of physiological function that offer protection from diseases resulting from a sedentary lifestyle. Such fitness can be improved and/or maintained through regular and moderate physical activity. Specific components of health-related fitness included cardiovascular fitness, body composition, abdominal strength and endurance, and flexibility. Currently, experts (Pangrazi, Corbin, & Welk, cited in Brewer, 2001) recommend that children be physically active at least 60 minutes everyday. If particular grade levels do not schedule recess every day or employ a specialized physical education teacher for classes, the classroom teacher must fulfill this responsibility through directed and nondirected play, a regular exercise program, and through movement activities in the classroom during the course of the day.

Cardiovascular fitness offers many health benefits and is often seen as the most important element of fitness. It includes the ability of the heart, the blood vessels, and the respiratory system to deliver oxygen efficiently over an extended period of time. In order to develop cardiovascular fitness, activities must be aerobic in nature (i.e., activities that are continuous and rhythmic in nature requiring that a continuous supply of oxygen be delivered to the muscle cells). Activities that stimulate development in this area are jogging, biking, rope jumping, aerobics, and swimming.

Body composition is an integral part of health-related fitness. It is the proportion of body fat to lean body mass. Attaining physical fitness is made more difficult when an individual's body composition is high in body fat.

Another component of health-related fitness is *flexibility,* the range and ease of motion of a joint. The amount of flexibility depends upon the structure and nature of the joints involved, the nature of the ligaments surrounding the joint, and the extensibility of the muscles connected to the joint. Through stretching activities, the length of the muscles, tendons, and ligaments is increased. Flexibility is important to fitness; a lack of flexibility can create health problems for individuals. For example, people who are flexible usually have good posture and may have less lower-back pain. Many physical activities demand a range of motion to generate maximum force such as serving a tennis ball and kicking a soccer ball.

Muscular strength and endurance are the other components of health-related fitness. *Muscular strength* is the amount of force that a muscle or group of muscles can exert. When muscular strength is desired as a training outcome, it is necessary to move near-maximum workloads with minimal repetitions. *Muscular endurance* is the ability of the muscles to continue to function over a long period of time. To develop muscular endurance, a low-resistance, high-repetition workload is suggested. For most, a balance of the two workloads is probably most useful. Climbing or pulling exercises and jumping rope are particularly effective for children's strength.

It is important to distinguish between health-related fitness and skill-related fitness. The focus of health-related fitness is to help youngsters understand how much activity is required for good health. Emphasis is placed on the process of *activity* and *participation* rather than on the product of high-level performance.

Skill-related fitness, on the other hand, helps *improve performance in motor tasks* related to sports and athletics. The ability to perform well is influenced to a significant degree by predetermined genetic characteristics. If skill-related fitness is taught in elementary school, it should be accompanied with an explanation about why some children and adults perform well with a minimum of effort whereas others, no matter how much they practice, never excel in certain areas. This may be due to height, body type, length of specific bones, or other factors but should not keep a person from enjoying a particular activity.

Once children are personally convinced that exercise is important for their own well-being, there is a good chance that physical activity will become a permanent part of their daily lives. It also appears that once a child's lifestyle moves in this direction, he or she will begin to modify his or her diet and other health factors to complement this positive and healthy way of living.

Consider the following practice question:

Mr. Pollack has his students find their heart rate after walking around the gymnasium for 3 minutes. They rest for a few minutes. Children are then to jog for 3 minutes and take their heart rate at the completion of the jog, followed by jumping rope for 3 minutes and finally followed by sprinting for 3 minutes. After each activity, students take their heart rate again. What is the most likely reason for doing this lesson?

A. To identify what types of activities place greater demands on the heart.
B. To complete a variety of cardiovascular activities in one session.
C. To maintain aerobic capacity for 12 minutes.
D. To identify how to measure heart rate effectively during a workout.

It is important for learners to understand that different activities place different demands on the heart. Having learners see the importance of the effect of different types of activities on the cardiorespiratory system is a valuable tool for understanding the concepts underlying the components of health-related fitness. The correct choice is option *A.* There is little to be gained by completing a variety of cardiovascular activities in a single session (*B*). Although an activity may be conducted for a significant length of time, it is the intensity of the activity that determines whether it is aerobic in nature. The walking phase of this activity does not constitute time spent in the *aerobic phase,* which is defined as when the cardiorespiratory system is able to meet the demands of the body's muscles and tissues with an adequate supply of oxygen.

Physical activity positively impacts the growth and development of children. Research supports the value of an active lifestyle for optimum growth and development. As clearly documented in the *Surgeon General's Report of Physical Activity and Health* (1996), there is an identifiable correlation between the incidence of health disorders and a sedentary lifestyle. Lifetime participation in physical activity often depends on early participation and gratification gained from such participation. Developing motor skills at an early age provides the tools needed to be physically active throughout life. A teacher's job is to integrate exciting activities in which children are physically active and in which they want to participate.

Despite the national interest in physical activity, the focus has not trickled down to elementary school children. Only about one-third of our children participate daily in school physical education programs nationwide. The need for activity as an integral part of children's lifestyles and education is strong. Participation in physical activity is more important than the concern to train children to pass fitness tests. Programs that focus on activity give all youngsters the opportunity for success and long-term health. Physical education programs must be designed to teach children how to live an active and healthy lifestyle. Teachers should advocate for children in support of such schoolwide programs.

Consider the following practice question:

During a fitness unit, students were required to keep a daily journal of activity and food consumed. These journal entries could benefit participants by which of the following?

A. Teaching students the importance of daily exercise for all people.
B. Teaching students how to monitor weight gain/loss by diet.
C. Teaching students the importance of diet and exercise as a lifetime commitment to better health.
D. Teaching students that diet is not a primary consideration in maintaining fitness.

Test taker #1 selects *B* because weight gain and loss is an indicator of health. Test taker #2 selected *A* because an important outcome of a physical education unit is to assure that children understand the value of daily exercise. Test taker #3 selects *C* because the commitment to lifetime fitness is the ultimate aspiration of a successful physical education program. Test taker #4 selects *D* because diet is not the primary consideration in maintaining fitness.

Choice *C* is correct. It is critical that students are made aware at an early age of the benefits of a lifelong commitment to the combination of physical activity and nutrition. As we age, the need for regular physical activity and a focus on proper nutrition becomes more evident and more critical. Selection *A* is not correct, since daily activity is not viable in many cases nor is it essential. Participation in moderate physical activity three to five times weekly will provide many health-related benefits. Monitoring weight gains and loss, as in choice *B*, is not meaningful unless children are taught the significance of weight gain and loss. Muscle weighs approximately 2.5 times the amount that fat weighs. As a result, weight gain does not always indicate a problem. If the ratio of percent fat to lean body mass (muscle) decreases, we are more fit. This is an important concept for children to understand. Choice *D* is incorrect. Diet is an essential component of fitness.

Movement

The TEKS guidelines in movement relate to skill development and developmentally appropriate activities. In the early years of elementary school, the emphasis is on applying movement concepts and principles to the learning and development of motor skills. Learners are first taught to demonstrate competency in fundamental movement patterns and proficiency in a few specialized movement forms. As children mature, they are expected to demonstrate appropriate use of levels in dynamic movement situations such as jumping high for a rebound and bending knees and lowering center of gravity when guarding an opponent. Smooth combinations of fundamental motor skills such as running and dodging and hop-step-jump as well as attention to form, power, accuracy, and follow-through in performing movement skills are emphasized. Controlled balance on a variety of objects such as balance boards, stilts, scooters, and skates are objectives of this standard, as are simple stunts that exhibit agility such as jumping challenges with proper landings.

Teaching physical skills is related to the psychomotor domain. The psychomotor domain consist of the following levels:

1. **Perception.** Sensory cues are used to focus on how to perform a skill (i.e., the learner pays attention to, notices, recognizes, senses, perceives, or detects).
2. **Set.** Think of "ready, set, go!" Set means that a learner becomes prepared (not only physically but mentally and emotionally) to do a skill (i.e., the learner is ready, prepared, takes steps, and desires to).
3. **Guided response.** This is the phase where a learner tries a skill as the instructor observes and coaches (i.e., the learner tries, performs, practices).
4. **Mechanism.** The learner practices enough to become proficient (i.e., the learner improves, increases skills in).
5. **Complex or overt response.** The learner can now use the skill very proficiently (i.e., the learner masters, excels in, perfects).
6. **Adaptation.** Now, the learner can perform new skills from the one learned by modification (i.e., the learner adapts, adjusts, accommodates).
7. **Origination.** The learner can create new skills that are based on the original skill, yet are completely original (the learner produces, originates). (Bloom et al., 1956, cited in Cruickshank, Jenkins, & Metcalf, 2002)

Try this practice question:

Lyn Addis teaches elementary physical education. Her program includes the skills of games, sports, and sequential gymnastics. Which of the following represents the appropriate sequence for kicking?

A. Kick the stationary ball, kick a rolling ball while running, kick a rolling ball from a stationary position.

B. Kick a rolling ball while using a running approach, kick a rolling ball, kick a stationary ball, kick action without the ball.

C. Kicking leg action without a ball, kicking a stationary ball, kicking a rolling ball, kicking a rolling ball while using a running approach.

D. Kick a rolling ball, kick a rolling ball while running, punting.

Test-taker #1 selected *D*, since this technique most closely approximates the skill of kicking. Test-taker #2 selected *C*, since this technique provides for the soundest progression or sequence of skill development. Test-taker #3 selected *A*, since kicking a stationary ball is the simplest technique for learners to use to develop appropriate kicking skill. Test-taker #4 chose *D*, since kicking is a skill mostly used in soccer, and soccer involves mostly kicking a moving ball.

The correct option is *C*. Using a kicking leg option without a ball allows for the establishment of the correct mechanics. Kicking a stationary ball, kicking a rolling ball, and kicking a rolling ball while using a running approach are techniques used to develop the skill of kicking in a sequential manner. Choices *B* and *D* involve initiating the development of the skill using an advanced approach. This can lead to frustration on the part of the learner.

Fundamental skills are those utilitarian skills that children use to enhance the quality of life. This group of skills is sometimes labeled basic or functional. Fundamental skills are basic attributes that help children function in the environment. Related to this experience is the opportunity to learn basic concepts about stability, force, leverage, and other factors related to efficient movement. Understanding genetic diversity among people, such as muscle type, cardiorespiratory endurance, and motor coordination, is requisite for helping students evaluate their physical capabilities. These *basic* or *fundamental skills* are divided into three categories—locomotor, nonlocomotor, and management skills.

Locomotor skills are used to move the body from one place to another or to project the body upward, as in jumping and hopping. Walking, running, galloping, skipping, and sliding are other examples of locomotor skills.

Nonlocomotor skills are performed in place, without appreciable spatial movement. These skills are not as well defined as locomotor skills. Included in this category are bending and stretching, pushing and pulling, raising and lowering, twisting and turning.

Body management skills are an important component of movement competency. Efficient movement demands integration of a number of physical traits, including agility, balance, flexibility, and coordination. A basic understanding of movement concepts and mechanical principles used in skill performance is necessary for quality movement.

Manipulative skills (developed when a child handles an object), *rhythmic movement skills* (involves motion that possesses regularity and a predictable pattern), *gymnastics skills* (which help develop body management skills without the need for equipment or apparatus), and *game skills* (which contribute to the child's total development by allowing children to experience success and accomplishment), and *sport skills* (learned in the context of application through an approach of skills, drills, and lead-up activities) are examples of *specialized motor skills*. In developing specialized skills, progression is attained through planned instruction and drills.

The *development of motor skills* follows an orderly sequence. During the stage known as early childhood (age 2 to approximately the end of the sixth year) a child develops the fundamental locomotor and nonlocomotor skills of running, jumping, leaping, hopping, skipping, sliding, dodging, stopping, swinging, twisting, bending, turning, and stretching. A child also begins to develop the basic manipulative skills of throwing, catching, and striking. Many of these fundamental motor skills are learned prior to kindergarten and, in most instances, through a process of exploration. During this time teachers should help children tune up awareness of how various parts of the body move separately and together to create coordinated patterns. For example, Mrs. Adams does this through teaching her class "The Duck Song," in which children "flap their wings," put their toes in a make-believe pond to test the water, and "fluff their tail feathers." During the first two years of elementary school, the continuing development of these fundamental skills should be through a program that emphasizes exploration of movement rather than refinement of skills. This is primarily important when a child is learning the basic manipulative skills of throwing, catching, and striking. The latter skills can be effectively learned through informal and creative games programs.

As children move into middle childhood, they begin to refine fundamental motor skills and to develop more complex combinations of locomotor, nonlocomotor, and manipulative skill patterns. Increased physical size and strength, coupled with improved perceptual and cognitive development, contribute to a child's ability to perform more coordinated movement patterns with greater speed and accuracy.

During the late childhood stage, the more specific movement skills required of games, dance, and gymnastics begin to show some refinement. In game activities the ability to move objects (e.g., balls) through a variety of complex game situations develops. Similarly, dance and gymnastics skills become more fluid and creative as the performer acquires greater skill and understanding of the finer aspects of an individual movement or sequence of movements. *Rhythm* is the ability to repeat an action or movement with regularity to a particular rhythmic pattern. It is an essential ingredient of all movement, whether throwing a ball, dodging a player, or dancing a waltz. Rhythmic activities play an essential role in individual development.

Consider the following practice question:

During a lesson for sixth graders on the fundamental movement skill of kicking, Mr. Iglesias organizes his students into groups of three for activity. The groups are to determine the optimum place on the ball to impart force for kicking the ball into the air and which part of the foot to use. The groups are to experiment with different ideas and develop a solution to be compared with other group's solutions. At the end of the lesson, the solutions will be written down, read, and discussed. This activity is appropriate for developing learners' motor skills because it primarily focuses on:

A. Refining the mechanics of the skill of kicking.
B. Improving the accuracy of the skill.
C. Retention through mental practice.
D. Variable practice.

Option *A* is the correct choice. This is a valuable method for teaching fundamental movement skills. Too often children are provided repeated opportunities for perfecting skills with little or no emphasis placed on the understanding of correct mechanics. By emphasizing understanding of correct mechanics, learners will be more likely to retain their skills and to be able to transfer their knowledge and ability to related activities.

Let's try another practice question:

Mrs. Huong has taught her class fundamental manipulative movement skills. Which of the following skills would be included in this instruction?

A. Throwing, kicking.
B. Turning, twisting.
C. Dancing.
D. Jumping, sliding.

While turning and twisting *(B)* and jumping and sliding *(D)* are fundamental skills, they are not classified as being fundamental manipulative movement skills. Neither is dancing *(C)*. The fundamental manipulative skills of throwing, catching, and striking are the foundation of all major individual and team sport activities. These skills involve controlling objects with the hands or feet. The correct option is *A*, throwing a baseball and kicking a soccer ball.

Growth and Development

Although the sequence of motor skill development is predictable, the *rate* at which these sequences appear may be quite variable. Each child is unique in that he or she has an individual timetable for developing. This phenomenon relates to a child's "readiness" to learn new skills, which refers to conditions that makes a particular task appropriate to master. Heredity, gender, nutrition, family size, the home environment, and culture all modify the basic developmental sequence. In physical education, we need to develop a foundation of psychological and perceptual-motor readiness, at the same time allowing the child to take full advantage of his or her present maturational level.

Three development patterns typify the growth of primary-grade children:

1. Generally, development proceeds from the head to the foot (*cephalocaudal*). Coordination and management of body parts occur in the upper body before they are observed in the lower extremities. This is the reason most students can learn to throw before they learn to kick.
2. Development occurs from inside to outside (*proximodistal*). Children can control their arms before they can control their hands.
3. Development proceeds from general to specific. Children become competent in *gross motor skills* (large body movement) before they develop refined motor patterns.

Without sound knowledge of the developmental aspects of motor behavior, one can only guess at the educational techniques and intervention procedures to use in skill development. The process of motor development should constantly remind us of the individuality of the learner. Each individual has his or own unique timetable for the acquisition and development of movement abilities. The EC-4 teacher should maintain his or her own records and provide activities that deal with changes in children's development (recording height and weight). Teachers should ensure that these activities not somehow suggest that "taller is better," etc., but that children understand that their bodies grow and change at different rates.

Girls are often separated for their talk on menstruation in the fourth grade. This onset can be a development that can be very difficult psychologically if it should come early. As girls mature earlier and earlier, even primary teachers need to be ready for this event and the difficulty that can accompany it as a health issue. Teachers should answer questions forthrightly, though with consideration to age-appropriateness.

Consider the following practice question:

The students in Mrs. Matthews' third-grade class have shown important variations in terms of their overall physical development and their current skill levels. Which principle should Mrs. Matthews follow in developing a physical education program to meet the students' needs in this class?

A. Plan units with activities that focus on relatively simple and basic objectives that all learners will be able to achieve.
B. Intersperse units requiring only relatively low skill levels with those that require substantially higher skill levels.

C. Plan units with activities that give all children opportunities to improve their current skill levels.

D. Minimize the total number of units planned in order to give all children ample time to develop and refine their skills.

Test-taker #1 selected C, since it is essential that students experience success. This teaching strategy will provide the greatest opportunity for success. Test-taker #2 selected A for the same reason. Test-taker #3 selected B, since this will permit the more skilled students to develop at a quicker pace. Test-taker #4 selected D. Using this strategy will result in accomplishment of more skill development.

The correct response is C. Children should be provided opportunities to enhance existing skills. Skilled students who are not given the opportunity to continue skill development can become bored and frustrated. The resultant behavior is often a lack of interest in activity or development of behavioral problems. This would be a likely result of alternative A. Answer B may cause frustration in both the skilled participants who do not need exposure to basic activities, as well as the unskilled participants who will not achieve the higher-level skills. Physical Education standards recommend that children be exposed to a variety of activities, with the goal of developing proficiency in many and competence in some. As a result, answer D is not in compliance with this standard.

Assessment and Evaluation

There are many kinds of assessment (both formal and informal) and evaluation, but all should be done to improve instruction and increase learning and skills. Ways to assess student learning and skills include the use of checklists, logs, tests, and scoring rubrics. Informal assessment is often done on the spot when a teacher observes and corrects or reinforces a student's performance.

Scoring rubrics are rating scales that list multiple criteria related to a task or motor skill performance. The criteria are performance levels students are expected to achieve. To employ this method of assessment requires accurate knowledge of different stages of acquiring skills so that a child's pattern of development can be observed and categorized.

Observation checklists are another means of gathering meaningful information about children. In this technique, criteria governing proper technique for the movement pattern are listed, and the child's performance is checked against these points. A teacher may want to keep a list of playground behaviors, recording such behaviors as (a) whether the child plays alone or in a group and for how long and how often, (b) the physical level of play [active: vigorous, rough and tumble, games with rules, etc.; or passive: talking, walking, sitting, waiting, etc.], (c) play with the same or opposite gender, (d) location of the play, and (e) if the play was adult directed or assisted (Daniels, Beaumont, & Doolin, 2002).

Skill checklists incorporate skills listed across the top of a roster in which class progress is recorded. The value of using this assessment tool is that it allows the instructor to be alerted to youngsters who are in need of special help. Checklists are usually most effective when skills are listed in the sequence in which they should be learned.

Standardized tests are useful in evaluating measurable outcomes. These types of tests have been administered to large samples of youngsters, and the results are useful for comparative purposes. These tests often require specialized equipment. The test results, or at least an interpreted summary, can be included in a child's health record and can be part of a periodic progress report to parents.

It is important to remember just how this information will be interpreted and used. Enough information must be collected to make a good judgment or recommendations, and the information on development must be communicated to parents and/or school health officials with proper concern for the child. If a teacher suspects that a child may have some physical developmental problems, it is wise to first consult with the school nurse and to collect information that would warrant further testing or medical attention, should it be needed.

Consider the following practice question:

How the curriculum is sequenced is important to the learner's sense of success. Which of the following statements represents a developmentally appropriate sequence?

I. Relays should be introduced to develop skills.
II. Competition should be introduced after skills are developed.
III. Lead-up games should be introduced to develop locomotor, nonlocomotor, and manipulative skills.
IV. Cooperative behavior should be established before competitive situations are introduced.

A. I and II only.
B. I and III only.
C. III and IV only.
D. II and IV only.

Test taker #1 selected *A* since relays and competition introduced after skills have been developed are an effective ways to develop skills. Test taker #2 selected *C*, since relays may not be effective, and they are a choice in *A* and *B*. Test taker #3 selected *D*, since relays do not result in skill development, and lead-up games do not enhance manipulative skills. Test taker #4 selected *B*. The correct answer is *D*. Introducing competition before skills are developed leads to frustration and often limits skill development. Although competition (II) is a healthy strategy, it should only be introduced *after* cooperative behavior has been established. Answers *A* and *B* can be eliminated, since introducing relays is not an effective skill development tool. *C* is incorrect since manipulative skills are not enhanced through lead-up games.

Positive Interactions and Personal Exploration in Physical Education

The TEKS in Physical Education state that students acquire the knowledge and skills for movement that provide the foundation for enjoyment, continued social development through physical activity, and access to a physically active lifestyle. In elementary school, children learn fundamental movement skills and begin to understand how the muscles, bones, heart, and lungs function in relation to physical activity. Learners begin to develop a vocabulary for movement and apply concepts dealing with space and body awareness. Learners are engaged in activities that develop basic levels of strength, endurance, and flexibility. In addition, children learn to work safely in groups, interdependently, and in individual movement settings. Team activities should reinforce working together to help all members achieve a goal and identify strengths that each member brings to a team. The best strategy for having children understand and obey rules is having them help establish desired guidelines. When children help make the rules, just as in classroom management, they feel more ownership and thus feel more compelled to comply. Occasionally they may play a standard well-known game with rules suspended (other than safety) to help them understand the rationale for following rules and maintaining fair play. As they progress through the elementary grades, learners can demonstrate mature form in fundamental locomotor and manipulative skills and can often maintain that form while participating in dynamic game situations.

Students should be taught key performance cues for basic movement patterns, such as throwing and catching, in the primary grades. They should learn game strategies, rules, and etiquette procedures for simple games and apply safety practices associated with physical activities. As learners mature, they combine locomotor and manipulative skills in dynamic situations with body control. The goal is for learners to demonstrate competence such as improved accuracy in manipulative skills in dynamic situations. Basic skills such as jumping rope, moving to a beat, and catching and throwing should be mastered and applied in gamelike situations.

Consider the following practice question:

Angelina Elementary School sets goals at the beginning of each school year. Competent motor skill acquisition is one of these goals. Which of the following activities is most likely to be chosen to meet this goal for the early elementary grades?

A. Team sports skills.
B. Locomotor skills and games.

C. Individual sports skills.
D. Aquatics program.

Test taker #1 selected *D,* since swimming involves a significant number of skills. Test taker #2 selected *A,* since skill in team sports is a good indicator of competent skill acquisition. Test taker #3 chose *B* because locomotor skills and games are prerequisite skills to the development of choices provided in each of the remaining choices. Test taker #4 chose *C* because individual sports skills are important for the elementary child.

The correct choice is *B.* Team sport skills should be used to apply motor skills after competency has been developed. Practitioners often introduce team sport skills early in the instructional process. The result of this practice typically is the reinforcement of poor habits or frustration on the part of the student who has not yet mastered the skill. While individual sports skills do provide an opportunity to teach competent motor skills, similar to team sport skills, they should be introduced *after* competent motor skills have been developed. Aquatics programs provide the opportunity to develop components of health-related fitness but are not efficient means of developing competent motor skills.

All people want to be skilled and competent in the area of motor performance. The elementary school years are an excellent time to teach motor skills because children have the time and predisposition to learn. The types and range of skills presented in physical education should be as unlimited as possible. Because children vary in genetic endowment and interest, they should have the opportunity to learn about their personal abilities in a variety of skill types. The school years should be the years of opportunity to explore and experience many different types of physical activity. Thus the curriculum should be expansive rather than restrictive. It should allow learners to better understand their strengths and limitations and to learn what types of activities are available in the real world and what activities they prefer.

Designing and Implementing Activities

Developmentally based teaching in physical education has received emphasis in recent years. A developmentally based curriculum focuses on several important factors. First, every child passes through a series of developmental stages. For example, in the process of learning how to throw a ball, every child progresses through an initial and somewhat jerky stage, to a more focused second stage, to a final automatic step in which the movement is performed smoothly and effortlessly. A second important factor is that, although the majority of children follow similar sequences of motor development and arrive at developmental points at approximately the same age level, the rate of motor development varies; hence, the rate of development is not age-dependent. Children pass through each developmental stage according to their own levels of maturity and ability, rather than according to an exact chronological age or grade level. Although it is impossible for a classroom teacher to completely individualize a program for each child, it is possible to use new organizational techniques, new content areas, and new teaching strategies to allow children within any given learning experience in physical education to develop and learn according to their own levels of interest, ability, and previous experience. Having children set individual goals helps strengthen skills based on the current skills of learners. Social, emotional, cognitive, and psychomotor development must all be understood if developmentally appropriate programs are to be achieved.

Consider the following practice question:

When scheduling units and activities in physical education, it would be most important for a teacher to follow which of the following guidelines?

A. Activities of greater interest to learners should be alternated with those of lesser interest in order to maintain learners' motivation.

B. Class activities should coincide with the professional sports in season at that time.

C. Activities that are more familiar to learners should be alternated with those that are less familiar to ensure that learners regularly experience success.

D. Activities should build upon learners' previous experience and skills and should progress from simpler to more complex.

In presenting activities that build upon previous experience and skills, the teacher is more assured of the developmentally appropriate nature of the activity. By doing so, learners' motivation will be greater; therefore, alternating activities, according to interest as suggested in options A and C, is not necessary. Scheduling activities based upon seasonal considerations related to professional sports programs is of little value in most cases. The best option is D.

What children learn can be applied in many settings. Learning is holistic; students use what they have learned in one area in many other areas. There is little doubt that learning to apply academic settings is an important process. Physical activity offers many opportunities for integrating subject matter and activity. For example, TAKS standards could be taught or reinforced by means of appropriate application of movement concepts. Examples of such academic integration include bringing together the fine arts and physical activity via posters, decorations, dancing, and costumes. Because the origins of physical education materials are diverse, geographical associations provide the classroom teacher with another source of learning experiences; games or dances of different cultures could be integrated into a lesson, for example. Studying geographical and climatic factors of various areas to see how they affect athletic performance is a natural integration of subject areas. Without using a great deal of imagination, it should be apparent how history, language arts, music, number concepts (mathematics), and so forth can serve in a symbiotic fashion along with physical activities.

Many children are kinesthetic learners who need movement in order to learn more quickly and better in all areas of learning. Providing for these learners can also increase movement while reaching the mode of these learners directly through movement activities such as forming letters with the body, creative movement (becoming a seed, for example, and moving through the growing process), large floor games, pantomime and charades, and dance.

Physical education has recently undergone dramatic change. Not only has the emphasis shifted from the development of sport skills to a more holistic approach that emphasizes interdisciplinary concepts, but the discipline has shifted its goals as well. Physical education plays a large role in enhancing the fitness and skill levels of learners so they have a background that allows them to develop an active lifestyle. People are commonly faced with many decisions that positively or negatively impact their level of wellness. The ability to make responsible decisions depends on a wide range of factors: (a) an understanding of one's feelings and clarification of personal values, (b) an ability to cope with stress and personal problems, (c) an ability to make decisions, and (d) understanding the impact of various lifestyles on health.

 ## SUMMARY

This chapter has explored the role of health and fitness within the context of the Generalist exam. Health and fitness are rapidly evolving fields. Much has changed from the "PE" classes that many of us may have had as students. These new developments have helped to solidify the roles of these disciplines in the educational process.

Data provided by the U.S. Surgeon General delineate the fact that ours is a "nation at risk." Lack of exercise and obesity have been determined to be as serious as smoking. Unlike previous conclusions regarding the amount of exercise required in order to maintain a healthy lifestyle, the Surgeon General, in concert with the Centers for Disease Control, now maintains that a moderate amount of exercise will meet the demands of healthy, active living. Healthy students are more physically and mentally ready to learn. Although recess has an important role in unstructured play and developing socialization skills in children, please do not perceive physical activity time as simply an opportunity to provide students with outside time. Physical activity is an essential component of the learning process and should be treated accordingly.

 ## REFERENCES

Brewer, J. A. (2001). *Introduction to early childhood education: Preschool through primary grades* (4th ed.). Boston: Allyn and Bacon.

Cruickshank, D., Jenkins, D., & Metcalf, C. (2002). *The act of teaching* (3rd ed.). Boston: McGraw-Hill.

Daniels, D., Beaumont, L., & Doolin, C. (2002). *Understanding children: An interview and observation guide for educators.* Boston: McGraw-Hill.

Eggen, P., & Kauchak, D. (2001). *Education psychology: Windows on classrooms.* Upper Saddle River, NJ: Merrill Prentice-Hall.

Goleman, D. (1995). *Emotional intelligence.* New York: Bantam Books.

Kagan, S. (1992). *Cooperative learning.* San Juan Capistrano, CA: Resources for Teachers, Inc.

Luepker R. V., Perry, C., McKinlay, S. M., et al. (1996). Outcomes of a field trial to improve children dietary patterns and physical activity. *Journal of the American Medical Association, 275,* 768–776.

Physical activity and health: A report of the Surgeon General (1996). Washington, DC: U.S. Department of Health and Human Services.

SUGGESTED READINGS

American Academy of Pediatrics. (1991). *Sports medicine: Health care for young athletes.* Elk Grove Village, IL: Author.

Anspaugh, D. J., & Ezell, G. (2001). *Teaching today's health.* Boston: Allyn and Bacon.

Gabbard, C., Leblanc, E., & Lowy, S. (1987). *Physical education for children.* Englewood Cliffs, NJ: Prentice-Hall.

Gallahue, D.L. (1987). *Developmental physical education for today's elementary school children.* New York: Macmillan.

Goals 2000: Educate America Act. (1994). M.R. 1804.

Gordon, A., & Brown, K. W. (1996). *Guiding young children in a diverse society.* Boston: Allyn and Bacon.

Graham, G., Holt-Hale, S. A., & Parker, M. (1993). *Children moving.* Mountain View, CA: Mayfield.

Hellison, D. (2003). *Teaching responsibility through physical activity.* Champaign, IL: Human Kinetics.

Landy, J. M., & Burridge, K. R. (1999). *Fundamental motor skills and movement activities for young children.* West Nyack, NY: The Center for Applied Research in Education.

Mosston, M., & Ashworth, S. (1994). *Teaching physical education* (4th ed.). New York: Macmillan.

Nichols, B. (1986*). Moving and learning—The elementary school physical education experience.* St. Louis: Times Mirror/Mosby.

Pangrazi, R. P. (2001a). *Dynamic physical education for elementary school children* (13th ed.). Boston: Allyn and Bacon.

Pangrazi, R. P. (2001b). *Lesson plans for dynamic physical education for elementary school students* (13th ed.). Boston: Allyn and Bacon.

Pangrazi, R. P., & Hastad, D. N. (1989). *Fitness in the elementary schools* (2nd ed.). Reston, VA: AAHPERD.

President's Council on Physical Fitness and Sports. (1991). *Get fit! A handbook for youth ages 6–17.* Washington, DC. President's Council on Physical Fitness and Sports.

Rink, J. E. (1993). *Teaching physical education for learning* (2nd ed.). St. Louis: Mosby.

Schmidt, R. A. (1991). *Motor learning and performance: From principles to practice.* Champaign, IL: Human Kinetics.

ABOUT THE AUTHORS

MEL E. FINKENBERG, Ed.D., is Regents Professor and Chair of the Department of Kinesiology and Health Science at Stephen F. Austin State University in Nacogdoches, Texas. Prior to his appointment at SFA, he served as Professor and Chair of the Department of Physical Education and Recreation/Leisure Studies at California State University, Los Angeles. Dr. Finkenberg has also been an exercise physiologist at NASA's Johnson Space Center and has taught elementary physical education. Dr. Finkenberg has been President of the Texas Association of Health, Physical Education, Recreation and Dance and was selected as the Association Scholar for 1999. He was awarded the Honor Award by this group as well. He served as Vice President for Physical Education for the Southern District American Alliance for Health, Physical Education, Recreation and Dance. He recently received this association's Honor Award. AT SFA he was named Distinguished Professor and selected as the Phi Delta Kappa Educator of the Year. Dr. Finkenberg has served as Vice President of the National Association for Physical Education in Higher Education. In 2001 he received that Association's Distinguished Administrator Award.

JANICE L. NATH, Ed.D., is a faculty member at the University of Houston-Downtown in the Urban Education Department. She is the co-editor of *Becoming a Teacher in Texas: A Course of Study for the Elementary and*

Secondary Professional Development ExCET (for the former state competencies), *Becoming an EC-4 Teacher in Texas: A Course of Study for the Pedagogy and Professional Responsibilities (PPR) TExES,* and *Forging Alliances in Community and Thought: Research in Professional Development Schools.* Teacher education is her main area of interest along with technology in teacher education, action research, and others. She has been actively involved in field-based teacher education for many years. She has also served as the president of the AERA (American Educational Research Association) Professional Development School Research SIG and president of the Texas Coordinators for Teacher Certification Testing (formerly, the ExCET Coordinators Association). Currently, she is a CSOTTE Board Member and officer.

JOHN RAMSEY, Ph.D., is Associate Professor of science education at the University of Houston. He has served as department chair, director of teacher education, doctoral and masters advisor, and principal investigator for funded projects. His professional experience includes more than thirty years in middle, secondary, and higher education. He has co-authored or co-edited nine books and published twenty-five refereed research articles. He has received the highest university teaching award granted at the University of Houston and was honored with the 2001 Research Excellence Award from the North American Association of Environmental Education. He has conducted more than 300 hundred international and national professional development workshops and presentations and has served as a consultant for the United Nations, national and state agencies, international governments, nongovernment organizations, and businesses.

Author Index

Subject Index